# PEACEMAKING

—

International and Security Affairs Series

Edwin G. Corr, General Editor

# PEACEMAKING

———

## The Inside Story of the
## 1994 Jordanian–Israeli Treaty

**ABDUL SALAM MAJALI**
**JAWAD A. ANANI**
AND
**MUNTHER J. HADDADIN**

FOREWORD BY
**HRH PRINCE EL HASSAN BIN TALAL OF JORDAN**

PREFACE BY
**DAVID L. BOREN**
PRESIDENT OF THE UNIVERSITY OF OKLAHOMA

**UNIVERSITY OF OKLAHOMA PRESS : NORMAN**

*Peacemaking: The Inside Story of the 1994 Jordanian–Israeli Treaty*
is Volume 4 in the International and Security Affairs Series.

U.S. edition copyright ©2006 Abdul Salam Majali, Jawad A. Anani,
and Munther J. Haddadin, published by the University
of Oklahoma Press, Norman, Publishing Division
of the University, by special arrangement with
Ithaca Press, an imprint of

Garnet Publishing Limited
8 Southern Court
South Street
Reading
RG1 4QS
UK

Library of Congress Cataloging-in-Publication Data

Majali, 'Abd al-Salam.
    Peacemaking : the inside story of the 1994 Jordanian-Israeli treaty / Abdul Salam Majali,
Jawad A. Anani, and Munther J. Haddadin ; foreword by HRH Prince El Hassan bin Talal of Jordan ;
preface by David L. Boren.
        p. cm. — (International and security affairs series; v. 4)
    Includes index.
    ISBN 0-8061-3765-7 (alk. paper)
    1.    Israel. Treaties, etc. Jordan, 1994 Oct. 26. 2.    Jordan—Foreign relations—Israel.
3.    Israel—Foreign relations—Jordan. 4.    Arab-Israeli conflict—1993—Peace. I. Anani,
Jawad Ahmed, 1943– II. Haddadin, Munther J. III. Hassan bin Talal, Prince of Jordan.
IV. Title. V. Series.
    DS154.16.I75M35 2006
    327.56940569509'049—dc22

                                                                                    2005055982

*Typeset by* Samantha Barden

Printed in Lebanon

# Contents

# Foreword

## by
## HRH Prince El Hassan bin Talal of Jordan

---

As Chairman of the Board of Advisors of the Center for Peace Studies of the International Programs Center of the University of Oklahoma, it has been a pleasure for me to work with President David L. Boren to promote knowledge and understanding of the Middle East as a means for peacemaking and peace-building.

This volume is one of a number of books focusing on the Middle East and associated with the University of Oklahoma Press with which I have been directly involved.

With that in mind, I commend to readers this latest publication: *Peacemaking: The Inside Story of the 1994 Jordanian–Israeli Treaty.* The authors present historical testimony on one of the most important chapters in the history of Middle East peace negotiations during the twentieth century.

*Peacemaking: The Inside Story of the 1994 Jordanian–Israeli Treaty* describes one of the most significant diplomatic achievements of the Hashemite Kingdom of Jordan under His Late Majesty King Hussein. His Late Majesty earned global recognition and respect for the positive role he played during the second half of the twentieth century in promoting a Middle East settlement based on a just, lasting and comprehensive peace in our region.

Israel has had eleven prime ministers since its establishment in 1948. The Hussein epoch was concurrent with all of them, except the last two. When my late brother assumed office, Israel's first Prime Minister, David Ben Gurion, was still in office. Moshe Sharett, Levi Eshkol, Golda Meir, Yitzhak Rabin, Menachem Begin, Yitzhak Shamir, Shimon Peres and Benjamin Netanyahu became Prime Minister during the forty-seven years of Hussein's reign. No wonder that no other world leader understood Israeli politics and the Middle East peace process as he did.

For thirty-four years (1965–1999) I stood, as Crown Prince, by the side of my late brother and supported all his efforts, including the enduring search for peace and justice.

It was George H. W. Bush, the eighth United States President during Hussein's reign, who finally convened in Madrid the international peace conference for which King Hussein had continuously called as a necessary first step to Arab-Israeli peace.

Together with my late brother we worked in partnership with successive U.S. administrations from Eisenhower to Kennedy, Johnson, Nixon, Ford, Carter, Reagan, Bush, and Clinton to achieve the required breakthrough.

The authors of this book were direct participants in the negotiations that culminated in the 1994 treaty conducted within the framework established by the Madrid Conference for bilateral and multilateral talks.

*Peacemaking: The Inside Story of the 1994 Jordanian–Israeli Treaty* is first of all a detailed first-hand account of Jordan's bilateral and multilateral negotiations. It also covers the Palestinians' participation in the peace process as part of a joint delegation with Jordan. Jordanian efforts to coordinate with other Arab delegations to the peace process are also described. Attention is paid to the Jordanian internal debate over negotiations with the Israelis.

The book contains valuable and interesting material not available anywhere else and is written with humour and an engaging style. I am confident that it will contribute to a better knowledge and understanding of the Middle East, which is the key objective of the Center for Peace Studies of the International Programs Center of the University of Oklahoma.

# Preface

by
David L. Boren, President of the
University of Oklahoma

---

I am honored and pleased to join with His Royal Highness Prince El Hassan bin Talal in providing information to the readers of *Peacemaking: The Inside Story of the 1994 Jordanian–Israeli Treaty*. His Royal Highness is the brother of His Late Majesty King Hussein, whom he served as Crown Prince, closest political adviser, confidant, deputy and Regent during his absences from the country from April 1965 until the changes in succession brought about by King Hussein in January 1999. Prince Hassan has honored the University of Oklahoma by ably serving as the Chair of the Board of Advisors of The University of Oklahoma Center for Peace Studies since 1999.

Jordanian peacemakers have not published accounts about negotiations of the 1994 Jordanian–Israeli Peace Treaty with the Israelis. On the Palestinian side, Hanan Ashrawi and Mahmoud Abbas (Abu Mazin) published their stories and opinions. Shimon Peres, Yossi Beilin, Uri Savir, Itamar Rabinovich and Eyton Benzar published Israeli accounts. This book makes available the experiences and views of Jordanian negotiators.

His Majesty King Hussein was a great leader for peace. His ascension in 1952, four years after the establishment of the State of Israel, coincided with the Egyptian revolution and the rise of Arab revolutionary movements. The bloody coup in Iraq in 1958 which terminated Hashemite rule there left the Hashemite Kingdom of Jordan somewhat alone in a hostile region. The growing strength of the Palestinian Liberation Organization (PLO) since its establishment by the Arab League in 1964 had implications for the Kingdom of Jordan which, more than any country, has accepted Palestinian refugees, treated them humanely, and accorded them Jordanian citizenship. The Jordanian Government for reasons of internal security, territorial jurisdiction and sovereignty was forced to expel Yasir Arafat and the PLO from Jordan in 1971. Notwithstanding this history, for two decades it was the Hashemite Kingdom that enabled Palestinians to participate directly and advance their national interests in international meetings.

Since the end of the 1967 War and the Israeli occupation of Arab territories, Jordan has played a lead role in practically all international efforts aiming at obliging Israel to restore the occupied territories. His Majesty King Hussein and his closest counselors understood that a political settlement was needed with their powerful neighbor Israel. King Hussein simultaneously remained committed to Arab consensus and would not sign a separate peace treaty with Israel unless other Arabs were willing to do so and steps were underway to resolve the 'Palestinian problem'. His Majesty King Hussein was the 'godfather' of United Nations Resolution 242 of 1967 that called for peace in exchange for territories.

The Egyptian–Israeli peace accord of 1979 brokered by President Jimmy Carter, the instability and civil war in Lebanon and its invasion by Israel in 1982, King Hussein's decision to abandon Jordan's territorial claim to the West Bank in 1988, and the first Gulf War in 1991, combined to prompt the United States to work diligently to bring Arabs and Israelis together at the negotiation table to peacefully resolve their protracted conflict. President George Bush and Secretary of State James Baker with support from the Soviet leaders succeeded in convening a Middle East Peace Conference in Madrid in October 1991. The letters of invitation to the parties provided the basis and opportunity for movement toward a comprehensive and lasting peace in the Middle East based on the land for peace formula. Jordan, as it had done since the mid-1970s in international meetings, and this time against strong domestic opposition, allowed the stateless Palestinians to participate as part of its delegation to the 1991 Madrid Conference. *Peacemaking* reveals the interactions and complexities of Jordanian, Israeli and Palestinian relations which add greatly to understanding of the peace process. The chapter which focuses upon the debates within Jordan on the pros and cons of making peace with Israel, especially the debates between the negotiating team and the most prominent Islamists in Jordan at the time, is particularly enlightening.

This book is an important contribution to literature on the Middle East. It joins other books on this region published by the University of Oklahoma Press and the University's International Programs Center, directed by Ambassador (ret.) Edward J. Perkins. These books on the Middle East have been inspired by and grown out of the programs and conferences of the Center for Peace Studies (which is part of the International Programs Center). The Center for Peace Studies is formed by Bethlehem University (Palestine), Haifa University, the Strategic Dialogue Center at Netanya Academic College (Israel), the Horizon Studies and Research Center (Jordan), and the Cairo Peace Association (Egypt) as well as the University of Oklahoma. The Chair of the University of Oklahoma Center for Peace Studies is Dr Christopher Howard and the Director is Dr Joseph Ginat. The general editor of the International and Security Affairs Series is Ambassador (ret.) Edwin G. Corr, Associate Director of the International Programs Center. I am proud to share with you the fourth volume in this series, *Peacemaking: The Inside Story of the 1994 Jordanian–Israeli Treaty.*

# Authors' Preface

This book tells the inside story of peacemaking between Jordan and Israel and the parallel efforts to make peace between Israel and the other Arab parties in as much as they impacted on Jordan. The authors were at the center of action throughout the peace process. Dr Majali was picked by King Hussein in October 1991 to lead the Jordanian delegation to the Jordanian–Israeli bilateral peace negotiations. He occupied that post until May 1993, when he was entrusted by His Majesty to form the Jordanian Cabinet. He became Jordan's Prime Minister, and during his tenure the negotiations with Israel culminated in the Peace Treaty. Dr Majali signed the Treaty on behalf of Jordan on Wednesday, October 26, 1994, and presented it to the Cabinet and to Parliament where it was approved by 55 votes out of 79 members of the Lower House who attended the session (with one absentee). The Treaty was then ratified by the King on November 11, 1994.

Dr Anani was a senior member of the Jordanian delegation to the bilateral negotiations, and was also head of the Jordanian delegation to the Multilateral Working Group on Refugees in the Multilateral Conference until May 1993, when he joined the Cabinet under Dr Majali. Dr Anani was given the portfolio of Minister of State and managed the negotiations with Israel.

Dr Haddadin was a senior member of the Jordanian delegation to the bilateral negotiations where he led the team to negotiate matters concerning water, energy and the environment, and participated in the negotiations over borders. He was concurrently the head of the Jordanian delegation to the Multilateral Working Group on Water Resources, and a member of the Jordanian delegation to the Steering Committee of the Multilateral Conference, and a member of the Jordanian delegation to the Trilateral Economic Committee (the United States, Jordan and Israel) to which he presented the plan for the integrated development of the Jordan Rift Valley. Dr Haddadin later joined the Cabinet under Dr Majali when he formed his second Cabinet in March 1997. He followed up on the implementation of the water Annex to the Peace Treaty, and on the development plan of the Jordan Rift Valley.

The authors were intimately involved with peacemaking (1991–4) and peace-building (1994–8) between Jordan and Israel as part of a comprehensive Middle East peace. They had designed the bilateral peace process in order to make progress on the Jordanian negotiations and to be in tandem with progress achieved on the other bilateral tracks of negotiations between the other Arab parties and Israel, and especially the Palestinians. The efforts culminated in a Jordanian–Israeli peace treaty after the Palestinians and Israel had exchanged recognition in September 1993 and had arrived at an agreement to set up a Palestinian Authority in May 1994, commencing with Gaza and Jericho. Parallel progress was made on the Israeli–Syrian track of negotiations and there were signs that the two parties would soon reach an agreement in the summer of 1994. All these encouraging achievements were made while moderate governments and strong political leadership were in power in the countries concerned. The political will to make peace on the part of the leadership and peoples of these countries existed and it was influential in overcoming the stumbling blocks on the way to peace. King Hussein led Jordan in that process while Prime Minister Yitzhak Rabin headed a coalition of moderate parties in Israel in the same process. The Palestine Liberation Organization (PLO), with Yassir Arafat as its Chairman, led the Palestinians in pursuit of a final status settlement with Israel. President Hafez Assad of Syria had the strength to lead Syria to a full peace with Israel based on the withdrawal of Israeli troops from their occupying position in the Syrian Golan heights. Except for Syria, the bilateral face-to-face contact by the leadership of the negotiating parties overcame the difficult issues encountered in the bilateral negotiations. The famous Washington Declaration of July 25, 1994 made jointly by Rabin and King Hussein and their subsequent meetings in the region gave impetus to the negotiations and accelerated agreements and resolution of several thorny issues concerning borders, security and water-related matters.

The personal involvement of the leaders proved necessary in the period that followed the 1994 Peace Treaty. The assassination of Prime Minister Rabin was a tremendous blow to this approach of higher diplomacy. Political power in Israel soon shifted to a coalition led by Likud and religious parties, and strain quickly loomed over the

Palestinian–Israeli contacts. King Hussein was influential in bringing the Palestinian and Israeli leadership to negotiate in 1996 over Hebron and again in 1998 during the Wye River negotiations. The sustained efforts also made by President Bill Clinton kept the Palestinians and the Israelis engaged. The death of King Hussein in January 1999 was another setback to the approach of higher diplomacy. President Clinton took it upon himself to stimulate the negotiations in the Middle East peace process. He attempted to narrow the differences between Syria and Israel and met with President Hafez Assad in Geneva in March 2000 but he did not succeed. Soon after, President Assad also passed away and his successor and son, Dr Bashar Assad, ascended to power with the negotiations with Israel stalled. Encouraged by the ascent to power in 1999 in Israel of a labour-led coalition headed by Prime Minister Ehud Barak, President Clinton decided to attempt to steer the negotiations between Israel and the Palestinians to a successful end before his presidential term expired. He brought the parties to another round of talks at Camp David in the summer of 2000 and again in the fall of that same year and an agreement on a final status between the Palestinians and Israel appeared to be very close. However, the issue of the right of return of Palestinian refugees proved the stumbling block and the negotiations collapsed.

In late August 2000, using a provocative visit to the Aqsa Mosque by the newly elected head of the Likud, General Ariel Sharon, the Palestinians responded the next day (after Friday prayers in the mosque) with riots and stone throwing. The Israeli reaction was more serious and blood was shed again. The event soon developed into a second Intifada that has raged since then. Elections were called in Israel and the combined effect of the failure of the Camp David talks and the new Intifada swayed the Israeli electorate to the right, and the Likud, headed by Ariel Sharon, triumphed at the elections. A violent confrontation was inevitable. The occupied Palestinian territories had never witnessed as much bloodshed as has occurred since the Intifada began. Israeli tanks violated the territories run by the Palestinian Authority and destroyed several refugee camps. The Israeli Defense Forces waged pre-emptive attacks against Palestinians suspected of 'terrorist' tendencies and targeted many Palestinian leaders for airborne assassination. The Palestinians responded with suicide bombers; victims fell on both sides, but the majority were Palestinians. The opposing extremists had their way, with no end yet in sight.

A crucial discouraging factor was the initial disengagement of the United States Administration that succeeded Clinton's. They were discouraged by the failure at Camp David and decided to put the Palestinian–Israeli conflict on the back burner. This eased the job of the new Israeli government in its violent confrontation with the Palestinians. General Ariel Sharon declared Arafat, Chairman of the PLO and President of the Palestinian Authority, as a supporter of terrorism and had him confined to his headquarters at Ramallah. Sharon further declared that there was no Palestinian partner to negotiate with.

The murderous attack on the American World Trade Center and the Pentagon on September 11, 2001 led to ramifications for the Palestinians. The United States launched a 'War on Terrorism', declared some Palestinian groupings as terrorist organizations, and froze their assets. Sharon's actions against the Palestinians were marketed on his behalf as part of the 'War on Terrorism'. Soon, the 'Honest Broker' of the Middle East peace process appeared to be taking sides, a move that pushed the Palestinians and the Arabs in a corner.

The situation worsened again in 2003 when the United States led a coalition to attack Iraq on the pretext of an imminent danger posed by the alleged acquisition by Iraq of weapons of mass destruction. Iraq's regime was forcibly changed amid worldwide protest. The coalition occupied Iraq and installed a provisional government to whom it attempted to restore sovereignty.

The situation at the time of writing is very different from the situation that prevailed after an earlier coalition led by the United States evicted Iraqi troops from Kuwait in 1991. Soon after that, the United States administration was capable of designing a peace process that was sponsored jointly by itself and the Soviet Union. The high expectations on the part of officials and the people in the region facilitated negotiations. The neutrality of the co-sponsors added to that facilitation. Some confidence building was necessary and that was not impossible. The parties met in Madrid on October 31, 1991 and the bilateral conference began. All concerned parties (except Syria and Lebanon) met in Moscow in late January 1992 along with other international parties and the multilateral conference was initiated. Progress gave hope of a better future shaped by peaceful relations and fruitful cooperation.

However the multilateral conference stalled soon after the Likud coalition took office in Israel in 1996, and the bilateral negotiations continued, only to terminate in 2000. A lot of damage has been done to Israeli–Palestinian relations and the image of the United States as a peace sponsor has been tarnished. The United States is no longer viewed as honest and neutral, but rather as taking the side of Israel, casting a negative vote in the United Nations Security Council whenever the Israeli operations were discussed. A lot of confidence rebuilding between the parties lies ahead before negotiations can be restarted with hope of any successful conclusion. Most recently, Israel, under the pretext of security, has been erecting a barrier of fences and walls that trespasses on occupied Palestinian territories. The barrier has been ruled illegal by the International Court of Justice, and a resolution against the barrier was passed by the General Assembly of the United Nations. Instead of cooling things down, developments have ignited hatred and re-established enmity. To add insult to injury, the internal Palestinian situation has been upset and a case close to chaos now prevails in the Gaza Strip. Remedial measures are needed to rectify the Palestinian internal front, and more work is needed to restore confidence in the sponsor and between the parties. A 'Road Map' leading to the final status between the Palestinians and the Israelis had been laid down. Sponsored by Russia, the European Union, the United Nations and the United States it currently forms the basis of the final settlement leading to two states, Israel and Palestine, living side by side in peace and harmony. The translation of this vision into actuality is a formidable task that requires courageous leadership and brave popular support.

This book details the events that the authors experienced during the negotiations and lays out the arguments put forth by the parties. Issues covered by colleagues are extracted from reports they submitted on the work of their Working Groups of the Multilateral Conference, but their accounts are carried simply to put the bilateral negotiations into perspective.

# Introduction

## Tribute to a Royal Peacemaker

The Princedom of Transjordan, the predecessor of the Hashemite Kingdom of Jordan, was established in 1921 in the wake of the Mandate over Palestine, Iraq, Syria and Lebanon. Abdallah Ibn al-Hussein, the second son of Hussein Bin Ali who led the Arab Revolt against the Ottoman Turks, was named the Emir (prince) of the new Emirate. His elder brother Ali was the Emir of Hijaz under his father, and his younger brother, Faysal, who ascended the throne of Syria for a short while, was chosen to be King of Iraq after the French ousted him from Syria. Their father, Sharif Hussein Bin Ali, died in Cyprus where he was exiled because of a dispute with the British Government over its unfulfilled promise to unite the Arab East in one Arab Kingdom under him, and over the British intention to establish a national home for the Jews in Palestine.

It was as he was leading troops from Hijaz to claim the throne of Syria that Abdallah was invited by the British Minister of the Colonies to a meeting in Jerusalem where he was offered the Emirate of Transjordan and was thus dissuaded from continuing his mission to regain Syria. Confident that the Hashemite plan for the unity of the Arab East would eventually come to fruition, Abdallah accepted the offer and established the first system of centralised government in what today is modern Jordan on April 11, 1921. Throughout his reign as head of the Emirate of Transjordan and the Hashemite Kingdom, Abdallah never lost sight of his basic goal of unifying the Arabs into one kingdom. He sought the unity of Greater Syria (Jordan, Palestine, Lebanon and Syria), and at times considered working for the unity of the Fertile Crescent by adding Iraq to the 'Syrian' states.

Emir Abdallah worked to loosen the grip of the British Mandate over Transjordan by concluding an Anglo-Jordanian Treaty on May 15, 1923. The British formal recognition of the Emirate of Transjordan as a state under the leadership of Emir Abdallah effectively truncated Transjordan from Palestine thereby reducing the area earmarked for a national home for the Jews under the Balfour Declaration of November 2, 1917. The Treaty stipulated that Transjordan would be prepared for independence under the general supervision of the British High Commissioner in Jerusalem.

In May 1925, immediately after Emir Ali was overthrown and Hijaz fell to the House of Saud after a Hashemite rule of 724 years (1201–1925), the Aqaba and Ma'an districts, then parts of Hijaz, became part of Transjordan. Between 1928 and 1946, a series of Anglo-Transjordanian treaties led to almost full independence for Transjordan. Emir Abdallah negotiated a new Anglo-Transjordanian Treaty on March 22, 1946, ending the Mandate and gaining full independence for Transjordan. In exchange for the provision of military facilities within Transjordan, Britain continued to pay a financial subsidy and supported the Arab Legion that it had helped set up and organize under the leadership of British officers, most notably General John Baggot Glubb. Two months later, on May 25, 1946, the Transjordanian parliament proclaimed Emir Abdallah king, while officially changing the name of the country from the Emirate of Transjordan to the Hashemite Kingdom of Jordan.

Abdallah realized that true stability could only be achieved by establishing representative institutions. As early as April 1928, he promulgated a Basic Law (constitution) that provided for an elected Legislative Council to exercise advisory powers. The first Legislative Council followed elections in February 1929. It comprised 21 members, seven appointed by the Emir.

The early years of the new Emirate of Transjordanian were dominated by the issue of Palestine. Under the British Mandate, this became the destination of Jewish migration from Europe. As Jewish immigration grew, Palestinians became increasingly worried. In Transjordanian political parties emerged opposing the entry of Jewish immigrants, or the purchase by Jews of lands in Transjordan. A minority did not fear Jewish entre-preneurship inside Transjordan, but no such Jewish activities were ever allowed by the British Mandate or by the Transjordanian Government. That did not prevent contacts being made by the Jewish Agency, part of the Zionist Movement, with persons inside Transjordan in the hope that opposition to the Zionist schemes for Palestine would be diluted. However, the connection between Palestine and Transjordan was strong, so much so that political parties spanned the River Jordan to include Palestinians and Jordanians in their membership. As Jewish immigration to Palestine continued unabated, the Palestinians organized themselves and staged their first 'Intifada' in 1936.

The British Government sent its first high-level Royal Commission in November 1936, headed by Earl Peel, former Secretary of State for India, to study the situation and make recommendations. The mission proposed the partition of Palestine into an Arab Palestinian state and a Jewish state, set a limit on Jewish immigration and specified a special status for Jerusalem. The mission's report angered both Palestinians and Zionists, who planned more immigration. The British Government sent a second mission, headed by Sir John Woodhead, whose report slightly amended the Peel Commission's recommendations.

Zionist efforts to increase Jewish immigration into Palestine were enhanced by the rise of Nazism in Europe. Throughout the period of the Second World War and thereafter, the Jewish influx into Palestine increased manifold, and the proposed ceilings for Jewish immigration set by both the Peel and the Woodhead Commissions were not enforced. The cauldron of Palestine reached boiling point in the years immediately after the Second World War. With international sympathy firmly behind the Jews in the wake of the Holocaust, Zionist leaders in Palestine brought pressure on the Mandate Administration through terrorism and other means. Finally, extracting itself from the situation, Britain declared in February 1947 that its mandate over Palestine would end on May 14, 1948.

The newly founded United Nations Organization (UN), successor of the League of Nations that had issued the Mandate, had to deal with the matter. After rejecting various plans, the UN voted for the partition of Palestine on November 29, 1947. More than half the territory of Palestine, including the fertile and valuable coastal plain, was allocated to the Jews who owned only 6 per cent of the land. Jerusalem would come under UN trusteeship.

The Palestinians and the Arabs were shocked, and conflict was inevitable. Serious clashes took place between the underground Jewish paramilitary organizations and the Jordan Arab Legion, whose three battalions had entered Palestine to assist the British Mandate in maintaining domestic peace. Additionally, well-armed and trained Jewish extremist groups waged attacks on Palestinian villages and killed and terrorized their inhabitants with the objective of having them flee their country. The flight of Palestinians started in the spring of 1948 to escape the terror of these Jewish groups with the belief that they would return to their homes as soon as law and order were established. Jordan was a natural destination for the Palestinian refugees, and so were the parts of Palestine with exclusive Arab inhabitants.

The British terminated their mandate over Palestine on May 14, 1948, and the Jews immediately proclaimed the establishment of the State of Israel. The new state was recognized and was admitted to membership of the United Nations. The United States White House, against the recommendation of the State Department, prepared the recognition announcement even before it knew what the name of the new state would be. Two days before the end of the Mandate, an Arab League meeting was held in Amman and concluded that Arab countries would send troops to Palestine to join forces with the Jordan Arab Legion there to defend the Palestinians against the Jewish atrocities. Lebanon, Syria, Egypt and Iraq sent regular troops to Palestine. The Arab League also started to mobilize volunteers under the leadership of Fawzi al-Qawuqji, a Lebanese national, to help protect Palestine against the Jewish takeover. The better prepared, trained, equipped and disciplined Israeli forces outnumbered the Arab forces and eventually had the upper hand in military confrontations with Arab regulars and volunteers, and the Israelis were able to occupy more territories of Palestine than the UN partition resolution allotted to them. Hundreds of thousands of Palestinians fled the horrors of war and took refuge in the predominantly Arab parts of Palestine (Gaza and the West Bank), the Hashemite Kingdom of Jordan, Syria, Lebanon, and Egypt.

The Jordan Arab Legion was able to rout Israeli forces from the old city of Jerusalem and keep possession of it and the surrounding Arab villages, including Latrun. The Arab Legion and Iraqi forces were able to defend the West Bank, and the Egyptian forces defended Gaza, while the Syrian forces were able to gain and keep a foothold in areas of Palestine north, east and south of Lake Tiberias. The war was interrupted by two UN-imposed truces and ended with the conclusion of four truce agreements between Israel and Egypt, Lebanon, Jordan and Syria respectively in February, March, April and July of 1949.

The Palestinians of the West Bank, who were saved from a Jewish takeover by the Arab Legion and Iraqi forces, decided in a conference held at Jericho to seek unification with the Hashemite Kingdom of Jordan.

Arrangements were made for the elections of a new Parliament on April 11, 1950 in which Palestinians had an equal number of representatives to the Jordanians. Thirteen days later, the Parliament unanimously approved a motion to unite the two banks of the Jordan, constitutionally expanding the Hashemite Kingdom of Jordan to include the West Bank. The move was consistent with the aspirations of Jordanians who saw it as a step toward greater Arab unity, and was responsive to the hopes of the Palestinians who feared Israeli expansion at their expense. It was also consistent with goals of the Hashemite king, Abdallah, whose efforts to unite Greater Syria never wavered.

King Abdallah's reign came to an end on July 20, 1951 when he was assassinated as he was entering al-Aqsa mosque in Jerusalem to perform Friday noon prayer. The assassin also fired a shot at the young prince Hussein, and had the bullet not ricocheted off a medal on his chest, he might also have perished.

Following the death of King Abdallah, the Jordanian throne passed to Crown Prince Talal, the late king's eldest son, who assumed the monarchy on September 6, 1951. For health reasons, King Talal had to abdicate less than a year later, on August 11, 1952, in favor of his eldest son, Prince Hussein. During his brief reign, King Talal enacted a modern constitution on January 1, 1952. The document made the government collectively, and the ministers individually, responsible to the parliament. The young King Hussein could not assume power until he became 18 lunar years of age, and a Regency Council performed his functions until he assumed constitutional powers on May 2, 1953. The smoothness of the transfer of power from Abdallah to Talal and from Talal to Hussein was remarkable, indicating the extent to which King Abdallah had succeeded in achieving constitutional order in Transjordan. The smoothness of transition was further confirmed as the world witnessed the assumption of constitutional powers by King Abdallah II Ibn al-Hussein on February 7, 1999 upon the death of his father, King Hussein.

King Hussein reigned during difficult times in the Middle East region. The 1950s witnessed multiple military coups in Syria, one in Egypt and another in Iraq. The most bloody was the Iraqi coup on July 14, 1958 when the Iraqi Royal Palace, Qasr al-Rihab, was stormed by rebellious troops and the young Hashemite King Faysal II, Hussein's cousin, was murdered along with all his relatives. The most notable events were frequent military clashes with Israel, the Suez Campaign, a decade of Arab cold war between 1957 and 1967, and one of armed tension in Yemen.

The Palestinian tragedy clouded Arab skies and overshadowed most other issues. In the midst of the Arab cold war, President Nasser of Egypt called for an Arab Summit in Cairo in January 1964 to work out plans to counter Israeli designs to divert the waters of the River Jordan. Another summit was convened in Alexandria, Egypt, in September of the same year at which the Palestine Liberation Organization (PLO) was created, and the late Ahmad Shuqeiry was installed at its head. The aim of the Arab leaders was to organize Palestinian efforts to recover their rights in their homeland, and to establish a Palestine Liberation Army that would join other Arab armies in the forthcoming battle over territory. A few months later, on January 1, 1965, a group of young Palestinian graduates, led by engineer Yassir Arafat, announced the formation of the Palestine National Liberation Movement (PNLM), better known by its acronym, FATH (Harakat al-Tahreer al-Filasteeni, read in reverse). Supported by leftist regimes of the Arab states, FATH conducted limited incursions into Israel from Syrian and Jordanian territories to carry out sabotage operations. (The Egyptian front was closed to such operations by virtue of the deployment of a UN Emergency Force after the Suez Campaign.) Such activities further worsened the fragile truce between Syria and Israel and between Jordan and Israel.

King Hussein's preoccupation with ending Israeli occupation after the June 1967 war did not cause him to neglect the economic and social development of what remained under his jurisdiction of the Kingdom. His brother, al-Hassan Bin Talal, Crown Prince for 34 years, was entrusted with a major role in the process of rehabilitation of the economy and its further development. The country achieved impressive rates of economic growth and social development through carefully prepared five-year plans. Throughout the reign of King Hussein the per capita income of Jordan soared from a modest $180 equivalent in 1952 to almost ten times that figure in 1988. It dipped in 1989 due to financial hardships and the drying up of Arab grants, but resumed its ascent in the 1990s to approach $1,600 by the end of the century. Strides were made in the various fields of social development, including education, health care, the role of women, public utility coverage of the entire country, and impressive rates of higher education among males and females.

As far as Palestine was concerned, the most devastating blow came in June 1967 with the defeat of the Arab armies, including the Jordanian Armed Forces that were put under Egyptian command, at the hands of Israel and the occupation by Israel of Egyptian Sinai, Syrian Golan Heights and whatever remained of Palestine (the West Bank including old Jerusalem, and Gaza). These events gave the PLO and FATH global prominence. Many other factions quickly emerged, some transformations of underground nationalistic parties. The number of organizations that existed after the war seeking the liberation of Palestine exceeded a dozen. They soon came under the umbrella of the PLO, and Yassir Arafat became its third leader in 1968, succeeding Ahmad Shuqeiry and Yahya Hammoudeh.

In Jordan King Hussein worked hard to rebuild the shattered Jordanian Armed Forces, and to secure the domestic situation that was threatened by the paramilitary presence of the various factions of the PLO. In a swift operation in September 1970, the Jordan Army succeeded in routing the PLO, and forced them to evacuate Amman in April of 1971. Regionally, the King maintained his drive to find a peaceful solution to the Middle East conflict, rallying the Arabs to adopt a solution through the convening of an international peace conference. Five devastating wars between Israel and the Arab parties had taken place but had failed to achieve the results people were after: peace and stability. King Hussein participated in each Arab Summit during his reign in an attempt to cement Arab solidarity in the face of common dangers. In one Arab Summit convened in Rabat, Morocco, the Arab leaders decreed that the PLO was the 'sole legitimate representative of the Palestinian people'. The King reluctantly went along with the Arab consensus that he had always respected.

Throughout the 1980s, King Hussein devoted his attention to Middle East peace. He attempted to coordinate closely with the PLO and reached agreement with Arafat on Palestinian-Jordanian representation in any peace conference, but that agreement was aborted in 1984. In July 1988, all administrative and legal ties between Jordan and the West Bank were severed to give the PLO a free rein to liberate the Palestinian territories from Israeli occupation.

American efforts to start a Middle East peace process resumed after the liberation of Kuwait from Iraqi occupation in January 1991.

American Secretary of State, James Baker, made history in bringing Arabs and Israelis to a peace conference. A peace process started in Madrid on October 30, 1991 and Jordan participated along with Syria and Lebanon. It enabled the Palestinians to participate under the state umbrella of Jordan. The bilateral negotiations between Jordan and Israel culminated in a Peace Treaty that was signed between the two countries on October 26, 1994, and witnessed by the President of the United States.

King Hussein was instrumental in overcoming serious stumbling blocks in negotiations between Israel and the Palestinians. He was behind the successful agreement to have the Israeli Army withdraw from Hebron in 1997, and he rushed from his hospital bed during his treatment for lymphoma to the aid of President Clinton when the Wye River negotiations almost collapsed in October 1998. 'We have no right,' said the King, 'to jeopardize the life of our children and our children's children. There has been enough destruction and enough hatred. It is time to make up for lost time.' Death, however, snatched the King away on February 7, 1999, and the peace process lost a primary player and an important stabilizer. The other major player was Israeli Prime Minister, Yitzhak Rabin, a hero in wars, and a hero in peace. Rabin lost his life on November 4, 1995 when an Israeli extremist shot him in a main Tel Aviv square after he participated in a celebration marking the first anniversary of the Peace Treaty with Jordan.

# 1

# A Call to Peace

───────

The President of the United States, George Bush, having organized a coalition of 33 countries against Iraq and forcing it out of Kuwait in 1991, decided to resume the quest for peace in the Middle East. His Secretary of State, James Baker III, shuttled between Egypt, Jordan, Syria, the Palestinian Territories, Lebanon, and Israel to conduct talks with top officials. There were many thorny issues to address, resolve, and remove from the path to peace.

On the Arab side, the atmosphere was tense in the wake of the war on Iraq, and the ranks were split. Jordan, having declined to join the American-led coalition to liberate Kuwait, was viewed as a supporter of the Iraqi invasion of Kuwait. The PLO Chairman, Yassir Arafat, and the leaders of Yemen, Sudan, Libya, Tunisia and Algeria were also considered to have sided with Iraq, only because they insisted on an Arab solution to the invasion they, in fact, deplored. Jordan suffered economic losses and almost total isolation from the rest of the world. Its only seaport, Aqaba, was blockaded by the US Navy, and ships visiting that port were subject to inspection to eliminate any possible flow of goods to Iraq from Aqaba in violation of a series of Security Council resolutions passed to enforce economic trade and military sanctions against Iraq.

Secretary Baker's efforts were a resumption of American peace efforts initiated during the Reagan administration and conducted in the region by his Secretary of State, George Schultz. A major obstacle was the representation of the Palestinians. The PLO, decreed by the Arab leaders as the sole legitimate representative of the Palestinian people, was not recognized by the United States, and contacts with it were prohibited. However, on November 15, 1988, the Palestine National Council (PNC) voted to recognize Israel's legitimacy, to accept all relevant UN resolutions going back to the Partition Resolution of November 29, 1947, and to adopt a two states solution for Palestine. The PLO subsequently denounced all forms of individual, group and state terrorism. This step prompted the United States to start a dialogue with the PLO in Tunis, led by the US Ambassador, Robert Pelletreau, but was not enough for the United States to override the Israeli veto against official or private contacts with the PLO. Yitzhak Shamir, Israel's prime minister, countered the Palestinian initiative on May 14, 1989 by presenting his Cabinet with a peace plan. He called for elections in the West Bank and Gaza to select a non-PLO leadership with whom Israel could negotiate an interim agreement for self-government based on the Camp David Accord.

On May 22, Secretary Baker spoke at an annual convention of the American-Israeli Public Affairs Committee (AIPAC) in Washington, DC. In his opening remarks, Baker highlighted the shared commitment to democratic values and the strong strategic partnership between America and Israel, and he welcomed the Shamir plan as 'an important and positive start down the road toward constructing workable negotiations'. But when Secretary Baker came to the fate of the Occupied Territories, his pronouncements differed very importantly from Shamir's proposal. The Secretary interpreted Resolution 242 as requiring the exchange of land for peace; he referred to 'territorial withdrawal' as the probable outcome of negotiations. In a pointed reference to Shamir's and many Jews' ideology, Baker said,

> For Israel, now is the time to lay aside, once and for all, the unrealistic vision of greater Israel. Israeli interests in the West Bank and Gaza – security and otherwise – can be accommodated in a settlement based on Resolution 242. Forswear annexation. Stop settlement activity. Allow schools to reopen. Reach out to Palestinians as neighbors who deserve political rights.

Secretary Baker's speech was not well received by his large Jewish-American audience, and it raised worries in Israel. It marked a shift toward a more active effort by the Bush administration to redesign the Shamir initiative into something that might be acceptable to the Palestinians. Such an approach found acceptance among Arabs and signaled to them Secretary Baker's commitment to be fair, serious and bold in his search for a common ground on which a peace process could be based. To define such common ground and get a process started required cooperation among the concerned parties. Innovative ideas and exceptional diplomatic skills were also mandatory. Secretary Baker possessed the needed skills and innovations. The Arab parties directly involved in the process were Jordan, the Palestinians, Syria and Lebanon. The influential regional parties among the Arabs were Saudi Arabia and Egypt.

The relations between the leaders of those countries left a great deal to be desired, especially after Iraq's invasion of Kuwait. Assad of Syria was hardly on speaking terms with Hussein of Jordan; he had severed all contacts with Arafat of the PLO. Leaders of Saudi Arabia and the Gulf States were not on speaking terms with Hussein or Arafat. Arafat always harbored suspicions toward Hussein fearing that he wanted the West Bank taken back into his Kingdom, and so on. Secretary Baker therefore had to bridge Arab rifts as well as get the Arabs and Israelis talking. The PLO was central to the initiation of the process, yet was not eligible to participate because of Israeli objections and American reservations. No public Palestinian figure would venture to step out of the PLO line, or to indulge into political talks with any other party without the consent of the PLO. A leaflet issued by the leadership of the Palestinian Intifada, after the Shamir Plan was announced, rejected Shamir's call for elections because they would occur under occupation, insisted there was no alternative to the PLO, and asserted that settlement of the Palestine–Israeli dispute could only be reached through an international conference with full powers.

The fiercest opposition to the Shamir Plan, not surprisingly, came from within Shamir's Likud party ranks. General Ariel Sharon, along with David Levy and Yitzhak Moda'i, accused Shamir of leading Israel toward destruction. They proposed four conditions, by which they hoped to thwart the Plan, and received the endorsement of the Likud Central Committee. The four conditions were: a) the Intifada (on the rise since December 1987) should be crushed, b) the Arabs of East Jerusalem should be prohibited from participating in the Palestinian elections, c) there must be no divisions in the western part of the Land of Israel (meaning west of the Jordan River and implying that there was a 'Land of Israel' east of it), and, d) there should be no contact with the PLO. Shamir did not fight for his plan and allowed the opposition to destroy his initiative.

The disagreements inside Israel over peace with the Arabs brought the national unity government to a crisis when Shamir dismissed Shimon Peres, vice premier and a Labor leader, from the government because

Peres had claimed that the government was not trying to advance the peace process. Peres' colleagues in the governing coalition walked out of the Cabinet and his Labor Party put a motion of no confidence in the government to the Knesset. The government fell. It was the first Israeli government to fall because of a no-confidence vote.

Shamir assembled a new coalition with a small majority in the Knesset that was composed of religious and ultra-rightist parties. The basic guidelines of the new government were: a) no Palestinian state, b) no negotiations with the PLO, c) Jerusalem to remain united under Israel's sovereignty, d) new settlements to be created and existing ones expanded, and, e) talks with the Arab states and non-PLO Palestinians to proceed on the basis of the Shamir Plan.

Secretary Baker shuttled between Cairo, Riyadh, Amman, Tel Aviv and Damascus seeking consensus to start the peace process. Difficulties faced him in each of these capitals. The Arab side, on the one hand, demanded that an international conference should be the mechanism through which the Arab–Israeli conflict should be resolved. This had been their position for a long time, frequently reiterated by King Hussein. The Israelis, on the other hand, insisted that the conflict should be resolved through bilateral negotiations conducted separately between Israel and each of its Arab rivals. Israel further opposed the participation of the PLO, a primary player in any peacemaking between the Arabs and Israel.

Secretary Baker achieved a breakthrough by combining the demands of both the Arabs and the Israelis. He proposed that the peace process would be composed of two conferences: a bilateral conference in which Israel would negotiate separately with each of its adversaries to resolve bilateral issues of dispute, political and otherwise; and a multilateral conference in which a number of countries would participate including the five permanent members of the Security Council. The multilateral conference would tackle issues that needed international involvement for resolution; and it would gain support for the bilateral negotiations, and reinforce peace and stability in the area.

Secretary Baker's second breakthrough was to pull Israel into the process. The Shamir government made conditions for its involvement in peace that were hard to satisfy. The strategy was to evade and defy American pressures. The Secretary skillfully used diplomatic tools available to him. Israel was in need of funding for the settlement of

Jewish immigrants pouring in from the collapsing Soviet Union. In addition to the annual US official aid package of $3 billion, Israel needed loan guarantees of $10 billion to fund a housing program for these immigrants. The United States had by then given Israel a total of $77 billion dollars in official aid, a per capita level unmatched in the history of foreign aid for any country. Secretary Baker made it clear to the Israelis they could keep the occupied Palestinian territories of which the rightist Israeli government was unwilling to let go, or keep the support of the United States. (The Bush administration probably did not feel it owed much to American Jewry, since President Bush got no more than 5 per cent of the Jewish vote in his bid for the presidency in 1988.)

Secretary Baker's third achievement was to bring the Palestinians into the peace process. Without bringing in the PLO, he saw to it that Palestinian representatives would have the PLO blessing but that Israel retained a veto power over any such representative. In this he was assisted by King Hussein who agreed to enable the stateless Palestinians to participate in the peace conferences under the state umbrella of Jordan in the form of a joint Jordanian-Palestinian delegation. He also assured the representation of Jerusalem in the Jordanian delegation, thus compensating for its absence from the Palestinian delegation by virtue of the Israeli veto.

The admirable work of Secretary James Baker, supported by President George Bush, made possible the convening of the peace conference in Madrid, Spain, on October 30, 1991. The Secretary issued letters of invitation to the conference, provided assurances to each participating party, and stipulated that the process would be based on Security Council Resolutions 242 and 338 and the principle of exchanging land for peace.

In preparation for the Madrid Conference, King Hussein called a Jordanian national meeting to which dignitaries, officials and Jordanians from all walks of life were invited. His Majesty announced in a speech that Jordan could not afford to stay behind while the future of the region was being shaped, and he provided convincing arguments, quoting from the Qur'an, for Jordan to join the peace process in Madrid with its other Arab brothers.

The King chose Dr Abdul Salam Majali,[1] a seasoned statesman with long experience of service to Jordan, to head the Jordanian delegation to the bilateral negotiations. Returning from a mission to

Paris for UNESCO, Majali received a briefing from King Hussein on the latest developments for the convening of a peace conference. On October 26, 1991, the King sent Majali an open letter of assignment, broadcast over the radio and television, in which the King extolled Majali's leadership and loyalty, and wished him good luck on his assignment. Majali's appointment was well received in the country. His dedication, loyalty, and public and private records have earned him the respect of all who have known him or heard of him. 'Your appointment is another call to arms,' noted one of his colleagues, 'except this time it is a battle for peace. I am sure it will be harder for you than the wars that you have been through.'

Honored to be chosen by the King, for his part Majali held sober views and perceptions of the Arab–Israeli conflict. He noted that the Zionist Movement, since its formal creation in 1897, was able to ally itself with the most powerful countries and force commitments out of influential leaders. The Arabs had practically no allies. In preparation for the Arab Revolt of 1916 against the Ottoman Turks, for example, the Arabs had allied themselves with Britain which, it turned out, was deeply committed to the Zionist Movement! He realized that the balance of power in the world scene was heavily in favor of the Jews. 'Throughout this century,' Majali would point out,

the Zionist Movement has been involved in hot wars and cold wars with the Arabs. We lost Palestine to the Zionists after they gained the support of the advanced western countries and the socialist bloc. There developed throughout the twentieth century a dichotomy in the world's perception of Palestine, a western perception and an Arab perception. In the countries of the West there has been deep sympathy with the Jews for many reasons; such as the religious linkages of Christianity with Judaism through the Old Testament, the sharing of western culture and value systems, the active presence of Jews in western societies, the stories of the horrors of the holocaust, the influence of Jewish interests in economic, financial, political, ideological, educational, scientific and other fields in the western world. Western perception of Palestine was gradually reinforced by a revival of the notion of the Promised Land for the Jews. Palestine also contains the Christian holy sites on which Christian Orthodoxy and Catholicism place high religious value. Western perceptions normally overlook Palestinian suffering and human aspirations to avoid moral and ethical questions over the support of western societies for the Jewish National Home in Palestine. Western perception, in addition, is not without the extensional effects of the Crusades of the twelfth and thirteenth centuries when the confrontation between the Arabs and Europe lasted for two centuries.

Palestinians as people do not enter the consciousness of Westerners; but when they do, they are almost always in the context of violence and are portrayed mostly as terrorists. There is no mention of their elite that have excelled in various branches of science, art and literature. Palestinians are way behind Israel in the contest for winning western public opinion.

People did not know what to expect. They remembered the United Nation's frustrated efforts to have Security Council Resolutions 242 and 338 implemented. They remembered the difficulties faced by the United States in its attempts to make peace in the Middle East in recent decades: The Roger's Plan in 1969; President Jimmy Carter's partial success at Camp David in 1978, making peace – but not a comprehensive one – between Egypt and Israel; President Ronald Reagan's Plan of 1982; and the shuttle diplomacy of Secretary of State George Schultz in the mid-1980s. Many recalled the reports of King Hussein's continuous efforts to initiate a peace conference and several of Majali's friends and colleagues wondered how it could be possible, after all this, to start a process now aimed at a comprehensive peace in the region.

Majali would reason thus:

The Cold War is over, thanks to Gorbachev's perestroika. The Gulf War is over. Iraq is all but destroyed and something has to be done to usher the region into a new era. Oil is critical to modern civilization and will continue to be important in the competition among the world's economic powers. In the previous era, before the end of the Cold War, the West depended on Israel to guard its interests in the oil fields. The Gulf War that the United States led against Iraq brought the western powers into the region, and they no longer have to depend on Israel to protect the oil fields. They can do it by themselves. No fire should be ignited next to that precious flammable wealth – oil – and the West must diffuse the potential for igniting such fire. The protracted conflict between the Arabs and Israel therefore has to be resolved. That conflict has been the major source of tension in the region, and it should be brought to an end.

'A new element recently emerged,' Majali stated.

It is Secretary of State Mr James Baker. His talents, diplomatic skills, intelligence and wit, his immense courage, fairness and persistence made a difference today. He has meticulously designed the process so that all parties who have a stake in the outcome will play a role of some kind. Many states, in addition to the permanent members of the Security Council, have interests in Middle East peace. Europe, Canada and Japan, and countries in Asia, Africa and South America have been affected in different ways by tensions in the Middle East. Their interests in peace should be accommodated.

Secretary Baker succeeded in formulating the peace process to accommodate demands by the Israelis and the Arabs; he also brought in the EU, Canada, Japan and the Soviets as partners.

The following days were very busy for Majali and for the leadership of the country. The Jordanian delegation to Madrid had to be selected, important homework had to be done, and done correctly in the short time left before October 30, 1991. Contacts with the sponsors of the peace process were continuous for clarification and coordination. Logistical support had to be put in place. The Royal Court became like a beehive and the Government of Taher al-Masri[2] worked at peak efficiency.

Crown Prince al-Hassan managed the preparations. He called on experts for consultation and counsel from the United States, the United Kingdom, Australia, Germany, and others. He met frequently in marathon sessions with the Jordanian delegates. He examined the draft position papers, asked critical questions and provided enlightening comments. Drawing on directions from Crown Prince al-Hassan, and on the provisions of the Letter of Invitation and Letter of Commitment that Jordan had received from the sponsors of the peace process, Majali conducted successive meetings with the Jordanian delegation at the Government's VIP Guest House in Jebal Amman. He reviewed the situation, appraised the stands each of the negotiators expressed, issued instructions, organized logistics, and set out rules of conduct.

The King ordered a special flight of a Royal Jordanian Airline Tri-Star to carry the Jordanians and Palestinians to Madrid. His Majesty presided over the official ceremony to bid farewell and wish good luck to the joint delegation at the Amman Airport. The Crown Prince, the Prime Minister, and Cabinet Ministers were present. In Madrid, the organization of the conference by the Spaniards was superb. Security was very tight. The opening session was historic.

The President of the United States, George Bush, the President of the USSR, Mikhail Gorbachev, and the Secretary General of the United Nations, Javier Perez de Cuellar, attended. The delegates took their seats in accordance with a pre-arranged understanding. The joint Jordanian-Palestinian delegation sat across from the Israeli delegation, and we Jordanians stared at our 'enemies', some with inhibition. Yizhak Shamir, Israel's Prime Minister, headed the Israeli delegation. The Minister of Foreign Affairs, Kamel Abu Jaber, headed the Jordanian-Palestinian delegation. The Syrian and Lebanese delegations were headed by their respective foreign ministers, Farouq al-Share' of Syria and Faris Boise of Lebanon. There were also regional delegates. Abdallah Bisharah represented the Gulf Cooperation Council and Foreign Minister Amr Musa represented Egypt. The European Union was also represented.

King Juan Carlos of Spain gave the opening speech, followed by the sponsors of the peace process, the President of the United States and the President of the USSR. The head of each delegation made a speech. Press coverage was unprecedented. It was a golden opportunity for Arab delegations to educate the world audience about their situation, hitherto much misunderstood by the West. The Palestinians had a wonderful and successful spokesperson in Dr Hanan Ashrawi, an eloquent, American-educated woman. She did a great job in presenting the case of the Palestinians. Never had the Palestinians had such an opportunity to appear as the civilized people that they are as when Ashrawi presented them to the world. Dr Haider Abdul Shafi, who headed the Palestinian delegation, also did an excellent job. With his sober character, superb English, deep understanding of his people and the world, Abdul Shafi commanded the admiration and respect of the press and the participants. From Madrid the Palestinian cause was able to enter the hearts and minds of people the world over, many of whom began to realize for the first time that there is, in fact, a Palestinian people, like all other civilized peoples in the world.

Jordan's spokesperson, Dr Marwan Muasher, together with Dr Abdul Salam Majali, made it dawn on the world that Jordan was not Palestine. This misunderstanding, which arguably suited the purposes of those in Israeli and Zionist circles seeking to confuse the nature of the conflict and to thwart the establishment of a Palestinian state on Palestinian soil, caused dread amongst Jordanians lest it should lead to Jordan becoming the 'alternative homeland' for the Palestinians.

On the opening day, the American delegation made arrangements for a bilateral negotiation session in Madrid and informed the delegations that these would be conducted in separate buildings at various times. The Syrian delegation protested and requested that the negotiations be conducted in one building and simultaneously. The intervention of the Saudi delegate, Prince Bandar Bin Sultan, Saudi Arabia's Ambassador to Washington, saved the day, and the Syrian delegation accepted the arrangement.

Majali abided by a request of the American delegation to meet one-on-one with his Israeli counterpart, Elyakim Rubinstein, before the bilateral negotiations commenced to agree on formats and procedures. Arrangements were that the three parties would be represented by an equal number of delegates, five members each. This was a huge breakthrough for the Palestinians – to be treated in parity with the Israelis and the Jordanians. In the general meetings of the plenary, the Jordanians and the Palestinians were each represented by seven members while Israel, Syria and Lebanon had fourteen delegates each. Jordan, in effect, gave up half its number of delegates to accommodate the Palestinians. Majali and Rubenstein, the two heads of delegation, met in a room adjacent to the negotiations hall where the bilateral negotiations between the joint Jordanian-Palestinian delegation and the Israeli delegation were scheduled to commence.

'Doctor,' said Rubinstein as the two men sat to talk, 'what is your idea of the mode of work now?'

'When we are seated I will make my speech,' answered Majali, 'then Dr Abdul Shafi will make his, then comes your turn to make yours.'

'Jordan that you represent is a state,' remarked Rubinstein, 'and Israel that I represent is a state too, but the Palestinians do not represent a state. Therefore, it is better that you make your speech first and I come second, then the Palestinian would be third.'

Majali promptly agreed because he thought Rubinstein's proposal would be better for the joint delegation. 'If the Israelis mention in their speech anything that we do not like and warrants a response,' thought Majali, 'then Abdul Shafi will have a chance to respond. The heads of delegations have only one chance to speak so Rubinstein will not have a chance to respond to Abdul Shafi.'

'You are a young man, a diplomat and an expert in negotiations,' said Majali, referring to Rubinstein's experience in negotiations with the Egyptians and the Lebanese. 'I am not like you,' he said.

I am a lot older, am a man of science and methodology, and not an expert in diplomacy and negotiations. I hate any attempt by anyone to fool me. Say what you like and I will respect your right to speak no matter how bitter your words may sound, and beware of attempts to sweeten your words. If I conclude that you intend to sweeten the bitter talk, you will not find me the same man thereafter!'

'I know all these qualities in you, and I promise you will not be disappointed,' Rubinstein said.

Before the meeting ended, Rubinstein asked: 'How do you want us to shake hands with each other?'

'It is really strange the importance you attach to this question,' said Majali. 'When you enter the negotiations and we enter it we can shake hands and say hello.'

'Does this mean you agree to shake hands?' asked Rubinstein.

'It is only natural and normal, and does not take arguments,' said Majali.

As we entered the hall, the Israelis through one door and the joint delegation through another, the news media, including television cameramen with their gear, followed. It appeared, however, that Rubinstein forgot about shaking hands, so the delegates took their seats without a handshake. Majali made his speech after the media representatives left. Rubinstein followed, and in each paragraph of his speech he displayed tough positions. When Abdul Shafi's turn came, he was not ready. The session was adjourned for fifteen minutes to give Abdul Shafi time to prepare. His speech had not arrived from the PLO leadership in Tunis. The delay took more than an hour.

Before we returned to the hall to hear Abdul Shafi, Rubinstein approached Majali: 'I am sorry, Dr Majali, but there are press correspondents who did not have a chance to take photos when our session first started. They are asking permission to enter the hall and take photos at this time. Do you have any objection?'

Majali realized that Rubinstein was asking for a second chance to take photos to make up for what he had forgotten the first time around – the handshake. As they entered the hall, Rubinstein informed Majali that the Palestinians had increased the number of their delegates, so he had increased the number of the Israeli delegation. Majali was not happy about the abrupt change.

'Why is there an increment in your delegation?' Majali asked Abdul Shafi.

'I will explain later,' answered Abdul Shafi.

Majali was not happy. He looked at Rubinstein who was calling for the television cameras to come. However, the television crew was a bit late, so Majali requested that the talks begin. Rubinstein asked for a few more minutes until the crew arrived. 'We are not here for television, we are here for negotiations,' Majali responded angrily.

The session started with the speech of Abdul Shafi. It was strong in its criticism of Israel and its behavior. Rubinstein looked angry and as soon as Abdul Shafi finished his speech, Rubinstein started to respond to him. Majali got angrier and demanded that Rubinstein stop talking because there was no right for any head of delegation to respond to the speech of either of the other two heads. Rubinstein apologized and terminated his response.

After the speeches, they started to talk about the venue of future negotiations. The Israelis suggested that it be some place in the Middle East, in Jordan and Israel in particular. Rubinstein looked at Majali and said: 'Why don't we have one round of negotiations in Karak [Jordan], and the following one in Beer Sheba [Israel], for example?' Majali refused the suggestion. In his view, the mere meeting of Arab and Israeli officials was shock enough to Arab publics.

After much debate, they agreed that each party would write down its preferred venues for future negotiations, and would leave it to the sponsors of the peace process to select the proper venue. Lists of preferred world capitals were prepared. Rubinstein approached Majali in the hallway after the meeting with the same proposal to have the venue alternate between Israel and Jordan.

'What guarantees do you have to give me,' replied Majali, 'that Israel, upon establishing a presence in Jordan at this time, will not claim Karak as part of Israel!'

A communiqué had to be issued after the meeting. Majali and Abdul Shafi preferred to issue a separate communiqué. Rubinstein preferred a joint one.

'No, no, Ambassador,' responded Majali, 'I think that each party should issue its own communiqué.' He then communicated with Abdul Shafi and agreed that the two would issue a joint communiqué stating that there would be an Arab–Israeli track of bilateral negotiations.

'May I, Dr Majali,' asked Rubinstein, "be allowed to share the communiqué with you and sign it as a third party?'

'No,' said Majali, 'this is a Jordanian-Palestinian communiqué, but you may read it.'

Rubinstein responded, 'But where is Jordan, Dr Majali? Where is Jordan in this statement? I suggest that the communiqué state that there will be a Jordanian–Israeli track, and a Palestinian–Israeli track.'

Majali agreed quickly because Israel had just proposed a separate negotiations track for the Palestinians, a first step towards recognition of their national status, and he further agreed that the communiqué be joint with the Israelis. Rubinstein made the correction to the communiqué with his own handwriting. It was the first time the two tracks were established and accepted by the Israelis, a notable achievement.

Majali read the joint communiqué to the press with Rubinstein and Abdul Shafi standing at his side. Rubinstein agreed with the communiqué as read, while expressing reservation concerning a separate agenda for Israel's negotiations with the Palestinians. He wanted those talks to cover only the interim period leading to final status negotiations. As the parties expressed their support for the communiqué, Rubinstein extended a hand to Majali for a handshake. Majali took Rubinstein's hand and gave it a good shake, and so did Abdul Shafi. At Madrid, the Palestinian entity became known to the whole world, and it was generally viewed with sympathy and approval. As the session ended, Majali hugged Abdul Shafi.

As the plane carrying them back to Amman landed, Majali said to Abdul Shafi, 'Congratulations, congratulations, and a happy take-off!' They were pleasantly surprised to see from the windows of the plane that King Hussein had elected to be at their reception. As the plane came to a stop, the King was at the bottom of the stairs. Before the door opened, Ashrawi insisted that Abdul Shafi stay behind until all the Jordanian delegation had disembarked. She wanted the Palestinian delegation to be separate and distinct. Majali disembarked and shook the King's hand.

'Where are the guests?' His Majesty asked Majali quietly.

'Still up there. Ashrawi wanted them to disembark separately.' His Majesty shook the hands of each and every delegate, and thanked them for their wonderful performance in Madrid. Prime Minister Taher al-Masri was also in the receiving party, and the homecoming included a celebration party for the joint delegation.

# NOTES

1 Dr Abdul Salam Majali earned an advanced medical degree in 'Ear, Nose and Throat' from the United Kingdom. He enlisted in the Royal Medical Services in 1948 and was immediately sent to Palestine to serve the 5th and 1st battalions of the Arab Legion that participated in the fighting with Israel. He ascended in military ranks to become Director of the Royal Medical Services in 1960; became a Minister of Health in 1969; and was appointed President of Jordan University (1971–6) and for another term (1980–5).

2 Mr Taher al Masri was a member of the Lower House of Parliament when the King entrusted him with forming a government that lasted a few months (June 19 to November 21, 1991). Masri's Cabinet took the decision to go to Madrid and named the delegates. The delegation consisted of seven members, two of whom were Jordanians of Palestinian origin in Jerusalem. Seven other members were to join from the Palestinian side to form the joint delegation.

# 2

## Pre-Talk Talks/Sofa Diplomacy

Secretary Baker, acting on behalf of the United States government, issued a letter of invitation to the core parties[1] (Appendix 1) inviting them to Washington, DC to engage in bilateral negotiations on December 4, 1991. Our Jordanian delegation[2] and the Palestinian delegation,[3] after about eleven hours of delay, boarded a special flight at Amman Queen Alia International Airport on Monday December 2, 1991 to Dullas International Airport in Virginia, USA. The Palestinians were delayed because of a problem they tried to resolve with the US Embassy in Amman concerning one of their colleagues in the support staff who had been denied an entry visa to the USA because he was a resident of Jerusalem. In the meantime, we Jordanian delegation members, some of whom came from ambassadorial posts overseas, got to know each other better, some meeting for the first time. When the Palestinians finally showed up, the members of the two delegations were introduced to each other. It was the first time that many of us had met.

The two delegations had not conducted any coordination meetings. It was widely rumored amongst the Jordanians that the Palestinian delegation members were resolved to display Palestinian independence at every opportunity. We respected the Palestinians' wishes and avoided any act of insensitivity. Jordan, among all Arab states, was in a particularly difficult situation, as the union of the West Bank with the Hashemite Kingdom in 1950 was still fresh in the memory, and radical Palestinians and the Arab states still harbored resentment toward that union. Radical Palestinian resentment was further fueled by events in 1970 leading to the eviction of PLO forces from Jordan, and the Rabat Arab Summit resolution of 1974 prompted the PLO quickly to replace Jordan in its responsibility for the occupied West Bank. The ongoing Palestinian Intifada enhanced the status of the PLO as the Arab party standing up to the Israeli occupation. Relations between Jordan and the PLO, however, alternated between hot and cold for two decades and disagreement between them was not unusual. These mixed feelings were reflected inside the plane as the members boarded. Instead of the members mixing with each other, only the two heads sat next to each other. The Jordanians occupied seats on the left-hand side of the aircraft, and the Palestinians occupied seats on the right-hand side.

While the two heads, Majali and Shafi, conversed and socialized, the members of the two delegations did so only intermittently. Anis al-Qassim of the Palestinians joined al-Khasawneh and Haddadin of the Jordanian delegation who were exchanging recitals of beautiful classical Arabic poetry. Saeb Ereikat of the Palestinian delegation joined the Jordanian support staff in the rear of the aircraft. When Haddadin happened to pass Ereikat, he introduced himself and chatted with him.

'You know the Ereikat in Palestine are originally of the Huweitat bedouin tribe of south Jordan,' Saeb told Haddadin. 'Oh really?' Haddadin said, 'and we have lots of relatives in Ramallah, Palestine. Practically all the Christian families there are originally Haddadin.'

'This testifies to the historic strong links between Jordan and Palestine,' noted Ereikat.

'Yes, it surely does; let us keep up the strength of those links. We are in many ways the same people.'

The flight landed for refueling in Frankfurt and we were allowed to disembark to stretch our legs. Elias Freij, mayor of Bethlehem and member of the Palestinian delegation, took a stroll with Haddadin in the transit hall and expressed his dismay at the dry atmosphere between the two delegations.

When it was time to disembark, Dr Hanan Ashrawi, the spokesperson of the Palestinian delegation, approached Abdul Shafi.

'Do not disembark with the Jordan delegation,' Ashrawi said with authority; 'we disembark separately.'

As the delegates waited for their luggage Haddadin approached Ashrawi and reminded her of her family's origins in the East Bank[4] before they immigrated to Palestine in the sixteenth century due to tribal disputes, and of how the Majali tribe was instrumental in ridding the south of Jordan of the tyrant tribes that caused the conflicts and subsequent immigration.

'Tribally speaking, we owe the Majali tribe a great deal over the centuries. We ought to show respect to Dr Majali,' said Haddadin.

'Okay, cousin!' agreed Ashrawi.

Outside the airport the two delegations made separate statements to the press. Majali was at his best, and so were Ashrawi and Abdul Shafi. They then proceeded to two separate hotels in Washington, several blocks apart. The Jordanians went to the Willard Intercontinental Hotel and the Palestinians to the Grand Hotel. The symbolism involved reinforced the feelings of Palestinian independence from Jordan, but was not conducive to close coordination between the members of what was supposed to be a joint delegation.

The day following the arrival of the delegations in Washington, a meeting was called for the Arab delegations at the Grand Hotel. The international press was all over the hotel, as well as in a hall earmarked for press use. Majali spoke of the need to coordinate on a daily basis between the Arab delegations during the negotiation process. Suheil Shammas, head of the Lebanese delegation, showed a deep understanding of the forthcoming difficulties. Muwaffaq Allaf, head of the Syrian delegation, spoke briefly. Abdul Shafi spoke, and Hanan Ashrawi spoke also, both outlining the Palestinian concerns. They focused on the importance of having an independent track of negotiations for the Palestinians. There was excitement and there were worries expressed by the heads of delegations, some concerning form and others concerning substance. Anxieties centred on seating arrangements, reporting to the press, and the like; those about substance included the extent to which the Israelis could be trusted in their declared intentions to make peace, and the possible level of involvement of the peace sponsors in cases of disagreement.

However, as of December 3, the Israeli delegation had still not arrived in Washington, DC. This failure to attend was interpreted as an expression of the Israeli dissatisfaction with the choice of the venue on the part of the peace sponsors. The Israelis had insisted on a venue in the Middle East, but the peace sponsors, who were entrusted by the parties to make a choice of the venue, had selected Washington, DC.

Nevertheless, on Wednesday, December 4, 1991, at 9:30 a.m., the specified date for the commencement of negotiations, our delegation arrived at the C-Street entrance of the State Department building and was ushered in by Foreign Service officers of the Jordan Desk at the State Department. In the negotiations wing on the ground floor, we were soon joined by the Palestinian delegation. The two delegations were given an orientation tour of the wing. On the left-hand side was a room each for the two peace sponsors, and two other rooms for the delegations. One large room, partitioned in two, was to be for the joint delegation, and another room for the Israeli delegation. On the right-hand side were two larger rooms: one was assigned for the Jordanian–Israeli negotiations (Jordanian track), and the other for the Palestinian–Israeli negotiations (Palestinian track).

At 10:00 a.m. the Jordanians and the Palestinians took their seats in their respective negotiation rooms. The opposite side of the negotiation table in each room, the side set for the Israelis, was not occupied. The sponsors did not allow the press in to photograph the empty seats. An American observer in the hallway commented that letting the cameras in would be unfair to the Israelis and would be 'hitting below the belt'!

The Israeli delegation arrived on Sunday, December 8. No sooner had its members checked in to the Mayflower Hotel than Rubinstein, head of the Israeli delegation, made a call to Majali. He insisted that Israel was prepared to negotiate with a 'joint Jordanian-Palestinian delegation' and expressed opposition to any format that might imply a separate Palestinian entity. Majali advised Rubinstein that he was not authorized to speak on behalf of the Palestinians, and if Jordan were to do so, the first item on the negotiations agenda would be Israeli withdrawal from the West Bank, not the interim self-government arrangements suggested in the Letter of Invitation to Washington. The Israelis then contacted the sponsors and demanded that the negotiations be conducted in one room with a joint delegation, and not two rooms as the sponsors had arranged. The arrangement was quickly changed and one room was set for the negotiations instead of two. Majali met with Abdul Shafi, Hanan Ashrawi, Akram Haniyyeh, and Saeb Ereikat of the Palestinian delegation to discuss the matter. The Palestinians insisted on a separate delegation and a separate room for negotiations, but did not mind the presence of one Jordanian delegate to honor the character of the joint delegation. They also agreed that the heads of the three delegations could meet for half an hour the following morning to settle this issue.

On Tuesday, December 10 our delegation arrived again at the C-Street entrance of the State Department in black limousines. The sequence of the limousines reflected the hierarchy of the occupants' seniority. To the left of the entrance stood cameramen and press reporters. Dr Majali, who stepped out of the first black limousine, promised the anxiously waiting press crowd that he would make a statement before the day was over.

Once inside the State Department, Dr Majali asked whether the other delegations had arrived. 'Only the Israelis, the Palestinians are on their way,' the official reported. We then arrived at the security checkpoint located in the lobby of the State Department. As we went through the procedures so commonplace now, and were reassured that the checks were carried out on all delegates, each member was given a plastic blue and white tag attached to a chain, with a silhouette of a dove under which the title 'Middle East Bilateral Peace Negotiations' was printed.

'Why did they choose blue and white?' Aktham Quosous, the Jordanian official in charge of administration, wondered aloud as we marched in. 'These are the colors of the Israeli flag.'

'Yes, but they are also colors on the American flag, notice also the red stripe across the bottom of the tag; it completes the colors of the star-spangled banner,' Dr Anani commented.

As we were led to the negotiations wing by officials from the Jordan Desk, suddenly, the hum of conversation quieted down. The Israeli delegation was in full view, and some of them wore Yammakas.

Dr Haddadin whispered in Anani's ear, 'I will take my cross memento and hang it down my neck unto my chest. It seems that the Likud Party wants to cast on the negotiations a religious color.'

'Yes,' Anani answered, 'but does that mean I should wear a crescent on my chest? Faith is in the heart.'

The two delegations sized up one another at the short distance that separated their respective rooms, but with no meeting of the eyes. No one at that particular moment wanted to show any signs that might betray feelings of resentment or awe. The Jordan Desk officer and her aids ushered the delegation into the room, the front of which was assigned to the Jordanian delegation, and the back to the Palestinian delegation. On each side of the partition panel were many chairs arranged around a meeting table with a telephone set upon it. On the wall hung three framed pictures of flowers: one red, one blue, and one white.

Few of our delegation members had seen Israelis before. A few of us had been delegates to the Madrid Conference and had met Israelis there, but for most it was like encountering an enemy for the first time. There was a tense silence and Anani was prompted to break it. 'I guess we are lucky; these are lilies,' he said, pointing to one of the pictures on the wall. 'Remember the movie *Lilies of the Field*, starring Sidney Poitier and five nuns, which was directed by Ralf Nelson? He also played in the movie.'

'Come on, Jawad!' exclaimed Muasher, 'The next thing you will want to tell us is who the cinematographer, the key grip and the gaffers were.' This tension-relieving banter continued for some time, to be succeeded by silence once again, this time interrupted by the arrival of the Palestinian delegation. Dr Haider Abdul Shafi, head of the delegation, greeted Dr Majali. It was formal but cordial. The members of the delegations greeted each other, but, as is customary among Arabs, none introduced himself.

Dr Abdul Rahman al-Hamad of the Palestinian delegation commented: 'Okay, we have sort of one room for our joint use, but do we have separate rooms for negotiations?' More than one Jordanian answered, 'No.'

'We have to pursue this matter with the officials of the State Department,' said al-Hamad. It was obvious that the facilities were prepared for a joint delegation in conformity with the Madrid format. The partition that went up halfway to the ceiling symbolized the separation of the Jordanians and the Palestinians, while the shared room symbolized the joint delegation; the two 'separate' parts of the same room echoed the separate character of each delegation and the passageway leading from one part of the room to the other represented the linkage of the two parties in the one joint delegation.

Aktham Quosous, the Jordanian delegation administrator, had earlier protested at the shared room to State Department officials, and was promised that something would be done. When Edward Djerejian, the US Assistant Secretary of State for the Middle East, was questioned on the matter, he said that no such specific promise was made. Moreover, the Israelis insisted that these arrangements should reflect the Madrid Invitation in letter and spirit. From our delegation, Dr Tarawneh, Ambassador Talal al-Hassan, and Ambassador Nayef al-Qadi insisted that this should not become a pure Israeli–Palestinian issue. While Israel was a sovereign state, so was Jordan, and there was a clear sentiment that whatever Israel got Jordan should equally be given. Jordan's sovereignty should not be compromised simply because it had sought to help the peace process by providing a state umbrella for the Palestinians. Our sober and eloquent legal expert, Awn al-Khasawneh, asked Majali's permission to express an opinion.

I would beg of you at the outset of these historic negotiations to use words with utmost care. A word like 'sovereignty' is a sophisticated legal concept, and when you say that this or that action 'jeopardizes the sovereignty of the Hashemite Kingdom of Jordan,' you open the door for doubting Jordanian sovereignty itself. May I remind you that, while I am as zealous as any of you, my distinguished colleagues, in defending Jordan's sovereignty, we know that its sovereignty is not manifested in the size or location of a waiting space assigned to its delegation. We entered the peace process assured that the joint delegation will in no way diminish the stature of our independent, sovereign country. So please let us not make out of a small, insignificant matter a big deal.

Dr Majali was quick to concur with what Mr al-Khasawneh had said. However, he insisted that the delegation should always use the terms 'Jordanian delegation', and 'Palestinian delegation' as two separate entities.

'We look forward to the day when the Palestinians will have their own independent and sovereign state on their own soil. This notion had been repeatedly expressed by our leadership,' said al-Khasawneh, 'If the notion just advanced by Dr Majali can somehow be sustained and reinforced, it will be a very good achievement, primarily for the Palestinians. We Jordanians should not instigate any doubts that we are fearful of any such arrangements negatively impacting our sovereignty.'

'Listen Awn, the matter is less complicated than all of you think,' Dr Majali interjected, 'and listen well all of you. I am Abdul Salam Majali, head of the Jordan delegation. And Dr Haider Abdul Shafi is head of the Palestinian delegation. Can I claim that I am head of the joint delegation?' Majali looked around for an answer. 'The answer is clear,' he concluded after no answer was heard. Mr Awn al-Khasawneh nodded in agreement,

You are, Pasha, the head of the Jordanian delegation, period. But if I may, Pasha, point out that the issue is not as simple as the question is. We are a joint delegation but structured in a way particular to this unprecedented mode of representation in international negotiations. The 'joint' characteristic of the delegation is loose and embedded in it are the seeds of what you just explained – complete separation – albeit not now. We are a joint delegation with two heads, each caring for his own share of national interests, that is all there is to it at this time. Granted, it sounds like a tale in Greek mythology but we are not dealing, with all due respect, with a two-headed creature. We are dealing with a simple fact. That is all there is to it.

Dr Anani was in total agreement: 'Jordan's sovereignty should not be invoked, in the context of minor issues with any other party – not the Americans, not the Palestinians and certainly not the Israelis.' Al-Khasawneh added

> I believe we should support the Palestinian request for separate rooms and accept the outcome. On the issue of terminology, I believe we can use the Jordanian delegation and the Palestinian delegation, and at times throw in the terminology of the Jordanian-Palestinian delegations (in the plural), but not in official documents and trans-actions. The issue would become overheated if we were to exchange with the Israelis official documents carrying such terminology. I do not think the Israeli delegation would quietly concur.

'Okay, but remember our aim. We are to get to a situation where the Jordanians and the Palestinians have their respective separate and independent delegations and negotiation tracks.' Dr Majali responded. The others agreed.

Among the Palestinian delegation, however, this issue was not resolved, and they were busy communicating from their hotel with someone in their implicit higher authority, the PLO in Tunisia. Dr Sameh Kana'an of the Palestinian delegation mentioned that they could use the public telephones in the hallway to make overseas calls. 'This,' he said, 'can be done despite Israel's condition that the PLO was not to be part of the process, neither would any Palestinian delegated belong to any faction of the PLO.' Anani asked Kana'an whether the Israelis knew of this communications facility, and Kana'an shrugged his shoulders nonchalantly.

'Maybe they do,' he murmured with his soft tone, 'but nobody wants to talk about it.'

The Israeli delegation headed by Dr Elyakim Rubinstein utterly refused to accept any changes to the room arrangements – one negotiations room in which the Israeli delegation would face the joint Jordanian-Palestinian delegation. Dr Haider Abdul Shafi and Dr Hanan Ashrawi, who was following the negotiation remotely from the Grand Hotel, assisted by Raja Shehadeh, the delegation's legal expert, talked to

Ambassador Djerejian. He insisted that the joint delegation have one room to negotiate with the Israelis. The dynamics of this dispute were part of a larger, ongoing argument over symbolism, sometimes beneath the surface and sometimes threatening to capsize the negotiations. Dr Majali predicted a protracted and nerve-taxing test of will.

A short while later, Rubinstein approached the joint delegation's room and asked Quosous, who was standing by the door, to push the door ajar. Quosous did, and Rubinstein's head appeared through the half-open door. 'Good morning everyone,' he said. '*Sabakhi Khair* Dr Majali. Hi everyone,' he added, addressing the rest of us, who were seated around the table in the fore room. Dr Majali stood up and answered in Arabic, '*Sabah al-Khair*. Good morning.' Rubinstein continued, 'I think we should meet – you, Pasha, Dr Abdul Shafi and myself. Is it alright with you?'

'This is what we came here for,' said Dr Majali. As he looked around for any comments, we all nodded our approval.

'Watch out, Pasha, the man looks much younger than you are. Abdul Shafi is not young either. Just yell if you need help,' joked Haddadin.

'You think you are as young as you once were? A teenager?' retorted Majali, and he left the room echoing with a laugh that was big on the heart and short on the lungs. Our respected leader had some excess weight and a semi-inflamed throat.

The three heads of delegations found a sofa just at the entrance of the corridor and sat on it for their discussions.

The Palestinian and the Jordanian delegates did not find it easy to melt the ice. Dr Saeb Ereikat, with his large but athletic build, and black and white beard, made attempts to break the silence. Dr Sameh Kana'an ventured out into the corridor for a sip of water while the door was open. On his way back, he was spotted talking with an Israeli delegate right by the door of the delegation room. He returned to strange looks from both ends of the room. 'Why are you leering at me like that?' he asked.

'Of course,' remarked Zakaria al-Agha of the Palestinian delegation, 'it is easy for you to communicate with them. They are *khwalak* [your uncles on the mother's side].'

'So what if they are my uncles?' Dr Kana'an replied. Anani moved closer to Kana'an, 'Did I hear Dr al-Agha right . . . are your uncles Jewish?'

'Yes,' he said, 'my mother is Jewish.'

'That qualifies you to be a Jew,' Anani remarked. Kana'an responded passionately:

> It does, according to the Jews, as I am the son of a Jewish mother. According to Muslims and Arabs, however, I am the son of my father. The Israelis, as you may guess, know every one of us in the Palestinian delegation. We have been detained in their jails without trial or bail for long periods; some even served long sentences. They have analyzed each and every one of us – medically, psychologically, socially, and politically. They probably know more about me than I know about myself. You may think that I received better treatment in their jail because of my mother's background. No sir, they almost charged me with the most serious of charges: treason.

Anani looked with deep amazement and asked, 'But what was the charge against you to have you detained that long?' Kana'an replied that he was suspected of being one of the fedayeen or freedom fighters. 'We participated in many secret meetings to discuss the resistance to the Israeli occupation of our land and their suppression of our people, but I was never involved in killing or hurting any Israelis,' Kana'an explained.

Anani then left the room for a sip of water and to stretch his legs. As he passed the door and turned left, he came up against a crowd of Israeli delegates surrounding a table rich with cookies, soft drinks and beverages. The table was set against the wall between the door of the Israeli room and the joint delegation room. On one side of the table was a big coffee pot. Beside the coffee pot were disposable cups for cold drinks, tea bags and bottles of fruit juice. On the other side of the table was a pot of hot water with disposable cups, sugar, cream, napkins and a few bottles of mineral water next to it. If a Jordanian or Palestinian delegate wanted to drink tea, he would have to walk over to the side of the table closer to the Israeli room. On the other hand, if an Israeli wanted coffee, he would have to go the opposite side, closer to the joint delegation room. True to the norms of human behavior, Jordanians and Palestinians assembled around their side of the table, and Israelis did the same on their side. Few people of the Middle East take coffee or tea without sugar however, and thus some interaction was unavoidable because of the layout of the table!

It is not difficult to imagine the psychological strain we experienced in that environment. Jordanians, although perceived as moderates and much less antagonistic toward Israel, were not used to meeting Israelis, let alone negotiating with them over issues of such importance. So what if I bump into one Israeli, thought Anani; they are thousands of miles away from Abu Kbeir penitentiary [near Jerusalem] where I was once kept overnight. 'Excuse me! Excuse me!' he murmured as he made his way through a group of Israelis who assembled around their side of the table, grabbed two sugar sachets, stepped back to open space, only to find both sachets contained the artificial sugar he did not care to use. He had barely returned from another foray when he heard his name,

'*Sabakhi Khair* Dr Anani,' came an unfamiliar voice.

'*Sabah al-Khair, Bukra tov*,' Anani answered, returning the greeting in kind.

'I recognize you from your program on Jordan Television,' said the Israeli delegate, 'I am General Dan Rothschild.'

'Oh yes of course, I remember seeing you on Israeli television,' responded Anani. Another Israeli delegate approached with a smiling face, extended his hand and introduced himself as Ambassador Eitan Bentsur. 'I overheard you saying *Bukra tov*, Dr Anani,' said the Ambassador. 'Do you speak Hebrew?'

'No.'

General Dan Rothschild lit a cigarette and offered Anani one. The conversation ended after the first deep suck and puff, and Anani returned to the joint delegation room where only a few of us remained seated. The jocurality and banter which served so well to defuse the tension occupied us until Dr Majali returned. He did not look very happy. 'Get the delegates here, Aktham, call all of them in,' Majali instructed Quosous.

Once we were all assembled in the room, Majali ordered the door shut, and started a briefing on his session with Rubinstein and Abdul Shafi. The Israelis had reneged on their previous acceptance in Madrid of equal representation for the three entities. 'Obviously,' Majali said 'we have a disagreement on the basics.' Majali reported the following conversation between the three men:

Majali: 'I propose to take up this matter of disagreement with the sponsors. They are upstairs on the sixth floor.'

Rubinstein: 'No, I am not about to have the sponsors arbitrate on this crucial issue. What do you think Dr Abdul Shafi?'

Abdul Shafi (pretending he was half asleep): 'I go with whatever Dr Majali proposes on this particular matter.'

Majali: 'Ely [short for Elyakim], if you will not go to the sponsor, who, then, do you think could solve this impasse?'

Rubinstein: 'I do not know, maybe God will.'

Majali: 'Even when God decided to solve man's problems He sent prophets; He sent Moses, and He . . .'

Rubinstein: 'Moses was Jewish.'

Majali: 'He sent Jesus and He . . .'

Rubinstein: 'He too was Jewish.'

Majali: 'He sent Mohammad.'

At this point in the briefing, Haddadin interrupted: 'You sound, Pasha, like you have compromised the basic beliefs of some members of your delegation already,' he joked, referring to himself and to Marwan Muasher, both of the Greek Orthodox Christian faith. 'You let Rubinstein go uncorrected. He stated that Jesus, the Messiah, was Jewish and you did not rebuff his claim.'

'I am actually focusing more on methodology than on theology,' replied Majali.

As he went on, Haddadin took a few steps into the Palestinian part of the delegation room and asked Elias Freij, Mayor of Bethleham, to join the discussion in the Jordanian part of the room. 'Mr Mayor,' Haddadin said, 'the Messiah was born in your town. Was he Jewish?'

'No he was not,' responded Mr Freij with confidence!

Majali was keen to hear our views on his conversation with Abdul Shafi and Rubinstein. 'I think, Pasha, your patience and wisdom will eventually prevail over Rubinstein's short-term tactics,' said Tarawneh.

'Where do I get the patience when he reneges on agreements we had concluded in Madrid?' Majali said, alluding to the parity in representation.

'Pasha,' said al-Khasawneh,

> I think the negotiations will be as protracted as the conflict itself. It is clear to me that the Likud came to Madrid to avoid embarrassing Israel's most important supporter and ally, the USA. It seems as though Secretary of State Baker pulled Shamir by the nose to come to Madrid. He also told him and the other Likudnics to forget about their dream of Greater Israel. What you have witnessed should give us an insight into the future. We have to brace ourselves and expect them to renege on other agreements that we conclude with them further down the road.

'With all due respect to you, Pasha, and to my colleagues,' Haddadin interjected,

> I beg to disagree with you over your proposal to go to the sponsors for resolution of this early impasse. I know you expect the United States to pressure Israel to be reasonable and that backs your position at this time. But, Pasha, I think this is serious. With such an act, you open the door for the sponsor to put pressure on you later in favor of Israel, more likely over a lot more important issues than the issue of parity in representation. I think we should keep the sponsors out of it.

Anani's view was this: 'I think we should be solid in our position. We stick to the Madrid arrangement, and we warn Rubinstein that, otherwise, we reserve the right to change our minds and renege on matters we agree to down the road. He should know that what he is trying to do is serious, and could negatively impact our bilateral efforts in the future.'

'Okay, thank you all for your contributions. I will have to go back to the sofa, and I will keep matters under control,' said Majali.

The press, hungry for news from this historical event, soon picked up the 'Sofa Diplomacy'. Progress was stalled on the first day and for several days to come. Majali, Abdul Shafi and Rubinstein shared that three-seater baby-blue sofa while they debated the impasse. On the following day, the sofa attracted not only the curiosity of the press, but also that of all three delegations' members. Delegates would stroll in the corridor, sip coffee or tea, and look at the heads of the delegations sitting on the sofa trying to resolve that same issue.

On one particular occasion, Haddadin was standing in the corridor, not far from the sofa, with three other Palestinian delegates during the break. The Palestinians were Dr Mamdouh al-Ekir, Mr Freih Abu Meddein, and Dr Nabil Qassis. Rubinstein came down the hallway, apparently returning to the sofa after the break. He headed directly towards Haddadin, and extended his hand out for a handshake to which Haddadin responded in kind. As the two shook hands, Haddadin noticed that Rubinstein ignored the presence of the three Palestinian delegates standing with him.

Rubinstein (with a strong handshake): 'How are you?'
Haddadin (with an equally strong handshake): 'Fine, who are you?'
'Fine, fine!'

'I am asking who you are,' Haddadin said, pretending that he did not know who Rubinstein was.

'I am Elyakim Rubinstein, head of the Israeli delegation.'

'And I am Munther Haddadin, a member of the Jordanian delegation.'

'Oh, I know who you are. You were born in 1940 to a Christian family in the town of Maien. You earned a bachelor's degree in engineering from Alexandria University, Egypt, and a Master's degree and a PhD from the University of Washington in Seattle, Washington. You are married to an American lady, and you have three kids,' Rubinstein listed with a proud smile.

'Oh! Rubinstein! Then you are the fellow who has been stalling the talks since yesterday.'

'Yes I am.'

'Why are you doing that?'

'Basically because I am a very bad man!'

'Are you married?' asked Haddadin innocently, pretending again that he knew nothing about the head of the Israeli delegation.

'Yes,' answered Rubinstein, 'and have three daughters. They call me *Abu el Banat* [father of girls].'

'If you are this bad, how did you manage to get married?'

'I fooled my wife.'

'Well, I am so glad you know me and as much about me as you do, because you will realize that you cannot fool me like you fooled your wife!'

'Oh! I do not mean to. I have respect for you. And actually I love my wife very much.'

'Well, since we came to know each other this well, I feel obliged to offer you one piece of advice that you will not regret.'

'What is it?'

'You were quoted yesterday as saying that Christ was a Jew; you should never say that again,' Haddadin suggested.

'But he was,' insisted Rubinstein. Haddadin put on gestures of seriousness and disagreement. 'Christ is the son of God; is God Jewish?'

'We Jews take people after their mothers. His mother was Jewish.'

'Oh! Was she? Can you prove that? Besides, the Virgin Mary became the first Christian on earth; she became Christian from the moment of conception.' There was a pause interrupted by Haddadin: 'Do you know how my family became Christian as you rightly mentioned?'

'No, how did they become Christian?' Rubinstein asked.

'Through bilateral negotiations with the Lord Jesus himself; so by now you should realize that I have behind me two thousand years of negotiations experience backing me up!' cracked Haddadin.

'Okay, okay, Christ is whatever you say he is,' Rubinstein pretended to concede, and he hurried to the blue sofa to wait for Majali and Abdul Shafi.

'Did you see how he ignored us?' noted Qassis.

'Yes I have noted that; and I am sorry I could not remember any names except yours, Nabil. I should have introduced all of you before he left.' The trilateral debate between the heads of delegations was resumed. Rubinstein sat in the middle with Majali and Abdul Shafi on either side.

Another issue was the separation of the Jordanian and the Palestinian delegations. 'Listen, Ely,' Majali said to Rubinstein, 'Jordan's issues with Israel are different from the issues Israel has with the Palestinians. Besides, we do not want others to share our problems with us, nor do we, for that matter, want to participate in the discussion of any Palestinian–Israeli issue. Above all, I am not authorized to speak for or on behalf of the Palestinians.'

'I understand, Pasha, I understand. But believe me, if I accept parity in representation, or separate delegations, they will hang me when I go back to Israel.' Majali stood up and started to pace up and down in front of the sofa as Rubinstein kept talking. 'Why don't you sit down and listen to me?' asked Rubinstein.

'You want my eyes or my ears? I can hear you from where I am.'

The outcome of the sofa talks was the concern of every delegate. It would determine when the real talks would commence. As the heads of delegations debated, the rest of us drifted in our thoughts to further horizons, confided in each other, and sought comfort in Qur'anic verses and in poetry.

Dr Majali came into the delegation room, swinging his plastic tag counterclockwise around his index finger. Dr Abdul Shafi followed, with his plastic tag around his neck and his lips pursed tightly together. The Palestinians wanted to withdraw to their section of the room, but Dr Haider Abdul Shafi suggested that both delegations should caucus together because the discussion would be equally important for everyone. Dr Majali explained that Rubinstein still claimed that the formula devised in Madrid for parity in representation of the three delegations had almost lost him his job and position. He wanted the Israeli delegation to go into the negotiating room in a number equal to that of the joint Palestinian-Jordanian delegation.

Dr Abdul Shafi continued the conversation. 'I told him that the three of us would meet like we have been doing thus far. We will be the delegates and the other members on each delegation would be advisors. But he would not accept,' Shafi explained. 'Rubinstein insisted that he could not allow such an arrangement. He claims "they" [those in Israel] would hang him if he dared to send a message like that to the Israeli government.' Majali added that Rubinstein made the excuse that the Israeli delegation was carefully put together in order to represent the different political shades of the Likud and other opposition parties and also to represent both military and civilian wings of the Israeli administration. It would be impossible for him to be the sole delegate.

As the contents of the trilateral meeting unfolded, it became obvious that there was a deep crisis. Ed Djerejian, Aaron Miller, and Dan Kurtzer of the US peace team appeared in the corridor along with the sole Russian representative. As co-sponsors of the peace negotiations, the Americans and Russians now had to try to reconcile the differences. It was impossible even to enter the negotiation rooms until agreement was reached on the numbers of each delegation. There was no way that the Israelis would accept a seating arrangement in which they were outnumbered by the joint delegation; their position was clear.

There were of course other aspects to the negotiations, as there also were Israeli–Syrian and Israeli–Lebanese meetings. The issue of parity of numbers was not a problem in those other tracks; in each case the negotiating parties were internationally recognized sovereign states and active voting members of the United Nations. Their negotiation rooms were at a distance from each other and from the joint delegation. Actually, the other two negotiating tracks each had a separate entrance into the State Department and were located at opposite sides of the building. Their delegates went into their respective negotiation rooms without any trouble over numbers, which were equal on each side. The very fact of commencing negotiations was, in itself, exciting for their delegates, despite the lack of achievement in the substance of negotiation in either track. The Syrian and Israeli heads of delegations did not shake hands, and each read from a prepared text. Progress on the first day of Lebanese–Israeli negotiations was similar, although there was less inflexibility and locking of horns. News of these other meetings elsewhere in the State Department did nothing to instil optimism in us or encourage resolution of our problem over numbers.

At 1:15 p.m., on Wednesday December 11, 1991 Dr Majali left the State Department ground floor escorted by the Jordanian delegation. A large crowd of reporters and their cameras were waiting in their allocated space immediately to the right of the exit onto C-Street. Dr Majali stepped toward them, escorted by his American bodyguards, and accompanied by Dr Muasher, the delegation spokesman, and other delegates who opted to stand in front of the cameras. Majali told reporters that the delegations had not yet entered the negotiation rooms. He explained that there were certain formalities to be settled and constituted before negotiations could start in earnest and added that those formalities would be revisited the following day. We then left for the Willard Inter-Continental Hotel, one block away from the White House.

We took the elevators by the E-Street Hotel entrance to the sixth floor, visited our rooms, and proceeded to the dining area. A private dining facility had been set up for our delegation on the sixth floor, where most of the rooms were reserved for its members' stay. Two adjacent rooms, 626 and 628, connected by a door, were refurbished as a buffet restaurant with specified hours for breakfast, lunch and dinner. The amounts of food and the hours of service were satisfactory, and the food quality was above average despite the complaints of some delegates.

Dr Majali, whose love for Jordanian small chopped salad with olive oil soon became known, sat at a table in the second room, away from the buffet, and we soon understood that this seat was always reserved for him. After lunch, we were to meet for two hours to discuss the developments of the day and to look into the work needed for the following day. There was daily coordination with the Palestinians, and it was usually Tarawneh accompanied by two other delegates who went over to the Grand Hotel to meet with the Palestinians.

In the evening of Tuesday December 10, 1991, the heads of Arab delegations met at the invitation of the Lebanese head of delegation, Dr Suheil Shammas, to coordinate and exchange information. The Lebanese delegation and Dr Majali were kindred spirits; their chemistry was very good, and Dr Majali insisted that he should honor the invitation. After the meeting, Dr Majali called for the Jordanian delegates to meet in his suite. He explained the situation, diagnosed the problem as he saw it, and urged us to think positively. 'We did not come here to create problems; rather, we are here to solve them,' Majali said. 'A good way to comprehend the scale of a problem is to try to put your feet in the shoes of the opposite party, and to understand why he thinks and acts the way he does. Does anybody have a suggestion?'

Professor Walid al-Khalidi, the implicit de facto deputy head of the delegation, suggested that the problem be tackled scientifically. He emphasized that the Jordanians should try to read what the Israelis were after, understand their initial bargaining position and anticipate what trade-off they were likely to consider. Khalidi then proceeded to anatomize the Israeli position in a detailed manner. He recalled that Israel had sought to preclude any notion of an independent Palestinian entity emerging as a result of these negotiations:

> The Israelis always meant to have the Palestinian delegation continuously tucked under the Jordanian umbrella. It is clear to me that the Likud government is only interested in peace for peace, or peace for security. That is all. In asserting that, they will continue to insist on one Joint delegation of a number equal to the Israeli delegation.

Dr Mousa Breizat, the political scientist and close friend of Professor Khalidi, concurred.

> We are dealing here with a well-prepared Israeli delegation. They do not work with impressions, but rather they have a well-structured conceptual framework. They fully realize that the balance of power is in their favor, and they are here to make peace taking full advantage of that. I do not believe that they will move an inch from their position of today. They will say nice things like 'we will look into other options', but they will not budge.

Breizat's remarks irritated Majali, and they were a good excuse for him to respond without offending Khalidi, the symbol of Jerusalem in the Jordanian delegation – a very important element. 'We should not be so determinedly pessimistic,' he said. 'If we are confident of the Israeli position, and that they will not budge, then we should go home tomorrow.' Anani was given the floor.

I believe that we should continuously remind ourselves of the fact that we are negotiators. Our understanding of the Israeli way of thinking should not paralyze our own thinking; on the contrary, we should use that knowledge to effect a change . . . to look for a compromise. I am sure that an experienced and well-seasoned negotiator like Dr Rubinstein, a law expert and a former participant in the Israeli negotiations with Egypt in 1979 and also with Lebanon in the formulation of the 17 May 1983 Draft Agreement between Israel and Lebanon, must have lots of self-confidence. We should impress upon the Israeli delegation tomorrow that their position is unacceptable. We should also make them certain offers which by logical necessity they cannot refuse. First, let us all remember and also remind the Israeli delegation, that the Palestinians received their own separate invitations to both the Madrid Conference and to the bilateral negotiations in Washington. They were not part of the invitations that were sent to Jordan. Second, the Palestinians were given an independent Letter of Assurance from Secretary Baker which was different from the one sent to Jordan. Third, the Palestinian–Israeli negotiations were arranged in two stages, the first is to negotiate over an interim self-government that lasts for five years, and the second is to negotiate, starting the third year of the self-government, over the final status of the Palestinian entity and territory. The Jordanian–Israeli negotiations are not structured the same way.

'I agree,' said al-Khasawneh, 'and above all, Jordan is not Palestine, and the Jordanians speak for themselves and can never negotiate on behalf of the Palestinians nor interfere in their track of negotiations.'

'I hear voices of reason and wisdom,' said Majali; 'let us expand on these issues to prepare a counter-argument.'

'Pasha, as you well know, we do not have an interim status to be followed by a permanent status like the Palestinian-Israeli track,' Anani interjected. 'Moreover, the issues between us and the Israelis are very much different from those between the Israelis and the Palestinians. How can we then represent these separate concerns in an agenda of negotiations between Israel and one joint delegation? This, obviously, is not a workable, operational format for negotiation.'

Majali instructed al-Qadi and al-Hassan to draft a cable to the Prime Minister in Amman to brief him on developments and on the position the delegation would be taking. Ambassador al-Qadi, a lifetime career diplomat and a stickler when it came to diplomatic procedure, suggested that the memo be addressed to the Minister of Foreign Affairs, Dr Kamel Abu Jaber, but Majali stuck to his guns, knowing that the cable would be coded and sent on to His Majesty's Communications Unit in the Royal Palace.

It became a daily activity. The coordination meeting with the Palestinians, the deliberations among the Jordanians, and the drafting of the report to Amman. The report to Amman contained developments over the past 24 hours, analysis by the delegation, the outcome of coordination with the Palestinians and the other Arab delegations, and the views of the delegation concerning the day's events. Advice from Amman was sought when necessary. The report was signed by Majali, and addressed to the Prime Minister. It was then encoded by a special team with the delegation and faxed to the Communications Unit at the Royal Palace in Amman. It would then be distributed to the members of the Higher Committee for Peace Talks. The committee was headed by His Majesty the King, and comprised the Crown Prince, the Prime Minister, the Chief of the Royal Court, and the Minister of Foreign Affairs. Other officials were invited as necessary. By the following morning, Washington time, the response from Amman would be received on a coded fax machine operated by the delegation's special communications team. If Majali wanted to talk to King Hussein, he did so through the machines operated by that team.

Later on the evening of Wednesday December 11, Khalidi approached Haddadin and asked for a word with him outside the meeting room, which he feared was bugged. The two men strolled up and down the corridor on the sixth floor of the Willard. 'You never know how secure the suite is, nor how secure the rooms are,' remarked Khalidi as they started their stroll. 'That is why I opted to stay at the Washington Hotel next door. Besides, I am used to that hotel and I like it. Now, what do you think of today's deliberations among the delegates? What do you think of the idea of the two tracks?' Haddadin saw the need for separate trades, and that a separate track for the Palestinians would achieve the goal of enhancing their independent entity. However, there was one thing he dreaded:

> I fear that at some point down the road, the Arabs may come to agreements with the Israelis before the Palestinians do, and thus the Palestinians will be left out in the cold. If the Palestinians are to

finish their final status negotiations in five years from now, it is almost certain that the Arab delegations will come to terms with the Israelis before then.

'Granted, that is a possibility,' said Khalidi. 'But we should be careful to coordinate continuously with the Palestinians.'

'What can you say if the Israelis somehow quickly come to terms with Jordan in the Jordanian track? Would you say "No I do not accept because I want to wait for the Palestinians?"' asked Haddadin. 'So there is merit in a linkage between the two separate tracks, provided that such a linkage will not jeopardize the independent Palestinian entity.'

'Yes, I agree. Let us hope for the best,' said Khalidi. 'These Zionists are a pain in the neck to deal with.'

The following days of sofa diplomacy went on in the same fashion. Stand-offs almost became routine. One evening, while Dr Majali and four other Jordanian delegates in his company were at the coordination meeting with the Arab delegations at the Syrian delegation's quarters, Aktham Quosous knocked on Anani's door. When allowed in, he informed Anani that Ambassador Rubinstein was on the line asking for Dr Majali, or any prominent member of the Jordanian delegation. Anani hurried to Dr Majali's suite to receive the call. On the phone, Rubinstein's shrill voice came through:

Dr Anani, listen, uh, I am sorry to bother you. You know Abdul Salam [Majali] Pasha is not in and I had to talk to you. Jordan is a sovereign state, and Israel is also a sovereign state. The Palestinians, you know, they are not a state – they are not even a government. I tell you, both of us should agree on a number formula that would reflect your sovereignty, ours, and take into account the joint delegation. You see my point. Don't you agree?

Anani asked if there was a specific message to convey to Dr Majali.

'Well, tell him that we should both have equal numbers, but you can take two or three Palestinians in the delegation and the rest will be Jordanians. This way we can all avoid the nominal issues and begin negotiating the real issues,' Rubinstein suggested.

When Dr Majali and his company returned from the Arab co-ordination meeting, the remaining Jordanian delegates were summoned to Dr Majali's suite, which served as the delegation's headquarters, for a briefing on the coordination meeting. 'It appears that Youssi Addas, head of the Israeli delegation on the Syrian track, and Ambassador Allaf, head of the Syrian delegation, did not favorably impress one another,' said Majali. 'Allaf told of an arrogant, dictator-like Addas. Allaf reported that Addas would stand up, leave his chair, look at the ceiling, and walk around and talk to himself! He did that every time he heard Allaf say something he did not like.' On the Lebanese track, Ambassador Shammas had given a detailed account of what Mr Lubrani, head of the Israeli delegation, had told him. Shammas was thoroughly convinced that Lubrani was displeased with the Lebanese because of continued paramilitary activities near and across their common truce line, and within the 'security zone' unilaterally declared by Israel in Southern Lebanon. Shammas detected that Lubrani had a personal vendetta against the Lebanese because he was instrumental in the doomed May 17, 1983, Lebanese–Israeli Draft Agreement reached after the Israeli invasion of Lebanon. The Lebanese President, Amin Jumayyel, never ratified it and thus the accord had no meaningful value. 'However, the Arab heads of delegations have agreed to appoint a four-man coordination committee which will meet after each working day,' Majali concluded.

By the end of the second week, the State Department representative informed Dr Majali that Assistant Secretary of State Edward Djerejian wanted to meet with the head of each delegation and the respective country's ambassador to the United States to see if there was a way to break the deadlock. American diplomats, including Djerejian, always adopted the role that James Baker had successfully demarcated for the United States: a role of politeness, good will and of maneuvering all participants into meaningful negotiations. The Americans' prerogative was to be nice, non-committed and play an active conciliatory role, but not to be assertive or pressure the parties. American officials would not issue a verdict on any issue, even if they were dead sure of it. All of the verdicts, assurances and assertions which the American diplomacy could produce had been exhausted and consumed in the grueling efforts and long shuttle diplomacy undertaken by Baker and his deputies in setting the stage for these negotiations. Baker had endured many confrontational sessions with the Likud government of Israel. He had also had hot encounters with Faisal Hussaini and Hanan Ashrawi of the West Bank Palestinians, and with President Hafez al-Assad of Syria. Now, American policy, after Baker's success in convening the Madrid Conference and in having the bilateral negotiations start in Washington, was set on ensuring that the parties to the negotiations were crawling before they walked and were walking before they could run.

The first round ended with very little to speak of in terms of progress or understanding. The joint delegation never entered the negotiation rooms, and no agreement was reached concerning the numbers of delegates and the format of negotiation. On Saturday 22 December, the Jordanian delegation left for home and arrived there the next day. They were met at the airport and received warmly by Prince Ra'ad Ibn Zaid, His Majesty's Chief Chamberlain, and Foreign Minister Dr Kamel Abu Jaber.

Contacts to resume the negotiations started without much ado, and it was finally agreed that Tuesday, January 7, 1992, after the Christmas and New Year holidays, would be an appropriate date. The delegations were supposed to leave on Friday, January 3. However, a sudden hitch clouded the atmosphere. The Israeli government of Yitzhak Shamir decided to expel twelve Palestinian activists from Palestine to Lebanese territory. The deportees were selected by Israel because of their role in intensifying the celebrations of the fourth anniversary of the Intifada, the Palestinian uprising that had erupted on December 7, 1987.

The Palestinian delegation was completely indignant. Its members felt that Prime Minister Shamir, who was already not very well liked by President Bush and Secretary Baker, was now trying to antagonize them into boycotting the peace process to save him taking the unpopular step of interrupting it. With the expulsions, the Palestinian delegates found themselves in double jeopardy: if they proceeded to Washington, their position would be weakened in negotiations with the Israeli delegation on the one hand, and on the other hand, to their own constituency in the Occupied Territories, which they would appear to be compromising. If they boycotted the negotiations, it would seem to everyone that they were responsible for ending the peace process.

The Israeli delegation arrived in Washington on time. The Palestinian delegation, under pressure from both the PLO leadership in Tunis and other leftist factions in the PLO ranks, stated that it would not depart for Washington without the return of the expelled Palestinians. The other Arab delegates also delayed their departures to Washington because of the deportation of the Palestinians. Only when the UN

Security Council issued Resolution 726 on January 6, 1992 condemning Israel's action and demanding that it be revoked did the Arab delegations feel able to resume the peace process. The United States voted for the resolution, a good sign of its impartiality as a peace sponsor. The Jordanian-Palestinian delegation, as well as the other Arab delegations, arrived in Washington on Saturday January 11, 1992.

The corridor diplomacy resumed on Monday, January 13, as the second round of negotiations was convened, and by Thursday, January 16, things began to brighten up. The Jordanian delegates were cooped up in their usual room – laughing, smoking a little and getting more familiar with the decor.

The first breakthrough came when the Israelis admitted that there was an undeniable difference between the agendas of the Palestinians and the Jordanians in their negotiations with Israel. The most impressive statement that triggered the Israeli admission was made by Dr Majali and directed to Ambassador Rubinstein. 'If you insist that the Palestinian and Israeli issues be negotiated with a joint delegation, then it is only logical that we cancel the interim stage for the Palestinians and immediately dive into negotiations regarding a "peace for withdrawal" from all the lands occupied in 1967, I mean lands which were under Jordan's sovereignty,' Majali said. Rubinstein's immediate response was intelligent and it sounded as though he could be prepared to entertain Majali's idea. 'You mean Jordan has no sovereignty anymore on the West Bank? Did you give up sovereignty or jurisdiction there by your 1988 decision to sever administrative and legal ties with the West Bank?' he asked. Dr Majali was not willing to allow the shrewd Israeli ambassador to drag the conversation into his own arena of competence. Rubinstein said that he was willing to take responsibility for proposing the need to separate the original Palestinian issues into two categories: those which were Jordanian-related, and those which were not. Yet, this dichotomy, asserted Rubinstein, did not cut deep enough to warrant two separate series of meetings.

'Listen, Ely,' said Majali, 'I am in no mood now or later to speak for the Palestinians or interfere in their affairs. I know if I did and was able to have Israel give up Haifa and hand it over to the Palestinians, they would not be happy. They would say, and maybe justifiably so, if their matters were in their own hands they could have liberated Jaffa and Tel Aviv as well, not only Haifa. There is no sense, then, in dragging me into the Palestinian affairs.'

'I hear you, Pasha, but can you hear me?'

'Go ahead.'

'My delegation is protesting at what they call concessions on my part. They see us sitting: one Israeli and two Arabs. They claim this is a concession and they demand that two Israelis should sit to face two Arabs.'

'This is a good idea. They are reading my thoughts. All you have to do is have the groups sit in their respective negotiation rooms. There is one assigned to our track, and another to the Palestinians'. I think you should take your delegates' wishes seriously.'

Slowly, the face-to-face conversations, lobby chit-chats and casual questions among the delegates began to sound like a dialogue. The working week was over, but there were still no obvious solutions, nor did any appear in sight. The three heads of delegation met, and the security tag on Dr Majali's index finger still rotated counterclockwise. Reports continued to flow back to Amman from the Jordanian delegation, and to Israel from the Israeli delegation, and, most likely, to Tunis from the Palestinian delegation.

By the beginning of the second week of corridor diplomacy, all the other delegates were wondering why we Jordanians invariably laughed in desperate times. Laughter is contagious. Anani was mimicking everyone. He teased Ambassador al-Qadi as he told stories of their time at the same high school in Amman. Al-Qadi was a true bedouin, highly educated, and rich in diplomatic experience. Dr Muasher continued to be the skilled spokesperson and a great joke-teller, that is when he was not on his cellular phone. Dr Majali loved to be impersonated and would shoot out that famous laugh until he would run out of breath.

Monday witnessed the usual morning meeting of the three delegation heads. Dr Majali and Dr Abdul Shafi would come back to their delegations to consult. As the heads of the delegations met on the blue sofa, the delegates passed time in chats and jokes. Laughter grew louder with time until the stock of jokes ran out. 'Do you think the room is bugged?' someone asked. 'Of course it is,' was the collective answer.

The rest of the week followed a similar course. No new or good news emerged. News of new Israeli colonies to be built around Jerusalem poisoned the negotiation atmosphere. Muwaffaq Allaf and Suheil Shammas, heads of the Syrian and Lebanese delegations respectively, reported to the press that there was 'no progress in negotiations'. Benjamin Netanyahu, the Israeli delegation's chief spokesman, was trying to sell the idea that Israel could consider a Jordanian-Palestinian entity without Jerusalem even if the Palestinians enjoyed autonomy. Dr Ashrawi insisted that Israel's policies and actions were jeopardizing peace negotiations.

Throughout this long period, there was also the difficult task of explaining to the media, without pointing the finger at any other party, why negotiations had not started, and why the heads of delegation were conducting their talks on the blue sofa in the corridor. Inevitably the obstacles to progress, so serious to the delegates inside, seemed trivial to the outside world. The minimalist approach adopted towards the media did not help. There was an unspoken understanding: give the press enough information to continue their coverage, but not enough to blow the lid off the negotiations.

On Thursday, January 16, 1992, an agreement occurred that created a little momentum. The heads of delegation decided, after consulting with their respective teams, that the working week would be of four days only. The three-day weekend consisted of Friday for the Muslims, Saturday for Jews and Sunday for the Christians. Late that Thursday, it became obvious that an Israeli compromise was in the offing regarding separate Palestinian and Jordanian tracks. Yet, for this to materialize, the Israeli delegation insisted on two points. First, the three delegations would meet in a plenary session to discuss substantive issues before breaking into two groups; in one Jordanian–Israeli issues would be negotiated, and in the other the focus would be on Palestinian–Israeli issues. Secondly, Jordanian representation was to be guaranteed in the Palestinian group, and, likewise, Palestinians were to be represented in the Jordanian group. After a long debate, the two separate tracks were agreed, but there was disagreement on representation at the plenary sessions of the two tracks. Dr Saeb Ereikat, Dr Abdul Rahman al-Hamad and Dr Su'ad al-Amiri resented the Israeli proviso that there would be no parity in the number of delegates representing the three entities, and adamantly refused to accept that provision. After the Jordanian delegation carefully reviewed the Israeli proposal, all agreed that it was carefully phrased and that it opened the door to further bargaining. Naturally, the positive thinking of Majali, Anani, Tarawneh, al-Khasawneh and Haddadin fostered a constructive approach.

Several proposals and counter-proposals were exchanged in the form of a 'non-paper'.[5] We Jordanians were sensitive to the needs of the Palestinians, but so were we to the full sovereignty of our own country. The Israelis, on their part, would not accept a one-third share of representatives in the plenary session. The following day, a break-through was in the making, and it was achieved. The Israelis finally agreed to the formation of two tracks in which 11 delegates would occupy the seats of each entity. In the Jordanian track, 2 Palestinians would join 9 Jordanians, and they would face 11 Israelis; and in the Palestinian track, 2 Jordanians and 9 Palestinians would likewise face 11 Israelis. This mixed representation cleverly preserved the status of the joint delegation; but we Jordanians felt the pinch with our reduced numbers negotiating with our counterparts in the Jordanian track.

Things were more difficult in the plenary meeting. The Israelis never wanted to negotiate with an independent Palestinian entity. Their excuse was that the Palestinians did not have a state of their own, and that the peace process, including the Security Council resolutions on which it was founded, was a matter for a state. Deep down the Jordanians and the Palestinians knew that Israel, and the Likud for that matter, considered the Palestinians as individuals living in 'Eretz Israel'. Successive proposals came and went. First came the suggestion that the Jordanians would have 12 delegates, the Israelis another 12, and the Palestinians 6, a total of 30 delegates in the plenary. The Palestinians were not happy about this, and wanted more members. The Jordanians supported their request, and the number of Palestinian delegates was increased by one, and the Israeli number by one also, with the proviso that the thirteenth Israeli delegate sat in a back seat and not at the meeting table. The representation became Jordanians 12, Israelis 12 plus 1 and Palestinians 7. The Palestinians were still not happy.

Contacts continued, and the Palestinians pleaded with the Jordanians for more members. Nabil Sha'ath, along with four Palestinian delegates, conferred with Majali and a few other Jordanian delegates at the Willard Hotel. Sha'ath asked for more seats for the Palestinians at the expense of Jordan. Finally, we conceded one of our front seats to the Palestinians. We renegotiated the matter with the Israelis and got one additional back seat member. The plenary was to have 11 plus 1 Jordanians, 8 Palestinians and 12 plus 1 Israelis. The additional Jordanian and Israeli delegates would be back-seaters. Upon Majali's insistence, it was agreed that the plenary would be a simple meeting of the two tracks and not a track or a forum for negotiation.

Majali was pleased with the outcome, reached at 11:00 a.m. that day and he headed towards the delegation room to break the news. He came into the room, twirling his ID tag around his index finger. He looked stony-faced and his big eyes squinted behind his frame glasses. 'Pasha, you look like you have good news,' Tarawneh said with an enlarging smile.

'How do you know, you smart eloquent one?' Majali replied jokingly.

'Well, it is the way you twirl your ID tag. It is clockwise this time!'

'I am glad to tell you that we finally have reached agreement,' said Majali. 'We will have two separate tracks. One Jordanian–Israeli track and one Palestinian–Israeli track. Each track will meet once every working day. We shall alternate. One week the Jordanian track will meet mornings and the Palestinian in the afternoon, and we will switch timing the following week.'

'But how many Jordanians and Palestinians in each track? We want to know,' interrupted Musa Breizat.

'You know, God created the world in six days. He could have made it in one day, or one hour. He meant to teach us patience,' said Majali. 'Okay, now where are we? Oh, yes. As I was saying, we alternate mornings and afternoons; Rubinstein will have a hard day every day because he will be heading the Israeli delegations to both tracks. With respect to numbers, we will have in the Jordanian track 9 Jordanians and 2 Palestinians. The Israeli delegation will total 11. A similar arrangement applies to the Palestinian track: 9 Palestinian delegates and 2 Jordanians. By the way, those two Jordanians and two Palestinians will not take part in the negotiations. They will listen and act as observers. If they have any reservations, they will ask for permission to talk from the respective Jordanian or Palestinian head of delegation, and state their point as briefly as possible. This way I think we have resolved the matter.'

'But how about the plenary?' Anani asked.

'Well, we succeeded in convincing Rubinstein to consider it an event with which we begin and conclude each round of negotiations. It is the meeting of the two tracks. Rubinstein said that he would accept this arrangement, with the usual risk he claims, that they might hang him for it in Jerusalem.'

'Well, he always says that before he asks for something. He said that we should have two plenary meetings to discuss issues of common interest,' Anani added.

'You did not accept that, Pasha, did you?' Haddadin asked.

'No, please be patient. I lose track when I am interrupted,' said Majali.

'Which track would you lose, Pasha? Palestinian or Jordanian?' retorted Haddadin. All laughed happily. Majali continued:

Okay? Now, where was I? Yes, the plenary meeting will convene twice, but it will not – let me repeat – it will not negotiate, I stress *will not* negotiate, it will only discuss organizational issues. Moreover, it will look into inter-session activities and into dates for the following round. I proposed to the two of them, Rubinstein and Abdul Shafi, that we should consider the negotiations to be continuous and that we should break once in a while. The Palestinians did not want that, and the Israelis are still undecided.

Some members had reservations about the number of Jordanians in the plenary meeting being less by one delegate than their Israeli peers. They raised the issue of diminished sovereignty but Majali and al-Khasawneh reassured them. 'Anyway,' said Majali, 'let us send a fax to Amman. Fayez, please draft it with Jawad, Nayef and Talal. Munther you can help. Let us seek Amman's advice.'

From that time on, the blue sofa was not occupied as it had been since the beginning of the negotiations. It merely evoked a memory of the days when three wise men sat on it to try to make history.

On Sunday, 19 January, the High Committee for Negotiations endorsed the agreements, and advised the Jordanian delegation not to interfere in Palestinian affairs but to support the Palestinians as they negotiated their own issues with the Israelis.

On the following day the delegations arrived at the C-Street entrance to the State Department in time for a meeting at 10:00 a.m. Dr Majali and Ambassador Rubinstein held the tête-á-tête meeting that became a regular feature of every working day. 'These Palestinians,' said Rubinstein to Majali in their first such meeting, 'are puzzling. They are like some man who has just met a beautiful lady and said "hi" to her. When she answers back with a similar "hi", he immediately wants to take her to bed. They have to realize that it takes a bit more tactfulness than that abrupt approach. It takes holding hands, going out to dinner, sipping a bit of red wine, and the like before the subject of intimacy is brought up.'

'I forgot what it takes for two reasons,' said Majali, 'the first is that I am not as young today as I used to be when I chased girls in my early twenties, and the second . . . Oh! I forgot it!'

The two delegations then entered the negotiation room and held the first of many sessions of bilateral negotiations for peace. In the afternoon, the Palestinian delegation, with its two Jordanians, met with the Israeli delegation. The stand-off was finally over.

## NOTES

1 The core parties are the parties engaged in the bilateral negotiations. These are: Israel, Jordan and the Palestinians, Lebanon and Syria. The regional parties are Saudi Arabia, Egypt, and one of the North African Arab states in addition to the core parties.

2 Dr Abdul Salam Majali headed the delegation. The members were: General Abdul Hafez Marea al-Ka'abneh, Assistant Chief of Staff of the Jordan Armed Forces, Dr Jawad Anani several times a Cabinet Minister, Dr Fayez Tarawneh, a former Cabinet Minister, Dr Abdallah Toukan, Science Advisor to His Majesty King Hussein, Dr Munther Haddadin, former President of the Jordan valley Authority, Talal al-Hassan, Jordan's Ambassador to Belgium, the Netherlands and the European Union, Ambassador Nayef al-Qadi, Jordan's Ambassador to Qatar, Awn al-Khasawneh, Advisor to the Crown Prince and Member of the International Law Commission of the UN, Governor Anwar al-Khatib, Governor of Jerusalem before occupation, Professor Walid al-Khalidi, a Jerusalemite and Professor of Political Science at Harvard, Dr Musa Breizat, a political scientist with the Ministry of Foreign Affairs, Dr Ahmad Qatanani, Professor at the Jordan University, Dr Marwan Muasher, Director of the Jordan Information Bureau in Washington, DC, and Dr Mohammad Bani Hani, Undersecretary of the Ministry of Municipal and Rural Affairs and Environment. The delegation had modest support staff headed by Aktham Quosous. It is interesting to note that half of the fourteen Jordanian delegates came from the private sector (Majali, Anani, Tarawneh, Haddadin, Khalidi, Khatib, and Qatanani), five from the Foreign Service, one from the military, and one from the civil service.

3 Headed by Dr Haider Abdul Shafi, a medical doctor from Gaza. All its members were from the occupied Palestinian territories, but none from Jerusalem.

4 Ashrawi (whose maiden name is Mikhail) comes from one of the Christian families of Ramallah in the West Bank who trace their origins to the Haddadin family in the East Bank (the Hashemite Kingdom). They all migrated as a result of a bloody conflict with the Queisum branch of the Amr tribe in 1516.

5 The term 'non-paper' was introduced by the sponsors in order that a proposal contents could express views in writing without it becoming officially binding.

# 3

# Issues of Representation

The first bilateral meeting with the Israeli delegation on Monday January 20, 1992 was unforgettable. It was preceded by a plenary meeting of the two tracks with a huge press presence to cover the beginning of the formal peace negotiations. This meeting lasted for only a few minutes and then the parties agreed to start the bilateral negotiations right away.

As well as Dr Majali, eight other Jordanians and two Palestinian delegates were to attend the track meeting. The Palestinian delegates, Sameh Kana'an and Abdul Rahman al-Hamad, were named, but the eight Jordanians were not. Majali would not be the one to decide who, of his thirteen fellow delegates, would attend the track meeting. Instead, he left it to the delegates themselves to select eight of their number. '*Yalla* [come on!], agree among yourselves, it is time to get into the negotiation room,' Majali would say. Eventually, eight delegates were selected almost at random: General Abdul Hafez Marea, Anani, Tarawneh, al-Khasawneh, Haddadin, al-Hassan, al-Qadi, and Muasher, spokesman of the delegation.

We entered the negotiation room after Majali. There were two long tables with eleven chairs arranged on each side. Some Israeli members had already entered, and were quenching their thirst with the cold drinks laid on the table in one corner of the room. Members of the mixed Jordanian delegation took their seats in order of seniority, and the two Palestinian delegates sat at the two ends of the Jordanian row. Rubinstein arrived with the rest of the Israeli delegation and soon everyone took his seat. The reporters, who had been allowed in to cover the beginning of the bilateral negotiations, were cleared from the room and an awkward moment of silence followed. The two rows of men looked across at each other in a pensive mood. How could one look at another so fixedly and yet not see him? Anani later assured Tarawneh that he could see the wall through Ben Tsur, Zalman Shoval, General Dan Rothschild, Dr Robby Sabel, and the other Israeli delegates!

Some delegates smoked and used the ashtrays that had already been provided by the State Department. Later, the respective delegation heads did not hide their displeasure with smoking, and Majali and Rubinstein prohibited their delegates from lighting a cigarette inside the negotiation room.

Dr Majali put on a sweet smile and nodded his head to Ambassador Rubinstein, offering him to start first. 'Oh no . . . you are our *Ra'ees* [the arabic word for Chairman], we decided so in Madrid. Please start,' responded Rubinstein. Majali insisted. This is how it all began, cordial, very much alive and full of anticipation, yet void of emotion.

As the conversation of that first session unfolded, it became obvious to everyone that these negotiations would be unique, unlike other negotiations; there were no observers or third parties present. The co-sponsors of the peace process did not want to attend the sessions and came no closer than the corridor outside the closed doors. There was no one appointed to chair the sessions, nor was there an agreed agenda or set of priorities. Our delegation had a loose agenda that listed headings for the topics to be negotiated. These were: peace, security, water, refugees, withdrawal and cooperation. Peace was to be achieved on the basis of Resolutions 242 of 1967 and 338 of 1973, issued by the UN Security Council in the wake of the June 1967 Arab–Israeli War and of the October War of 1973 respectively. In a nutshell, the delegates had to start the negotiations in an environment of non-agendas, non-observers, non-chairman, and would soon use the terminology of 'non-paper' to describe a non-committal position or a proposal they would give in writing to the opposite party. After brief discussion in the first session, it was agreed not to bring in secretaries or stenographers to keep an official record, nor to use tape recorders.

'Dr Majali, and distinguished members of the Jordanian delegation,' noted Rubinstein, 'if we allow tape recorders in the room, I am afraid we will be talking to the machine for the record, and will tend to express extremist positions. So will be the case if we talk to cameras. It is best without these devices, wouldn't you agree, Pasha?'

'Our objective is to make peace, and not to make a show in the negotiation room. We all can do without these devices, especially if we intend to get deep into substance very soon,' answered Majali.

'I assure you, Dr Majali,' said Rubinstein, 'that we share with you the same objective, and we are prepared to get into substantive issues very soon like you are. But on the issue of recorders, really, I do not know how it is in Jordan, but in Israel if we use a tape recorder we all want to talk to it and not to each other.' He laughed 'in reverse', the pitch getting lower as he went on. Majali gave a big smile out of courtesy. 'Keeping record through tapes is tedious. It is better to take notes. They are time-saving and are usually to the point,' he said.

After a brief moment of silence, Majali said,

> I think it is a good idea to introduce our teams, and I start with mine. I am Abdul Salam Majali, head of the delegation; I am currently in retirement, a former Cabinet Minister, also a former General in the armed forces as Director of the Royal Medical Services. To my right is General Marea, Assistant Chief of Staff, and to my left is Dr Fayez Tarawneh, a former Cabinet Minister and currently unemployed. Next on my right is Dr Jawad Anani, a former Cabinet Minister and currently unemployed. Next to the right is Dr Munther Haddadin, former President of the Jordan Valley Authority, and currently unemployed.

Dr Majali continued introducing the team. 'Last, but not the least, is Dr Marwan Muasher, head of the Jordan Information Bureau in Washington, and spokesperson of the delegation,' he concluded.

Rubinstein took the floor. 'Before I make my introductions, Pasha, I cannot help but notice that most of the seniors in your delegation are unemployed. Would you consider offers by the Government of Israel for attractive jobs that fit your impressive backgrounds?' he asked jokingly.

'This is very kind of you. We may be unemployed as I reported, but we have track records of achievements that testify that we are doers, uninhibited doers, and good at removing obstacles from our way. This is why we have been selected to serve on this delegation,' Majali noted.

In introducing their respective teams, both heads of delegation had to labor through one or two names that, under the stress of the moment, suddenly escaped their memory. This occasioned several jokes.

By the end of the first session, the atmosphere in the room was filled with humor. Some of our Jordanian delegates, reclining in the seats of the limousines on their way back to the hotel, were critical of the immediate joking with the adversaries and of the humor exchanged with them. Others were worried about the chemistry they had seen developing between the two heads of delegation.

In the afternoon of the same day, Tarawneh and Anani went back to the State Department to attend the session of the Palestinian–Israeli track. The Israeli delegation was pretty much the same composition it had been in the morning for the Jordanian track. The Palestinian delegation members were tense, and so were the Israelis. Tarawneh and Anani could see the contrast in atmosphere between the two tracks, the ease and friendliness on the Jordanian track, and the tension and virtual hostility on the Palestinian track. The Jordanian delegation had its regular meeting that evening. Tarawneh and Anani reported on the Palestinian track. Majali reviewed and appraised the events of the day and expressed hope that the good start signified the onset of meaningful negotiations. At this point Professor Khalidi asked permission to offer his interpretation of the behavior of the Israeli delegation, and his understanding of what was behind Rubinstein's apparent innocence. Looking at Majali with all the civilized determination he could bring to his soft features, he dropped the bombshell:

> Tomorrow, Pasha, Rubinstein will hand you a draft peace agreement and will go out to the press to tell them that the Israeli delegation has proposed the accord in good faith in order to move ahead with the negotiations. If Rubinstein does that – and I am sure he will – you will find yourself in a catch-22 situation. You are doomed if you accept it, and you are doomed if you don't.

Majali was not prepared for a scenario like this so early in the negotiations. The rest of us had diverse reactions to Khalidi's prediction, but all agreed that starting with a peace treaty would be putting the cart before the horse, and urged Majali to ignore any attempt by Rubinstein to that effect.

Dr Tarawneh and Dr Anani briefed the meeting on the session of the Palestinian track. They noted that Rubinstein and some members of his team were hostile to Dr Haider Abdul Shafi's presentation, especially when he spoke of Palestinian rights to self-determination, Israeli settlements in the Occupied Territories, and Israeli violation of human rights when it came to the Palestinians under occupation. They noted that Rubinstein was not the gentle, respectful man that he was in the Jordanian track, but exactly the opposite. To Khalidi, this merely reinforced his theory. The Likud government was keen on progress with Jordan, but not with the Palestinians. Eretz Israel was inherent to their thinking, and especially important to the religious parties that were partners in the Likud coalition.

'Let us examine that,' said Majali. 'Egypt was an integral part of the Zionist dream. The sign "From the Euphrates to the Nile" is still hanging in the Knesset, but that does not mean the Likud was not willing to withdraw from Sinai. Let us remember that it was the Likud government that withdrew from Sinai, but it was a national unity government with a Labor head that had occupied it in 1967.'

'Likud or Labor or the shades in between,' said Haddadin, 'I just do not see how Israel would withdraw from the West Bank. Look at the number of colonies/settlements they have built, the number of settlers residing therein and the investments made in infrastructure, roads and the facilities to serve the settlements. Israelis have already annexed Jerusalem and some have settled in Hebron.'

'So what?' said al-Khasawneh,

These acts are not lawful in the eyes of the world community. Settlements are illegal, and they run contrary to the Fourth Geneva Convention. However, the thing that should cause us concern is the position the USA has taken on the settlements, and the development of that position over time. At first, the USA joined the world community in saying that the settlements were illegal. In the early eighties, during the Reagan administration, the USA suddenly described the settlements not as illegal, but as 'an obstacle to peace', and who knows how their position will further develop.

The discussion picked up steam. Finally we agreed that the scenario outlined by Professor Khalidi should be kept in mind, and that Majali should take the position of a categorical rejection of a premature draft peace treaty, on the grounds that the issues should be first negotiated and agreed upon. How did Khalidi reach the conclusion that Rubinstein would hand Majali a prepared draft peace treaty? Was this privileged information or thoughtful speculation? In the heat of the debate, nobody actually raised this question, although it occurred to Majali to make a bet with Khalidi.

'I am willing to bet $100 that Rubinstein will not hand me a copy of a peace treaty as you expect,' Majali said.

'And I accept the bet, let us shake on it!' replied Khalidi.

On the following day, we had the delegation room at the State Department to ourselves because the Palestinian delegation was to use it in the afternoon that week. The room looked much larger now that only one delegation occupied it. Strangely, we automatically stayed in our original section of the room and felt that we would be trespassing if we encroached on the Palestinian section. Dr Majali was uneasy that morning and he twirled his security tag around the index finger of his right hand in all directions.

'What if Dr Khalidi was right? What if Rubinstein hands me a draft treaty?' asked Majali.

'Are you worried you will lose the bet of $100 to Khalidi?!' said Haddadin jokingly. 'No, seriously, that would be bad news and you do not have to take it.'

'Yes, Pasha,' said Tarawneh, 'and we all agreed that you would reject it with the most acceptable diplomatic gesture.'

'Oh yeah, that simple. I really cannot believe the way some of you think sometimes, you intelligent ones,' responded Majali impatiently, reprimanding us in his characteristic way. 'I think that is what I will do,' he added on reflection. Yet still, he was a little anxious that Ambassador Rubinstein was late in bidding him good morning. 'He must be on the telephone talking to Shamir,' someone suggested.

'No,' said Anani, he cannot be. Shamir must be fast asleep now. However, the only one who would be found awake at 3:00 a.m. in the Middle East and working is Chairman Arafat.'

'Don't tell me Ruby is talking to Arafat!' said Talal al-Hassan.

'No, but I suggest the day will come when Israeli officials will be talking to Arafat, maybe not at 3:00 in the morning, but I can see it happening!' said Anani. Al-Khasawneh cited a poem in Persian. 'Hafez says, "the likelihood of the impossible happening is highest when it is least expected",' he translated.

'But,' said Haddadin, '*Feema at ta'alolu fiz zawra'i la watani biha wala naqati feeha wala jamali?* [Why should I claim joy over Baghdad when it is not my home, nor do I have in it my camel?]'

'Al-Tughra'ee!' exclaimed al-Khasawneh with joy.

'Yes, yes,' said Haddadin, 'it is al-Tughra'ee, the author of *Lamyyat al-Ajam*, the famous Arabic poem.' Majali snorted, 'Look at these guys,' he said. 'They are totally out of context. They are miles from me. I am in one wadi, and they are in a totally different wadi! While I am wondering what to expect from Rubinstein, they recite Persian poems and speak of Hafez and al-Tughra'ee! For crying out loud!' Haddadin continued in a similar vein, but Majali was spared any further annoyance by the arrival of Ambassador Rubinstein.

'*Sabah al-Khair Ya Abdul Salam Pasha,* good morning everybody,' Rubinstein said as he stood at the door with a close-shaved face and an ambiguous smile.

'You know, I do not like this smile of his,' said al-Qadi, 'nor do I like his looks. He looks so unfamiliar,' he added. Dr Majali stood up slowly, looking uninterested, and whispering '*Ya Sater*' (Oh Protector, meaning the Almighty). The two met privately for about an hour, and afterwards Dr Majali reported the results:

> When Ambassador Rubinstein and I sat to discuss some sort of a loose agenda for our bilateral meeting this morning, I noticed he was agreeable to everything that I had said. The ease with which he was agreeable surprised me. *Li'eb al-far fi ibbi* [a mouse was down my shirt]! I wondered what was up his sleeve that he was so easygoing.

Apparently Rubinstein then produced a document he had taken from his briefcase, saying:

> I have been instructed by my Government – by Prime Minister Shamir himself – to give you this copy of a peace treaty which was prepared by our legal, military and economic experts. It is not the Gospel or the Qur'an, and we're not wedded to each and every word of it. Actually, we can change anything you want by mutual agreement. Have a look at it, Pasha.

Majali sighed as he recalled the details, 'I was mad, I was furious.'

'What do you mean have a look at it?' Majali had yelled, looking Rubinstein straight in the eyes. 'Do you take me for a fool?' and he hit the desk with his right fist, refusing to take the document.

'Pasha, God forbid,' said Rubinstein quickly, 'Such a notion will never ever cross my mind. I hold a great deal of respect for you. But these are my instructions,' he explained.

'Just remember what I told you in our first meeting in Madrid. I hate to be fooled.'

'I remember, I remember,' said Rubinstein.

'It hit me as I looked him straight in the eyes that his ambitions were to convince me to accept the receipt of the document,' recalled Majali. 'If my hunch was right, then he would be willing to live with my refusal. So I decided to test the validity of my gut feeling,' added Majali in a rather excited tone.

'Look here, Ambassador Rubinstein,' Majali then said, 'I have a real problem with you. Regardless of whether I take your draft treaty or not, you will go to the media.' Majali could read behind Rubinstein's quickly moving eyes. He could see that his mind was going faster than his tongue. 'No . . . no,' said Rubinstein, 'if you take it, we can agree now that nothing about this will leak to the media. However, if you do not, I cannot assure you that I can control my delegation's desire to leak this information. You see, all shades of the Israeli political spectrum are represented in our delegation.' Majali then realized that there was room for maneuverability. 'I told Rubinstein,' he continued, 'that we knew that he wanted to use Jordan to persuade the American administration on the $10 billion dollar loan guarantees for Israel, a request that the United States had denied Israel on the grounds that it would make the situation in the West Bank worse by financing the expansion of settlements.' He was beginning to gain the conversational advantage over Rubinstein:

> I really do not see how this is going to work for you: I can take the draft treaty from you and say that we need at least two years of hard work to have it analyzed, negotiated and to hopefully agree on a final text. This would take away the element of optimism from your surprise. But look here my friend, I think that President Bush and Secretary Baker have sealed an understanding with both the Senate and the House. Both men made sure that any attempt by your advocates and supporters there to reverse the situation would be futile. Incidentally, I can also go to the press with a statement of the type I told you, or maybe worse.

As the debate continued, Majali reported to his colleagues, it seemed as though Rubinstein was walking a tightrope.

'Please, Pasha, don't tell us that you felt sorry for him, or that your heart was bleeding over his agony,' said Haddadin. 'This is the time for bargaining.'

'Exactly,' said Majali.

'Exactly what? Did your heart bleed for him?' snapped Anani. Majali reported with passion:

> You guys are impossible. Poor Rubinstein, he does not know yet what kind of people he has to deal with in negotiations. If I cannot

control you guys, how can he dream of getting anything from any of you, for crying out loud. I view it this way. He is my negotiation counterpart. I could do him a favor by pulling him out of the hole he was in, and have him work in a better environment than the tightrope he was walking. Besides, I genuinely respect the man and have even developed a liking for him. He and I should not be engaged in a zero-sum game nor in a winner-takes-all bet. On his part, I could tell how perplexed he was. It was not easy for him to admit to himself that I was honest. It was as though his heart said 'aye' but his brain said 'nay'. The heart was right.

Majali's dialogue with Rubinstein had continued.

'Why don't you take a peak at the draft treaty, just have a quick glance?' Rubinstein pleaded.

'No, Ely, no. To me this is not only a taboo, but it would be condoning the crazy notion of putting the cart in front of the horse,' Majali answered, and added, 'You are married, Ely, aren't you?'

'Yes.'

'And a rabbi conducted your wedding?'

'Yes.'

'When you asked for your wife's hand from her family, did you tell her father what you would be doing in bed with their daughter right after the wedding party was over?'

'No, I did not,' answered Rubinstein.

'Why not?'

'Because they would not give me their daughter.'

'But why?'

'Because telling them about the happy ending in bed would be demeaning to her family,' answered Rubinstein.

'But that was what would be happening between you and their daughter after she became your wife.'

'Yes, but one does not go around telling it to others.'

'Okay then, do you realize what it means to us to mention the treaty at this time, before we get to negotiate? It is like telling your would-be father-in-law what you and his daughter would be doing in bed!'

That metaphor ended Rubinstein's unyielding insistence on considering the draft peace treaty. Majali took advantage of the silence, and wanted to show some flexibility. 'Ely, I have a better workable idea. Why don't we agree to exchange our visions of peace? We will tell you right at the outset what and how we think of peace, what it is to us and to you, what it entails in terms of gains and pains to us all.' Rubinstein appeared to be making some rapid calculations.

'Okay, Dr Majali, I will take your proposal on the exchange of visions back to my colleagues. I am also afraid I have to call my boss back in Jerusalem to seek guidance on the next steps. You do not know, Pasha, what a mess I am in,' said Rubinstein.

'Messy or neat, I am afraid it is your own doing. Who, in his right mind, would think to learn the alphabet starting with Z? You start, as all people do, with A,B,C and so on,' said Majali. 'But I am willing to help you out. We can compare notes on what and how each of us thinks of peace. This is not a bad deal after all.'

That exchange was a litmus test for the rapport which began to evolve between Majali and Rubinstein. Although their relationship was never completely informal, each began to accept the other the way he was. In fact they had several things in common. Both were religious men. Majali observed all five pillars of Islam, and was keen to attend Friday prayers in the mosque of the Washington Islamic Center or at other mosques. Rubinstein observed the rituals of Judaism including prayers, kosher food for meals, and learning most of the Old Testament by heart. Both firmly believed that peace between their two countries would be an historical achievement. Both were career public officials, and despite the difference in age (they were almost 22 years apart as the younger Rubinstein was 48 at that time), they both saw themselves climbing the professional ladder. Rubinstein's acknowledged career goal was a high-level judicial post in Israel, while Majali hoped his career would culminate in the top political job of prime minister, something he both deserved and was qualified for. Both men wanted very much to succeed, and Rubinstein always thought of the Jordanian track as his favorite and realistic attempt at success and goal achievement. You could say that the door to Rubinstein's Eden, in a way, was guarded by an angel called Majali, and vice versa.

After an exchange of cables with Amman, permission was given for the submission of a peace vision which rested basically on the resolution of substantive issues such as the comprehensiveness of peace, withdrawal, mutual political recognition, resolution of the issue of refugees and displaced persons in accordance with the relevant UN resolutions, and Jordan's rights to waters of the shared rivers, etc. Once these issues had been successfully resolved, the two countries could move toward building a permanent, just and comprehensive peace between them. The directives from Amman were quite clear in terms of content, prioritization and position. Actually, there were no surprises in any of these directives. The task of writing, delivering and presenting the issues in the form of a vision of peace fell to the delegation. Great tact was needed both to stimulate negotiation and to safeguard its continuation and fruitful end. In marathon-like meetings held in one of the rooms in Majali's hotel suite, we decided on a direct and formal presentation that would summarize Jordan's position as we had always viewed it. There would be three major parts to the vision, the first of which would include:

a)   an overview of the causes of conflict and the impact it had on host states and on people who were dispersed as refugees, the mitigation of such impact, and an overview of peace as Jordan perceives it, its components, cooperative environment and rewards,

b)   an account of the political dimensions of peace and its comprehensiveness, and,

c)   a review of Jordan's historical role in the pursuit of peace.

In the course of this part of the presentation, we would make it very clear to our Israeli counterparts that Jordan would be taking no part in the responsibilities of the Palestinians; and would confirm and adhere to the disengagement decision of 1988 that had severed Jordan's legal and administrative links with the West Bank. In clear terms, Jordan would never negotiate on behalf of the Palestinians, who would do so responsibly on their own.

The second part of the Jordanian peace vision would explain the legal underpinning of Jordan's position. In this, we meant to anticipate the counter-questions which the Israelis might have in mind, and provide legal arguments to answer such questions. Internal debate and brainstorming led to the following bewildering issues, most of which basically emanated from the issue of Jordan's disengagement from the West Bank. While the disengagement was rationalized politically, its status in regard to Jordan's constitution was in question. The second article of Jordan's constitution stipulates that the Hashemite Kingdom of Jordan (including the West Bank), is an integral whole and no part of it may be ceded. The text of the article is absolute and has no ifs or buts nor any exemption clauses that could constitutionally justify the ceding of any part of the Kingdom under any circumstance. The constitutional and legal interpretation of the decision to disengage from the West Bank was unanimous among scholars and constitutional lawyers. However, some constitutional and legal brains in Jordan became reconciled to the disengagement after discussions with His Majesty the King.

Notwithstanding that decision, the Jordan delegation felt that the applicability of UN Resolutions 242 and 338 on the Jordanian–Israeli track could be seriously tested. Israel occupied the West Bank during the war of June 1967 when the West Bank was part of the Hashemite Kingdom of Jordan. The Security Council issued Resolution 242 on November 22, 1967 which called for: withdrawal of Israeli armed forces from territories occupied in the recent conflict; termination of all claims or states of belligerency and respect for and acknowledgement of the sovereignty, territorial integrity and political independence of every State in the area and their right to live in peace within secure and recognized boundaries free from threats or acts of force. It affirmed further the necessity: for guaranteeing freedom of navigation through international waterways in the area; for achieving a just settlement of the refugee problem; for guaranteeing the territorial inviolability and political independence of every State in the area, through measures including the establishment of demilitarized zones. The Security Council also issued Resolution 338 in 1973: 'The Security Council 1. calls upon all parties to the present fighting to cease all firing and terminate all military activity immediately, no later than 12 hours after the moment of the adoption of this decision, in the positions they now occupy; 2. calls upon the parties concerned to start immediately after the cease-fire the implementation of Security Council Resolution 242 (1967) in all of its parts; 3. decides that, immediately and concurrently with the cease-fire, negotiations shall start between the parties concerned under appropriate auspices aimed at establishing a just and durable peace in the Middle East.' It could be argued that Resolutions 242 and 338 do not apply to any territories acquired before the outbreak of war in 1967, nor to any other territories acquired after the ceasefire, or the date Resolution 242 was passed (November 22, 1967). With the exception of the West Bank, all of Jordan's territories under Israeli domination and control were acquired by Israel either before the outbreak of the 1967 War, or after the ceasefire was put into effect. The peace process was launched with

Resolutions 242 and 338 serving as a frame of reference. Although the West Bank falls within the territories covered by 242 and 338, since Jordan had severed its ties with the West Bank, one could successfully argue that Jordan does not claim any territory under 242 or 338.

On the issue of refugees, of which Jordan was host to at least one million in 1991, the Israelis could say that this was not a bilateral, but rather a multilateral issue in which the world community would contribute to resolution. Our response to that would be that as the Palestinian refugees in Jordan (those who took refuge during and after 1967) are citizens of Jordan by their own free choice, Jordan, and not the world community, is the defender of their rights through negotiations with Israel. Moreover, it would be unthinkable for Jordan to ignore the hopes and aspirations of a sizeable portion of its population to return to the homes and properties they left behind when they took refuge in Jordan.

In the wake of the brainstorm, it was decided that the peace vision should also include a thoroughly prepared but concise legal presentation defending Jordan's right to claim those of its territories occupied by Israel.

The third part of the peace vision covered Jordan's views on bilateral economic relations. In essence, we included this part to answer Israeli aspirations to establish normal economic relations between the two countries and because the Madrid Invitation included economic cooperation as one of the objectives of the peace process. As a matter of fact, Jordan's invitation to Madrid referred, in particular, to that objective. All these factors notwithstanding, the Jordanians intended to send, through their vision of peace, a loud and clear message to the Israelis that Jordan was not interested in conflict resolution alone, but was thinking beyond the peacemaking effort to an era of peace-building.

Majali's views formed the backbone of the first part, and the outline of the vision was then drawn up by Anani, al-Khasawneh, Haddadin, and Breizat. We discussed and debated a draft version before producing the final document. The topics of the vision would form the basis for Jordan's proposal for an agenda for later negotiations.

On the following day, Wednesday, the one-on-one meeting between the heads of the two delegations was not as cordial as its predecessors, but yet there was room for humor. Rubinstein said that he was reprimanded by his boss, Yitzhak Shamir, because he had not delivered the draft treaty to Majali. Majali, who had already informed Amman that the treaty document incident was behind them, was not pleased to find the issue still haunting his counterpart. 'No,' he said, 'I cannot even raise the issue of a treaty now. It is too early.' Rubinstein answered that he only wanted to announce together with Majali that their purpose was to arrive at a peace treaty and that this was the objective of the negotiations. 'There is more than one way to skin a cat!' Majali reminded his counterpart. The two heads talked about the political opposition in their respective countries, and how those parties and groups could cause problems and retard the peace efforts.

'Even the "Peace Now Movement" in Israel expects you and I to announce that we agree from now on the eventuality of reaching a treaty of peace,' remarked Rubinstein.

The tit-for-tat ping-pong debate went on and, at certain moments, it almost spun out of control. Rubinstein respected Majali and treated him like a senior colleague. Somehow, Rubinstein had studied Majali's tribal background so that he could appeal to his sense of 'sheikhdom', coercing Majali to respond favorably. Rubinstein beseeched Majali to accept his proposal but Majali was not ready to do so. Majali then softened his accent and said that he could tolerate a discussion of the idea of a peace treaty in the track session. When the session convened ten minutes later, Rubinstein repeated almost verbatim what he had just told Majali: 'I mean, I really do not see why the word "treaty" should be treated as a dirty word. It has five letters, not four.'

'You know Ambassador,' Majali responded, 'a friendly act could at times be construed as offensive. If I say "good evening" when it is morning, you might find that insulting.' Ambassador Zalman Shoval, Israel's Ambassador to the United States, took the floor to try his luck in pursuing the mater. 'Why don't we agree on using the term "treaty of peace" now?' he wondered.

'Simply because we might arrive at a peace accord or some other terminus, like a peace instrument, not a treaty,' responded Awn al-Khasawneh, the legal expert on the Jordan delegation. 'Why should we prejudge the outcome of our negotiations and deny ourselves other feasible possibilities?'

'Ambassador Shoval,' intervened Anani, 'can you also say that we both agreed to arrive at a peace treaty under which Israel would withdraw from Jordan's occupied territory, uphold the rights of the Jordanians of Palestinian origin, and return Jordan's rightful shares in the waters of the Yarmouk and the Jordan Rivers.'

'Well what is wrong with peace for peace?' Shoval answered coldly. There was collective silence and the atmosphere suddenly became tense as a result of Shoval's notion. The whole peace process was based on the 'land for peace' principle, and Shoval's proposal of peace for peace, if seriously intended, would undermine the whole process. Majali said that Shoval's comment should be taken as a joke and should not be allowed to cloud the atmosphere. 'Well . . . well . . . I am a strong believer in peace. My name, al-Salam, means peace. Despite the difficulties we encountered today I still feel optimistic. When there is a will there is a way.' At that moment, Rubinstein could not resist the temptation to crack a joke. 'Pasha, we say in Israel, when there is a will, there are many relatives,' and everybody laughed. 'Excuse me, Dr Majali, are you through?' asked Rubinstein.

'Yes for this session, basically yes. If you do not have more things to say, we can probably adjourn,' answered Majali.

The chemistry between Majali and Rubinstein was moving faster than the chemistry among the rest of us. Moreover, not all of the Jordanian delegates appreciated Rubinstein's sense of humor or his manipulation of words and tones. They thought that even his off-the-cuff jokes were loaded with political insinuations. If there were two possible interpretations, one good and one bad, the bad one was considered more likely to be intended. They believed that his seeming simplicity concealed his ability to be sly. Well, no matter what the Jordanian delegates felt about Rubinstein, he was certainly making an impression. A good negotiator, however, is one who can choose when to get angry, against whom, for what reason and to what level. A negotiator, we would say, knows how to dress, what to dress and when to dress what.

'So do you think that Dr Majali is a good actor?' asked Dr Mohammed Bani Hani.

'Yes,' answered Anani, 'and he is the best type, because he does it so naturally that nobody knows he is actually acting.'

The third round of negotiations in Washington ended on Thursday, January 23. The Israeli delegation left for home the same day. Reports of the meetings in the media were very dismal. There had been progress on the form and format of negotiations, but no substantive issues had been discussed or negotiated as yet. No talk had been initiated on a negotiations agenda that the two sides would agree to. This would be the main task of the two delegations in the rounds to come. According to Richard Boucher, the State Department spokesperson, 'the key is to remain on the road, and the only way to move down this road is for the parties to engage in direct discussion of their differences.'

The greatest achievement of this round was removing those obstacles that could have prevented it from convening. The United States sought to reassure the Israelis that it was not going to use its leverage to pressure Israel into any concessions. Both the Bush administration and the Israeli government were aware of the fact that elections in the United States and Israel were approaching later that year. While each secretly hoped for the failure of the other, neither could act publicly in a manner that would betray their true hopes.

Upon arrival in Jordan on Sunday the Jordanian delegation was summoned the next day to the Royal Palace for an audience with His Majesty King Hussein. It was a late afternoon meeting attended by His Royal Highness Prince al-Hassan Bin Talal, the Prime Minister, the Chief of the Royal Hashemite Court, the Minister of Foreign Affairs and the Jordan Representative to the UN, Adnan Abu Odeh. As usual, the King praised our relentless efforts. He especially praised Dr Majali and reminded those present of the reasons he had chosen him to lead the negotiations. When the King first chose Majali, the parties opposed to peace with Israel circulated a rumor that Majali was the only person to accept leading the negotiations with Israel! 'Yes,' the King went on, 'he was the one we could trust with this critical mission.' The King seldom gave such an explicit gesture of support.

'I would like to ask you a question,' said the King. 'How did our brothers, the Palestinians, perform? Did they arrive at an agenda with the Israelis, or was the time spent on formalities and procedures?' Hardly anybody volunteered an answer. Adnan Abu Odeh, a candid and long-time advisor to the King, who was born and raised in Nablus in the West Bank, rephrased the question: 'What I believe *Sayyedna* wants to know is whether the Palestinian delegation was more interested in the Palestinian issues or in representation issues. Did the delegates act to promote Palestinian issues or the PLO?' Dr Majali was quick to answer that Dr Haider Abdul Shafi and others were extremely interested in promoting the Palestinian cause. He recalled that some of them, like Elias Freij, the Palestinian delegate and Mayor of Bethlehem, were actually critical of the delegation's tendency to address the media and stave off the main course of the negotiations.

Tarawneh asked for the floor. 'If *Jalalet Sayyedna* [His Majesty our Lord] permits, I want to speak of our experience with the Palestinians. They behave as though we are a threat to them, not their supporters. It is clear to me that most of them, maybe with the exception of Elias Freij, are members of the PLO, and are not particularly fond of Jordan or the era of the union with Jordan.' The King nodded his head, tensing his upper jaw against his lower jaw.

> It is our destiny, among all our Arab brethren, to live the pains of Palestine. We are destined to support them in every way we can. This is why we accepted to provide an umbrella for them to enable them to participate in an international conference. We do not do that to seek their gratefulness. It is the destiny of the nation and of our future generations.

This was a subtle remark by His Majesty; he did not want to be quoted as being even slightly critical of the Palestinian delegation attitudes. He also had a deep respect for Abdul Shafi who was a friend of his late father King Talal.

Abu Odeh indicated that His Majesty did not get a clear answer, and suggested that Anani might have something to say. Anani pointed out that the Palestinian delegation was very much interested in symbolism and issues of representation. For instance, the Palestinian delegates knew full well that they had been directly approved by the Israelis because Shamir had insisted on the right to exclude any Palestinian delegate, a right that Secretary Baker had tactfully managed with the Palestinians. It was known that in the last days before the Madrid Conference Secretary Baker exerted great efforts to convince Ashrawi and Husseini (with whom he was negotiating) of the structure of the Palestinian delegation to attend the peace talks, a delegation devoid of a member from Jerusalem or from the diaspora. Jordan had to fill the gap by choosing more than one Jerusalemite in its delegation. The Palestinian delegation insisted on an independent identity from the days of Madrid throughout the first two rounds in Washington. 'Yes, symbolism was still high on their agenda,' affirmed Anani.

> As long as the Israeli government insists on setting conditions on membership of the Palestinian delegation, the legitimacy of the delegation and its representation would remain in question. The

Israelis need to be totally assured that Jordan would not negotiate on behalf of the Palestinians. If Israel was assured of this, it would have to find a solution for a problem which it has created, namely, Palestinians' commitment to whatever agreement the Israelis may reach with them.' Anani thought that the Palestinians had weighed these factors and that they wanted to tell the Israelis that they insisted on political recognition. For this reason all Palestinian delegates were oblivious to comments discrediting Jordan, describing it as an occupier when it united with the West Bank.

The King nodded his head, a sign of general concurrence with the analysis he had heard and the meeting concluded with encouraging words from him. While Majali was asked to wait for another closed meeting, the other delegates were excused. In that closed meeting, the King decided that it was necessary to establish contacts with Arafat through his Ambassador in Amman, Tayyeb Abdul Raheem. From that day on, it was obvious that Jordan's negotiations with the Palestinians were as complicated as those with the Israelis. Yet, coordination with the Palestinians and other Arab delegations was of utmost necessity. The days ahead were to be very interesting indeed.

# 4

# Jordanians' Attitudes to Peace

The mood in Jordan over the prospects of peace after the second round of bilateral negotiations was optimistic. People were under the impression that once the Arab parties, victims of the creation of the State of Israel, finally decided to make up with Israel, then things should move very quickly towards peace. It is a cultural assumption characteristic of Arab peoples that a bloody conflict can easily be resolved once the victim accepts to make peace in lieu of taking revenge. There were, undoubtedly, opponents to making peace with Israel or accepting it as a state in the region. The peace opponents could not come to terms with the fact that Israel was there to stay, and that the Arab-Muslim character of Palestine would be modified for both the foreseeable and unforeseeable future. The mood of the general public favored the termination of the state of war and looked forward to an era of honorable peace in which the rights of all would be respected and preserved. However, unlike the general public, the opponents to peace were better organized and were more ideologically motivated. Followers of such political parties as the Islamic Action Front, which is the political arm of the Muslim Brotherhood Movement; the Arab Nationalists Movement, which was reorganized into PLO factions such as the Popular Front for the Liberation of Palestine (PFLP) and its sister organizations, the Arab Ba'ath Socialist Party; and others were spearheading the opposition to peace. Their presence was more felt on the streets, in public political activities and in the ranks of professional associations and unions. The opposition to peace presented itself from the right and left of the moderate center of the political spectrum, the center embracing the peace proponents. The weight of King Hussein and the stand of his government helped keep those opponents checked within the bounds of law. The intellectual forums, including the universities, unions and professional associations, and the centers for strategic studies, were very eager to offer a platform for the proponents of peace to give speeches and answer questions, and, if at all feasible, for them to conduct a dialogue with those opposed to peace with Israel.

In the time between negotiation rounds, we members of the Jordanian delegation prepared ourselves for the following round. We consulted with colleagues, retrieved official relevant documents, made in-house presentations, and reached out for public support. It was important to counter the stands taken by the opponents to peace, and to appear in public forums as frequently as time permitted. Haddadin received an invitation to speak at the Professional Association Center in Amman, the main hub of political opposition. Its various councils are usually dominated by Islamists and leftist nationalists. Anani received an invitation to speak at Yarmouk University, Irbid, in a forum shared with representatives of the Islamic Movement, known to be vocal in their opposition to peace with Israel. Other delegates were invited for interviews with the press, and on the government television channels.

At the Professional Association Center, the hall was full. Haddadin could see familiar faces and faces of colleagues and sympathizers, if not with the peace process then with his own person; he was, after all, a member of the Engineering Association and had been elected to serve on the Executive Committee of the Civil Engineering branch in 1972. He was introduced by the head of the educational committee. Haddadin made a presentation on the status of the peace negotiations, described the environment of the encounter with the Israeli delegation, and went over the primary issues to be negotiated with the Israelis with regard to borders, security, water rights, and Palestinian refugees hosted by Jordan. A question and answer period followed. All the questions came from outspoken professionals known for their nationalistic leanings. 'I do not see who has the authority to cede any part of the Arab lands. Our constitution, for example, prohibits the ceding of any part of the Kingdom,' commented one senior engineer who was obviously referring to the Palestinian territories. 'Why do you accept to be part of a process that would ultimately cede parts of Palestine to aliens?' he added. Haddadin's response was measured:

> Well, my dear friend, I have respect for your viewpoint, and I hope you will allow me to express mine. The Jordanian delegation will not cede any part of the Hashemite Kingdom. Remember, when the union with the West Bank was made back in 1950, it was stated that such union will not prejudice the rights of the Palestinians. You also

remember the Rabat Arab Summit of 1974 and its resolution that named the PLO the sole legitimate representative of the Palestinian people. Let us also remember the decision to disengage with the West Bank in 1988, which decision gave a way for the PLO to exercise its responsibilities to pursue the rights of the Palestinian people. The Palestinian territories, including the West Bank and Gaza have become, by Palestinian insistence and Arab consensus, the responsibility of the Palestinians, and the PLO is their sole legitimate representative. We stand to support them in every way we can, and Jordan has, already, facilitated their participation in the peace process by providing them with the state umbrella and agreeing to a joint delegation.

The mood in the hall was supportive of the Palestinian rights, particularly their right to return to their homes in cities and towns taken by Israel. The level of support for peace with Israel was not very audible. Haddadin was aware of such sentiments in the ranks of the professional associations, and accommodated the ideological inclinations of most of those who asked questions.

'Palestine is Arab from the dawn of history. Jerusalem is Arab from before the dawn of history. In fact, Diar Bakr of Anatolia is Arab. Why do we accept to negotiate with those who have, by the force of arms, usurped our lands?' asked a medical doctor known to be a member of the Arab Ba'ath Party, whose slogans call for Arab Unity, the recovery of all Arab territories, and for freedom and socialism. Once again Haddadin answered carefully:

Well, doctor, you dropped a few regions from your list of usurped Arab lands. May I remind you that al-Ahwaz, now within Iranian territory, is Arab, and so are the three islands in the Arabian Gulf of Greater Tunb, the Lesser Tunb, and Abu Musa, taken over by Iran. Also Arab are Antioch and Alexandretta of Syria, now in Turkish hands. I do not want to go far back in history as you did, sir, when you claimed Diar Bakr as Arab which it used to be, because I am afraid if I go that far back, I will have to remind us all that Andalusia of Spain is Arab too. We can hardly cope with one problem of occupation – occupation of land and occupation of Arab people by Israel – and you want me to take on Iran, Turkey, and maybe Spain? I am sorry we are not able to do that, at least in my lifetime!

The outcome of the event at the Professional Association Center was good. People were thankful for the information they received, and expressed their trust in the competence and zeal of most of the negotiation team. A tea party followed the presentation, and it was interesting to see the supporters come up to Haddadin and reaffirm their support. None, however, ventured to do that publicly in the lecture hall. The presentation, questions and answers were carried by the newspapers the following day, and the coverage was positive.

Out in Irbid, Yarmouk University organized a forum in which two peace opponents would debate with two peace proponents. The event attracted more than 1,500 people. Opposition to peace was represented by two Islamists: Laith Shbeilat, an elected member of parliament who had been the President of the Jordan Engineering Association, and Ziad Abu Ghanimeh, an outspoken member of the Muslim Brotherhood Movement who was born and raised in Irbid. Facing these two gentlemen on the platform were the proponents of peace: retired General Abdul Hadi Majali, a younger brother of Dr Abdul Salam Majali, and head of the newly established political party, al-Ahd (the Pledge), and Dr Jawad Anani. It looked like the Islamist peace opponents had mobilized their own supporters as they filled most of the seats in that auditorium.

General Majali, who also had served as the Jordanian Ambassador to the United States, and earlier as Chief of Public Security, after he had served as Chief of the General Staff of the Jordan Armed Forces, emphasized that Jordan had always called for peace. The Hashemites, according to him, suffered a great deal because of their zeal for the cause of peace. Viewing the issue from a political point of view, Majali reminded the audience of the shift in the international power balance after Gorbachev's Perestroika and Glasnost in the former Soviet Union. He stated that the United States had just emerged from the coalition war against Iraq, virtually unrivaled in the world. In effect, he said, the USA had become the world's only superpower. Jordan, which had positioned itself against an international solution to the Kuwait occupation by Iraq, and stood virtually isolated, could be subjected to the wrath of the international coalition that freed Kuwait. The peace process provided Jordan with a forum in which it could be influential. Peace to Jordan was safety, security and salvation. Majali ended his address by calling on every one to support the negotiating team because they were men of courage fighting the honorable battle of peace on Jordan's behalf.

Laith Shbeilat followed. He was fiery and a speaker who selected his words, and skillfully made quotations from the Qur'an and from the

Prophet Mohammad's Hadith to support his argument against making peace with Israel. His main focus was on refuting General Majali's justification of Jordan's decision to seek peace with Israel. He alluded to the disparity in power between the Arabs and Israel which would mean the results of the negotiations were bound to be in Israel's favor. Shbeilat shouted in the microphone:

> If we are weak, who is responsible for our weakness? The Arab peoples have been subjected by their rulers over the last 400 years to all sorts of oppression, injustice and mayhem. Now these leaders tell us we have no choice but to make a humiliating peace with our Zionist enemy. I say that those who accepted the principle of negotiations had not read the Qur'an. Did not they know better than to forget God's words who made jihad a duty of every Muslim, male and female, until the occupied holy lands are fully restored and the Islamic flag is flying over them?

The hall was in utter silence, and Shbeilat quoted from the Qur'an to capture the audience even more: 'Those who support peace try to fool us by reference to the Qur'anic verse [*Ayah*] which says that "if they opt for peace, so shall thou opt". But they take it out of context. Those who negotiate with the Jews, our enemies, overlook what the Qur'an instructs us to do.' He quoted several verses calling for revenge, 'Thou shall kill them wherever you find them, and shall evict them from wherever they had evicted you. Thou shall not fight them by the holy mosque until they fight you in it, and if they fight you there you shall kill them.' By this time, Shbeilat was in full command of the audience.

Shbeilat's command of the Qur'an and Hadith was in a way surprising given his background as a graduate of the American University of Beirut which is an American secular institution open to Western culture and short on courses of Qur'anic teachings, Hadith and Fiqeh (religious jurisdiction). He pointed to the cultural dangers that could result from close contacts with the 'Jews'. According to him, Jews were out to destroy Islam as both a religion and a political movement. To him, negotiations for peacemaking between Jordan and the Jews was like attempting peacemaking between a lamb and a wolf. 'People like Anani should know better than to fall into the "shameful abyss" of talking to the enemies of God, enemies of the Prophet Mohammad, and enemies of Arabs and Muslims the world over,' he shouted. He concluded his statement by raising his eyes and the index finger of his right hand to the ceiling, and he shouted, 'I have warned, and may God be my witness.'

His speech was received with overwhelming appreciation and thundering applause. Many students shouted '*Allahu Akbar . . . Allahu Akbar*' (God is the greatest, God is the greatest). Muslims have been using this term since the early days of Islam when the Prophet started his mission in Mecca and it is especially used to signify Muslims' defiance against the overwhelming power of ruling tyrants or of foreign enemies.

Abu Ghanimeh followed, and his manner was sharp but considerate. He had two challenges to cope with: the first was to outmatch Shbeilat, who was not from the Muslim Brotherhood Movement as Abu Ghanimeh was; and the second was to anticipate what Anani would say after him, and try to undermine Anani's logic in support of the peace process. Ghanimeh supported Shbeilat's opinions of the Jews. In a way, he glorified them when he spoke of their influence, for example, in the Western press media, the film industry, the US Congress, the Soviet Politburo and Supreme Council, the United Kingdom's Houses of Commons and Lords, and Germany's Bundestag. He stated that the Jews were influential in economic circles through their control of banks, stock markets and financial intermediary companies, in addition to famous chainstores in Europe, North America and other countries.

Ghanimeh then focused on a story from the Qur'an in which God asked the Jews to sacrifice a cow through his beloved messenger Mousa (Moses). Being only nominal believers, the Jews, through Moses, asked God to be more specific and give them a lead to help locate the cow. The answer came that they were to look for a middle-aged cow with no particular marks. Unwilling to sacrifice and fond of argumentation, they asked the messenger to tell God that he should be more specific because all cows looked alike. Finally, God specified it as a yellow cow, which was unique. 'You see, the Qur'an tells us that Jews love to argue and debate, but at the end they will not give anything,' Abu Ghanimeh said.

By the time Abu Ghanimeh's presentation was over, members of the audience – who were predominantly devout Muslims and leaned more towards Shbeilat's rhetoric, had floated their allegiance in the currents of the arguments presented thus far. Abu Ghanimeh, within his own field of knowledge and information, believed that he was telling the truth by addressing people's minds and not their hearts. Anani was the last speaker. He took on Shbeilat for a starter and asked him if he would, under Islamic teachings, advise a Muslim male not to marry a Jewish girl that he had fallen in love with. 'If Muslim men are allowed to marry Jewish girls and Christian girls as our great religion decrees, how could you say it is sinful to negotiate with Jews?' Anani asked emphatically as he made his point. 'Show me one Qur'anic verse or one Hadith which clearly forbids negotiating with the enemy, whether Jewish or others? Or are you going to tell me that Muslim males are allowed, under Islamic shariah, to marry Jewish lasses but that they cannot talk to them? What kind of a marriage would that be?' There was hearty laughter. The audience was bemused and Anani went on.

Both of my friends, Shbeilat and Abu Ghanimeh quoted profusely from the Qur'an to scare me off because I cannot, God forbid, challenge the word of God. Of course I cannot, and will not. But I shall defy your understanding and your conception of the Qur'anic verses you quoted. Gentlemen, we are just fresh out of the Gulf War. There were Imams (religious leaders) who quoted the Qur'an in order to support the argument that Iraq was right in doing what it did to Kuwait. Other Imams quoted other Qur'anic verses that supported Kuwait and Saudi Arabia in inviting American troops to fight on their side against the Iraqis, their brethren in Islam. Who is right? Both, unfortunately, had appealed to the authority of the Qur'an. If history has taught us anything, it is that we should never carry the Qur'an on the blades of our daggers or the edges of our swords. The Qur'an is far more sublime than to be employed by humans to service their own mundane goals.

I shall address the gentlemen's arguments, not because I claim monopoly over the truth, but to offer you alternative insights. The Qur'an, the eternal word of God since the beginning of creation, and the symbol of active revolutionary thought, should be critical of all other existing religions and their believers, especially those which the new religion, Islam, had encounters with. Qur'anic verses are critical of Jews, Christians, Maji, pagans, hypocrites, disbelievers, and certainly of nomadic Arabs. Does the fact that the Qur'an was critical of all of those peoples mean that we are not allowed as Muslims to talk to or negotiate with any of them? Who else in this wide world, other than ourselves, can we then talk to?

Mr Abu Ghanimeh, referred to the story of the cow which God asked the Jews to slaughter in sacrifice. You must have noticed that he never finished the story, because if he did, the inference that is derived from it will not serve his purpose. The story ends with the Jews ultimately slaughtering the cow in sacrifice, and they barely did so. But they finally did. Yes, Jews love to argue. Even in the Qur'an we see that the Prophet Mohammad speaks to God with total submission. Earlier prophets mentioned in the Qur'an, the sweeping majority of whom were Jewish Hebrews, did argue with God for the sake of self-reassurance. Moses argued with God in Sinai, Ibrahim [Abraham] did so when he asked God to show him how He restores life to the dead, and so did others. Moses had a hard time with those relatives whom he had saved in the desert. Well, they argue, and if you listen to the Jews joking, they refer to their love of argumentation. Don't you think that they do so because, by nature, they are suspicious and inquisitive? Why was it that the best economists, psychologists, physicists, doctors, etc. happened to be Jews? I think that is because they argue back and forth. They eventually deliver when they see the optimal path.

Now I shall take only five minutes of your time to answer some of the historical issues which my colleague, Mr Shbeilat has raised. He says that our rulers in the Arab world are responsible for what we, in the Arab world, suffer from. We, therefore, should not accept their logic when they tell us that we have to negotiate because we are too weak to fight. Well, I really do not know what to say except to raise one question. Do you know of any other people in the world, other than Arabs as you say, who have endured four consecutive centuries of oppression and mayhem? Do you think that we, as people, deserve better leaders when we surrender in humiliating submission to those leaders for four centuries? First of all, historically you are wrong. Second, there is a cyclical pattern to history. Moses who sat on the top did not last there forever. Lastly, the decision to negotiate with Israel was only raised in the last 25 years or so; it does not date back to the year 1516, the year the Ottoman Turks occupied the Arab lands and stayed here for four centuries.

I am really amazed, that all the debate today in the presence of about 1,500 people did not even touch upon the topic of 'negotiations'. We did not even nibble on the edges. We discussed the principle of negotiations. Do you not think that it is too late for that now? These arguments should have been waged before the negotiations even started. Now we should concentrate our efforts on how to score the best results. That is what we should debate. I hope the question and answer period will bridge this gap.

Shbeilat rebutted by saying that Anani was trying to task himself out of the main point. 'Gentlemen,' Shbeilat said in protest, 'he ignored that there is a clash of civilizations that has been recurring for centuries. Islam has been on one hand, and Judaism and Christianity on the other.'

Furthermore, he added that this civilizational conflict is not new and would continue for centuries to come. 'Go ahead and make your peace. But you know it will not last. The Jews look at you, not as a peer, but as a party negotiating from a position of weakness,' Shbeilat said.

Abu Ghanimeh wondered how Anani could forget the blood of the martyrs who fell in Palestine throughout the protracted conflict with the Zionists.

> Martyrs fell in the revolution of 1936, in the war of 1948, and in the encounters of 1956, 1967, 1973, 1982, and the many border clashes and exchanges of fire between Jordan and its enemies in the days and months separating those events. Are you going to tell the martyrs and their children that you are negotiating on behalf of Palestine? Are you going to forget the right of refugees? How could anybody with a memory and a heart do that?

Ghanimeh's words raised high emotions. Anani reiterated Majali's view that Jordan had always opted for peace. Had the atmosphere and political and economic conditions been favorable, Jordan would have negotiated a peace treaty with Israel in 1948. The late King Abdullah had the vision, awareness and understanding of world politics, and was accurate in his assessment of the odds the Palestinians were facing in the light of the disparity in power between the Arabs and the Western powers that backed the establishment of a national home for the Jews in Palestine. 'Instead of being listened to,' Anani asserted, 'he was defied and called names. Additionally, after the defeat of 1967 and the loss of the West Bank, peace with Israel was within Jordan's reach in return for the West Bank without Jerusalem, but His Majesty King Hussein refused to entertain the idea of losing Jerusalem.' Anani recalled that after the Camp David Accord in 1979, Jordan seriously pursued peace in response to the Reagan initiative and again in 1987 and thereafter. 'We are proud of our track record in searching for an honorable peace, and were disappointed when our attempts did not bear fruits,' Anani said. 'His Majesty King Hussein has said,' he added, 'that peacemaking in this part of the world has been a sad history of missed opportunities.'

He went on to deny that the clashing of civilizations was the destiny of the Middle East. In reviewing the major wars that had taken place over the past few centuries, he noted that they started between European nations, belonging to the same Western civilization. In contrast to that,

Muslims and Jews had lived side by side and both peoples had made valuable contributions to human civilization and to Arab-Islamic culture. Those seeking to voice criticisms of the Jews never gained an audience throughout the long history of Muslim–Jewish interaction. Only in the twentieth century had Muslim–Jewish relations been severely strained because of the Zionists' designs on Palestine and Western support for those designs. He spoke with passion:

> Our Qur'an tells of Moses as the prophet of God, of Ibrahim, David, and Solomon the Wise as prophets as well. Our Qur'an took sides with Moses against Pharoah and with Solomon against the Arab Queen of Sheba; I can cite many examples in our history when Jews' only refuge from Western persecution was in Arab lands.
>
> It is not our fate that we should be enemies with the Jews forever; it is a waste of energy and resources and the conflict has caused so much agony to people. Now Jordanians are willing to go to peace, and I think we should. The fact that the Israelis are superior to us in power should not bother us. If only equals negotiated, half of the world's needs would not be met.
>
> As for the martyrs, we have always honored them, and we shall always do. Jordanian martyrs died in battle as brave soldiers. They did not kill children, women, or old people. They did not destroy civilian properties or cut-down trees. They fought to defend and they fought with honor. I do not think those martyrs would be happy in their eternal life if they see us send more of our boys to war.

The debate was followed by a long question and answer session. The subject of the Palestinian Intifada that erupted in December 1987 against the Israeli occupation dominated the discussion. A participant wondered if 'going to peace' would abort the Intifada without achieving its legitimate goal, and whether the boys and girls who were killed in fueling the Intifada had lost their lives in vain. 'No,' Anani answered.

> The Intifada has contributed to changing the image of Palestinians in the world. They are no more the terrorists that Israel has tagged them; rather, the Palestinians have portrayed themselves as people who stand up to defend themselves against oppression. On the other hand, the Intifada made the Israeli army look ridiculous as their soldiers, armed with tanks and machine guns, confronted unarmed Palestinian women and children who were doing nothing more than throwing stones. I believe that the Intifada has brought

home in Israel the belief that peace is as important for them as it is for the Arabs. However, the Intifada could not, on its own, liberate the land from occupation.

The reaction was mixed but mainly favorable to the peace proponents.

The Islamic movement was, in principle, against negotiations and peace with Israel. However, in the course of Arab–Israeli peace negotiations the Islamists' position branched out in two different directions. One represented the unwavering position that the whole area of Palestine – from the Mediterranean Sea to the River Jordan – was part of the Holy Land hugging al-Aqsa Mosque. Supporters of this belief thought that Jews should be welcome to live in Palestine as citizens, as long as they remained under Islamic rule. Until then, every Muslim must carry out the holy duty of jihad (fight or struggle) to defend the Holy Land. Most of the adherents to this hardline thinking were Palestinian refugees. They never accepted Israel either as a notion or as a nation. From a utilitarian point of view, they believed that the maximum gains that negotiations could bring them, as refugees, would never match even the minimum of what they saw as fair. Realizing the overwhelming power of Israel, and the influence it had on the world stage, these Palestinian refugees resorted to a rationale entrenched in a religious doctrine of divine vengeance – somehow God would punish those who had driven them from their homes and caused them so much suffering. They did not see any real benefits coming their way from the peace process. Other groups with the same views, such as the Muslim Brotherhood Movement, were basically motivated by the same belief. Young idealists, fed up with foreign cultural paradigms and attracted to the cause, most of them young men and women, shifted their position as they matured and faced the realities of adult life.

The second branch of the Islamic movement was essentially born and raised on the East Bank of the River Jordan. The Muslim Brotherhood Movement, founded in Egypt in the late 1920s and early 1930s, had offices across the Arab World and carried out its activities as a humanitarian organization. In Jordan, it was licensed in 1946 and maintained cordial ties with the King and government. However, the Movement suffered a serious setback in 1954 when its members were charged with conspiracy to assassinate Nasser on October 26, and they were hunted down, particularly in such countries as Egypt, Syria, and Iraq. In Saudi Arabia, although not officially licensed, the Brotherhood maintained friendly and cordial relations with the country's rulers who themselves kept a watchful eye on Nasser's plans for influence in Arab countries. In Jordan the Muslim Brotherhood Movement gained momentum. The ban on political parties (1957–89), which forced other parties underground, did not apply to it.

On the issue of Palestine, the Muslim Brotherhood distanced itself from the PLO. Although the founders of Fatah, the Palestine Liberation Movement, were known in 1965 for their Brotherhood leanings, the movement did not align itself with the PLO, especially when the Rabat Arab Summit decreed in 1974 that the PLO was the sole legitimate representative of the Palestinian people. To the Brotherhood, the entire Palestinian question was the responsibility of the Islamic Umma (whole constituency). By transferring this huge responsibility to Palestinians alone, as the PLO had demanded of the Summit and got, the Arab heads of state, in effect, had relieved their countries, themselves and the other Islamic rulers of that collective responsibility. They could then say 'Let the Palestinians do it and we will help in every way we can.' King Hussein, who was pressured into accepting the Rabat Resolution regarding the PLO, found solace in the Muslim Brothers' position, which was shared by the Ba'ath Party, other leftist movements and many Jordanian West Bankers who had moved to the East Bank. They distrusted Chairman Arafat and insisted that the two Banks (East and West) should remain united under the Hashemites. They contended that, in pursuing that decree from the Arab Summit in Rabat, the PLO had, in effect, compromised the national Arab interest for the sake of its own.

In the occupied Palestinian territories the Muslim Brotherhood Movement manifested itself in a new organization called Hamas (*Harakat almuqawamah al-Islamia*, Islamic Resistance Movement). It gained ground quickly and got much of the credit for igniting the 1987 Intifada. The other factors which contributed indirectly, but critically, to the rise of Hamas were related to the Israeli policies in the Occupied Territories, and the actions taken to subdue and humiliate the populace there. Basic infrastructure was deteriorating, and the living conditions of Palestinians, especially in Gaza, were intolerable. Their dignity was assaulted and their basic needs ignored. Hamas attracted those who opposed Arafat and had been followers of other political parties, some with communist leaning. (Of course within the PLO there were already at least two factions with leftist leanings and communist sympathy and support – the Popular Front for the Liberation of Palestine (PFLP), and the Popular Democratic Front for the Liberation of Palestine (PDFLP).)

The philosophy of the leading Israeli political parties also enhanced the success of Hamas. They were adamantly against the notion of an independent Palestinian state on security grounds. To many Israelis, demographic reality was the worst enemy, and one that would get stronger with time. The Palestinians have one of the highest birth rates. In refugee camps, to give an extreme example, the crude estimate of the birth rate in the 1980s was between 45 and 50 births per thousand. The average Palestinian family numbered more than seven. Israel's natural population growth, by way of comparison, was about 1 per cent. To those Israelis, having a Palestinian state next door meant a new entity that would, with time, provide a springboard for a holy war against Israel.

The Muslim Brotherhood Movement in Jordan is still, of course, a staunch supporter of Hamas and highly critical of Arafat and the PLO. In their Friday sessions, the Movement's leaders lecture against the peace process and single out the PLO and Arafat for their most injurious criticisms.

Islamic movements gained political and financial support after the 1979 Islamic revolution in Iran, when the country was overtaken by an Islamic regime. The euphoria with which Arab Islamic movements welcomed the return of Ayatollah Khomeini to Tehran was beyond description. The Palestinians were jubilant over the decisions by the new Islamic government in Iran to sever relations with Israel and stop exporting Iranian oil to Eilat.

The Muslim Brotherhood grew in strength and influence. Syria, which was a strong ally of the Iranian Revolution in 1979 and supported it right from the start, had itself to cope in 1979–80 with the rising militancy of the underground Muslim Brotherhood Movement. Jordan gradually found itself and the Brotherhood as strange bedfellows. They needed each other, and yet did not see eye to eye on many issues. Pragmatists within the Brotherhood did not wish to do anything to cause embarrassment to their host country, yet the Muslim Brothers knew that keeping Jordan as a sole ally could prove to be rather burdensome to Jordan. Thus they stepped up their relations with the Iranian government and maintained cordial relations with Saudi Arabia, which had adopted the Qur'an as its law and constitution. The Brotherhood's biggest gain was to branch back into the West Bank and Gaza. The Intifada of 1987 allowed it to boost its standing and to campaign vigorously for what it believed in.

In Jordan, in April 1989, the King made one of the most important and visionary decisions in his long reign. Following an economic and fiscal setback, he decreed a return to democracy after decades of living under the emergency defense law. He promised to allow political parties, banned since 1957, to operate under legal license. He formed a pluralistic committee representing all political streams and shades in Jordan to formulate a national charter which would determine the country's political, economic, social, cultural and diplomatic goals and objectives. That same year, he called for general elections. The Muslim Brotherhood, overtly active since 1946, scored a decisive victory, gaining 26 of 80 seats in the Jordanian parliament. Seven other candidates, either from other Islamic movements or independent Muslim zealots, were also elected. The results qualified the Islamists to join the government, and five of them became ministers in 1989. They declined participation in the government that was formed in August 1991 in preparation for the Madrid Conference. Additionally, the leftist minister in that government resigned when it was announced that Jordan would join the peace process.

So the Islamic movement in Jordan commanded great support among the public and was the strongest of all political parties. In the next general elections, Islamist candidates fared well, albeit a little less so than in the 1989 elections. Those elected maintained their opposition to peace with Israel, and were a force to reckon with in the course of peace negotiations as were the leftist elements and the nationalists. There were times when that opposition performed a useful function in the peace process, as shall be revealed later.

# 5

## Visions and Revisions

---

The efforts involved in managing the negotiation rounds, starting anew and dealing with unexpected obstacles were all time-consuming and patience-taxing. Negotiators and strategists alike were like travelers caught in a field with two feet of snow, unable to return, and thus compelled to find their way on. America, the sponsor of peace, encouraged all parties to move along, committed to the belief that as long as all were giving the process their best efforts, a solution was bound to emerge.

To some, the mere fact of the continuity of the process indicated that there would eventually be an outcome to please everybody. For Arab negotiators, the outlook was different. An Arab is always risk-averse. He must know the nature and the stability of the ground he intends to step on. Adnan Abu Odeh once described the basic differences that caused frustration between Arabs and Americans – for example, in their approach to negotiations – by comparing the desert culture to the forest culture:

> In a forest you can afford risk because you can always count on finding something to eat, liquids to drink, a place to sleep and a hideaway when danger strikes. In the desert, you have to know ahead of time where you are going and when you will get to your destination. In the desert there is nothing you can depend on but open territory, a lot of heat and no water. There is no place to hide nor a shady corner to sleep in.

The fourth round of bilateral negotiations started on 24 February 1992. We were prepared to start with the presentation of the Vision of Peace as agreed in the third round. In their one-on-one meeting, Majali and Rubinstein entertained the idea of having an informal exchange of views over difficult issues such as water. A side meeting would be arranged for a smaller group of delegates who could start an exchange of views and maybe a debate over the points of conflict.

In the meeting of the Jordanian track, Majali presented the Jordanian vision of peace and Rubinstein and his colleagues listened with visible interest. The presentation, a well-prepared, diplomatic and visionary piece, was impressive. It went over the lost time of confrontation, the loss of resources in wars, the agonies caused, and the bright opportunities that a peace era had in hiding for the parties to unveil and exploit. Majali stressed the sympathy Jordan harbored for the agony of the Jewish people and represented that the mitigation of Jewish suffering should not be through inflicting suffering on other peoples, especially the Palestinians.

> Peace to us is a call to bury the past animosity and to work hand in hand for a better and secure future for all. Peace is a call to reallocate our resources for the welfare of our people and the welfare of the region. Peace is a genuine effort on the part of all parties in the region to rid it of the weapons of mass destruction and to cooperate in making it the place of opportunities and hope. Peace, after all, has to be comprehensive among all antagonists in the region, based on justice and mutual respect. It has to be the peace that is accepted and defended by the current generations and the generations to come. Let us remember that we all are the children of Abraham, and it is time that we act like we should, members of one big family.

Majali then gave the floor to Anani who supplemented Majali's presentation with an eloquent elaboration on the economic, social and human costs of the confrontations and wars that the Middle East had gone through, and the lost benefits that would have accrued but for several missed opportunities to make peace. There was silence as the speakers finished, and there were clear signs on the faces of the Israeli delegates that they had made a good impression.

'Pasha, Dr Majali,' said Rubinstein with a clear tone of admiration and respect, 'we have great respect for you and your vision of peace, and for the eloquent presentation made by Dr Anani as well. In fact Israelis admire the efforts that Jordan and His Majesty have exerted to have the peace process started. But may I, Dr Majali, with all due respect, tell you the prevailing notion among Israelis of peace with the Arabs?' 'Please, Ambassador, proceed,' said Dr Majali. Rubinstein began:

> In your far history, two Arab tribes lived on opposite sides of a water pool [and he looked at Haddadin as he mentioned water]. They agreed to divide the pool in half between them, so that each

would use its own half. One day, the female camel that belonged to the son of the chief of the tribe on the north side, strolled around to the southern side and quenched her thirst. The son of the southern tribe's chief got upset that the camel of the northern tribe trespassed against the water of the southern tribe, and, with his sword, killed the trespassing camel. The owner, son of the northern tribe's chief, retaliated by stabbing and killing the assailant. It was not like an eye for an eye, it was rather a young man for a camel! Because of that, a long bloody war erupted between the two tribes who were soon joined by their respective tribal allies. That war ·was bloody and lasted for forty years. It is called *Harb al-Basous* in your history.

The Jordanians were taken by surprise, not only by the details of Rubinstein's story, but also by the implications of his response – an impression on the part of the Israelis that the Arabs can go to war with their own neighbors for trivial reasons, and that they do not mind if the bloodshed lasts for forty years. There was a long pause. Haddadin asked for the floor, and, aware of Rubinstein's familiarity with Arabic literature, said: 'Ambassador Rubinstein, your recounting of *Harb al-Basous* is not quite accurate. Regardless, you overlooked one fact that is pertinent to our mission here. Throughout the bloody years of that war, the best of Arabic poetry was written. As a matter of fact, one epic was written by an Arab Jew, Samawa'al.' Haddadin went on to quote from Samawa'al's famous poem. 'There was evidence,' Haddadin continued, 'that, while the tribes were fighting, Jews who did not ally themselves with either party were never harmed, and they enjoyed a peaceful progressive life by evidence of their poetry. What is it then to you, sir, if Arabs engage in a rather long spell of interfighting while Jews are kept unharmed?' 'Dr Haddadin,' Rubinstein replied, 'I always thought that water, unlike its role in triggering the fight between the tribes in Arab old history, would be the gate to our understanding and cooperative relations. I just hope that the gate to water will not be a Watergate!'

'Rest assured, Ambassador, that I am not a plumber!' Haddadin retorted. There was laughter, and the atmosphere went back to normal.

During the 15-minute coffee break, Majali called Haddadin into the delegation room, and said, 'We agreed, Rubinstein and I, to start a side dialogue over water. I want you to head our group and steer the talks. I think you should take Bani Hani in with you. Who else do you want?' Haddadin gave a considered response:

Sir, I feel that we have to combine more topics than water. My reason is simple. We have a clear interest in recovering what we think are our water rights, and they will resist. I know they have an interest in the environment, and they will seek our consent to cooperate in that field. A third related topic is energy, and I know they will have a similar interest in pursuing cooperation in energy, and we have some interests in that too. So, integrating the three topics in one side group is a better arrangement for us. We can use their interests in environment and energy cooperation to promote our own interests in water. Besides, there are physical linkages between the three.

'I see your point. I will raise the issue with Rubinstein a bit later. Until then, go in the other room, you and Bani Hani. Rubinstein will assign some of his men to the task,' Majali said.

After the break, Haddadin accompanied Bani Hani and Toukan into an adjacent room, assigned to the Russian representative. Dr Elyahu Rosenthal, a prominent Israeli hydrogeologist, joined them. 'You do not know me, Dr Haddadin,' said Rosenthal, 'but I know who you are. As a matter of fact, the water community in Israel knows who you are and we have high respect for your abilities. I cannot possibly match you,' Rosenthal added, with politeness and modesty. Haddadin responded in kind, complimenting Rosenthal on various papers he had published.

The talk remained general and full of courtesy. 'I myself have great respect for the Jordan Armed Forces,' said Rosenthal.

I was in the reserve in June 1967. My wife was due to deliver the 5th or 6th of June of that year. I was driving her to the hospital on the 5th when I heard the call of my unit from the reserve to active duty. I left my wife at the hospital and rushed back to report to duty at a military camp in Jerusalem. I was issued my uniform and I went in to put it on.

I had one leg inside the pair of pants, and was trying to put the other in, when hell broke loose. The Jordanian Army opened fire from the mount where the United Nations quarters were. The Jordanians had occupied that neutral area, and their fire on the Jerusalem camp was heavy. They really hit hard and on target. Their fire never stopped. Boy, I am telling you, that was the scare of my life!

'Well,' said Haddadin, 'aren't you glad we are not in a battlefield with tanks and guns. I am sure glad we do not have to shoot and kill at this time.'

'I mean to say that Israel never wanted to strike at Jordan or occupy the West Bank; it was Jordan that opened fire first, and Israel responded,' claimed Rosenthal.

'Think of it another way,' said Toukan, 'it is because of that war and the other wars between our two countries that we are here to make peace. Let us work to make the future better than the past.'

The conversation did not focus on the substance of the topics the group was supposed to discuss, and the group agreed to meet the following day.

Back at the main track meeting, we were revisiting the issue of a peace treaty. 'Pasha, we really understand the sensitivities you have in connection with speaking about a peace treaty at this time,' said Rubinstein.

> You also understand our sensitivities to the terminology of occupation and withdrawal that you frequently use to describe our presence in certain territories. We know why we are here. We know that our goal is to arrive at a peace treaty with Jordan through our bilateral negotiations here. Now why can't we agree on that goal and get on with our business?

Al-Khasawneh asked for the floor. 'Ambassador Rubinstein,' he started with his British accent, 'entry into negotiations does not automatically lead to the conclusion of a treaty of peace.' Rubinstein looked at Robby Sabel, the international law expert in the Israeli delegation, and asked him to respond. 'What is it then that our negotiations may culminate with?' asked Dr Sabel.

'An accord, maybe an understanding, or, to be more exact, we can end up with a legal instrument of peace,' al-Khasawneh answered.

'The normal instrument is a treaty of peace, wouldn't you say, Dr al-Khasawneh?' Sabel asked.

'No, not necessarily. I ask you to look at the case of the Allies against Germany after the end of the Second World War. There was no peace treaty. Other examples are ample,' answered al-Khasawneh.

'I take your point, Dr al-Khasawneh,' said Rubinstein, 'but may I ask why not a treaty of peace?'

'You know, Ambassador Rubinstein,' said al-Khasawneh,

> your question reminds me of a personal story back when I was young in age and green in judgment. I was enamored of a certain

young lady who unfortunately was more interested in philosophy than in friendship. Whenever I asked her out for dinner, she would think about it thoroughly and say: 'Why not? But on the other hand, why?' and this is exactly our answer to your question, and our position with regard to the conclusion of a treaty of peace.

There was laughter and a short exchange of jokes ensued, for which Rubinstein was famous.

Anani gave a superb presentation about the Palestinian refugees hosted by Jordan and made frequent reference to the resolutions passed by the United Nations over the years, starting with Resolution 194 of 11 December 1948, giving the refugees the right to repatriation and compensation. Rubinstein responded:

I would like to assert here that Israel was not responsible for the plight of the Palestinian refugees. It was the Arab rulers who encouraged the refugees to leave their homes because they promised them they would be back soon. The Arab states waged the war on Israel the day it was pronounced independent, and it is their actions and promises that led to the plight of the Palestinian refugees. Besides, the problem of refugees is not only a Jordanian problem. Israel, too, has received waves of Jewish refugees that came to it from Arab countries. Their problem is to be resolved too.

Majali reminded Rubinstein that there was no gain to any party in denying the plight of the Palestinian refugees and the causes thereof. 'The whole world recognized that,' Majali said, 'and one just cannot argue over axioms and simple facts.'

Haddadin asked for the floor and addressed Rubinstein: 'Ambassador, Anani has just cited the number of Palestinian refugees that Jordan hosted because of Israel. Could you please tell us how many Jewish refugees came to Israel from Jordan?' Rubinstein, taken by surprise by an unexpected question, said 'None to my recollection.'

'Thank you, Ambassador,' Haddadin replied.

We are here in a bilateral track of negotiations, and the bilaterals, as you know, have been Israel's condition to have the peace process started. Anani has presented to you a bilateral problem for resolution in our bilateral talks, and you responded by referring to Jewish refugees from other Arab countries. Do you mean to bring here with us in this room delegates representing Iraq? Egypt? Or maybe

Yemen? If so we look forward to integrating the Arab delegations in one.

'No! No! Dr Haddadin, this is not what we are after, nor it is what I meant,' said Rubinstein. 'I mean . . . I mean . . . the problem of refugees can only be resolved within an international context. I am sure that Dr Anani understands what I mean. He heads the Jordan delegation to the Working Group on Refugees in the multilateral peace talks. That forum, I think, is the place and the context in which the problem of refugees should be addressed.'

'No! No! This cannot be tolerated,' said Majali. 'The problem of Palestinian refugees is part and parcel of the political settlement that we are seeking through bilateral negotiations. I am sorry, Ambassador Rubinstein, this will have to be dealt with on our bilateral agenda.'

Al-Khasawneh took the floor and went over the provisions of international law on the declaration of human rights, and on the circumstances under which the United Nations Relief Works Agency (UNRWA) was established. He quoted George Santayana and other philosophers to support his points. Sabel responded by saying that Israelis do not consider UN resolutions as part of international law! Al-Khasawneh rebuffed that argument and cited the legal opinions of world famous jurists on this matter.

It must have become very clear to Rubinstein that the Jordanians would not entertain the idea of a treaty of peace before the issues of conflict were negotiated and resolved satisfactorily. But that did not stop him and his delegates from asking for 'confidence-building measures' (CBMs) on several occasions during this and succeeding rounds. 'Okay, if talking about a peace treaty is viewed as sinful,' remarked Rubinstein at one point, 'let us consider something that is to us quite kosher. Why don't we talk about some meaningful confidence-building measures?'

'Like what?' Majali asked. Rubinstein replied,

I would say, Pasha, let us do something in communications, like have telephone links. By the way, do you know, Pasha, that Jerusalem is the only place on earth where a call to heaven is a local call? No seriously, we can think of telephone links . . . direct telephone links. We can also think of electricity connections, of mail, we can think of joint security patrols along our common borders.

'I think we have more urgent issues at hand. I think we want to avoid putting the cart before the horse; we have to agree on the common borders before we can think of joint patrols along them,' Majali responded. Al-Khasawneh asked for the floor,

> Ambassador, in this respect, a few lines of poetry jump to mind:
>
>> 'O! innocent victim of cupid,
>> Hear this terse little verse,
>> To let a fool kiss you is stupid,
>> To let a kiss fool you is worse.'
>
> So much for your proposal of CBMs, Ambassador.

The conversations went on and on. We insisted that before any meaningful CBMs were addressed, the Israelis had to commit themselves to withdrawal from occupied Jordanian territories. The Israelis kept rejecting the use of the word 'withdrawal' and we rejected the use of the term 'peace treaty'.

If not much was achieved in the Jordanian track, in the Syrian track the talks were running in a vicious circle. The Israelis wanted to talk about normalization of relations, and the Syrians wanted to talk about full withdrawal from the Syrian territories that Israel occupied in 1967. The Syrian preferred phrase was 'full withdrawal', and the Israelis countered by 'full normalization'. No progress was achieved there either. The Lebanese track was not more successful. The Israelis were weary of what they figured was the Syrian influence over Lebanon. They wanted to talk about a peace treaty with Lebanon, and the Lebanese wanted to have Israel implement without delay Security Council Resolutions 425 and 426 that called for Israeli withdrawal from the territories it occupied in South Lebanon. These talks went in a vicious circle as well.

On March 25, 1992 Majali and Rubinstein reviewed the work of the day before. Majali brought up the subject of combining water, energy and the environment in one subset of talks, and Rubinstein readily agreed. He contacted his colleagues and formed an Israeli group of four.[1] A fifth delegate, representing the Ministry of Foreign Affairs, would sometimes join. They were all members of the Israeli delegation.

## Water

Jordan's available water resources were much short of what was needed. The case in Israel was a bit brighter. Of particular importance to Jordan was the abrupt increase in the demand for water as a result of the return of some 300,000 Jordanians from Kuwait and the Gulf States in the wake of Iraq's invasion of Kuwait. Those returnees crowded Amman and its environs. Municipal water to Amman could be increased by pumping from the Jordan valley, drawing on the Yarmouk River, the subject of the negotiations. The water-sharing issues around the basin of the River Jordan and its largest tributary, the Yarmouk, had been addressed through mediation by the United States between October 1953 and October 1955. After four rounds of shuttle diplomacy, the American envoy, Ambassador Eric Johnston, had succeeded in having the parties agree, on the technical level, to a unified plan for the development of the Jordan valley, with water-sharing a primary component of it. The Johnston Plan, although it was not endorsed on the political level, served as the basis for the involvement of the United States in water projects in the basin.

In its pursuit of Syrian approval for a dam project on the Yarmouk, Jordan yielded to Syrian conditions and replaced its Yarmouk treaty with Syria in 1987. The new treaty upset the allocations stipulated in the Unified Plan. It gave to Syria an estimated annual amount of 200 million cubic meters (mcm) compared to its share of 90 mcm under Johnston's allocations. The Johnston Plan was later seen by subsequent American mediators (such as the late Ambassador Philip Habib) as 'unrealistic'. By 1992, when the peace talks started, the number of riparian parties had increased by one (Palestinians) on account of Jordan's disengagement from the West Bank. On the Yarmouk, Jordan was able to use only about 35 per cent of its share as specified in the Plan. Israel was using 240 per cent of its share, and Syria was using 240 per cent of its share also. Jordan had to negotiate to restore the applicability of the Unified Plan, and was unlikely to receive the support of either the Israelis or the Americans, nor, of course would it appeal to the Syrians. Since the Plan was finalized, Israel had won several military encounters with the Arabs, and was in a much stronger position to negotiate a new water-sharing formula that could give it more gains than Johnston did back in 1955.

The first meeting of the subgroup on water, energy and the environment, held on March 25, 1992, was more of an introduction, both of people and of the subject. At the end of the meeting, the Israelis asked for a Jordanian proposal on the wording of an item on water for the agenda for negotiations within the Jordanian–Israeli track. That afternoon and evening, Haddadin sat down and drafted a few proposals for an agenda item on water. He chose one and debated it with Awn al-Khasawneh. Awn's background on water in international law was substantial. He also happened to be a member of the International Law Commission of the United Nations that had been working on the draft convention on 'Non-Navigational Uses of International Water Courses', and his contributions in that area were known to Haddadin. Between the two of them, a draft clause was finalized, which was discussed and approved by the rest of us in our meeting that evening. The text under item 3, 'Water', was as follows:

a)   Securing the rightful shares of the riparians in the Yarmouk and the Jordan Rivers.
b)   Searching for ways to alleviate water shortage.
c)   Controlling the level of the Dead Sea.

The informal meeting of the Jordanian–Israeli group on water, energy and the environment convened the following day, March 26, 1992. It did not cost the Jordanians much effort to debate their draft proposal with the Israelis and have it adopted with slight modification. The final text read:

a)   Securing the rightful water shares of the two sides in the Yarmouk River and the Jordan River.
b)   Searching for ways to alleviate water shortage.

The difference between the two texts was that the first item addressed the rightful shares of the two sides, and not of the riparians, whose number exceeded two (they include Syria, Lebanon and the Palestinians in addition to Jordan and Israel), and that the control of the Dead Sea level was shifted to another article of the common agenda that addressed bilateral cooperation within a regional context. After the text was agreed between the two sides, Haddadin suggested that the group go into substantive discussions of the intent of the text. 'We do not propose to start from scratch, although we could,' said Haddadin. 'We propose to save time and energy, and jointly to adopt the compromise that was accepted by the Arabs and Israel back in 1955.' 'Failing that,' he added, 'I am afraid we will have to disregard all our past commitments and start from the very beginning.' Sabel asked to come back to the issue early in the next round.

The discussion then moved on to the environment. The Israelis complained of several issues. 'We have big environmental problems that we have to cooperate on and solve,' said Prujenin. 'We have the problem of houseflies. They make the resort areas south of the Dead Sea difficult to visit and enjoy.'

'I do not want to downplay the importance of such issues, Mr Prujenin,' snapped Haddadin, 'but have you given a thought to the miserable life of people who have been living in shacks in refugee camps? Don't you think that we should be talking about their misery too?'

'Well, this is outside our jurisdiction here. We have a mandate to talk about water, energy and the environment,' interjected Sabel.

'This *is* an issue of the environment,' insisted Haddadin. 'Anything that impacts human life and nature falls under the umbrella of environment. At any rate, we will have plenty of time to debate all these issues.'

'Oh! Another important issue,' said Prujenin. 'I am sure Ambassador Rubinstein must have mentioned it in the track meeting. It is the problem of pigeons that freely cross the borders between our two countries. Wild pigeons feed on grain around your grain silos at the port of Aqaba, and they fly over to Eilat and drop their packages on the hotel balconies and on the tourist on the beaches of Eilat.'

'There will be time, there will be time,' said Haddadin, 'but right now, I am afraid we have to catch our rides back to the hotel.' Over lunch, Haddadin briefed Majali and the delegates who sat with them at the lunch table. Majali was pleased. 'Now we have at least one item of the common agenda agreed to. Don't forget to help Nayef al-Qadi draft the cable to Amman tonight.'

## The Palestinian track

In the Palestinian track, there were Jordanian participants, Fayez Tarawneh with one other delegate of his and Majali's choice. In this fourth round, he once chose Dr Munther Haddadin to accompany him to an afternoon session. The day before, the Palestinians had given the Israeli delegation a non-paper outline of their views concerning the conflict and the topics to be negotiated. It contained terminology that the Israelis disliked, such as 'Palestine', 'our Palestinian homeland', 'the inalienable rights of the Palestinian people'. The Palestinians also expressed their views about the character of the Palestinian Interim Self-Governing Authority (PISGA), and the nature of relations with Israel.

The session started with Abdul Shafi asking Rubinstein about the Israeli response to the Palestinian non-paper. The Jordanian delegation had not been given a copy of the Palestinian non-paper, nor were the Jordanians briefed about it. The Jordanian representatives with the Palestinian delegation listened to the debate over the contents of the non-paper in the track session. In his response, Rubinstein was unkind to the Palestinians. He blasted the contents of their non-paper and was almost shouting as he talked. 'You say that Palestine is your country? This is Israel. You should be grateful that we let you bury your dead in Eretz Israel . . . You talk of a history that you have in it? I will tell you what history you have. It is Haj Ameen al-Hussaini who allied himself with the Nazis during the War . . .'

Abdul Shafi interrupted with his calm dignified voice, 'Out of fairness to the man . . .'

'He does not deserve any fairness,' Rubinstein shot back. Abdul Shafi continued, 'Yes, he does. He allied himself with the Nazis for the same reasons your protectors and mentors, the British, allied themselves with Stalin.'

'Your history is full of acts of terrorism. Your history is the terrorist Mohammad Abbas and his assaults on the beaches of Israel, and on the Italian cruise ship *Achilli Laro*. Your history is that corrupt Yassir Arafat who buys allegiance from people through bribes. He has been bribing people with cars and money,' Rubinstein replied.

'You are obviously going against all norms of protocols, and past all red lines. Arafat is the President of the State of Palestine, and we will not allow any derogatory remarks to be said about him,' said Abdul Shafi.

Rubinstein continued to lecture the Palestinians on what he considered the history of events in Palestine. 'Just one thing you should always keep in mind. You have never had a state throughout your entire presence in Eretz Israel. You say Judea and Samaria is occupied? It was Jordan that occupied it between 1948 and 1967, and Israel's Defense Forces liberated it from the Jordanian occupation.' The atmosphere was tense. Abdul Shafi took the floor and said a few sober and meaningful words. He then gave the floor to Mamdouh al-Ekir, a prominent Palestinian dentist from Nablus, who politely disagreed with everything Rubinstein delivered. While Mamdouh was talking, Haddadin leaned over to his left and whispered in Tarawneh's ear: 'I am going to take on that bastard. The Palestinians here come from the Occupied Territories and they would not dare give him an equal and opposite reaction.'

'I prefer not,' said Tarawneh. 'We have not coordinated such a thing with the Palestinians beforehand. Now they will accuse you of spoiling their presentation and jeopardizing their case. Please don't.' Haddadin took note of what Tarawneh had to say, but signaled to Abdul Shafi, asking for the floor. Abdul Shafi nodded in recognition of Haddadin's request. When Mamdouh was through, Abdul Shafi turned to his right, the side where the Jordanians were sitting among other delegates, and gave the floor to Keilani, a veteran of Israeli detentions from Nablus, then to Nabil Qassis, a university professor from Ramallah teaching at Beir Zeit University in the West Bank. He then gave the floor back to Rubinstein without giving Haddadin the opportunity to speak. 'Dr Abdul Shafi, what in the world has happened?' Haddadin said in Arabic, addressing the head of the Palestinian delegation. 'I asked you for the floor.' Abdul Shafi did not respond because Rubinstein had started to speak. Hearing Haddadin's words to Abdul Shafi, Rubinstein realized with his knowledge of Arabic that Haddadin wanted the floor. 'Dr Haddadin, you want to say something?' he asked.

'Yes, Ambassador,' Haddadin replied.

'You have the floor, please,' Rubinstein said. Haddadin stood.

Thank you, Ambassador. I just want to put on record my reservation as a Jordanian delegate about every word you said concerning Jordan and the West Bank that you strangely referred to as Judea and Samaria. I want also to put on record that we reserve the right to respond to your comments about this matter in the proper track at the proper time.

As the session ended and the delegates rose to file out, Haddadin walked next to Dr al-Ja'bari, a Palestinian delegate. His family were from the city of Hebron, and his late father, Sheikh Mohammad Ali Ja'bari, was a strong proponent of the West Bank union with Jordan. Sheikh Ja'bari held ministerial posts in the Kingdom several times after the union in 1950, and he was Minister of Education when Haddadin went to grade school. 'Dr Ja'bari, what a loss!' Haddadin said. 'You all heard Rubinstein speak of Jordanian occupation of the West Bank, and no one rebuffed his disregard of our union. Who was pulling our ears when we were kids in class but your own father. We accepted that because we were one united country. How come you did not say a word?'

'You want me to speak out in support of the union of the two Banks,' answered Ja'bari, 'so that they [the Palestinians] would call me a traitor, son of a traitor?' Haddadin was stunned by this attitude so early in the talks. He realized that his future participation in the Palestinian track would bring friction, not only with the Israelis, but also with the Palestinians – and that he could do without.


Back at the Willard Hotel, Tarawneh and Haddadin reported to Majali what had happened in the Palestinian track. Majali immediately sent for al-Khasawneh, the legal expert on the delegation. Al-Khasawneh worked all evening formulating the Jordanian response to the Israeli allegations of a Jordanian occupation of the West Bank. He used the best of language in his written rebuff, and was equally superb in his argument the following morning in the session of the Jordanian–Israeli track.

Al-Khasawneh had a good idea of what position Dr Sabel (the Israeli legal expert) would take with respect to the West Bank. Sabel repeatedly reiterated the position developed by a number of Israeli and pro-Israeli Jewish lawyers around the world. Their argument was that Israel had a better claim to the West Bank than Jordan, whose status they viewed as that of a belligerent occupier. They formulated exotic legal argumentation 'proving' that the West Bank was terranullius, i.e., territory without a sovereign. One of the arguments was that Israel's title was superior because it entered the West Bank in self defense.

In his counter-argument, al-Khasawneh asserted that initially Israel had acknowledged its position as a belligerent occupier and issued military orders to administer the territories, which, in accordance with the Geneva Convention of 1949, was the right thing for an occupier to do. It was only later that a group of lawyers including Yehuda Blum,

Stephan Schwebell and Eliahu Lauterpacht started developing arguments aimed at releasing Israel from its obligation under the Fourth Geneva Convention. He then reviewed all these arguments and delivered responses to them including, inter alia, the frequent pronouncements by the UN Security Council and General Assembly requiring Israel to comply with its obligations as a military occupier. With regard to the claim of 'a war of self defense', al-Khasawneh quoted from Judge Jennings that, 'title to the territory cannot be predicated upon subjectively asserted notions of self defense'.[2] This was all the more so in this case, since the Security Council never came to a determination as to who was the aggressor or who was acting in self defense in 1967. Al-Khasawneh, furthermore, quoted the late Israeli Prime Minister Menachim Begin, who was replying to his critics after the invasion of Lebanon in 1982. In response to the critics who said that Begin's war in Lebanon was unnecessary, Begin said, 'All Israel's previous wars were unnecessary. We knew, for example, that Nasser was not going to attack in 1967.' Begin himself was a member of the Eshkol Government in Israel that waged the 1967 War which now some advocates of Israel wanted to claim as a war of self defense.

Rubinstein was obviously impressed and gave the floor to his legal advisor, Dr Sabel. The legal debate went on for a short while and then Rubinstein interjected: 'Even if your arguments are all correct, Mr al-Khasawneh, the fact remains that only two states, the United Kingdom and Pakistan, recognized the legality of Jordan's presence in the West Bank.' Al-Khasawneh answered:

> The effects of implied recognition are no different from those of explicit recognition, and it is fair to say that the international community at large dealt with Jordan in a way that cannot but be construed as recognizing Jordanian sovereignty in the West Bank. This is a direct result of the lack of reservation to Jordan's entry into the United Nations in 1955, and the hundreds of international agreements that Jordan entered into without a single reservation by others as to their applicability to the West Bank. And in any case, even if your argument about the United Kingdom and Pakistan is entertained, that leaves Jordan with two states on its side more than Israel, whose presence in the West Bank is recognized by no one, implicitly or explicitly.

In their argument back and forth, Sabel used to read from a prepared text quoting a General Assembly resolution on 'Friendly Relations Among States in Accordance With International Law'. Al-Khasawneh would respond by similar quotations from the same resolution, different paragraphs, except he was quoting from memory, with no prepared text, which stunned his counterpart. 'Obviously,' Sabel said, 'you definitely know your international law.'

'This is partly why I am here,' responded al-Khasawneh with obvious wit.

Dr Majali then went on to tell the Israelis what Jordan had done to develop the West Bank, then an integral part of the Kingdom, socially and economically. He alluded to the special attention the West Bank had received from His Majesty and his governments. He cited the medical services as an example, and how he himself played a role in providing medical services in the West Bank when he was Director of the Royal Medical Services of the Jordan Armed Forces. Majali compared the rate of development before Israel's occupation with the corresponding rate after the Israeli occupation of the West Bank, and showed how superior Jordanian efforts had been.

At the end of the round, Majali inquired from Rubinstein about their response to the Jordanian proposal for the negotiations agenda that was handed over to him in January. Rubinstein promised to have a response in the following round. The fourth round ended and we flew back home. As usual, Majali held meetings for us to review progress and prepare for the coming round. The meetings were held at the Government's Guest House in Jabal Amman. Majali impressed on those attending to do their homework, prepare all necessary references, and get ready for the historic encounter. 'The Egyptians, with all the size and weight of Egypt, had difficulties in negotiating with the Israelis in Camp David and afterwards. We should be doubly prepared and more cautious,' he advised.

Majali asked that the proposal for a negotiations agenda with the Israelis be revisited. This simple, outline agenda had been prepared before Madrid and handed to Rubinstein at the end of the third round in January. At the onset of the fourth round, the Israelis presented us with a counter-proposal to our draft agenda. The Israeli draft accommodated the five points of the Jordanian summary agenda, added to them, and went into more detail (see Appendix 2). The

Israelis were adamant in rejecting the word 'withdrawal' and opted to call the Jordanian occupied lands 'disputed lands'. They wanted to have the negotiations culminate in a peace treaty while we cited the goal as reaching a just, lasting and comprehensive peace in the Middle East. The Israelis proposed that discussion of security issues focus on an understanding not to use force against one another. We demanded a freeze on the building of Israeli settlements, and a mutual renunciation of nuclear, biological and chemical weapons. We also elaborated on the issue of water and demanded that the problem of refugees and displaced persons be resolved in accordance with the relevant UN resolutions. The Israelis focused on 'improving the quality of life' in refugee camps, and on cooperation with others to resolve refugees' problem.

'Pasha, with all due respect,' said Rubinstein, 'we in Israel look upon the right of refugees to repatriation as a form of definite suicide!'

'Conversely,' asserted Majali, 'we in Jordan look upon the denial of the rights of the Palestinian refugees to repatriation and compensation, as decreed by the UN, as a recipe for a troubled Middle East. There can be no peace or quiet so long as the refugees' problem is not settled in a fair and square way.'

'But, Dr Majali,' answered Rubinstein, 'this is beyond our capability. It has to be an international effort. Until then, we propose that the quality of life in the refugee camps be improved.'

Finally, the Israelis wanted Jordan to assume some kind of ambiguous role in the Interim Self-Governing Authority of the Palestinians, something we Jordanians adamantly refused to consider. There was simply no way to bridge the gap between the two positions, or at least, it was very difficult to reconcile the differences.

The delegations returned to their home bases. Those members involved in the multilateral peace talks got ready for the second round. The working groups for the multilateral talks had different venues that were a world apart in geography and time zones. Water was discussed in Vienna, Refugees in Ottawa, Security in Washington, Environment in Tokyo, and Economic Cooperation in Brussels. Yet, the Director of the Special Office at the Ministry of Foreign Affairs, Abdul Ilah al-Khatib, did a marvelous job in coordinating their work, communicating official instructions, briefing each group on what went on in the meetings of the other groups, and giving suggestions.

The fifth round of bilateral negotiations was to convene in the same venue, Washington, on April 20. At the beginning of that round, Haddadin was in Majali's suite sharing with him his favorite pastime, playing cards. Aktham Quosous and Musa Majali, the security officer, made up the four players for a game of Hands Remie. Pleased and relaxed after a streak of wins, Majali looked at Haddadin after the game ended. 'What did you say about the agenda for negotiations?' he asked.

'I thought maybe we can draft an updated agenda that would narrow the differences with the Israelis, and would expand on the summary topics. It could avoid the bracketed language that the Israeli counter-proposal contains, maintain our position and spell out issues and their resolution,' Haddadin answered.

'Okay,' said Majali, 'would you like to take a shot at it?'

'Gladly,' said Haddadin, and he retreated to his room to start work. He drafted a proposal for a Common Agenda for discussion by the delegation, to be sent back to Amman for comments and approval, and then presented to the Israelis. He had it done before he went to bed that night. The following morning, he handed it to Seita, the able office manager of the Minister of Foreign Affairs who was among the support staff of the delegation. Seita typed the draft Common Agenda on April 27, 1992. It was presented to a meeting of the delegation that same day, commented upon and amended (see Appendix 2). The amended draft was forwarded to Amman the following day, and was put in final form on August 28. Haddadin handed a copy of it to Abdul Rahman al-Hamad, the Palestinian delegate attending the Jordanian track, and Majali handed over another copy to Abdul Shafi and the other heads of the Arab delegations in the coordination meeting the following day.

That proposal was submitted as a 'non-paper' over which the bilateral track with Jordan had most of its discussions throughout the sixth and seventh rounds. The more the negotiations dragged on, the more the positions became clearer, but no agreement was reached on the Common Agenda.

In the corridor of the negotiations wing, and during a coffee break, Haddadin brought up the subject of controlling the Dead Sea level with Dr Uri Wurzburger, Director General of Israel's Ministry of Energy. This topic had been included in the first draft of the agenda item on water that had been agreed upon during the previous round. Haddadin knew the solution the Israelis favored, namely to transport water from the

Mediterranean Sea to the Dead Sea to raise its declining level. Jordan, on the other hand, favored a linkage with the Red Sea and a water conduit that would traverse Wadi Araba. Wurzburger indicated that the Israelis were prepared to consider the Red–Dead linkage, and expressed a willingness to start a joint study of the project as soon as possible. Haddadin was not ready to advocate a joint study with the Israelis before the dispute was settled and cooperation between the two countries commenced.

The fifth round ended on April 30, 1992 and the delegations went home. Our delegation and the Palestinian delegation held coordination talks at the Ministry of Foreign Affairs in Amman, in the presence of Dr Kamel Abu Jaber, the Jordanian Minister of Foreign Affairs and Mahmoud Abbas, Secretary General of the PLO's Executive Committee. A side meeting was held at the Jordan Higher Council for Science and Technology to look into the arrangements needed by the Palestinians to establish the PISGA. Inevitably the conversation came round to the forthcoming Israeli elections. 'Obviously, we will have our own elections for PISGA,' said Hanan Ashrawi. 'We have not embarked on the issue of who is going to vote.'

'Who do you think should be eligible to vote for the council of the PISGA?' asked Haddadin.

'All Palestinians in the West Bank and Gaza, and we are hoping that the Palestinian refugee camps would also be given the right to vote for PISGA. In this respect, we would like to have voting booths in the refugee camps in Jordan,' Ashrawi said.

'What?' exclaimed Haddadin. 'But these people are Jordanian citizens, and the soil they are on is Jordanian! How would a Palestinian general election be conducted in Jordan?'

'It is our hope that Jordan will cooperate and support this notion,' said Ereikat.

'I do not know how the official decision would be; but offhand, I would think that such elections would only reinforce the notion of the extremists in Israel, like General Sharon, that Palestine is actually Jordan,' said Haddadin. 'We have to think much deeper and find an alternative to the voting of Palestinians in diaspora.' There was silence, and the conversation went back to the Israeli elections.

On their way to Washington for the sixth round, Awn al-Khasawneh and Haddadin, sitting next to each other on the plane, spent a good part of the time on the flight to Amsterdam reciting Arabic poetry. Suddenly, Awn switched the topic, 'I am afraid that this will turn out to be a thankless job, my friend,' he said.

'Which job?' asked Haddadin. Awn replied,

> The task we are doing, our efforts to make peace with Israel. Look at the time you are spending, and you are not a government official or employee. You are a member of the bilateral delegation, you are also the head of the multilateral delegation on water, and you are a member of the steering committee of the multilaterals. You are working full-time like you are drafted in the service. Our government pays for your meals and lodging at a time when you have your own business for which you have no time left.

'And look at you, you are full-time as well,' commented Haddadin. 'You are pivotal in the bilateral negotiations, you are a member of the Jordanian delegation to the refugees working group of the multilaterals. You are also a member of the steering committee of the multilaterals, and you are on call continuously to prepare position papers where international law is important.'

'Yes, but I am afraid that by the end of the day, we will be targets not of appreciation, but of blame and thanklessness,' said Awn.

> Awn, my friend, I look at what we are doing as a duty like the military draft. We are doing our duty towards the motherland. We are giving our energies and our time for its sake, but our giving is still not enough. Look at those who gave their lives in its defense. We are among the lucky, Awn, thanklessness or gratefulness, we are among the lucky. We are alive and are doing our sacred duty. It is close to having the cake and eating it at the same time.

'I guess you are right, Munther, but brace yourself for the worse,' Awn said.

The sixth round convened on August 24 and lasted until September 23, 1992. The long break between the rounds was because of the planned Israeli general elections in June that would bring about a new government as well. The excitement of the negotiations started to taper off, and the coverage of the talks in the press became nominal. In Israel, Labor and the Greens were able to form a coalition government headed by Yitzhak Rabin. Likud and its extremist partners became the opposition.

Majali showed signs of toughness coupled with impatience as time passed without substantial achievements. Impatience was not among the qualities that Majali was famed for, but lack of progress when he was in charge irritated him. The Israelis were eager to start meetings of specialized groups to discuss various topics of negotiations and were willing to call them anything: subcommittees, subgroups, working teams, or any other suitable name provided that the two delegations would split in as many teams as was practically possible. Majali got the message and wondered if Rubinstein's easy agreement to an informal group on water, energy and the environment concealed a covert intention to split that group up into smaller ones.

## Water, energy and the environment

A new head for the Israeli team in the water, energy and environment group arrived, taking over from Dr Elyahu Rosenthal. He was Noah Kinarti who was by no means a newcomer to water issues, especially issues over the Yarmouk. Meeting him informally over coffee, Marwan Muasher of the Jordanian delegation introduced himself to Kinarti and pointed out his Jordanian counterpart on water, Munther Haddadin.

'I know of him, and I do not like him,' said Kinarti.

'But why? He is a very nice man. I am sure you will get to like him once you get to know him well,' said Muasher.

'Your Dr Haddadin fooled us many times over the Yarmouk. He will know what I am talking about,' said Kinarti. Muasher was quick to relate to Haddadin his short conversation with the newcomer. 'I know who he is. Kinarti heads the kibbutzim in what they call the Jordan valley. We have been in competition over the waters of the Yarmouk since 1979,' said Haddadin.

'He really does not like you. I could tell from the way he looked when I told him about you!' said Muasher.

'I played hide-and-seek with them over the Yarmouk waters. They are not difficult to beat. Their fallback position has always been the Israeli Army – they called it in and I did not like that for obvious reasons!'

'Maybe that is why he does not like you,' said Muasher.

'What do you expect? Not liking me is an understatement. He is trying to disguise his extremist attitudes. But I am looking forward to a period of fun in the negotiations!' said Haddadin.

Kinarti was a recently appointed advisor to the Minister of Defense, Prime Minister Yitzhak Rabin. He was said to have contributed to the victory of Rabin (Labor) in the recent elections. Kinarti was active in the Jordan valley and had secured the majority of votes for Rabin. He showed a rather snobbish attitude from the first meeting he attended with the team of water, energy and environment, but Haddadin responded in kind.

Substantive talks started on water. As he stated in the previous round, Robby Sabel, the Israeli legal advisor, wanted to comment on Haddadin's proposal to go back to the agreed compromise achieved during the Johnston mission of 1955. Obviously, there had been violations of that Plan by Israel and by Syria. Sabel read from a prepared text:

> The Johnston Project was vague. What is your understanding of it and your position regarding it? You said that you have a document that shows your commitment to it. Can we have a copy of that document?
>
> Tell us, what is the share of Syria in accordance with the Johnston Plan, and are the Syrians abiding by that share?
>
> You concluded an agreement with Syria in 1987. How much did you allow the Syrians to withdraw from the Yarmouk flow? How do you conclude an agreement over the Yarmouk without the approval of Israel who is the third partner? How do you compare the share of Syria in the 1987 Agreement with its share under the Johnston Plan, and with the quantities they currently abstract from the river?
>
> Did you take into any consideration the interests of the West Bank in the 1987 Agreement?
>
> What was the quantity of flow that Jordan was supposed to deliver to the West Bank through the siphon across the Jordan River? What was the capacity of that siphon?
>
> Of the 100 mcm stipulated by the Johnston Plan to be drawn from Lake Tiberias, what was the percentage of the brackish water included in them?
>
> Since Jordan did not deliver any water to the West Bank, where is that water now?

His voice was clipped and dry. Haddadin responded:

> I am surprised that the Israeli side is posing questions the answers to which they know very well. The presentation sounds like that of a plaintiff in a court of law. We would be prepared to present a defense of the defendant if this were a court of law, in which case we need a jury and a judge. They are close. They must be in this same building [referring to the United States officials]. Let us bring them

in so that they hear the charges and the defense, and we both should accept the verdict.

Sabel understood the sarcastic response, declined the proposal and politely apologized for the tone of his presentation.

'Your repeated reference to Syria puzzles me,' Haddadin resumed, and, remembering that the bilateral negotiations were an Israeli demand, he added,

> Do you want the Syrians with us here or don't you? They are negotiating with Israel in the other wing of this same building. We are prepared to work either way.
>
> If there are parties who would testify to our consideration of the rights of others on the Yarmouk, Israel should be the first such party. Israel should be the last to complain about being ignored in any venture Jordan has undertaken on the Yarmouk. The detailed designs of the Maqarin dam [renamed Wehda dam] were forwarded to you via the American intermediary from the outset. We also found out that our consultant, Harza Engineering Company, received a delegate from your Water Commission to explain the designs to him and answer his questions. That was done without our consent, and yet we did not fire our consultant for being that liberal in the disposition of our material. We understand the factors and the pressures that prompted our consultant to abide by the requests of outsiders.

'But that was . . .' interrupted Dr Sabel.

'Now, please,' interrupted Haddadin firmly, 'I gave you all the time you needed without any interruption. I expect you and your colleagues to reciprocate.' There was an extreme silence that was obviously to Haddadin's advantage and he deliberately remained quiet for a few more seconds, and then resumed:

> As for the 1987 Agreement with Syria, its cornerstone is the Wehda dam, and such an agreement should be of value when the dam is built. We will be prepared to look into any grievance you have when we come to build that dam. Therefore, it is a waste of time to enter into a debate over an agreement that has no effect unless the dam is built. Besides, we are not responsible for what Syria does in the river basin, and we have informed them of our objections on several occasions before 1987.
>
> With respect to the Palestinian rights under the 1987 Agreement, Syria has never recognized the West Bank as part of the

Hashemite Kingdom. Therefore, Syria's talk with Jordan does not apply to the West Bank. As a matter of fact, Jordan and Syria both consider the PLO as the sole legitimate representative of the Palestinian people.

Jordan did not deliver any water to the West Bank because the share of the West Bank was to come from Lake Tiberias which has been under Israeli control all along. The Palestinian share would be delivered to the King Abdallah Canal from Lake Tiberias, and Jordan, in turn, would deliver it to the West Bank through a siphon under the Jordan River. So you see that the share of the West Bank under the Plan is still in Israeli hands.

We never have disregarded the Palestinian rights, but we have refused, and still do, that Israel speak on behalf of the West Bank. As for the quantities we intended to give to the Palestinians, it is for us and the Palestinians to decide, although Israel has a role there pertaining to the number of Palestinians who would exercise the right of return to Palestine and Israel.

Israel's protest over being ignored in the 1987 Agreement would have been sustained were the contracting parties not in a state of war with Israel.

Syria's share in the Yarmouk under the Johnston Plan is 90 mcm per year, which was the same share implied in the 1953 Agreement we had with them.

The percentage of salt water to be included in the 100 mcm from Tiberias is not more than 15.

We are prepared to exchange documents with you. We are ready to give you a copy of our commitment to abide by our share in the Unified [Johnston] Plan provided you give us a copy of your commitment to your share under that Plan. You issued such a document as a condition precedent to receiving financial aid from the United States to build the Tiberias–Beit Shean pipeline, and the National Water Carrier.

The Israeli side appreciated the Jordanian explanation, but insisted that Israel's share in the Yarmouk of 25 mcm was only the summer allocation! They asked that a share in the winter months be negotiated and agreed upon. This was a repetition of their old position during the negotiations with Eric Johnston, in which they insisted that their annual share from the Yarmouk was 40 mcm. The Jordanian side rejected their claim and insisted that the annual, not the summer, Israeli share in the Yarmouk was 25 mcm.

'Let us now break into three groups, one for water, one for energy, and one for environment,' suggested Kinarti in a confident manner.

'We are fine the way we are. We do not want to miss points on any of these three topics. We sit in one group and discuss any topic we like together,' said Haddadin.

'But why, it is more practical to split in groups of specialty. You and I will head a subgroup on water. Dr Abdallah Toukan and Mr Uri Wuerzburger will handle the energy, and Dr Duraid Mahasneh, head of the Ports Corporation in Jordan and Mr Amran Prujenin will handle the environment,' insisted Kinarti.

'You see, Mr Kinarti,' responded Haddadin, 'I am appointed to head Jordan's teams on each of the three topics. Obviously, I cannot be in three different locations at the same time.'

'You and I can supervise the three groups by checking on them. The only way to achieve progress is to split in three subgroups. If you are not willing to do so, we might as well forget about negotiations,' said Kinarti.

'Listen fellow, I have been trying to sound nice but you are heavily taxing my patience. Be my guest, if you do not want to negotiate in one group I will be cooperative and respond to your suggestion to forget about negotiations,' said Haddadin, and he left his seat and headed towards the soft drinks and coffee in the left fore-corner of the room. Kinarti left the room and went out. After a little while, Rubinstein came to Majali in the delegation room. 'Dr Majali, Haddadin is not willing to cooperate. He refuses to have the group of delegates split up in workable sizes and talk special topics. What can we do to please your Haddadin?' he said. Majali called Haddadin in and respectfully asked him to explain, which he did. As the two men conversed, Rubinstein tried to step in through the open door of the Jordanian delegation room. Majali slammed the door shut with his foot in a clear message of anger to Rubinstein. 'Okay, Haddadin,' said Majali, 'Do not budge until I ask you to.'

As Majali clearly anticipated, Rubinstein tried to contact him again. Soon, Quosous knocked at the door, opened it and addressed Majali: 'Pasha, Rubinstein looks very worried and he wants to talk to you. I advise that you please be kind to him.'

Majali agreed to speak to Rubinstein. 'Listen *walah* [you],' he said in an insulting tone of voice, 'I told you at the very beginning. I told you never ever to try and fool me, and you do not seem to benefit from that advice of mine. If you think I am rough at times, this Haddadin is known to be rough all the time. I could turn him loose and you deal with him.' Rubinstein was quick to appease him:

No Pasha, no. I am not trying to fool you, nor is Mr Kinarti trying to fool Haddadin. We are just trying to get our job done. You are lucky with Haddadin who can conduct the talks in any one of their topics. I have no one like him. Kinarti can talk only water, Wurzburger can talk only energy, and Amran Prujenin can talk only environment. I cannot squeeze three of them in one. This is all.

'This matter is for Haddadin to decide. You and I should not interfere,' said Majali.

'You know how strongminded Haddadin is, he will never give in. Please, Doctor, please help us with him,' pleaded Rubinstein. Majali walked back to Haddadin, and whispered, 'It is okay if you let the three groups meet for five minutes each in the different corners of the same room, and you walk around to oversee their conversation. Tell them not to talk about anything substantive.'

'Yes Sir,' said Haddadin. He headed back to the negotiation room and Kinarti followed.

Haddadin organized his team in three groups, instructed them what to do, and the three subgroups met for less than five minutes in three corners of the room. The rest of the round, the meeting was in one group, and they agreed to start working on a subagenda for water, energy and the environment.

In that sixth round there was some progress, as agreement was achieved on certain items on the draft common agenda. The wording of other items, especially those relating to security, refugees and borders, remained subjects of non-agreement.

## NOTES

1 The Israeli team consisted of Dr Uri Wurzburger, the Director General of the Ministry of Energy, Mr Amran Prujenin, Deputy Director of the Ministry of the Environment, Dr Rosenthal, and Dr Sabel, the legal advisor to the delegation. The Jordanian team was headed by Haddadin and had in it Dr Mohammad Bani Hani, Dr Abdallah Toukan and Ambassador Talal al-Ḥassan. The members of both sides changed over the course of the negotiations.

2 R. Y. Jennings, 'Acquisition of Territory in International Law', Manchester University Press, Oceana Publications, 1963. Manchester, New York.

# 6

## Developments in the Round

Between the second and sixth rounds of bilateral negotiations at the State Department, various international developments had one effect or another on the negotiations. The peace process itself achieved more success as the multilateral conference convened in Moscow on January 28, 1992, and formed five working groups. With a new Israeli government in June 1992, although the Israeli team composition did not change much, the attitude shifted towards a more serious intention to reach peace agreements. Within Jordan, the success of surgery that King Hussein underwent in September, 1992 to remove a cancerous growth prompted a show of extreme loyalty, giving him a stronger hand in the peace process and helping to quieten the opposition to peace amongst Jordanians.

### The Palestinian track

The Palestinian track was probably the most important; any breakthrough in that track would promote progress in other tracks. However, it was evident from the first two rounds that the Israeli tactic with the joint Jordanian-Palestinian delegation was to suppress Palestinian identity. The Israelis were prepared to give the Palestinians some sort of autonomy with vague notions of jurisdiction/sovereignty, and to sign a peace treaty with Jordan which included minimum land and water concessions. As elections in Israel were drawing nearer, the Likud government was keen to strike a deal with the Palestinians in Washington that would give the Palestinians little but would end the Intifada in the Occupied Territories. The Likud did not mind idling in the negotiations and the Israeli authorities made a habit of kicking up a fuss just before any round of negotiations started. They would, for example, delay some Palestinian delegates from leaving the Occupied Territories or issue a deportation order against some Palestinian activists. The Americans urged the Palestinian delegation not to let short-term misgivings abort the constructive efforts of peacemaking. The long-term strategic objective should be the guide, not the noise that Israel created every now and then.

In Palestinian–Israeli negotiations, two terms were in circulation: The ISGA (Interim Self-Governing Arrangement) as interpreted by the Israelis, and the PISGA (Palestinian Interim Self-Government Authority) as interpreted by the Palestinians. The different interpretation of the terms reflected what each delegation thought of the ongoing transitory stage before the final status of the Occupied Territories and of the Palestinians was settled. The Israelis wanted the interim arrangement to be simply a delegation of certain responsibilities assumed by Israel in the Palestinian territories to some Palestinian executive body to be agreed upon and to be limited only to the Palestinian residents in 'Judea and Samaria' (the West Bank) and Gaza, and to be without any territorial jurisdiction or sovereignty. Israel also preferred to assign some kind of a role to Jordan in this arrangement.

The Palestinian delegation, on the other hand, had a different concept altogether. They wanted the transitory stage to serve as a bridge toward an independent Palestinian State, the seeds of which needed to be planted through the negotiations. The Palestinians wanted the Israeli delegation to commit itself to the applicability of Security Council Resolution 242 to the occupied Palestinian territories. That meant an exchange of occupied Palestinian lands for peace with the Palestinians. Moreover, they wanted the word 'Palestinian' to appear before ISGA, and the A to stand for 'Authority' and not 'Arrangement'. Last but not least, the Palestinians wanted authority to be transferred and not delegated to them from Israel. Saeb Ereikat would say, 'If Israel delegates authorities or responsibilities to us, it then can, likewise, retract them.'

Jordan, for its part, refused to entertain any notion of a Jordanian role in the Occupied Territories, and firmly stated that it was a Palestinian responsibility to negotiate and create terms which they themselves could accept. The Jordanian delegation repeated that position and assured the Palestinian delegation of every possible support.

Palestinian–Israeli sessions were marred by continuous debates over what Israel called 'acts of terror and disorder', meaning the Palestinian Intifada, and over what the Palestinians referred to as 'Israeli violations of human rights' and the Israeli delegation referred to as 'security measures'. At the opening of the sessions, Dr Haider Abdul Shafi would read a list of Israeli violations, to which Ambassador Elyakim Rubinstein would respond by asking the Palestinian delegation to stop issuing statements to the press that would incite riots in the 'territories'. Another basic difference between the Palestinians and the Israelis was the name each had for the West Bank and Gaza. Whereas the Palestinians, and indeed all the world, considers them the Occupied Territories, Israel called the West Bank 'Judea and Samaria' and regarded these areas and Gaza as 'Eretz Israel', that was liberated in 1967.

The issue of Israeli settlements was another hotly debated topic. At that time, the Likud government had been actively expropriating lands and building new settlements. 'No one has the right to deny Jews the right to settle anywhere in Eretz Israel,' Rubinstein would frequently declare.

The Palestinians often raised this issue with American diplomats who had impressed upon the Palestinians not to yield to Likud tactics. In general, American policy was against settlements and it used the $10 billion loan guarantee aimed at absorbing new Jewish immigrants from Russia to dissuade the Israeli government from building new settlements or houses in the Occupied Territories. The Likud could not see eye to eye with the others on these matters. In February, 1991, Ambassador Zalman Shoval, Israeli Ambassador to the US, made statements critical of the United States in regard to its conditions for financial support for Israel. These statements were met by open American criticism; Secretary Baker reprimanded the Israeli Ambassador, and Ambassador Dennis Ross, the American peace coordinator, continued to insist that the $10 billion loan guarantee was to support the absorption of Jewish immigrants inside Israel, and not to build new settlements in the Palestinian territories. Yet American diplomacy was also keen not to appear in opposition to Israel – such opposition could elevate Arab expectations from American diplomacy to the point that the Administration would lose favor with the Congress and with the American people. Should this happen, the reluctant Likud government, which Secretary Baker had to lure to Madrid, could use the opportunity as an excuse to abandon the peace process altogether.

The Palestinians, Jordanians and other Arab delegations showed their relentless resentment of Israel's settlement policy, which was a clear violation of the invitation to Madrid. The acceptance of the division of the Israeli–Palestinian negotiations into 'Interim' and 'Final Status' stages was not intended to give Israel a chance to change the status quo on the ground so much that there would be practically no land left to negotiate over in the Final Status stage. At the beginning of each negotiation session, the issue of new settlements would be raised, and the Israeli side would simply restate the Israelis' right to settle anywhere in 'Judea, Samaria and Gaza'.

A war of words was waged through reporters on the subject of settlements too. The eloquence of Dr Hanan Ashrawi was not a source of comfort to the Israeli delegation. Yet, within the Palestinian delegation itself, other members wanted to share the celebrity status that Dr Ashrawi had achieved. Dr Nabil Sha'ath, who started coming to Washington with the delegation, was active with the media and did rather well. Dr Saeb Ereikat was also camera-happy. While not as eloquent and as good at improvising as Nabil Sha'ath, he would, once in a while, devise an expression that would become in vogue. His description of Israel's settlement policy as the 'salami approach' was well received. Later on, Sha'ath came up with another reference to Israel's ISGA proposal, calling it 'the Swiss cheese' approach.

By the third round, the Palestinian–Israeli and the Jordanian–Israeli tracks had become separate to all intents and purposes. The joint delegation was joint in name alone, save occasional symbolic gestures. The Palestinian and Israeli delegations agreed to minimize their full track meetings by meeting in two committees to discuss settlements and Resolution 242. Each delegation was represented by four individuals on each committee, and Jordanian delegates were thus effectively prevented from participating in Palestinian negotiations. Such a measure was approved by the Israelis who wished to redirect the focus of the debate with the Palestinians over ISGA. Jordan's response was also supportive.

Likewise, the exchange of documents between the Israeli and Palestinian delegations was confined to their respective delegates. Although Dr Majali kept the Palestinian delegation fully in the picture by handing them copies of what the Jordanian delegation provided or received, the Palestinians did not reciprocate. Ambassador Rubinstein often handed copies of Palestinian proposals to Dr Majali, in a gesture that suggested Israeli–Jordanian cooperation in the absence of Palestinian communication. Majali grew resentful about this practice and reminded the Palestinian delegation to deal with its Jordanian counterpart on a basis of reciprocity. However, his advice was seldom heeded.

On the Jordanian–Israeli track, the discussions gradually narrowed down to a number of topics that were mutually accepted by both sides. The debate in the second round over the relevance of Resolution 242 to Jordan continued through the third and fourth rounds. We Jordanian delegates were given specific instructions in the recess between the second and third rounds that priority should be given to three agenda items: land, refugees and water. The issues were debated in a meeting in Prince Hassan's residence attended by Prime Minister Sharif Zaid Bin Shaker, Foreign Minister Kamel Abu Jaber, Majali, Anani, Tarawneh, al-Khasawneh and Haddadin. Anani and al-Khasawneh felt that the refugee issue should be given top priority. The knowledge that the Israelis would resist concessions on this issue fueled their desire to make it the highest priority. They believed that as long as the problem of refugees was not adequately resolved, the peace treaty so sought after by the Israelis could not be reached. The others at the meeting feared that this notion could drive the Israelis into a stubborn and uncompromising position. Also, it was argued, the issue of refugees had not been raised by the Palestinian delegations in any serious manner so far. Finally we agreed to prioritize Jordan's concerns in descending order: land, water and refugees.

The peace treaty was indeed important to Israel. The Israelis always stressed the fact that they wanted a peace treaty mentioned in some form in the agreed agenda for negotiations. Ambassador Rubinstein used all his skill to convince the Jordanians of the need to include a reference to a peace treaty, but we maintained our position of refusal. On the issue of economic cooperation, Majali was more lenient, and this item was added to the list of negotiation topics while the Israeli delegation almost dropped its insistence on including Jordanian-related issues on the Israeli–Palestinian track. The issue of security was agreed upon as an item, but the gap over its interpretation was almost unbridgeable when it first emerged as an agenda item.

To construct an agenda, a number of hurdles, some of which seemed insurmountable at times, had to be overcome. One way to sidestep these issues was to compose an agenda using only seven or eight words: land, security, water, refugees, cooperation, other issues, etc. The Israeli delegation made a proposal on such generic terms and presented it in a document that had no addresses, titles, signatures, dates, or any indication as to its origin or destination. By this formula, the Israeli delegation dropped references to a peace treaty and to a comprehensive peace. In return, Jordan was supposed to be ready to sign a peace treaty when the items on the agenda were satisfactorily resolved. If this proposal were adopted, Jordan, would not have to wait for the completion of the other Arab negotiation tracks. However, any attempt by Jordan, at that time, to break away from Arab ranks, so to speak, would have met with a strong backlash from Arab countries, and for this reason it refused the Israeli idea of a neutral and ambiguous structure for the agenda.

Delegates pondered other formulae that sought to use more structural language and employ brackets whenever agreement over a term or item proved to be remote. Each bracketed item would begin either (Israel:) or (Jordan:), to indicate which of the two parties had requested the particular bracketed language. This second suggestion was similar to the previous one in the sense that it postponed thorny issues for later sessions after greater mutual understanding and increased confidence had been achieved. The Jordanian delegation was not in favor of this idea, considering it an attempt to 'sweep problems under the carpet'.

The third and only feasible approach was to sit down and negotiate an unbracketed common agenda. Once the two negotiating teams had agreed on its entire language, they would in effect have resolved many differences in positions and could look forward to smoother sailing from that point onward. Such an approach would differ from regular negotiations where the parties in contention agree on an agenda, a prioritized list of topics, which they then select to negotiate one at a time. However, this more common style of negotiation only works if the contending parties are able to reach a general consensus on the definitions of key phrases constituting the cornerstones of future agreements, and no such consensus existed here. Despite the cordiality and the determination of the two delegations to conduct the negotiations in a gentlemanly, business-like way, there were always times when a tough exchange of views and positions proved necessary. Deeply held convictions had to withstand the test of the other side's reactions.

And so, the third option it was. The discussion focused on the meaning of Resolution 242. In reality, this Resolution (of November 22, 1967) was the theme of intense debate on both the Jordanian and Palestinian tracks. The Israeli delegation contended that the absence of the definite article 'the' in operative clause 1(i) of the Resolution actually meant partial, not total, Israeli withdrawal from the territories it occupied in 1967. In other words, Israel had the prerogative to make partial withdrawals on all fronts, partial withdrawals on some fronts, or complete withdrawal on one front, as they did with Egypt. Accordingly, they already had completely complied with the 'land for peace' article of the Resolution when they withdrew from Sinai, and felt they did not have to withdraw from any other territory like the West Bank, Gaza, or the Golan Heights. However, the words 'withdrawal' and 'occupied' were not acceptable to the Israelis, and they insisted that they would in no way accept the use of either word in the agenda. Moreover, the Israeli delegation insisted on revisiting the issue by posing questions to the Jordanian delegation, such as: 'What is your envisaged relation with the West Bank?' and 'Are you willing to go into confederation with the Palestinians or some sort of a permanent arrangement in the future?' Such questions kept popping up with no direct Jordanian answer. An answer could not be given before a Palestinian entity was created and its jurisdiction defined. 'We will not negotiate on behalf of the Palestinians, nor will we sign or ratify any agreement involving the West Bank. However, we will help in any way we can,' was Dr Majali's typical answer.

The debate over the interpretation of Resolution 242 went round and round in circles. On the Palestinian track, the Israeli delegation was more adamant. They would not give the Palestinian delegation a chance to debate the issue on the grounds that all the issues emanating from that Resolution, if any, were 'Final Status' issues to be negotiated three years down the road. They reiterated a position they had held for some time, that 242 provisions applied to member states of the UN, and therefore the resolution did not apply to the stateless Palestinians. When they had exhausted all these arguments, the Israelis asserted that the Palestinian agenda was solely to tackle issues of the interim arrangements (ISGA).

During the fourth round (between February 24 and March 3, 1992) it became evident to the Palestinians that Israel was stonewalling them while they were debating issues of substance with Jordan. On February 26, the Israeli and Jordanian heads of delegation discussed the possibility of creating subcommittees (Israel) or working groups (Jordan) to discuss a number of prominent issues. Dr Majali refused the idea of working groups after consulting with the rest of us, but it was agreed that an ad hoc meeting would take place between Jordanian and Israeli experts to discuss steps leading to the implementation of Resolution 242 but not its content. On that same day, the meeting of experts took place. News of the meeting reached the media, resulting in misreporting that provoked critical reactions from the Palestinian delegation and other Arab delegates. The media reported that the experts were discussing the content of Resolution 242, and the Palestinian delegation saw this as an attempt to undermine their negotiations with Israel. In Amman, the Palestinian Ambassador, Tayyeb Abdul Raheem, conveyed an urgent message to the Jordanian Foreign Minister expressing deep concern regarding the meeting of experts. Amman immediately instructed us to defuse the crisis and end the experts' working group.

Majali did not share Amman's conservative attitude towards negotiations, nor did he share the view of some of his delegates that Rubinstein was maneuvering him into agreement to measures that served Israeli interests. To him, the negotiations were still at a stage too early to determine any outcome. Majali believed that the different arrangements and configurations that any track might employ to explore each other's opinions and positions should neither be the concern nor the business of the other tracks. The fact that the conduct of our delegation was transparent to the Palestinian delegation but not vice versa did not mean that the Palestinians had the right to interfere in the way we managed our affairs with Israel. At the time, Majali's moral and predictable approach was thought by some to be unsubtle for the careful and calculating Ambassador Rubinstein. In the final analysis, Majali had to inform Rubinstein of his government's decision to suspend the experts' group and resume business in the track meetings.

The rest of the third round was spent probing ideas on refugees, security, and economic cooperation. Although the jokes and repartee continued, the zest of the negotiations round faded after February 26. When the round ended, the Israeli delegation made a strong case for moving the negotiations out of Washington and to the Middle East. The Israeli case was somehow strengthened by apparent American indifference to keeping the negotiations in Washington. The Americans said that they would not in any way oppose moving the negotiations if the parties agreed that Rome was an acceptable location. When the Syrians and the Lebanese stated their strong opposition to changing the venue until substantial progress had been achieved in all tracks on the basic issues, some believed that the real American position, camouflaged by cool indifference, tallied with the Syrian–Lebanese one. American diplomats did not need to assert their insistence on keeping the negotiations in Washington as long as the Syrians and Lebanese were doing it for them. At that time, the Likud government did not see eye to eye with the US administration and believed that the Americans were intent on seeing them lose the forthcoming June elections in Israel. A change of venue would be a plus on the Likud's balance sheet although no one else wanted such a change.

It was commonly understood that the third round of negotiations in Washington would be the last such meeting before Israeli elections. This understanding was proved wrong, and the delegation teams met again in late April for a fresh round of negotiations. The Likud government wanted a chance to appear more dove-ish and to assert that the negotiations could provide a realistic chance of the peaceful settlement that the majority of Israelis favored. Violent acts had intensified in the month of February and impacted on Israeli public opinion. The rise of the Islamic movement in the territories as a new resistance force gave depth to the resistance itself and rekindled Israeli fears. Yitzhak Rabin's campaign motto of economic deliverance and security in return for peace and some of the lands scored well with the Israeli public. The Arab delegates agreed to participate in a new short round with the understanding that the Likud government was willing to make substantial changes in its position. If this was the case, a minimum negotiating position with Israel would have been established regardless of which party ruled in Israel.

## Palestinian developments

The rise of Islamic resistance in the Occupied Territories at the time when negotiations were stalling and producing no glimpse of hope also put pressure on the PLO. In the period between the fourth and fifth rounds, after six months of negotiations since Madrid, and having settled for a hidden background role, the PLO felt that it was slipping in the eyes of Palestinians. In an attempt to salvage its position, it began to press two issues to the fore with the help of the Palestinian negotiators. The first was the suggestion to enter into a confederation with Jordan. On Monday, April 27, 1992, the *Boston Globe* featured an article by reporters Etan Brunner and Ghadeer Taher which stated,

> What the PLO is suddenly urging on Jordan – in something of a turnaround – is that the Hashemite Kingdom should declare its sovereignty over the West Bank, which was captured by Israel in 1967. Then, once it can negotiate the land away from Israel, it should hand it over to the PLO to form a Palestine State that would exist in confederation with Jordan.

Although no PLO leader or spokesperson would go as far as urging Jordan to declare its sovereignty over the West Bank, the idea was floated across the media and indirectly to Jordanian decision-makers.

Jordanian officials interpreted the entire matter as an act of publicity and reiterated Jordan's official position that talks of future relations be postponed until a time when the Palestinian people were in a position to express their free will. In other words, Jordan was not willing to shoulder the responsibility of negotiating a settlement with Israel on behalf of the PLO. Despite the fact that the current mode of Palestinian negotiations clearly was not going to produce tangible results, Jordan felt that the Palestinians would reject any settlement it could reach with Israel over the territories regardless of how successful that settlement could be. Moreover, Jordanian officials doubted the seriousness of this Palestinian proposal which they considered to be a test balloon and a publicity stunt to influence the outcome of the fifth round of bilateral negotiations. PLO officials were trying to allay Israeli fears of an independent Palestinian State by suggesting that such a state could confederate with Jordan. Jordanian officials were not pleased with the underlying assumption implicit in the proposal of a confederation that Jordan was a better guarantee for Israeli security. At that time, the feedback the PLO received was not as it had hoped.

The second Palestinian proposal, which met with more sympathy, was for a relaxation of the Israeli-imposed conditions on the composition of the Palestinian delegation to the peace process. The first opportunity to accommodate this demand had presented itself in the multilateral talks, kicked off in Moscow on January 28, 1992. The Palestinian delegation to the Moscow Conference opted not to participate in the opening session because of the limitation put on the number of their representatives in a joint Jordanian-Palestinian delegation. The Jordanian Foreign Minister who headed the joint delegation did his best to convince the sponsors to accommodate the Palestinian aspiration for a full delegation (six members) and to relax the restriction on the membership by allowing them to include members from outside the Occupied Territories. The sponsor insisted on the agreed arrangement of the 'Madrid Formula' that the joint delegation would be composed of seven members including its head, the Foreign Minister of Jordan. The meetings were boycotted by Syria and Lebanon as were all the subsequent meetings of the multilaterals. Both the Syrians and Lebanese felt that the multilateral negotiations were mainly designed to rearrange the priorities of the bilateral negotiations by focusing on 'normalization' before the resolution of the substantive issues of the bilateral negotiations. Despite assurances by the co-sponsors and the Europeans to the contrary, the Syrians and the Lebanese refused to take part in the multilaterals.

With these developments, Jordan and Israel were the only two core parties that attended the opening of the multilateral talks in Moscow. Other parties from the region were invited, and Saudi Arabia, Kuwait, Egypt, Algeria, among others, eventually participated. Jordanian officials who insisted that Jordan participate in the five working groups of the multilateral negotiations made it also clear that Jordan preferred to see all its Arab brethren in attendance as well. Americans could not even ponder the failure to deliver multilateral negotiations. To them, the multilateral talks were designed to allow international involvement in and commitment to the concurrent bilateral Arab–Israeli peace negotiations. On a more strategic level, the Americans were keen not to involve their western allies in the peace process, and the optimal vehicle to achieve this was by inviting their allies to take an active role in the multilaterals. European countries and other allies harbored ill feelings towards the Americans after the Gulf War. They thought that the Americans were the primary beneficiary from that war as the reconstruction contracts and armament undertakings of the Gulf States were awarded mainly to American companies.

Without the Palestinian presence in the negotiations, the multilaterals would be devoid of an essential element. The Arab oil-producing countries in the Gulf and countries in North Africa would find the multilaterals meaningless without the core Arab parties, especially the Palestinians. American diplomats focused on giving the Palestinians more elbow room by relaxing the conditions which affected the selection of Palestinian delegates to the multilaterals. The American proposal would allow Palestinians in exile, sometimes referred to as Palestinians in diaspora, to attend the multilateral talks. Moreover, the US proposal would expand the number of Palestinian delegates to the multilateral working groups to a number equal that of the Jordanian delegation and the Israeli delegation. The Israeli response was negative until April 27, 1992, during the fifth round of bilateral negotiations (started April 20), when they accepted the participation in the multilaterals of Palestinians who were resident in Arab countries but not in exile at large.

Americans, however, tried their luck with another new compromise which sought to allow Palestinians in exile to participate in the multilateral working groups on refugees and regional economic cooperation but not on the other three (water, environment, and arms control and security). Both the Israelis and Palestinians threatened to boycott the meetings of the working groups where their respective conditions on Palestinian representation would not be met. The Palestinian delegation achieved a limited gain in the debate over representation in the multilateral talks, namely relaxed conditions on the specifications of representatives and a number equal to that of the sovereign states of Jordan and Israel. The gain was not decisive, but it paved the way for further relaxed conditions regarding the active and direct participation of the PLO in the peace process.

Inside the bilateral Palestinian track of negotiations, Israel's long-awaited new proposals were not as constructive as had been hoped. To the Palestinians, the Israeli offer was basically made up of two new elements. The first was to allow the Palestinians to run health, education, welfare and some municipal affairs through functional committees, but not through departments. In order to demonstrate their seriousness, the Israelis proposed that they immediately turn over the operation of 14 hospitals to the Palestinians. In reality, Israeli participation in the administration of those hospitals had been nominal as even Israeli spokesman Benjamin Netanyahu came close to acknowledging. Naturally, the Palestinians rejected the notions of functionality without a jurisdictional concept. They also rejected the use of the term 'give to the Palestinians' in reference to delegation of authorities. They suggested, instead, that the proposal use the term 'transfer'.

The second Israeli offer to the Palestinians was to conduct municipal elections in certain towns. The Palestinian delegation had been consistently demanding general elections from which an executive council or Cabinet would evolve. The Israelis were not oblivious to the Palestinian objective that would create a Palestinian legislative council from which an executive council or executive authority would be selected. Added to the existing judiciary authorities that were carried over from the administration before occupation and were allowed to operate in accordance with the law of the land (Jordanian law), the arrangement of general elections would plant the seeds of a Palestinian State, something that the Likud was adamantly against. The Israeli offer of municipal elections (Jerusalem not included) was, as expected, scoffed at by the Palestinian delegation. In the final analysis, the new Israeli offers only helped to open the discussion of certain issues of some substance without achieving any tangible progress.

On the Jordanian track, a Jordanian proposal for a common agenda was finalized and handed over to the Israelis before the fifth round ended, and copies were also handed over to the Palestinians, Syrians, and Lebanese. It was to be the subject of serious negotiations in the following rounds.

On both the Syrian and Lebanese tracks, the debate moved to substantive issues as the Syrians had demanded. Yet, the Israelis did not consider themselves as arriving at peace with Syria simply by declaring their intention to withdraw from the Golan Heights. The Israeli head of delegation, Yossi Ben Hadas, insisted that Syria should explain its concept of peace. To the Israelis, the absence of war was not peace. Peace to the Israelis meant the exchange of diplomatic missions, opening of borders to trade, and investment and agreement on security matters. The Syrians, who had made a positive gesture prior to the convening of this round, found that the Israeli position was in essence still the same. The Syrian gesture had been the decision by President Hafez al-Assad to allow Syrian Jews to migrate anywhere they wanted except Israel. This provision was in reality a non-condition because it would only result in requiring Syrian Jews to take a longer and more expensive route to Israel. Yet, there were some Syrian Jews who did not want to migrate and preferred to stay in Syria.

On April 30, 1992, the fourth round of bilateral negotiations ended. After six months of intensive negotiations since the Madrid Conference, the engagement in talks had produced very few results that could be communicated to the waiting public in Jordan, Syria, Lebanon, Israel, the Occupied Territories, to Jews and Palestinians all over the world, or to the Americans. The arguments that the negotiating parties had dealt with substantive issues or that progress was possible so long as the process was kept alive became predictable responses that failed to arouse any enthusiasm or hope. Even the multilateral talks looked oblique and futile at the end of April 1992, as both Israelis and Palestinians cast dark shadows over their engagement in the five working groups. In addition, the Syrians and Lebanese refused the principle of holding the multilaterals before tangible progress was achieved in the bilaterals, and the results of the last bilateral round could scarcely convince them to reconsider.

For whatever it was worth in retrospect, the main stumbling block to the smooth sailing of the peace process as a whole was the doctrinaire, uncompromising attitude of the Likud government. Yitzhak Shamir, the Prime Minister of Israel, was in reality engaged in dilatory tactics until the zeal for negotiations was diminished completely and the Americans had found new international arenas in which to score greater successes in peacemaking. The American administration would obviously favor a victory of the Israeli Labor Party in the forthcoming Israeli elections in June, 1992. If the Labor Coalition could win and Yitzhak Rabin, head of the Israel Labor Party, could become the Prime Minister, negotiations would then be given a second chance.

In the meantime, the peace process attracted the attention of several academic institutions and other non-government organizations, and centers for strategic and international studies. The academic interest in Middle East peace, especially among political scientists, triggered constructive academic activities aimed at promoting the conditions for peace. Seminars, conferences, lectures, publications and other forms and forums of contributions became frequent. The University of California at San Diego, Harvard University's Kennedy School of Government, The Institute for Social and Economic Policy in the Middle East, the Washington Institute for Near East Policy were amongst the institutions that made substantial contributions through what was called Track Two of talks.

Track Two presented the opportunity for Jews, Arabs, Americans, Europeans and Asians who were keen on joining the peace process to make their voices heard. Individuals affiliated with the Washington Institute for Near East Policy, the Council on Foreign Relations, the B'nai B'rith, and the British Institute of Strategic Studies, as well as former congressmen, officials and diplomats who had at one time or another been involved in Middle East politics and the Arab–Israeli conflict, all wanted to have a role or be given an opportunity to impart their wisdom. Some of these individuals secured definite positions and were called upon to give a helping hand in tackling certain complicated matters. However, the greatest advantage of Track Two meetings was the ability to address issues openly and to probe possible innovative solutions that the formal tracks found difficult to address.

The publicity that the negotiations had received prompted the Jordanian delegation to reach out and talk to the people in America. Majali, Anani, Tarawneh, Haddadin, al-Khasawneh, Bani Hani, Toukan and others made organized trips to several states and delivered lectures about Jordan and its role in the peace process. We were met with enthusiasm but also by some skeptics. The long weekends and the recess periods enabled us to cover many of the states and present Jordan's point of view and that of the Arabs. Majali made special efforts to make contact with Clinton's campaign officials, for he was at that time the Democratic Party candidate running against President George Bush. Majali succeeded in visiting his headquarters and in talking to a senior campaign official.

By the end of the sixth round of negotiations on September 23, little progress was manifesting itself in the agreement in the Jordanian-Israeli track on the wording of some items of the draft common agenda, and in the engagement of their delegates in substantive talks on water sharing. Progress on the Palestinian track was minimal if any at all. The Israelis and Palestinians kept reiterating their positions regarding the 'ISGA' versus 'PISGA', the delegation of authority versus the transfer thereof, the functional assumption by Palestinians of certain municipal and health responsibilities, the rejection by Israel to have Resolution 242 apply to the Palestinian territories, and extreme differences over the expansion of existing settlements and the construction of new ones. The exchange of divergent positions between the Syrians and the Israelis continued on the Syrian track, and the Lebanese scored no progress either.

Almost eleven months had elapsed since the Madrid Conference in October 1991, and virtually no progress had been made. The seventh round would prove to be critical as it coincided with the first anniversary of the Madrid Conference. Jordan felt it was important to come up with some positive report on that occasion.

# 7

# Multilaterals

Wars in the Middle East were never bilateral. At least two regional parties and the world powers were always involved. Since its wars were multilateral, its peace, it would seem, should involve more than just the combatants. When war broke out in the Middle East, superpowers armed and rearmed the regional parties to the conflict, before going on to cooperate over ceasefires and issue United Nations resolutions. No conflict demonstrated their defiance of bilateralism more than the 1991 coalition led by the United States to evict Iraq out of Kuwait.

Needless to say making peace in the Middle East has never been easy. It took members of the UN Security Council five months of hard negotiations to agree on the language of Resolution 242 that spelled out the basis for resolving the dispute between the Arabs and Israel. However, as it turned out, the resolution had neither the teeth nor the mechanism to put its clauses into effect. It took another war, six years later, before a new Resolution, 338, was adopted, requiring prompt commencement of negotiations among the parties to arrive at peace. The structure of the mechanism and the identification of the parties were left ambiguous. In honor of Resolution 338, Jordan, with Egypt, Syria and Israel attended a peace conference in 1974 in Geneva that lasted for a few days before it folded without any success. In a peculiar but uncanny way, that Geneva peace conference proved the theory that substantive Middle Eastern issues like occupation, cross-boundary security, and withdrawal of troops, could only be resolved on a bilateral, one-on-one basis.

While bilateralism can be justified, on grounds of practicality and expediency, to resolve substantive issues, in this case it could not ensure the durability of peace. There had to be an inclusive approach, necessitating multilateral involvement. No one understood the need to involve the international community in the making of Middle East peace better than King Hussein. He repeatedly called for the convening of an international peace conference, with participation of the five permanent members of the UN Security Council, under whose umbrella the warring parties of the Middle East could engage in meaningful negotiations towards peace. The Israelis, on the other hand, insisted on bilateral negotiations to end the conflict and establish peace. With the end of the cold war and the rise of the United States to the status of uncontested world power, a modified form of that idea was agreed upon and made part of the peace process. Secretary of State, James Baker, succeeded in his formidable efforts to structure a peace process that responded to the demands of the adversaries: a bilateral conference in which Israel would negotiate separately with Lebanon, Syria and a Jordanian-Palestinian delegation, and a multilateral conference in which other concerned countries of the world would participate. The Madrid Conference gave way to these two other conferences, and the first round of the bilateral negotiations convened in Madrid immediately after the opening session of the Madrid Conference. The multilateral conference was to convene in Moscow on January 28, 1992. The multilaterals were to reinforce the work of the bilaterals and would address such important topics as regional economic development, regional security and arms control, water resources, environment, and Palestinian refugees.

Among the core parties that responded positively to the invitation extended by the sponsors were Jordan and the Palestinians, who would participate in a joint delegation, and Israel. The other two core parties, Syria and Lebanon, opted out because they felt that such a conference would aim at normalizing contacts with Israel before progress took place in the all-important bilateral negotiations. The other parties from the region responded positively, and attended the conference. These were Egypt, Saudi Arabia and Tunisia. Egypt represented the then Arab Cooperation Council (Iraq, Egypt, Jordan and Yemen); Saudi Arabia represented the Gulf Cooperation Council (Saudi Arabia, Kuwait, Oman, the United Arab Emirates, Qatar and Bahrain); and Tunisia represented the Maghareb Union (Libya, Tunisia, Algeria, Morocco, and Mauritania).

King Hussein stressed that the multilateral talks, to be attended by more than 40 countries, were an international forum such as the Arabs had always called for. Such a gathering presented a unique opportunity to promote the interests of the Arab core parties. For Jordan, the success of the peace process was crucial and it was eager to contribute to its success. As well as this, it needed to redeem its international image, which had suffered during the Iraqi occupation of Kuwait. Aqaba, its only seaport, was under siege by the US Navy since the boycott of Iraq in 1990 and that caused a big problem for Jordan's trade. Commercial airlines had avoided Jordan since the Gulf War, and the Royal Jordanian airline was the only carrier that serviced the country. Indeed, some analysts thought that, with the economic hardships it was facing and the damage to its international reputation, Jordan was doomed, and it was only a matter of time before it would fall apart. It was therefore virtually impossible for Jordan to refuse participation in the multilaterals. Syria, on the other hand, did not have such problems. It enjoyed the benefits of its participation in the coalition against Iraq in Operation Desert Storm, and had no interest in attending a multilateral conference in which its rivals, Israel and Turkey, were participating.

There were, of course, other reasons for Jordan to attend the multilateral negotiations – the issues being discussed were central to Jordan's overall concerns, whether as part of a peace process or not. On the issue of refugees and displaced persons, Jordan had received the influx of three waves of refugees: the first in 1948, the second in June 1967, and the third during the Gulf War from August to January 1991. Palestinian refugees and displaced persons who chose Jordan as their destination exceeded 1.5 million, representing 30 per cent of Jordan's population in 1992 and about 40 per cent of the Palestinian refugee population, according to UN records at the time.

Regarding water issues, Jordan suffered delays in securing its share of the Yarmouk River only to have both Syria and Israel benefit from that share. Potential economic cooperation between Israel and Jordan would serve Jordan's interests too, for the country's vital natural resources fell within a 7-mile-wide strip that extended along the 300-mile-long border between the two countries. Some 70 per cent of Jordan's renewable water resources, and the Dead Sea industries, are located in the Jordan valley. Environmental problems in the Jordan valley, and in and around the Dead Sea and the Gulf of Aqaba, were mounting and the state of belligerence between Jordan and Israel had prevented the two countries from engaging in any meaningful dialogue to resolve them.

Arms control and security were of utmost importance for the two countries, and Jordan often expressed deep anxiety over Israel's nearby Dimona nuclear reactor. While Jordan and Israel had in essence opposing views on how to handle arms control and security issues, both shared a vision of keeping the Middle East clear of weapons of mass destruction or great harm.

In the light of these facts, Jordan's motivation in attending the multilateral conference was bifocal: self-interest dictated by facts on the ground, and aspirations for a long-lasting peace growing from grass roots instead of one dictated by the superpowers.

The Minister of Foreign Affairs of Jordan, Dr Kamel Abu Jaber, took it upon himself to steer and organize the Jordanian delegation to the Moscow conference. He convened several meetings with Jordanian experts to help him formulate Jordan's positions. Crown Prince al-Hassan frequently chaired those meetings. Haddadin was invited to them and was identified as one member of the delegation to the conference.

'Say, Munther,' said Abu Jaber one day after a meeting held at the Higher Council for Science and Technology, 'who would you nominate as an expert on the environment?'

'Do you want him as a delegate to Moscow?' Haddadin asked.

'Yes,' replied the Foreign Minister, 'you know there will be a group on the environment.'

'I would nominate Dr Murad Beino of the Royal Scientific Society, and I would also nominate Mr Anis Muasher, Chairman of the Royal Society for the Conservation of Nature,' said Haddadin.

'Good, thank you,' said the Foreign Minister. 'I think I have the different groups taken care of. You will head the Water Group for sure. I will have to make further consultations for the rest. Please keep this information to yourself.'

'Okay, but we are due to go on a round of bilateral negotiations in a few days,' said Haddadin, 'I hope the bilateral round will end in time for us to catch the flight to Moscow.'

'It will end in time for you to come back here, attend a meeting, clear the position papers, and take off for Moscow,' said Abu Jaber. 'Tomorrow I need you to attend a meeting at the Ministry of Foreign Affairs. Minister Kawar [of Water and Irrigation] is coming.'

Dr Majali, Jordan's head of delegation to the bilateral negotiations, strongly argued that Jordan's key representatives to the multilaterals should come from the bilateral delegation. Specifically, he demanded that Jordan should adopt an integrated approach to both bilateral and multilateral talks, which in practical terms meant that the head of Jordan's delegation to the bilaterals should be the head of the multilaterals, and that key negotiators in the bilaterals should head Jordan's delegations to the various working groups of the multilaterals. Majali's rationale was well noted and justified, but it was interpreted by officials in the Ministry of Foreign Affairs as an attempt on his part to widen his sphere of influence and keep Ministry officials outside the circle of negotiations. The Ministry officials already begrudged the fact that Majali never addressed them directly and instead reported to the Prime Minister. Abu Jaber insisted that his Ministry would handle the multilateral negotiations. He gave the reason that they should be separated from the bilaterals because it was not humanly possible for Dr Majali to shoulder the two sets of negotiations with the intensity that they merited. Fayez Tarawneh was appointed head of the delegation to Regional Economic Development; Jawad Anani would head the Refugees delegation, Munther Haddadin would head the Water Resources delegation, Abdallah Toukan would head the delegation to Regional Security and Arms Control, and Anis Muasher would head the delegation to Environment. With the exception of Anis Muasher, the other four delegates were key members of the bilateral negotiations. Moreover, the most senior members in every Jordanian multilateral delegation were also senior bilateral delegates.

The meeting convened the following day at the Ministry of Foreign Affairs, attended by Minister Kawar and the Minister of Planning, Ziad Fariz. Those present reviewed the invitation to Moscow, and the preparations made for the occasion. The speech to be delivered by the Jordanian Minister of Foreign Affairs, Kamel Abu Jaber, was drafted using two proposals for that speech made by Haddadin and Dr Rima Khalaf (later Minister of Planning).

The delegation to Moscow was named by the Council of Ministers upon the recommendation of the Minister of Foreign Affairs.[1] The delegation left on a Royal Jordanian flight to Larnaca, Cyprus, and from there an Aeroflot flight took the delegation to Moscow, arriving on Saturday 24 January. The Soviet security around the hotel and the conference hall was tight. Abu Jaber made contacts with the sponsors and called for a meeting of the Jordanian delegation the following day.

Each delegation of the core parties (joint Jordanian–Palestinian, Israeli) was allowed seven seats including the head of that delegation. For the Jordanians, this meant that only Abu Jaber and three other members of the delegation could attend the conference. The three other seats were reserved for the Palestinian delegation. After a consultation, it was agreed that General Marea, Tarawneh and Haddadin would take up the three seats at the opening session. But Haddadin was concerned that in the whole peace process thus far there had not been any representation of Jordanians living south of Karak. Now, with Ambassador Saleh Kabariti from the city of Aqaba in the extreme south of Jordan, there was an opportunity to redress the balance. For this reason he gave up his seat in the opening session to Kabariti, who was most grateful.

Haddadin joined Dr Mustafa Hamarneh and others that evening for a chat in the hotel lobby. They also met members of the Palestinian delegation, and were surprised to see a couple of prominent members of the PLO Executive Committee, including Suleiman Najjab. 'Quite a shift from previous positions,' said Haddadin to Hamarneh. 'PLO officials were not allowed to participate in the peace process.'

'Maybe they are here for guidance from behind the curtain,' said Hamarneh.

'Maybe, and let us hope that the PLO will finally surface in the negotiations.' Haddadin went to bed and enjoyed a good night sleep. He was sound asleep at around 8:00 a.m. the following morning when he was awakened by an urgent knocking at his door. 'Wake up, sir, wake up,' said the caller. Haddadin opened the door, half asleep, and saw a diplomat from the Jordanian Embassy in Moscow. 'Good morning, sir,' said the diplomat, who looked like he was in a hurry.

'Good morning; what is the matter?' Haddadin asked.

'The Minister is waiting for you in the lobby. He asked me to tell you to be dressed and to hurry up,' answered the diplomat.

'Are you sure that it is me who the Minister sent for?' asked Haddadin.

'Yes sir, absolutely.'

Knowing that it had been decided the day before that he would be replaced by Ambassador Kabariti for the opening session, Haddadin asked, 'Do you know who I am? What is my name?'

'Your name is Dr Munther Haddadin,' said the caller with confidence. Haddadin rushed into the bathroom, got a quick shave with a few cuts to the chin, dressed and hurried down to the lobby. There was Dr Kamel Abu Jaber with Ambassador Mohammad Adwan, Dr Fayez Tarawneh, General Abdul Hafez Marea and Ambassador Kabariti, looking serious. Something was wrong. 'Good morning, Excellency, change of plans?' Haddadin asked the Minister.

'Yes,' said the Minister, 'the Palestinians would not accept three seats, they said they have to have a full delegation. We are doing our best. In the meanwhile, we are to be ready to occupy all seven seats.'

Toukan soon joined the group in the lobby, and the delegation rushed to the waiting cars that drove to the building of the Labour Union where the conference was to be held. The Jordanian delegation hurried up to the entrance, and lined up in the long line of participants who were shaking hands at the top of the stairs with the Soviet Foreign Minister, Edward Shevardnadze, and the US Secretary of State, James Baker. As Minister Abu Jaber reached the ministers, he shook hands with the host Soviet Minister and then stood with Secretary Baker debating with him the rights of the Palestinians to have a full delegation. Abu Jaber wanted Baker to heed the demands of the Palestinians, to agree to them attending with six delegates under his chairmanship to maintain the joint character of the delegation. Baker adamantly refused, and so did his staff without exception. The rest of the Jordanian delegation proceeded to the conference hall but Abu Jaber stayed behind to talk to the Americans and to seek help from the Russians in saving the day for the Palestinians and in starting the conference. Finally, Abu Jaber came in and Haddadin, who had checked the seating arrangements, was at the door waiting for him. 'What happened?' asked Haddadin.

'No use, the Americans have a deaf ear, worse than my right ear that you well know,' the Minister replied.

The Palestinians were not allowed the number of delegates they wanted in parity with the other core parties, and therefore they stayed out of the meeting and did not attend the conference.

'Our seats are next to the Israelis, and they are headed by their Foreign Minister, Mr David Levi,' said Haddadin.

'Please, please,' insisted Abu Jaber, 'walk next to me and stay always between me and the Israelis. I do not want to see any of them, let alone shake hands.'

The Israeli delegation occupied seven seats to the left of the Jordanian delegation. None of them was from the bilateral delegation. Haddadin was the member seated closest to them. 'Hi,' said the Israeli delegate sitting closest to Haddadin.

'Hallo,' responded Haddadin. 'How you doing?' The Israeli delegate stood up and so did Haddadin.

'I am David Kimche,' he said.

[133]

'And I am Munther Haddadin.'

'I know who you are. Come, let me introduce you to our Minister,' said Kimche. Haddadin stood there, and the Israeli Minister of Foreign Affairs, David Levi, walked towards him. He spoke in Hebrew and Kimche translated.

'He says he knows about you from the good work you have done in the Jordan valley,' said Kimche.

'Thank him for me,' said Haddadin. During the session, Haddadin leaned and whispered in Toukan's ear: 'Have you noticed, Abdallah, what I have noticed?'

'What?' replied Dr Abdallah Toukan.

'Look, four out of the seven Jordanian delegates are married to American wives – you, me, Abu Jaber, and Adwan,' said Haddadin.

'You are right,' said Toukan. 'If that is made public, a rumor would spread that the Jordanian delegation is run by Americans!'

In the coffee break, Kimche approached Haddadin and said, 'You know, you and I can solve this protracted conflict in the Middle East in no time. In a couple of sessions we can solve it.'

'How? Shoot!' said Haddadin.

'No shooting please! I said we will make peace in no time, and you ask me to shoot!' said Kimche with a laugh.

'You may be right. I will tell you how we can solve it right now. Pull back to the June 4 lines, recognize the right of the Palestinians to a sovereign state, recognize the right of Palestinian refugees to repatriation, and those who opt not to return are to be compensated for property and damages, and . . .'

'Wait a minute,' interrupted Kimche. 'How can we withdraw to the June 4 lines without you recognizing our legitimate security concerns? Do you want me to pull out from the Golan without security arrangements?'

'What kind of security are you talking about? Who in his right mind would think that the Golan can stand between an imminent Syrian attack and Israel in this age of advanced rocketry and weapons of mass destruction,' said Haddadin.

'Well, rockets do not occupy territory; tanks do,' snapped Kimche.

'You see, you are playing the same record that your colleagues are playing in the bilateral negotiations. I am glad we are here in a multilateral conference and not in a bilateral negotiation session. I could differ with you from here to eternity,' said Haddadin.

At that opening session of the multilaterals it was decided that five different working groups would be established:

- The Regional Security and Arms Control Working Group, for which Russia and the USA would alternate as chair.
- The Regional Economic Development Working Group that came to be known by its acronym, REDWG (pronounced redwig), presided over by the European Union.
- The Refugees Working Group, for which Canada held the chair.
- The Water Resources Working Group, chaired by the USA.
- The Environment Working Group, chaired by Japan.

Finally, the works of all these groups would be followed up and reviewed by a Steering Group to be jointly chaired by the USA and Russia. The distribution of the working groups and the dispensing of organizational responsibilities was carefully studied and approved. The distribution of chairing responsibility gave the major non-regional players a direct involvement in the peace process, in areas for which they considered themselves to be qualified and sufficiently experienced to handle. Several assistants were appointed to each chair, to further spread responsibility and involvement. At Jordan's suggestion, observers were later invited, primarily the World Bank, to attend the meetings of the Water Resources Working Group and of the Regional Economic Development Working Group. A Group committee was created for each of the working groups with the gavel-holder as chair and the countries presiding over the other groups as members, along with the core parties and the regional parties (Egypt, Saudi Arabia and the representative of the Maghareb Union of North African Arab states).

The role the United States had been playing in the water resources sector in the region was substantial. Millions of dollars in capital and technical assistance funds were advanced to Jordan and to Israel from the United States to build their water projects in the Jordan River basin. Their chairmanship of the Water Resources Working Group was not surprising. The Japanese wanted to steer a working group that they felt was within their sphere of competence and which would be as apolitical as possible, and the Environment Working Group seemed to fit most of these requirements. For the European Union, economic development was a natural interest, given Europe's long-standing economic relations and strategic interests in the Middle East, and thus they were very satisfied to be given the opportunity to chair REDWG. The very complex and divisive issue of refugees could not have been handled with more deftness and skill than the Canadians. Moreover, Canada has its share of Palestinian immigrants and has always contributed to the emergency and human relief funds for Palestinian refugees. Russia and the USA oversaw the working group for Arms Control and Regional Security as both were major suppliers of weapons to the belligerent parties in the Middle East, and both had concerns for the security of their respective allies in the region. This was the optimal distribution of assignments.

The Jordanian delegation wanted to introduce two new working groups: one on Jerusalem and another on human rights. The idea did not gather much support. Some Arab regional parties opposed the idea of a working group on human rights for fear of hot debates and accusations of human rights violations in Arab countries. The major western parties attending the conference did not want to rock the boat and wanted to go along with the arrangements that had been worked out already before the multilateral conference convened. It was claimed that Jerusalem itself had not been singled out as an issue in either of the UN Resolutions 242 or 338. As the Arab section of Jerusalem was part of the Occupied Territories, Jerusalem would be the heart and soul of the bilateral negotiations. Thus, the issue of establishing two new working groups was deferred. The decision whether to act on suggestions of this nature was entrusted to the Steering Committee, which would meet after every round of multilateral negotiations to assess conclusions, review progress, and take action to implement the decisions arrived at in the various multilateral working groups.

On the second day of the Moscow Conference, the working groups held their first introductory meeting. Jordan was prepared and the delegates took their respective seats in those meetings. Haddadin headed the Jordan delegation to the Water Resources, Tarawneh to REDWG, Toukan to Regional Security and Arms Control, Murad Beino to the Environment, and Adwan filled in for the Refugees Working Group. The delegation to Water Resources had done its homework already, and suggested an agenda for the discussions of that Group. It also helped shape the agenda that was presented to the Group in the following round of the Group's meetings.

Minister Abu Jaber asked Haddadin to join him in a press conference after the conference was concluded. Abu Jaber did very well in presenting Jordan's positions on the various peace issues. His approach was diplomatic, comprehensive, and conformed to the moderate position that Jordan had consistently assumed. 'How serious do you think the water question will be, Minister,' asked one senior correspondent.

'We know,' answered the Minister, 'that there is a distortion in the water resources–population equation. That distortion would handicap the efforts to achieve a balanced social and economic development.'

'Would cooperation with Israel be helpful in removing that handicap?'

'Undoubtedly, the diversion of defense expenditures to development would help, but it is too early to call on potential cooperation at this time. My colleague, Dr Haddadin, may want to elaborate.'

'We see a potential for cooperation whereby the result would have a positive conclusion with benefits for all participants. However, there is a sequence we have to observe to start cooperation and make it meaningful. That sequence is restoration, mitigation, cooperation,' said Haddadin.

'Could you please be clear about this slogan?' demanded another correspondent.

> Yes, of course. We start with restoration of rights, and when that is done we proceed to mitigation of the damage that this protracted conflict has caused, and when that is agreed and started, we proceed to cooperation. Clearly, one cannot cooperate with a party one does not trust, nor can one think of such cooperation if one's rights, usurped by the other party, are not restored.

After the meeting in Moscow, Jordan declared its intention of participating in all of the working groups. It was, however, disheartened by Syrian and Lebanese attitudes towards the multilaterals and their Arab participants. The Syrian media published statements and commentaries that criticized those who had joined the multilaterals before any tangible progress was made in the bilaterals. The Palestinians, on the other hand, decided to postpone their decision to attend until the Shamir government accepted Palestinians in exile as participants in the meetings.

The main operational challenge for the multilateral working groups was the need to delineate with meticulous clarity the terms of reference for each so that they would not duplicate any part of the bilateral negotiations.

The first round of the multilaterals held on the second day of the Moscow Conference alluded to the need to formulate agendas for the different working groups, and addressed the issue of venues for the following meetings. The chair of each working group asked members for proposals on venues for the following meeting of the group. In the Water Resources Group, Austria and Turkey extended invitations. Canada extended an invitation to the Refugees Group; Brussels to the REDWG meeting; Japan to the Environment, and the USA to the Regional Security and Arms Control. The sponsors consulted with the core parties on the venue for the next water meeting, and Jordan opted for Vienna so that Syria would not be further alienated by the group meeting in Turkey.

Upon the conclusion of the fifth bilateral round in late April 1992, political analysts and negotiators estimated that the bilateral negotiations could not be resumed for a minimum of three or four months after that round. Israeli elections would take place in June and, judging from historical precedence, it would take at least one month after the elections to form a Cabinet. This delay was determined to be too long to keep negotiations alive and on track. Thus, the best possible move was to invite the parties to the second round of multilateral negotiations.

## Water Resources Working Group, Vienna

The second round of the multilateral talks for the Water Resources Working Group convened in Vienna on May 12, 1992, and it was eventful. The Jordanians were the first to arrive at the Conference Center that morning. Soon after them came the Algerians, and then the other delegations followed. The Arab delegates, at the initiative of the head of the Palestinian delegation, Dr Riyadh al-Khudary, caucused and decided to appoint Dr Haddadin as their spokesperson.

The seating inside the meeting hall, arranged in alphabetical order, placed the Jordanian-Palestinian delegation between the Kuwaitis on one side, and Italy, separating them from Israel, on the other. With the vote of confidence that he had received from all Arab delegates, Haddadin felt more assured. He played the Israeli chief of delegation, the Water Commissioner Dan Zaslovsky, right and left through arguments and counter-arguments that appealed to the audience from 38 countries. During the coffee break, many delegates came to congratulate Haddadin on a superb and exciting discussion. The chief German delegate confided in Haddadin that, 'The Israeli chief delegate looked for trouble and you gave him what he deserved.' The Arab delegates expressed similar feelings and Haddadin's fellow Jordanian delegates were very proud.

Thereafter, the Israeli Water Commissioner was cautious, and so were his colleagues. The Jordanians and the Palestinians dominated the debate. In the afternoon break, Zaslovsky approached Haddadin before he was able to get to the coffee pots, and asked for a private conversation. From the four bilateral rounds that had taken place, Zaslovsky must have had several briefings from the Israeli delegates on Haddadin's attitudes towards a water settlement with Israel. The two chiefs of delegation stood in the conference hall while the delegates were having coffee in the lobby outside. 'What is it that you are after in the settlement of our conflict over water?' asked Zaslovsky.

'You know the answer to your own question, so why do you ask?' Haddadin responded.

'I know, I know,' said Zaslovsky. 'You are after the Eric Johnston formula of water-sharing. But how much of the share stipulated for the Hashemite Kingdom in that formula would you earmark for the Palestinians?'

'Pardon me, but this is none of your business; it is a pure Palestinian-Jordanian matter. However, I would give you the role of a remote observer because, in a way, you are connected.'

'How, in your thinking, are we connected?' asked Zaslovsky.

'Well, it depends on how many Palestinians will be allowed to exercise the right of return,' answered Haddadin. 'Those who are allowed to return will carry their water share with them because, as you know, their rights are in the Jordan River waters, and that water could be pumped either to the east of the river, or to its west, depending where the rightful owners will eventually choose to settle.'

'Okay, I understand now, but a lot of cooperation will have to be assumed by all three parties to define that end condition.'

'Agreed,' said Haddadin.

'Okay, the next round of multilateral negotiations will be in Washington, DC in September. I will be heading the Israeli delegation, and I will bring with me the maps on which we shall jointly work to develop a solution based on what you just mentioned: the Johnston allocations,' said Zaslovsky.

'Great,' said Haddadin. 'So I will see you in Washington with the maps.'

'Certainly,' said Zaslovsky. 'See you there.'

At the end of the day, Haddadin stood before the cameras of the international press. The Saudi chief delegate approached him. 'Let me tell you how proud we are at what we have seen and heard today from you,' the Saudi delegate said.

'Thank you,' Haddadin said. 'The credit goes to the unequivocal support and mandate given to me this morning by you and other Arab colleagues.'

Haddadin used the facilities of the Royal Jordanian Airline, who maintained an office at the Hilton Hotel, to communicate with Jordan. Abdul Ilah al-Khatib, the energetic director of the Special Office at the Ministry of Foreign Affairs, put in an extraordinary effort to synchronize the work of the five Jordanian delegations to the five working groups whose meetings were spread over the time zones of the world in Tokyo, Moscow, Brussels, Ottawa, and Vienna.

The second day was as eventful and challenging as the first. Under the chair, Allan Kieswetter, the conferees worked out the agenda for the group, and the Jordanian delegation was pioneering in that effort.

On their way back from the sixth round of bilateral negotiations, al-Khasawneh and Haddadin were asked by the Jordanian government to stop in Rome. Their mission was to attend a preparatory meeting of a Mediterranean water conference aimed at drafting a Mediterranean Water Charter. During the first session of that water conference, Haddadin and al-Khasawneh worked with caution to insert clauses in the draft charter that would help in laying down principles for water use, giving priority to in-basin uses of river waters, and they succeeded. In the coffee break, the Israeli delegate, Ambassador Amos Ganor, approached Haddadin. 'I am afraid they will cut off my balls when they find out in Israel how I may have been fooled here. I just hope that you will not invoke this principle of in-basin use at the bilateral talks,' said Ganor.

'Your balls must have taken the usual course of duty and achieved their mission. Do you really want them at this age, aren't they expired?' Haddadin joked.

'No! Heavens no! Besides, who wants to lose his balls? I also have a granddaughter I want to enjoy, so please be understanding.'

'I will, I will, don't worry. Your balls are clearly an important asset that we all have reasons to preserve!'

'In the bilateral negotiations, we know that you enter the room to negotiate water either alone or accompanied by someone else who doesn't actively participate in the negotiations. But how many Israelis come into the same room to do the negotiations?'

'Five, sometimes six,' Haddadin answered.

'Why, do you think, is there this disparity in representation?' asked Ambassador Ganor.

'An Israeli delegate handles water, a second handles the environment, the third handles energy, the fourth is a legal advisor, the fifth represents the Foreign Ministry, and the sixth comes in, maybe, for moral support,' Haddadin answered.

'No, no,' said Ganor, 'but do not quote me on this. In Israel we believe that it takes this many people to match you!'

'I am flattered,' said Haddadin, 'but this is not the first nor the only time the Israelis exaggerate and make a mistake!' When Haddadin told that to al-Khasawneh five minute later, Khasawneh said, 'They are right! And I think that number is not sufficient for the intended purpose!'

## REDWG, Brussels

Dr Fayez Tarawneh headed the Jordanian delegation to the Working Group on Regional Economic Development, held in Brussels. Its meetings ended one day before the Water Working Group. He had with him in the delegation Ambassador Khalid Madadha, Jordanian Ambassador to Brussels and the EU.[2]

It was only a matter of expediency and tacit diplomacy as to when the issue of the Arab economic boycott of Israel would be raised. This boycott was an Arab League decision taken back in 1949 to besiege Israel economically. According to the original decision, the boycott would operate on three levels. The primary boycott would prohibit Arab individuals, NGOs, and public and private institutions from engaging in any economic deal with Israel in the region and anywhere else in the world. (It should go without saying that, in principle, individuals of any Arab country would not be allowed to contact, directly or indirectly, the citizens of any enemy country.) The secondary boycott stipulated that foreign companies that invest in Israel would be boycotted by Arab countries without exception. The tertiary boycott declared that companies or individuals who bought Israeli goods and services as imports or sold finished Israeli goods and services should be boycotted as well. The secondary and tertiary boycotts were, in effect, directed against third party countries dealing with Israel. The Arab League boycott office was stationed in Damascus, Syria, and kept a black list of third party country companies that violated Arab economic boycott regulations.

The European Union, the United States and some other countries including Canada and Norway considered the secondary and tertiary Arab boycott to have caused more damage to their own economies than it had to Israel. This argument alone was used from 1977 until the beginning of the peace negotiations. In the Brussels meeting of REDWG, the point was made that ending the Arab boycott of Israel would serve as a prelude to opening Arab markets and their integration in the world economy. It would further serve as a confidence-building measure and would convince the Israelis of the Arabs' sincere desire to make peace with them. In fact, by 1991, the Arab economic boycott had lost its cutting edge and become a pure formality. Countries of North Africa and the Gulf States became weary of the Arab League boycott office in Damascus, and some of them accused it of corruption.

REDWG focused its attention on the deteriorating economic conditions in the Occupied Territories, particularly the Gaza Strip. This area, not exceeding 280 square miles, had a population of more than one million people. The city of Gaza itself had one of the highest population densities in the world, and its resources and infrastructure were insufficient to provide for a decent standard of living. REDWG members thus decided to ask the World Bank to conduct a study of the development requirements in the Occupied Territories.

## Refugees Working Group, Ottawa

The issue of refugees was a lot more complex. The group met in Ottawa on May 7, 1992 with delegates from 38 countries attending. Israel did not send delegates because of its expectations that exiled Palestinians would be among the Palestinian delegates. The question was to determine which refugee issues should be discussed in the multilaterals. The

Canadian chair, Marc Peron, and his aides, envisaged an agenda comprising topics such as job creation in refugee camps, data banks on the social and economic conditions of refugees, exchange of studies on refugees and the collection of a bibliography, family reunification through the competent UN agencies and the International Red Cross, and the improvement of infrastructure in the camps. The proposed agenda revealed a great deal of ingenuity, but aroused deep suspicions that the Refugee Working Group had the unstated intention of helping refugees settle in their current places of residence in an attempt to abolish the right of return.

The Palestinian delegation arrived into Ottawa, headed by Dr Salim Tamari, a Palestinian professor who lived in France and taught at the University of Paris, and including other Palestinians from the 'diaspora'. Each core party delegation was allowed six delegates to sit at the negotiating table, while the other delegations were allowed two. There were six Palestinians and six Jordanians. At the head table there were two chairs under one sign that read, 'Joint Jordanian-Palestinian Delegation'. The Palestinian head of delegation, supported by Anani, head of the Jordanian delegation, asked for two separate signs indicating the 'Palestinian Delegation' and 'Jordanian Delegation', but the Canadian chair and the American sponsors turned them down. Dan Kurtzer, head of the American delegation, was keen from the beginning not to allow any changes which would further antagonize the Israelis. As everything was negotiable, the Canadian chair agreed to acknowledge the Jordanian and Palestinian heads of delegation separately, each in his own capacity, when either asked for and was given the floor. With this compromise, the Palestinians felt that they had taken one extra symbolic step toward their recognition as a separate and independent entity. Moreover, the Canadian authorities had, presumably with the prior consent of the US State Department, issued entry visas to two prominent PLO members to supervise, from behind the scenes, the performance of their delegates. The two PLO officials were Shafiq al-Hout and Akram Haniyyeh. They spent their time in a hotel that was a beautifully refurbished train depot and was a short walking distance from the meeting hall.

The meeting started with a statement from the chair, Marc Peron, a senior diplomat of the Canadian foreign ministry. He emphasized that the multilateral group meetings were to promote and advance the bilateral negotiations and not to serve as a substitute for them. Accordingly, he expressed the hope that those core parties who could not join the multi-laterals (meaning Syria and Lebanon) would reconsider their position. The speeches delivered by the delegates of the United States, Russia, the European Union and Japan carried similar messages and expressed the hope that the current meetings would be business-like and would avoid posturing and the use of sensitive language which could divert attention away from the business in hand.

A draft agenda had been distributed the night before and now needed agreement. Marc Peron had considered the order of priority carefully, placing the less controversial topics first and ending with the most problematic, which was family reunification. Both Jordanian and Palestinian heads of delegation raised the question of priority just before Peron managed to finalize agreement on the agenda. In the absence of any 'nay' votes, he had almost ruled the agenda approved as he circled with an ephemeral glance at the delegates but avoiding looking in the direction of the joint Jordanian-Palestinian delegation. His maneuver, however, did not work, as the compelling hand-waving finally caught his eye. 'I recognize the head of the joint Jordanian-Palestinian delegation,' said Peron.

'But such a person, ex-officio, does not exist,' said Anani.

'No, he does not,' reinforced the head of the Palestinian delegation.

Peron, puzzled and careful, tried again, 'Okay, I recognize the head of the Jordanian delegation within the joint Jordanian-Palestinian delegation.' Long, dreary and boring as it sounded, it coaxed a smile out of the audience.

'May I, Mr Gavel-holder, ask about the wisdom behind the insertion of the item of "family reunification" at the tail end of the agenda items?' asked Anani. The answer was not convincing, and the longer the justification took, the less credible it sounded.

'I think it is safe for me to say that family reunification can be discussed regardless of its location in the list of agenda items,' said Peron in an attempt to proceed with the adoption of the agenda. The point was made and this compromise was acceptable to both Jordanians and Palestinians.

The core parties were allowed to make two statements lasting no more than 15 minutes each before the discussion on the agenda ended. The Palestinian head of delegation had a prepared speech. It explained in detail the sources of the Palestinian refugee problem, and he demanded that the group endorse UN Resolution 194, issued in 1948. According to operative clause 11 of the resolution, Palestinian refugees have the right to return to their homes or, for those who opt not to return, the right of compensation for properties damaged or forgone as a result of the 1948 War.

The head of the Jordanian delegation explained the size of the refugee problem in Jordan and how Jordan coped with the influx of refugees since the beginning of the Arab–Israeli War in 1948. He also demanded that the Working Group on Refugees study the ways to implement Resolution 194, because, in so doing, the multilateral forum would promote and facilitate the work of the bilateral negotiation, thus exactly fulfilling its expected role.

Dan Kurtzer and Marc Peron were uncomfortable after listening to the Palestinian and Jordanian statements. Kurtzer emphasized the fact that this meeting was not strictly political and was not a substitute for the bilateral talks. He stated that the Refugee Working Group should adhere to its terms of reference, which did not include the discussion of relevant UN resolutions. He also said that such an issue was central to the bilateral negotiations. He was right in a way, but Anani felt that the lack of a clear-cut division of remit between the bilateral and multilateral negotiations regarding the multitude of refugee issues could give Israel a pretext to preclude such important issues as the right of return and the right to compensation. The Israelis could make such issues bounce between bilateral and multilateral tracks of negotiations with no meaningful treatment in either. The ambiguity of the terms of reference could further complicate bilateral negotiations. Yet, the gavel-holder understood the motives behind mentioning the UN resolution over refugees in the opening statement. By bringing up this issue from the beginning, the Palestinian delegation paved the way to have such refugee issues discussed by the Working Group notwithstanding any Israeli protests or attempts to bounce them between the two tracks, or have them deferred until the 'final status' negotiations with the Palestinians.

Anxious to retain the Israeli presence at future meetings, Dan Kurtzer and Aaron Miller of the American delegation reminded the meeting that decisions adopted by the Working Group had to be by consensus and should, in particular, be approved by the core parties to the bilateral negotiations. In other words, each of the core parties or any other delegation present had the power to block any potential decision the group tried to take. The Palestinian delegation objected to this on the grounds that it would only empower the Israeli delegation in future meetings to veto any decision pertaining to family reunion or the right of return. On the other hand, the Jordanian delegation saw the rule as an advantage to those delegations finding themselves in a defensive position – a position in which they believed that they, along with the Palestinians, could find themselves in the course of those meetings. However, it was too late to argue over the 'consensus rule' because it applied to all working groups and its adoption had been intended to reassure all core parties that they had a last-resort option to refuse any decision that violated their basic positions or interests.

The discussion of the agenda items pertaining to humanitarian concerns, statistics and data-gathering for refugees passed with relative ease. The number of topics covered and decisions approved on the first day was impressive. Yet experience had taught that extrapolations based on past successes could be most misleading.

The smooth sailing on the first day was offset by a bitter and testing ordeal faced on the second day when the chair labored to have a document approved summarizing the conclusions of the two-day meeting. To save time and adjourn the meetings at noon, Peron worked closely with the American and Palestinian delegates ahead of time on the summary statement. The Palestinian delegation was unhappy that the draft did not include any reference to UN Resolution 194 or to the right of return and insisted on the inclusion of a statement to that effect. Ignoring these issues altogether in an international forum of Middle East peace, especially in the absence of an Israeli delegation as was the case in Ottawa, would infer that the whole world community was shying away from the Resolution, and not just Israel. Such an inference would make it ever more difficult to use UN Resolution 194 as a basis for resolving the refugee question.

But Peron was deeply worried that the Palestinians' insistence would make the Refugee Working Group unable to function, and thus put a sad end to it from the very beginning. He, nonetheless, did his best to appear and sound neutral on the issue, but occasional slips revealed a bias for the American position. That morning, Dr Breizat of the Jordanian delegation briefed Anani on the gavel-holder's draft concluding statement and tipped him that Peron was ardently debating it with the Palestinian and American delegations. Anani and al-Khasawneh hurried to the meeting hall and demanded a copy of the statement. They discovered that it made no mention of the issue of the right of return and they insisted that this should be rectified. They said that the final statement should be an honest reflection of the actual deliberations that took place in the Working Group. Marc Peron promised to work on this provided that, in return for his flexibility, he could decide which statements to include. Otherwise he would consider the delegates as interfering in the work of the gavel-holder, something that he would never accept.

When the meeting reconvened, a crisis was looming. A side panel that was entrusted with handling the issue of family reunification failed to come to meaningful conclusions. The conferees agreed that family reunification programs should be respected by all parties and that Israel's policy toward accepting applications for reunification should be made more transparent. The Jordanian delegation pointed to the plight of 85,000 Palestinians, on their way home, who were stranded in Jordan because the Israeli authorities denied them re-entry into the occupied territories. Those people had obtained expensive permits to leave the Occupied Territories legally in order to stay abroad for long periods to work, attend universities or seek medical treatment, and to then return to their homes. Anani asserted that this issue was of extreme importance to Jordan and the Palestinians. People were separated from their families, and it was the responsibility of the Refugee Working Group to tackle their problem. The chair took note of this remark and promised to include it on the agenda of the next meeting of the Group.

When discussions of the agenda items were concluded, the meeting recessed for a short period to allow Peron time to put the final touches to his closing summary statement. It was disclosed during the recess that the Palestinian delegation, which was keen on inserting some kind of reference to the right of return, had accepted a light reference to it. The Jordanian delegation thought such a diluted reference would jeopardize the issue more than its exclusion. The text read: '. . . while some delegates stressed the importance of the right of the Palestinian refugees to return or be compensated in accordance with Resolution 194 and the subsequent UN General Assembly Resolutions re-iterated until 1991, other delegates did not.' The Jordanian delegation objected to this text on the grounds of objectivity. Not a single delegation expressed any reservation or disapproval of the contents of Resolution 194. The delegation pointed out a more serious ramification of the gavel-holder's statement: it would cast a doubt on the unanimity which 194 and succeeding resolutions commanded in the UN General Assembly. In this regard, it was useful to mention that when Resolution 194 was submitted in December 1948 to the UN General Assembly, US President Harry S. Truman and his Secretary of State, Dean Atcheson, insisted that the Israeli government of David Ben Gurion accept the resolution and implied penalties to Israel otherwise. The resolution was passed unanimously and Israel did not vote against it, but abstained. Since that date, the same resolution was routinely re-adopted by the General Assembly without much debate.

After three hours of debate among the Jordanian, Palestinian, American and Canadian delegations, it became obvious that the parties would not arrive at a consensus. The delegates were allowed a lunch break and were asked to return to a final meeting at 3:00 p.m. During the recess, two members from each of the above four delegations were invited to a closed meeting. Kurtzer insisted that he could not include a statement that showed no reservations whatsoever on the inclusion of the right of return because doing so would hinder the prospects of Israel joining the Group. Anani and al-Khasawneh argued that Israel's failure to attend the Group's meeting was reason enough to keep the statement as suggested by the Jordanian delegation. Kurtzer and Aaron Miller saw that the best way out of the impasse was to delete the entire text that referred to Resolution 194, a proposal that threw the Palestinian delegation out of balance.

The meeting reconvened at 3:00 p.m. for the closing session, while the ad hoc committee of four had not yet reached an agreement. The delegates were all standing in a circle, around the delegates of the four parties. Anani challenged Kurtzer to name the countries that had made statements of reservation against Resolution 194 of 1948. Kurtzer explained that the European delegations and delegations from other regions had refrained from voicing their reservations for fear of triggering a crisis. In bilateral private conversations, Kurtzer told Anani that Americans would not be happy to hear discussions of Resolution 194 or any political issues in the Refugee Group's meetings.

By this time, the Anani-Khasawneh versus Kurtzer-Miller debate had become a test of personal willpower. The dispute reached its peak when Kurtzer threatened to go to the podium and declare that the US position was, in effect, against Resolution 194. Anani and al-Khasawneh decided to call his bluff, and dared Kurtzer to make the announcement. It was then, and only then, that Kurtzer was ready to compromise.

Al-Khasawneh eventually came up with the language that was finally agreed:

> Some delegates insisted on the rights of return and/or compensation as stipulated in the General Assembly Resolution 194 and the subsequent resolutions issued on the same issue until 1991, while other delegates showed reservation. However, this position does not in any way prejudice the right of the negotiating parties to use Resolution 194 as a basis for resolving the Palestinian refugee issue.

The statement was acceptable, and the Jordanian delegation covered the potential misuse of the deficient text by adding the saving clause. The dispute over this text consumed about eight hours of difficult negotiations. Anani and al-Khasawneh also succeeded in another matter. It was to invite the UN Relief and Works Agency for Palestinian Refugees (UNRWA) to attend future meetings. UNRWA had been involved in the affairs of Palestinian refugees since its establishment in 1949, and had in its files a wealth of data, information, and projects awaiting financing. These resources proved to be extremely valuable.

## Regional Security and Arms Control Working Group, Washington

The meetings of the Regional Security and Arms Control Working Group were beset by thematic issues. The Israeli delegation was not in a mood to admit that Israel produced, amassed, and was able to deliver weapons of mass destruction, nuclear, chemical and biological. Nor was it willing to answer questions regarding Israel's refusal to sign and ratify the Nuclear Non-Proliferation Treaty (NPT), or any similar UN-sponsored undertakings. The Israelis argued that signing peace with their immediate neighbors did not guarantee Israeli security because it conceived of other dangerous enemies far afield, like Iraq, Iran, and Central Asian republics. Israel's perception of security went beyond those immediate neighbors to encompass the nuclear capability of other Islamic countries. Israeli military experts stated that the area that should be free from weapons of mass destruction in the region extended from Israel to Iran, Pakistan and all the way to Kazakhstan and Uzbekistan. To expand the region under consideration to those territories was a non-starter; it amounted to an excuse used by Israel to duck the issue and monopolize the stockpiling and delivery facilities of weapons of mass destruction. This, however, became a primary issue on the agenda for bilateral negotiations between Jordan and Israel.

The Israelis also wanted cooperation with their neighbors to stem terrorist acts and violence. The Arab countries that attended the Working Group on Regional Security and Arms Control were never a threat to Israel in that regard. The Palestinians, who were not invited to this meeting in Washington, did not accept Israel's reference to their Intifada as a form of terrorism. It was a legitimate right of the occupied to resist occupation. Syria and Jordan were very strict in guarding their borders against attempts to violate them and sabotage Israel. Yet, the Israelis wanted this working group, in effect, to adopt measures that would enhance its own perceptions of security. The Jordanian head of delegation, Dr Abdallah Toukan, was known for his interests in military technological advances, armaments and the strategic implications thereof. He was softly spoken, well educated, and aware of the requirements of security and the need for arms control. His approach was quiet and business-like. 'If the Israelis do not appreciate a proposal,' Toukan would say, 'do what the Israelis always do: give them another proposal.'

The meetings proceeded without noticeable tensions or problems. It seemed that the absence of a Palestinian delegation helped pacify Israeli anxieties, and the talks were professional, cordial, but lacking in progress.

## Environment Working Group, Tokyo

The Environment Working Group was able to identify two major areas of immediate environmental concern for potential cooperation in the future. The Dead Sea and the Red Sea are both unique in the world. The religious significance of the Dead Sea, whose surface is the lowest contour on earth, is reinforced by the fact that it also contains valuable dissolved minerals and that its waters possess the highest natural density of all waters. The high rate of evaporation and the continuous diversion of the waters from its primary feeder, the River Jordan, had caused its level to drop by about 50 feet in the preceding 40 years, and this was continuing. Unless mitigated, the Dead Sea surface would shrink further and its ability to limit the inflow from surrounding ground-water aquifers would be diminished. The local and regional environment would also be negatively impacted. The Red Sea, some 110 miles to the south of the Dead Sea, contained the most beautiful coral reefs in the world. The Gulf of Aqaba, about four miles in width, had two rapidly expanding cities on its shores, Aqaba in Jordan and Eilat in Israel, and faced serious hazards of contamination from commercial navigation. A joint regional effort was needed to avert future ecological disasters that could have immense economic consequences. Additionally, the fragile environment of the Wadi Araba, the inland desert terrains on both Jordan's and Israel's sides of their common borders stretching between the outskirts of the Dead Sea and the Red Sea, demanded attention and cooperation between Jordan and Israel if it was to be preserved. The Working Group on the Environment was a suitable forum to discuss these topics and come up with workable joint arrangements. The talks on the environment went smoothly. Obviously, the Jordanians, the Israelis and the Palestinians each had a stake in laying the grounds for cooperation because it would yield benefits to each party. The positive tone of the talks amongst the adversaries encouraged the participating international parties, and Japan indicated a willingness to help finance projects of cooperation on the environment. Success in that field would also reflect well on the gavel-holder of the Working Group, Japan itself.

When all the Jordanian delegations to the multilateral groups returned home, they convened a meeting in Amman at the end of May, 1992. Each delegation head submitted a detailed report of the proceedings of his own group, and an evaluation of its session in general. The conclusion of deliberations called for diligent care, not gloomy despair. Prince al-Hassan Bin Talal, who presided over the appraisal meetings, reminded everyone that these multilateral sessions were only the beginning and that delegates should be fully aware of the fact that these were open talks with the world community in contrast with the bilaterals that were closed meetings with no joint summary for each round as was the case in the multilaterals. Even if the multilaterals did not produce tangible immediate results, Jordan should benefit from the exposure in that forum and should present its case clearly, carefully and moderately. Prince al-Hassan viewed the multilateral working groups as having a single topic: the human environment in its wider concept. Each of the five working groups, he pointed out, addressed a topic that is at the heart of the human environment. Economic development, improvement of the fortunes of refugees and securing family reunions, providing the basic amenities like water to the people of the region, protecting the environment, and enhancing security for all. These are important means to enhance human dignity, preserve human rights, and provide for better living. The prince emphasized three themes that he thought Jordan should pursue in the multilaterals: democracy and human rights, just and durable peace, and meaningful regional cooperation. In the process, efforts should also be directed at mitigating the adverse impacts of the confrontation between man and man, and between man and nature. The resources for success were both human and natural, but the basic role of the multilaterals was to serve these goals.

The multilaterals eventually picked up momentum as the bilateral peace negotiations proceeded. Although Syria and Lebanon did not participate directly, they were very interested in following up the results of each round. The test of time proved that some of these working groups were destined to succeed with flying colors while others were doomed to lose momentum and stagnate. However, the agendas set in the first round of each group continued to set the tone for the succeeding multilateral rounds. Although multilateral negotiation never became a substitute for bilateral negotiation, in many ways it proved to be very useful.

## NOTES

1 It was headed by the Minister himself, and had in its membership Tarawneh, Haddadin, Marea, Abdallah Toukan, Ambassador Mohammad Adwan (Moscow), Ambassador Saleh Kabariti (Turkey). Others in the delegation included Dr Safwan Toukan, Dr Murad Beino, Dr Mustafa Hamarneh.

2 Madadha's father was a prominent Jordanian who served as Minister of the Interior in the 1950s. He was a tough Minister who cracked down on leftist activists and opponents to the monarch, even though his son, Khalid, was such an activist at the time. The father was code-named 'Traitor' by the leftists (Communists, Ba'athists, and Arab Nationalists). These parties claimed to be the champions of the people's interests. They had slogans calling for the 'liberation of Palestine', and the removal of the Jewish state. Dozens of them were detained in 1957 for interrogation, and some were kept in detention in a desert outpost without trial. The meeting in Brussels was Madadha's first experience of the peace process. On the first day he leaned over and whispered to Tarawneh, 'Say, Fayez, I can hear the voice of my father asking me from his grave: "Who is the traitor now?" and it looks like he needs no evidence to prove that we are!'

# 8

# The Process Survives

The time that lapsed between the end of the fifth and the beginning of the sixth rounds of bilateral negotiations was long, extending almost four months from April 30 until August 24, 1992. The recess was mandated by the general elections in Israel, and the formation of a new Cabinet. The Israeli election outcome was crucial to the continuity and success of the peace process. While opinions among Arab political analysts varied widely over Labor's zeal for peace, there was unanimity in the belief that re-electing Likud would mean the death of negotiations. Jordanians, in particular, viewed a Labor victory as a catalyst to peacemaking. Yitzhak Rabin himself, Jordanians thought, had come to the conclusion that wars with the Arabs were not going to secure Israel's security; peace would. The Palestinians also favored a Likud defeat and a Labor victory for much the same reason. The public Syrian position on the matter was that both represented the aggression of Zionism against Arabs, and hard negotiations were to be expected.

During this pause in negotiations, proponents and opponents of peace in Jordan and Israel on all fronts were busy hammering out their positions and solidifying gains in their respective appeals to the public.

Jordanian opponents of peace shifted from evoking anti-negotiation sentiments on religious and nationalistic grounds to a more mundane issue, namely the Israeli elections. They based their opposition on five arguments, linked by a chain of intellectual niceties. The first argument was that the peace process, brokered by America, was triggered only after the remaining hope for Arab power, Iraq, was essentially demolished by an act led by the peace sponsor. The second was that the contenders for the Israeli leadership, Yitzhak Rabin and Yitzhak Shamir, were essentially adherents to the same Zionist philosophy, but with different styles for its implementation. As a matter of fact, Shamir to them was the lesser of the two evils because he did not use euphemisms or silk gloves to hide his intentions, and his lack of popularity in the West helped to unveil the realities of Zionist schemes. The third argument rested on Rabin, whom many Jordanians remembered as a Jew involved in the establishment of Israel from day one; a soldier who spent most of his life in military service, served as Chief of Staff in the 1967 War, and was the Defense Minister in 1988 who set the policy of breaking the bones of Palestinian children to extinguish the Intifada. The fourth argument of the opposition emanated from the ongoing change in the Israeli political scene in which no single party had commanded a majority of votes in the Knesset, the Israeli parliament, in more than a decade. Thus, small religious parties had a golden opportunity to influence Israeli politics because they held the votes that tipped the balance. In fact Arabs opposed to peace found in Jordan and elsewhere remote and unsolicited support on the other side. Ultra-right groups in Israel opposed peace with the Arabs in much the same way as nationalist and Islamist Arabs were opposed to peace with Israel. Jordanian opponents comforted themselves with the hope that the political parties in Israel would do the job for them in blocking peace.

The fifth and last argument was spun out of speculation over future American elections. Opponents to peace in Jordan pointed out that after 12 years of a Republican administration, and in the light of the economic slowdown and the rise in unemployment, the American electoral mood could shift and a majority of voters could support the Democratic Party. Since the Democratic Party had nominated Clinton, his election to the presidency of the United States would result in a total pro-Israel bias by the superpower sponsoring the negotiations. In the minds of Arabs, Democratic presidents identified more strongly with pro-Israel liberalism than their Republican peers. They reached that conclusion by analyzing the historical profile of the US response to the changing circumstances in the Middle East. While President Truman, the Democrat, helped create Israel in 1948 and secure its admission to the UN, President Eisenhower, the Republican, was the one who issued an ultimatum to the aggressors in the 1956 Suez campaign, spearheaded by Israel, to pull out of Egypt. In 1967, the year of the crushing Arab defeat, Lyndon Baines Johnson was the US President who appeared on television expressing relief at the outcome of the war. Moreover, it was President Jimmy Carter, the Democrat, who brokered in 1979 the Camp David Accord that neutralized Egypt, the Arab heavyweight champion in the protracted conflict with Israel. When these five arguments were combined, Arab prospects looked potentially grim.

Culturally, Jordanians expected quick results from the peace process and forthright concessions by the Israelis. After all, Jordanians thought, it is the Jews that made the lives of Jordanians and Palestinians very miserable. Jews came from remote areas in Europe and fought with the rightful owners, the indigenous people of the land. They killed many Jordanians and Palestinians, and evicted many Palestinians from their land. In Arab culture, the aggressor's (and his family's) obligation is to pay all the damages to the victim's family when the latter agrees to make peace. Viewed in this context, it seemed strange that the Israelis were dragging their feet in accepting their obligations, since they were the aggressors. When His Majesty King Hussein had convened a National Conference to announce Jordan's decision to go to Madrid along with the other Arab parties, two elderly fellows, so the story goes, were playing the popular game of *siejeh* in the village of Kufr Yuba in north Jordan. 'Well,' said the player who was about to lose the game, 'we finally accepted to make peace with Israel after the *Jaha* [group of dignitaries] came to us from the United States.'

'Yes,' said the other, 'I wonder how much the Israelis will pay in land and money to make up for all they have done to us; it must be considerable compensation to justify our agreement to make peace.'

When no quick and tangible results came from the peace negotiations, after the first or second rounds, it cast a dark shadow over future prospects among all Jordanians, whether indigenous or of Palestinian origin. The lack of progress also reinforced the arguments of the Jordanian opposition. It gave no evidence for the peace proponents to offer to justify the hopes for peace.

The Israeli election results renewed hope that Israel, which was the central peace interlocutor, had decided to change its position and seek peace. The most telling result of the June, 1992, Israeli elections was not the victory of the Labor Party, which totaled 44 seats in the new Knesset, but the defeat of the Likud Party, which now had only 22 seats. More reassuring was the victory of new, pro-peace parties in Israel. Meretz, a strong liberal party and a staunch supporter of the land for peace formula, won 12 seats, and two Arab parties won five seats combined. A Labor-led government did not need the religious parties to win a vote of confidence in the 120-seat Knesset. The 1992 Israeli elections seemed to mark a watershed in Israel's sense of national identity. On the last day in office, Shamir was quoted as saying, 'The Jewish State cannot exist without a unique ideological content . . . We will not exist for long if we become just another country that is mostly devoted to the welfare of its citizens. We must provide our sons and daughters with motivations of values and challenge.' In contrast, in his opening address to the new Knesset, Rabin said,

> In the last decade of the twentieth century, the atlases, history and geography books no longer present an up-to-date picture of the world. Walls of enmity have fallen; borders have disappeared. Powers have crumbled and ideologies collapsed; states have been born, states have died, and the gates of emigration have been flung open. And it is our duty, to ourselves and to our children, to see the new world as it is now, to discern its dangers, explore its prospects and do everything possible so that the state of Israel will fit into this new world.

Once the Israeli Cabinet was formed, it became obvious that the broad-based government which Rabin had struggled to structure was not going to come through. The two Arab parties were denied Cabinet positions; Rabin wanted their support but did not need it, as their votes would not make or break his government's chances of survival. He solicited the support of Shas, a relatively new religious party with a social agenda. The structure of the government commanded only 61 votes of Jewish Knesset members but could count on the votes of the Arab members of the Knesset on matters related to the promotion of peace. It was evident that the ultra-conservative Zionists (Likud, Tsomet, and a score of other religious parties) were not in the decision-making process of government, but were rather in the opposition.

Developments within Israeli society were also echoed in Jordan. As a matter of fact, the Jordanian parliamentary elections of 1989 revealed the extent of the public's interest in economic reform with social justice. Jordanians shifted their focus, as peace negotiations did not yield quick results, to combat the high poverty and unemployment in their country. In some strange way, the opposition, political Islamists and Arab nationalists, had associated the program of economic adjustment, assisted and coordinated by the International Monetary Fund (IMF), with the US-sponsored peace process. Both movements, the opposition claimed, caused Jordan a great deal of unnecessary pain. The peace process, they predicted, would end in disastrous failure, and would only exacerbate economic hardship. The linkage the opposition made between the pains of economic structural adjustment and the peace process was difficult to argue against with a dissatisfied public. A successful economic and social development program could disprove the opposition's economic argument, and could at least dilute their political argument. The term 'peace dividend' began to invade Jordan's lexicon and proceeded eventually to become a household word. The common question raised was: 'So what is this peace going to do for us? Let us see.' The peace antithesis shifted argument from a religious to a socio-economic base. It was initially based on the notion that the land of Palestine is an Islamic Waqf that nobody has any right in ceding any part of to any other party (i.e. Israel). The opponents of peace shifted the focus of their argument to socio-economic secular matters, casting the sort of doubts mentioned above on the peace process. However, the shift from a religious to a secular argument was more of a change of mind than a change of heart.

During the lull in negotiations, the Jordanian Parliament passed a new (political) Parties Law in 1992 which allowed for a group of at least 50 Jordanian adults to caucus, write a charter and bylaws, and submit an application to form a political party. It would be licensed de facto unless the basic surmountable conditions were violated. Thirty political parties emerged of which ten were the offspring of previous covert or overt parties in Jordan. The old Communist Party broke into three, the Ba'ath Party into three also, the Islamic parties into two, and two other Pan-Arab nationalist parties, nostalgic for Egypt's Nasser, broke apart into several factions. With the exception of the Muslim Brotherhood Movement, the other nine parties that opposed peace were considered small and politically lightweight.

The other new parties were basically local in nature, although each one presented itself as broader in focus to avoid the stigma of appearing too narrow. The goals of the other 20 new parties constituted the bulk of Jordanian interests, namely: a better future for their children through economic development and performance, better job opportunities, and, above all, security and stability. To Jordanians, stability and economic prosperity are synonymous – this conviction held not as an ideal, but as a result of long experience of being at the center of a Middle East beset by tumults, wars, civil riots, military coups, sieges, boycotts, and bloodshed.

King Hussein's steady steps toward cementing 'irrevocable' paths to democracy and peace were articulated by Prince al-Hassan's visionary formulations of the future Middle East. In the spring of 1992, the King gave a speech to businessmen and economists in the Hague, Netherlands. He articulated the Jordanian vision of the principles that must be observed in order to achieve domestic stability and regional security throughout the Middle East. His Majesty listed eight such principles to reach this goal:

(1) legitimate constitutional regimes that respect individual citizens' rights;
(2) balanced international support of the Middle East;
(3) the right of the people in the region to utilize their resources for their own economic and social development;
(4) democracy and respect of human rights;
(5) open opportunities for education, allowing access to other cultures and technology;
(6) freedom from weapons of mass destruction;
(7) an integrated approach to address the problems of security, development and human rights; and
(8) the establishment of a healthy, stable Middle East order by establishing a similar order in its larger circle, the Arab World.

The significance of these points lay in the King's identification of the 'Middle East region' as a subset of a wider region comprising the Arab world, thus building his vision for the Middle East with Israel as an indigenous part of it. The main issue then was not negotiating peace with all its bureaucratic details, but to address the wider issue of building a future. At the helm in both Jordan and Israel were now two men who knew and respected each other, and whose strategic, geopolitical and security interests were so mutual that they were likely to bond in the future – as they did, in fact, on July 25, 1994 at the White House under the auspices of the US President.

On the Palestinian side, it was obvious that the victory of the Labor Party (or better, the defeat of Likud Party) was of great importance. It was Shamir who had denied any role for the PLO, disbarred Palestinian residents of Jerusalem from the Palestinian delegations to the peace process, and resisted any linkage between interim and permanent status negotiations. The consistent abortion of Palestinian attempts to steer the negotiations toward a meaningful resolution frustrated the Palestinian delegation beyond perseverance. When Rabin formed his government, he immediately adopted certain goodwill measures to set the trend for his future policies and break away from the Likud style of negotiating tactics. Most of Rabin's early confidence-building measures were of a symbolic nature, such as lifting barbed wires that surrounded the Palestinian refugee camps in the West Bank and the Gaza Strip. The more important ones he kept for the negotiations.

Rabin's first visit to the United States after his election came shortly after Secretary James Baker was appointed as the White House Chief of Staff, and President Bush's campaign manager. Lawrence Eagleberger, who had taken Baker's place at the State Department, was a long associate of Henry Kissinger and well versed in Middle East politics. Rabin's visit in itself helped solidify his position with the Bush administration and was also helpful in redefining the role of Jewish lobbyists such AIPAC (American Israeli Public Affairs Committee), which had been very active during the gloomy period of soured American–Israeli relations during Shamir's premiership. Rabin, it was reported, told AIPAC officers that they should not expect their organization to define Israel's negotiation positions, nor would they be allowed to draw up Israel's negotiation strategy. The honeymoon AIPAC had with the Israeli government during the supremacy of the Israeli conservative Likud coalition had apparently ended.

The Palestinians became more eager to be given bolder recognition by the sponsors of the peace process, and they did get incremental recognition. They could attend the five multilateral working groups under the tacitly PLO label, experts from amongst Palestinians in exile would join the bilateral negotiations, and consistent harassment of the Palestinian delegates in the West Bank and Gaza would stop once and for all. That was one primary gain for the Palestinians with the end of the Shamir era.

Washington, DC continued to be the venue of bilateral negotiations. The sixth round lasted a month, from August 24 until September 23, 1992, interrupted by Labor Day and some Jewish holidays. A few days before the resumption of the sixth round, the Palestinian delegation pressed the Americans for more details on the status of a proposed $10 billion in loan guarantees that the US intended to extend to the Israelis.

The Bush administration had withheld that facility until Israel undertook not to use any of its proceeds to build further colonies in the West Bank and Gaza. Rabin, who in his first speech to the Knesset had promised to freeze such colonies/settlements, went the extra mile needed to abide by US conditions and terminated settlement expansion altogether.

On the morning the negotiations commenced on August 24, the Israeli press center in the Mayflower Hotel in Washington issued a communiqué to the media explaining the confidence-building measures taken by the Prime Minister and Minister of Defense, Yitzhak Rabin, 'in order to improve the atmosphere among the Arab residents'. The four measures were:

a)     the relaxation of the age limit from 60 to 50 for Palestinians who need special permits to work and trade in Israel,

b)     the release of 800 Palestinian political prisoners who had completed two-thirds of their sentences,

c)     gradual lifting of street and alley closures subject to reconsideration in the case of riots, and,

d)     the reopening of houses which had been sealed for five years or more.

The language of the communiqué, which referred to the West Bank as 'Judea and Samaria' and to Palestinians in the West Bank as 'residents', diluted the positive tone of the measures, especially among the technically oriented and legally minded experts in both the Jordanian and Palestinian delegations. Al-Khasawneh, the Jordanian delegate and legal expert, asserted that the language of both Elyakim Rubinstein and Robby Sabel were imprinted all over the translation of the communiqué issued by the Israeli Press Center. Yet, the most intriguing confidence-building measure that the new Prime Minister had taken 'in coordination with senior defense officials' was the cancellation of the deportation orders issued eight months earlier against 11 residents of the Occupied Territories. The Israeli Supreme Court in December 1991 had ordered the orders to be frozen, but Rabin annulled them altogether on August 23, 1992.

When the negotiations resumed the following day, the Jordanian and Israeli delegates met and, through strong handshakes and warm words, expressed that they had missed each other. Four months had passed since they had last met. In their bilateral meeting, Rubinstein dampened the high expectations of the Jordanians and indicated that though the new Israeli government was more flexible than its predecessor, it was within the limits imposed by public opinion. Majali pointed out that, judging from Rabin's policy statements, there was an emphasis placed on the Syrian and Palestinian tracks. 'Jordan,' said Majali, 'is not only indifferent to such strategy, but is actually supportive of it in many ways.'

'Really?' exclaimed Rubinstein. 'How so?'

'Because,' Majali explained, 'the only way to have peace endure is to make it comprehensive.'

'But the new Prime Minister', said Rubinstein, 'is strongly interested in the Jordanian track of negotiations, and subscribes to the principle of comprehensiveness.'

'You can see that we are not against that,' said Majali.

The new Israeli Cabinet did not effect significant alterations to the composition and membership of its bilateral peace delegations. The chief negotiator with Syria, the Likudist Youssi Ben Aharon, was replaced by a renowned academic, Itamar Rabinovich; a new water negotiator was appointed to the Israeli delegation, Noah Kinarti, a strong supporter of Prime Minister Yitzhak Rabin. The most notable non-change was maintaining Rubinstein as head of the Israeli delegation, negotiating with both Jordanians and Palestinians. This very decision caused a great deal of disappointment to Palestinian delegates who thought of him as a haughty religious idealist whose hidden mission was to foil negotiations with the Palestinians and have them blamed for it. The Jordanians did not mind the continuity of Rubinstein's tenure. Actually, they went by the old saying, 'the devil that you know is better than the angel you don't know'. Moreover, a working relationship characterized by mutual respect had developed between the two delegations.

An Israeli perception of the Palestinian attitude towards Rubinstein was echoed by Aliza Wallach in the Israeli paper, *Davar*, and was quoted in the September 2, 1992 issue of the *Mid East Mirror*. Wallach wrote,

> The Palestinians have difficulty digesting Rubinstein, Shamir's rep-resentative, as Rabin's representative. Maybe the Palestinians have bad eyesight or are hard of hearing, but that is the way they perceive him and what he represents. And that should not surprise us. In fact, it's surprising we are surprised that the Palestinians do not understand that the hands are Rubinstein's hands, but the voice is Rabin's.

Contrary to the views of some American columnists who asserted that Israel's priority was the Palestinian negotiations, the Jordanian track was critical to Israel's ability to make peace. Uncomplicated as the Jordanian track may have appeared it was actually more challenging than most analysts noted. The challenge in the Jordanian–Israeli negotiations lay in the topics they would address that the Palestinian track was not allowed to touch on before the negotiations of Final Status. The Israelis were not oblivious to these challenges, nor did they downplay them.

If changing the chief negotiator was necessary to alter the atmosphere in the negotiations room, it was not sufficient to ensure progress. The strategy had to be amended, reworded, and made more accommodating. This was visible in the Israeli approach to the Palestinians and the tactical gains the Palestinians were allowed in terms of representation and respect. In the Syrian track, where the Israeli chief negotiator was replaced, there was no change in the strategy of either side, and no substantive progress was achieved.

## The Syrian track

Encouraged by the style of negotiations in the Jordanian–Israeli track, the Syrians gave the new Israeli chief negotiator a document describing the 'vision for peace', to break the deadlock in their track of negotiations. This document excited the Israelis to the extent that their Foreign Minister, Shimon Peres, considered it progress. However, the other Arab teams of negotiators heard about it only after the Israelis announced it on Israeli television nine days after they received it. The secrecy with which the Syrian delegation operated did not appeal to the other Arab delegations. The event gave proof that the daily coordination meetings among the four Arab delegations did not serve the purpose they were meant to serve. To the Jordanians who put on the table all the developments that took place in their track, this Syrian secrecy added to the disappointment they frequently felt concerning Palestinian secrecy. The Palestinian delegation refrained from sharing with the Jordanians the documents that they submitted to the Israelis despite the fact that they were both part of a joint delegation. All the evidence indicated that in reality there was no coordination.

After the American and Jewish holidays, negotiations resumed on September 13, 1992. Rabin made a statement that day to the effect that Israel would not open dialogue with Syria over the return of the Golan Heights until Syria demonstrated its will to make peace. When the two delegations met in Washington a few hours later, optimism began to evaporate into thin air. The same old cycle of 'who blinked first' was set in motion again. The left-wing Israeli newspaper, *Al Hamishmar*, reported in its Monday edition that one week earlier King Hussein had met in London with Shimon Peres, Israel's foreign minister, and that Peres had spoken through the Jordanians on the telephone with Farouq al-Share', Syria's foreign minister. Peres had proposed to al-Shara'a that Israel was willing to discuss several options regarding the future of the occupied Golan Heights, including 'the notion that Syria be ready to lease the area to Israel on a long-term basis'. Syria publicly rejected that idea, considering the proposal of a lease as another means to maintain the status quo. Jordan never refuted officially the rumored meeting between the King and Peres, although many Jordanians, including some of us in the Jordanian delegation, thought the rumor was highly plausible. Dr Majali suggested that the Syrians should have considered the alternatives and should have publicly interpreted the offer by Israel as Israel's recognition of Syrian sovereignty over the Golan Heights. According to Majali, the Syrians should have stated that they acknowledged Israel's recognition of sovereignty but were still awaiting more genuine proposals to arrive at peace. However, the Syrians would not have entertained Majali's proposal because, according to them, this would throw suspicion on the Golan being an integral part of Syria, a possibility the Syrians would never tolerate under any circumstances.

## The Palestinian track

The Palestinians were also disappointed by the Israeli response to their written proposals. The Israeli delegation would not entertain Palestinian aspirations to a meaningful self-governance that entailed authority, jurisdiction and political elections. Instead the Israelis offered the Palestinians detailed municipal responsibilities. The Palestinians countered the Israeli proposal with two documents: a proposed common agenda, and one dealing with the structure and jurisdiction of the interim self-government arrangements (ISGA). The Palestinian delegation insisted on discussing human rights in the Occupied Territories from the perspective of the Fourth Geneva Convention that dealt with the obligations of the occupying power toward the occupied; and on addressing the issues of Jerusalem, Israeli settlements, and the structure of the Palestinian authority. Even on issues where some agreement was reached, such as election modalities, the two parties had categorically different views on the function and size of the elected body. Majali tried to use Jordanian offices to bridge the gap. In private, Rubinstein would tell him that the Rabin government was willing to walk the distance toward the Palestinians, provided that the Palestinian delegation was willing to confine its discussions to items in the Madrid Invitation. On the other hand, Majali tried to convince the Palestinians to endorse the positive aspects of the Israeli proposals, and to aim for cumulative gains. He also cautioned them against accelerating their demands through written proposals to the Israelis. Such a tactic would scare the Israelis away from even the limited positive offers they had included in their written proposal, and they would then blame the Palestinians for such a backward step. But the Palestinians feared that an incremental gain tactic of the type Majali proposed could lead them into a Rubinstein trap. However, toward the end of the round, the Palestinians and Israelis agreed to have small groups of experts that, because of their informal nature and small size, would exclude the Jordanian representatives who participated in the full track meeting. The Jordanians did not complain. They themselves developed the same mechanism of informal talks without the participation of either of the two Palestinian delegates attached to their full track meetings.

## The Jordanian track

On the Jordanian side, the mood of the negotiations oscillated from highs to lows, but was full of fun. However, the lack of visible progress by the end of the first week of the round that ended on Thursday, August 27, 1992, caused disappointment and the media's interest in the Jordan–Israel track faded. But at the same time the two sides were engaged in serious discussions of the items of the draft common agenda proposed by the Jordanians in the fifth round. Section A of that draft stated that the goal of negotiations was 'the achievement of a just, lasting and comprehensive peace between the Arab states, the Palestinians and Israel as per the Madrid invitation'. The Jordanians wanted to use the word 'comprehensive' to qualify the goal of peace, but the Israelis thought that the Jordanian definition of 'comprehensiveness' had a negative connotation that spilled over from the Syrian–Israeli track. To the Israeli delegation, the emphasis on comprehensiveness threatened to diminish the benefit Israel thought it could get from purely bilateral negotiations where it could foster disparity between the various tracks of negotiations to its own advantage. The Jordanians explained that this section was general in nature and, if the discussion was caught up in semantics, it could go on forever. On the other hand, the Israelis were worried that Jordan would slow down its negotiations with Israel tactically to keep pace with other stalled negotiation tracks, thus, the purely bilateral nature of the talks would be compromised. In fact, Rubinstein tried to maneuver his way into getting a commitment from the Jordanians to sign a peace treaty if all Jordanian–Israeli agenda topics were satisfactorily resolved.

For its part, the Jordanian delegation had reservations about the wording the Israelis proposed to use with reference to the parties to peace. Israel favored the use of 'achieving peace between Israel and its neighbors', a phrase that would drop the mention of Palestinians and make Israel sound as if it was at the center of the region. The Jordanians argued that in such a phrase, the word 'Israel' would be the only definite term while 'its Arab neighbors' seemed like a burdensome adjunct. The two sides agreed eventually on the wording 'between neighboring Arab countries, the Palestinians and Israel'.

The second part of the proposed agenda, Section B, cited Resolution 242 to form the basis of negotiations on topics of contention. The Israeli understanding of Resolution 242 was again debated. The famous article 'the' and the connotations of dropping it from the English text of the Resolution was debated to no avail. Israel insisted that it had abided by the requirements of the Resolution when it withdrew from Sinai, and that it was not about to make generous concessions and withdraw from more territories. By this time, both sides had elucidated their position thoroughly, and the assimilation of their points of view on the issue needed a high-level understanding, or a package deal. The Israeli delegation did not arouse Jordanian fears over the applicability of Resolution 242 to Jordanian lands that Israel had occupied, but expressed their nagging worry that Jordan would some day include the West Bank among the Jordanian territories that should be the subject of withdrawal. Majali, al-Khasawneh and Tarawneh all indicated that Jordan had made its decision not to negotiate, in lieu of the Palestinians or on their behalf, Israeli withdrawal from the West Bank or any other occupied Palestinian land.

On the issue of security, the two sides had their differences over the item addressing the stockpiling and the potential deployment and use of weapons of mass destruction. The Israeli delegation would never accept the use of the word 'deployment', pointing out that this would be a limiting factor to Israel's right to self-defense against other regional enemies such as Iran and Iraq.

On the issue of refugees and displaced persons, the Jordanians insisted that these issues be resolved in accordance with the relevant United Nations resolutions. The Israelis suggested that these two categories be referred to in one item, stating that the issues of refugees and displaced persons would be resolved in accordance with mutually accepted international instruments. It was curious that the Israeli proposal used the phrase 'accepted international instruments', as this had been introduced by al-Khasawneh instead of 'peace treaty' in reference to the culmination of the bilateral negotiations.

On water, there was almost an immediate agreement, although both Israeli and Jordanian water negotiators were considered tough and unyielding. The prompt agreement was the result of informal talks that the side committee on water, energy and the environment had conducted, starting in the third round. The wording did not touch on the details of water rights, thereby postponing any disagreements to a later time in the negotiations.

It was during the sixth round of negotiations that King Hussein underwent surgery for cancer at the Mayo Clinic in Rochester, Minnesota in August, 1992. When he was released a week later from the hospital, he and her Majesty, Queen Noor, went to their riverside home in Maryland, near Washington, for a period of convalescence. While they were there, our delegation was able to visit them. We sat with the King on the terrace of his Maryland home, where he informed us that he and Queen Noor would be having dinner the following day with President and Mrs Bush, a piece of news that pleased us immensely. He then asked about the negotiations and how they were going, and touched on important issues including water. The King surprised the delegation with his command of the detail of the water issue.

'It is worth it to struggle to recover our water rights when it is public knowledge that the unaccounted-for water is so high in our country? How much is the percentage of unaccounted-for water?' he asked.

'Around 56 per cent for Amman in 1991, Your Majesty,' replied Haddadin.

'This is more than half of the water supplied. This is too much. Measures have to be taken to minimize it to acceptable limits,' said the King.

'Yes Sire; fixing the leaks is less expensive than bringing in more supplies,' confirmed Haddadin.

The third round of multilateral talks of the Water Resources Working Group was to be convened in Washington during the second leg of the sixth round of the bilateral negotiations. As was agreed between Haddadin and Zaslovsky in Vienna in May, the Israeli Water Commissioner was due to bring his map and work out the settlement of the water rights in accordance with the Johnston allocations. An important matter like that could not be left without reporting to the King the likelihood of agreement over water with the Israelis. On his way out of the King's home with the other delegates, Haddadin briefed the King on what he was expecting from the Israelis on the occasion of the multilateral session scheduled for September 14–16. The King considered the possibility very good news, and despatched Haddadin and al-Khasawneh to Amman to brief the Negotiation's High Committee, headed in the King's absence by his brother and Crown Prince, al-Hassan. Haddadin and al-Khasawneh spent five days in Amman and received much encouragement from Prince al-Hassan and the High Committee.

The problem with the key issue of land for peace was not the refusal of the Israeli delegation to acknowledge Jordan's rights to recover its territories that had been under Israeli control, but rather the insistence of Rubinstein that this issue be linked to the 'Final Status'. The use of this term, that applied only to the Palestinians, in the Jordanian track invoked a strong Jordanian response. There was no way that Jordan would accept the division of its negotiations into two stages paralleling the Palestinian negotiations. The Jordanians wanted to ensure the separateness of the two tracks and would reject any suggestion that Jordan should play a role in Palestinian affairs or in the fate of

Palestinian territories, something the Jordanians thought the Israelis would like to invite.

The two delegations went through a laborious list of issues that could be the subject of bilateral cooperation within a regional context (item 6 of the draft agenda, Appendix 3). These included environment, health, transportation, energy, and communications, and other matters.

## Water Resources Working Group, Washington

The second leg of the bilateral negotiations started on Monday September 13. The third round of the multilateral talks on Water Resources was scheduled to start on the Tuesday in Washington. Dan Zaslovsky, the head of the Israeli delegation to the Water Resources Working Group, arrived on Sunday September 12, and gave Haddadin a call to set an appointment for the following day. The informal meeting between Israelis and Jordanians on Monday was disappointing. No deal was struck, and it appeared as though the Water Commissioner was reneging on what he pledged in Vienna four months earlier. Haddadin attributed that to the results of the Israeli elections that brought to power the Labor Party. He soon heard rumors that the Water Commissioner would be replaced. There was another co-chair of the Israeli delegation, Avraham Katz-Oz, a former Labor Minister of Agriculture. That afternoon, Haddadin went to meet with the gavel-holder of the Water Resources Working Group, Alan Kieswetter. Kieswetter told Haddadin that the multilateral meeting, due to convene the following day, would recognize 'progress' made in the bilateral tracks, and would call for more interaction between the core parties of the multilaterals, i.e, Jordan, Israel and the Palestinians. Haddadin denied there was progress warranting closer interaction, at least on the Jordanian and Palestinian tracks. 'Besides, Mr Kieswetter,' said Haddadin, 'the multilateral talks are meant to induce progress in the bilateral negotiations, not the reverse.'

Kieswetter was obviously eager to achieve progress in the work of his group, and to build a momentum of meaningful progress. Haddadin sensed an atmosphere of pressure on Jordan to come up with ideas for cooperation with Israel, or run the risk of having ideas imposed on it. He felt he had to avert such pressures. Haddadin had two bosses in the peace process: on the multilaterals, he reported directly to the Minister of Foreign Affairs, and on the bilaterals, he reported to Majali. He was, in that particular round, a soldier in the field with two commanders.

The next day, Tuesday, the Water Resources Working Group session was opened with a speech from the gavel-holder, followed by another from the delegate of Japan, and a third from the representative of the EU. They all alluded to and praised the 'progress' made in the bilaterals. Haddadin, dismayed at Zaslovsky's retreat from his pledge, understood the message. When he was given the floor for a speech as a core party delegate, Haddadin read from a written text that he had prepared, but departed from the text to say, 'As a participant in the bilateral negotiations, I take the liberty to say that there has not been progress to speak of there, not unless we consider sipping coffee and exchanging a few jokes progress! Today, we are no closer to peace than we were in Madrid a year ago.'

At that point, Haddadin noticed one Israeli delegate leave the room. The chair started the discussions of the items on the agenda. The Palestinians, unable to deliver reports asked for by the chair in the second session in Vienna, claimed their inability to deliver was dictated by the Israeli monopoly on water resources data, and Israeli denial of Palestinian access to them. 'Residents of Judea and Samaria are welcome to any data they need. All they have to do is ask,' commented an Israeli delegate.

Haddadin leaned over to Riyadh al-Khudary, head of the Palestinian delegation, saying 'What is this inconsiderate remark? What is this Judea and Samaria business? Do not let it go. It is both insulting and inappropriate.'

'Mr Chairman,' said al-Khudary, 'the Israeli delegate pledges things he does not deliver. He always makes these claims but he never delivers when we ask.'

'Judea and Samaria,' whispered Haddadin to al-Khudary, 'make a strike on that one.'

Al-Khudary asked for the floor for one of his delegates to speak. Marwan Haddad approached the microphone, and said a few words about the Israelis using the term Judea and Samaria, and so did Abdul Rahman al-Tameemi, another Palestinian delegate. Haddadin was not impressed with their interventions, however. The Israeli delegate took the floor and repeated the use of the term, and insisted that he would give information and data to the Palestinians should they ask for any. Haddadin felt he had to take on the issue, and asked for the floor:

Mr Chairman, distinguished delegates, we have heard the distinguished representative of Israel use archaic terminology in modern times. We have all heard him refer to what we all know as the occupied West Bank as Judea and Samaria. I seek your understanding, then, when I say that, should he repeat this again, I shall refer to all the territories that lie between the Mediterranean and the Jordan River as Palestine.

There was commotion on the floor. The Israeli delegate asked for the floor and he presented arguments to justify the use of the term Judea and Samaria. Haddadin returned the argument and demanded that the Israeli delegation apologize. He exchanged public comments with the Israeli delegation for about twenty minutes.

'We are sorry,' said Amos Ganor of the Israeli delegation as he was given the floor. 'We did not use the term in the context Haddadin is resenting. We were only using the terminology that our own people use. That is all there is to it.'

'I, too, have been using the term our own people use,' said Haddadin after taking the floor.

Finally, the gavel-holder decreed that the Working Group was better off without the use of sensitive terminology; another Israeli delegate left the room.

The outcome of the first day was good for the Jordanian delegation. They coordinated very well with the Palestinians, and with their PLO supervisors, who stayed at the hotel because they were not accredited to the multilaterals.

In the evening, Haddadin was writing his report to send to the Foreign Minister. Bashir Rawashdeh, of the support staff, came and told Haddadin that Majali wanted to see him. After he finished his duty of reporting the multilateral to the Foreign Minister in Amman, an exhausted Haddadin went up to Majali's suite.

'What happened today at the multilateral session?' asked Majali.

'Why do you ask, *sidi*?' asked Haddadin.

'Because it upset our work on the bilateral track.'

'And how did that happen?'

'Well,' said Majali with all the patience for which the Majalis are known, 'I was sitting with Rubinstein in our usual preparation pre-track meeting. He was commending you and said he wished he had two like you in his own delegation. He went on and on praising how well rounded you are, and then there was a knock at the door.'

Haddadin remembered the first Israeli delegate who had left the multilateral session, and asked, 'What time was that?'

'Around ten-thirty. Anyway, Rubinstein answered, and he went outside. Pretty soon he came back, and his face was almost red with anger.'

'What is this Haddadin of yours!' Rubinstein had exclaimed.

'Why? What happened?' Majali had asked.

'He is criticizing you and me. He says that you and I are spending our time sipping coffee and exchanging jokes!'

'There must be a misquote. There must be something wrong,' Majali had said. 'But the thing that really got him and stalled our work was when he called Tarawneh, some half-hour later, and protested to him about you. He informed Tarawneh that he – Rubinstein – was going upstairs to file a complaint against the Jordanians because their Dr Haddadin insulted the State of Israel and denies its existence.'

Rubinstein had obviously been briefed by the second Israeli delegate who left the multilateral session, and was outraged by the Judea and Samaria argument that had taken place in the multilateral meeting that morning.

'If you do not recognize that we exist, why do you negotiate with us?' Rubinstein had yelled at Tarawneh. 'Otherwise, you have to find a solution to this Dr Haddadin of yours.'

'So,' Majali told Haddadin, 'I am asking you so that I can answer Amman when they ask questions.'

'If they do, Pasha, I beg that I answer the questions. This is a multi-lateral track, and, with due respect, I am the one in charge of it here.'

'Can you then, for my own record, write me a brief note?' Majali asked.

'You bet, Pasha, we are your soldiers either way.'

Haddadin wrote Majali a brief note, attached to it a copy of his speech in the opening session of the multilaterals, and retired for the day at about 1:30 a.m., totally exhausted.

After breakfast the following day, Haddadin decided to attend the morning session of the bilateral delegation to follow up developments on the common agenda negotiations. He went to the meeting at Majali's suite at 8:30 a.m. on Wednesday, September 15. When Majali opened the meeting, he asked Haddadin to report on developments in the multilaterals the day before. Haddadin was taken by surprise, and refused to report because the matter was not the concern of the bilaterals. Majali protested at this attitude, and said that the smooth sailing he had enjoyed with Rubinstein had turned rough because of the developments in the multilaterals. He asked Anani for help but Haddadin would not budge. A long day was ahead of him looking after the multilaterals, and he excused himself. As he walked out, he addressed his fellow delegates in an obvious tone of protest:

> Please colleagues, remember always that your adversary is still your enemy. We are no closer to peace now than we have ever been. I will go to the multilateral second session today. I was hoping for your support as I go to encounter them this morning, but I can do without it just as well. I know how to handle my enemy, and I hope you do. Good day, gentlemen.

That was the first time there had ever been friction between Haddadin and Majali, who had known each other well for 21 years. Haddadin looked upon Majali as an older brother, a guardian of Jordanian interests, and a prominent man who enjoyed respect from all. He truly regretted the encounter and comforted himself with the fact that he had not sought it. He thought that perhaps Majali wanted to prove that the dichotomy between the bilaterals and the multilaterals was not beneficial, an idea he had held all along.

Although the sixth round of the bilaterals did not end with the anticipated results, the concurrent third multilateral session on water ended with some success when the Japanese donated a pilot desalination plant for Jordan, and the Europeans donated one for Gaza. Haddadin was instrumental in obtaining these two pledges. Dan Zaslovsky was replaced by a new Water Commissioner, and he left the multilaterals and went back to his post as a professor at Technion (Israel Institute of Technology). The anticipated quick agreement over water allocations never materialized before he was replaced.

## Refugees Working Group, Ottawa

Anani led the Jordanian delegation to Ottawa. The mood was sobering, and the memory of the first meeting a few months before was still fresh in everyone's mind. Dan Kurtzer, head of the American delegation, and Marc Perot, the Canadian gavel-holder, made early contacts with Jordanian, Palestinian, Egyptian and other Arab delegates to reiterate the American and Canadian desire to see the meetings move smoothly. The Israeli delegation, attending for the first time since Moscow, was given warm words of welcome in the opening session by Perot, and by the American, European, Russian and Japanese delegates. Ben Ami, Israel's former Ambassador to Spain and a rising star at the time, led Israel's delegation. He gave a long opening statement and answered, politely and professionally, some of the points that were raised by the Palestinian head of delegation in the previous meeting of the Refugees Working Group that the Shamir government had refused to attend. Ami did his best to strike a conciliatory tone, but his attempt had to concede to the biting reality of the issues at hand.

The discussion was good and items on the agenda sailed smoothly until the item of 'family reunification' was discussed. Anani insisted that Israel should allow Palestinians who were denied re-entry to the Occupied Territories and stranded in Jordan to return to their homes. As these people would return to homes in the Territories and not to Israel, Anani wanted the Working Group on Refugees to adopt a decision on this matter and choose an independent third party to study the conditions of those stranded people and report on Israel's policy of denying their return home. Bajoulet, the French representative, supported the motion and was immediately nominated by the Jordanian and Palestinian delegations to head the proposed mission. The Israeli delegation consulted with its government and later reported in private that Prime Minister Rabin himself had refused the idea. History repeated itself, and at the last meeting, when the gavel-holder read his final report, Anani asked for the floor. 'I see there is no mention of the mission to be dispatched to study the conditions of the citizens of the West Bank and Gaza stranded in Jordan,' he protested.

'There is no consensus on this matter, Dr Anani,' answered the gavel-holder.

'Neither is there on several other parts of the report you just read. I did not agree on some and my Palestinian colleague expressed reservations on others. Despite this, we hear them included in the report.'

The Palestinian delegate concurred. Again, it took hours of haggling between Anani and al-Khasawneh of the Jordanian delegation, and Ben Ami and Freddie Katz of the Israeli delegation, in addition to representatives of the US and European delegations, before there was hope that the report would be endorsed. Anani was willing to compromise and suggested that if Israel reconsidered its position by the next meeting, the Jordanians and Palestinians would rescind their reservation (which actually amounted to a veto). Two months later, the Israeli government changed its mind. The veto was lifted and Bajoulet undertook the mission and wrote a report that he later submitted at the fourth meeting of the Refugee Working Group in Oslo, Norway.

When the sixth round folded and the heads of delegations held their final press conferences, the evaluation was mixed and contradictory. Itamar Rabinovich said, 'Progress has been made in substance, and some progress has also been made on procedure.' Syria's spokesperson, Bushra Kanafani, told Egyptian radio that 'we made no progress in this round'. Palestinian spokesperson, Dr Hanan Ashrawi, was quoted as saying, 'This peace process has brought the Palestinians nothing but more suffering.' The Jordanian delegation was more reserved in its public statements. While Dr Muasher, our spokesperson, liked to tell it as it was, he was discouraged from making cynical or pessimistic categorical statements. Majali told reporters in Amman, upon his return on September 27, that both Jordan and Israel engaged in serious and business-like negotiations, and both were trying seriously to bridge gaps over the agenda.

On his way back to Amman, Majali found himself in the plane with Sheikh Abdul Mun'em Abu Zunt of the Muslim Brotherhood, member of the Jordanian Lower House of Parliament. 'Dr Majali,' said Abu Zunt, 'you come from a prominent family with a distinguished history in its service of the country. Why do you accept to meet and negotiate with the Israelis? They will never return to you anything.'

'I do that in service of the country,' said Majali, 'and I am sure we will recover all the Jordanian rights that Israel had usurped.'

'I bet they will not give you back anything they already have.'

'Okay, I am willing to bet that they will. What is the bet that you like?' asked Majali.

'A big tray of *Nabulsi Kinafeh* [a sweet dish for which the town of Nablus in the West Bank is famous] for each square kilometer of Jordanian land the Israelis will return, and likewise, for you, for each square kilometer the Israelis will not return.'

'I accept the bet,' said Majali.

Almost two years later after the signing of the Peace Treaty, Majali met Abu Zunt under the dome of the Parliament and asked him to honor that bet. Abu Zunt claimed that he meant that Majali would bring back the territories by war! That response showed the futility of trying to convince the Islamists of the utility of peacemaking with Israel.

The close of the sixth round of the bilaterals also brought together the heads of the Arab delegations to assess the reality of the situation and to consult on what to advise their respective governments. Muwaffaq Allaf, the head of the Syrian delegation, presented a gloomy picture of the state of the negotiations on their track, and expressed pessimism about future progress. 'What do we advise our governments?' Majali asked Allaf. 'Shall we advise them to have us join a next round or not?'

'Of course we should advise them to join the next round,' answered Allaf without hesitation.

'How could that be in light of your pessimistic assessment?'

'Well, maybe the Israelis will change their positions.'

On the way back to the hotel from the coordination meeting, Ambassador Shaker Arabiyyat, who had joined the Jordanian delegation, was deep in thought. 'I was thinking, in light of Allaf's attitude,' said Arabiyyat, 'of the two guys from my home town, Sult, who went to see a movie.'

'What about them?' asked Majali.

'The good guy in the movie was on a chase to get the bad guy and kill him. So this Sulti guy was excited and made a bet with his companion that the bad guy would escape when all indications were to the otherwise. Soon the good guy got the bad guy within range, shot and killed him.'

'So what is there to think about?' asked Majali. Arabiyyat explained that the Sulti guy lost the bet and paid it on their way home. He then confessed to the winner that he actually had seen the movie the day before, and saw that the bad guy was actually killed. But he thought that the stupid bad guy would have learned a lesson by the next day and would manage to escape the killing! Majali laughed.

'And this much for the Israelis changing their position,' added Arabiyyat.

# 9

# The Common Agenda

The seventh round was convened on October 21, 1992 and was interrupted for ten days because of the general and presidential elections in the United States. The first anniversary of the Madrid Conference, October 30, was fast approaching at a time when the state of negotiations on all tracks was not encouraging.

For Jordanians and Israelis, and compared to the previous rounds, the seventh round deserved the label 'most exciting'. During the first leg of this round, the Jordanian and Israeli delegations vigorously negotiated their proposals for a common agenda, consolidating the commonalities between them and working to reach common ground on other issues. It looked like the Rabin government had become certain of Jordan's determination not to negotiate for or on behalf of the Palestinians, nor would Jordan negotiate the return of any non-Jordanian occupied territories. In effect, the disengagement between Jordanian and Palestinian tracks had to take its natural course in the minds of Israeli strategists long after it had matured in the minds of the Jordanians and Palestinians themselves. Moreover, it dawned upon the Israeli government that the Syrian track of negotiations could drag on for a long time. In acknowledgment of Bush's strong support for Rabin, the Israeli government felt that it ought to support Bush by reaching a peace agreement with at least one of the Arab countries during his term in office. A breakthrough in the peace process that Bush had ushered would sure be an asset for him as he conducted an uphill campaign for his re-election, haunted by polls showing him trailing behind Bill Clinton. The Jordanian track was the one in which success seemed most plausible, as it was the most reliable track in terms of the delegates' behavior, consistency and professional, down-to-earth attitudes. In the world of politics, success on the Jordanian track was welcomed by all Israelis with the exception of a few ultra-religious groups. The Israeli government did not need to invest in any rigorous publicity campaigns to win support for its plan to make peace with Jordan.

While the Syrian–Israeli track showed signs of retraction and fatigue, the Palestinians continued to hover in metastatic analysis of the issues. The Jordanians scored a noticeable measure of success with their Israeli counterparts, but this was not particularly welcomed by the other Arab delegations as long as their own tracks were practically stagnant.

Right from the first day of the round, Rubinstein informed Majali in their one-on-one morning meeting that he had instructions from his government to accommodate the Jordanian positions and language within the limits which had been set in the previous round. Rubinstein requested in return that our delegation accommodate Israel's need to make a clear-cut reference to a treaty of peace. Majali sensed Israeli willingness to make progress and consulted with Amman on the Israeli request. The answer from Amman was positive and included, as usual, one or two cautioning remarks to guard Jordan's parametric positions and vital interests. The two delegations engaged in an intensive, business-like discussion, and it was Awn al-Khasawneh, the poet, who always sought a positive solution to all the impediments that appeared along the way in order to make the first tangible achievement in these peace negotiations. Majali made sure that the two Palestinian representatives were informed and given up-to-date information on every new development made on the Jordanian–Israeli track. In reality, the outspoken Abdul Rahman al-Hamad used to protest at the rate of potential progress and claim that certain points of Israeli–Jordanian agreements harmed Palestinian interests. Majali would heed all of al-Hamad's remarks, although most of them were unfounded and based on suspicion.

With regard to the draft agenda's Section A, the Goal, it was agreed that the text should read 'The Achievement of just, lasting and comprehensive peace between the Arab States, the Palestinians, and Israel as per the Madrid Invitation.'

Section B dealt with the bilateral issues to be resolved between Jordan and Israel. Its objective took a long time to resolve because of Rubinstein's prior insistence on the inclusion of a clear-cut reference to a peace treaty as the end point of successful negotiations. Majali and al-Khasawneh, withholding approval of that, argued that the goal of peace was clearly indicated in Resolutions 242 and 338, and the inclusion of a statement to that effect would take care of the Israeli delegation's request. Finally, both parties agreed on the following text for the first objective of Section B: 'Searching for steps to arrive at a state of peace based on Security Council Resolutions 242 and 338 in all their aspects.'

The issue of security and arms control consisted of five points. Al-Khasawneh's attempt to convince the Israelis to list refugees as a security issue did not succeed; this was because the Israeli delegation thought that Jordan would invoke the right of return as a security concern for Jordan.

The issue of refugees had to overcome a major hurdle. The Israelis wanted the bilateral talks to resolve the bilateral issues justly, as the statement in Resolution 242 had stipulated. The Jordanians wanted a just resolution of the refugee problem that did not ignore the relevant UN resolutions on refugees and displaced persons. After lengthy consultations with Professor Fragrath, a German legal expert often consulted by the Jordanians, it was agreed that a resolution of the refugee problem in accordance with international law would take care of Jordan's concerns. It was finally agreed that the text concerning refugees would read as follows: 'Achieving an agreed, just solution to the bilateral aspects of the problem of refugees and displaced persons in accordance with international law.' Paradoxically, and amusingly to some, both parties agreed on the phrase 'in accordance with international law' because each delegation understood the text to serve its own objectives. The Israelis argued that international law did not include UN resolutions, while we believed it did. By disagreeing on its interpretation, both parties agreed to the text. It was a classic case of constructive ambiguity.

While the two delegations were fully engrossed in battles of wit, they still had time for humor. Awn al-Khasawneh, a lover of poetry, had an excellent memory for it. When discussing the language of the agenda item 4 on refugees, Awn recited a line of Persian poetry, which said, no matter how long and crooked the course of the river is, it always flows into the sea. Rubinstein laughed and said, 'Yes, but even if all rivers flow to the sea they never fill it.'

On the issue of water, Haddadin and his Israeli counterparts had already an agreed-upon text for it and the item was passed without arguments. Rubinstein's comment was, 'I really do not understand how Dr Haddadin always waters down the water issues.' He further hoped that joint water projects would be worked out with similar ease.

Addressing Dr Abdullah Toukan, the arms control expert on the Jordanian side, Rubinstein said, 'Please, the word project is not derived from projectile.' Jokes were exchanged, but Rubinstein always made sure that his jokes induced relaxation; only on rare occasions did his jokes play on words and send a 'sinister' political message.

On October 26, the two delegations allowed the momentum of our cooperative spirit to push for an extraordinary effort to arrive at a language on which we mutually agreed. Two major points and other minor ones needed to be sorted out in a marathon-like, eleventh-hour session. The Israeli delegation adamantly refused any use of the words 'withdrawal' or 'occupied', and our delegation was fully cognizant of this Israeli sensitivity. The negotiation room ceased to be the cold, formal meeting place of the two opposing delegations. Most of the Jordanian and Israeli delegates withdrew to their respective delegate rooms or strolled up and down the corridors to allow blood to circulate in their numb legs. Anani, Haddadin and al-Khasawneh from our side battled with Rubinstein, Sabel, and Ben-Ari from the Israeli delegation to devise a common language for the item relating to borders and territorial matters. We were all united in the search for a positive outcome. In the end, al-Khasawneh and Haddadin insisted on a text for the item on borders that the Israelis did not readily accept. The Jordanian text read:

> Settlement of territorial matters and agreed definitive delimitation and demarcation of the international boundary between Jordan and Israel with reference to the boundary definition under the Mandate, without prejudice to the status of the territories presently under Israeli military government control. Both parties shall respect these international borders.

With Jordan's 1988 decision to disengage from the West Bank and to turn over responsibility for the West Bank to the PLO (and the Palestinian delegation to the peace process), Jordan's borders with Israel would have to fall back to the borders of Transjordan with Palestine, defined in 1922 and adjusted near Aqaba in 1946. The sensitive point to be attended to was the status of the West Bank, including Jerusalem, that was occupied from the Hashemite Kingdom in 1967. The saving clause 'without prejudice' was meant to point out that the definition of borders would not prejudice the status of those territories; in other words, the delineation of borders would not mean that the Occupied Territories became part of Israel.

At that time, we Jordanians intently refused the Israeli notion of 'secure' borders because it catered for Israel's appetite for keeping control of Arab lands under the pretext of security. There was ample evidence that the territorial requirements of security stood in the way of smooth negotiations between Syria and Israel, and would do so in the negotiations between Israel and the Palestinians.

On Tuesday, October 27, the Jordanian track was to meet in the afternoon. Majali emerged from his usual preparatory session with Rubinstein, and called Haddadin to the hallway. 'I just agreed with Rubinstein to have a small group of delegates go into the negotiations room and hammer out the remaining differences over the Common Agenda,' said Majali. 'The group is to keep negotiating until an agreement on the agenda is reached.'

'Good,' said Haddadin, 'it is just about time. Who would be the small group?'

'Rubinstein said he would head his small team that would include Robby Sabel and Ahaz Ben-Ari,' said Majali. 'They are, as you know, the legal advisors of the Foreign Ministry and the Ministry of Defense respectively. He asked me who I would bring in with me.'

Majali put on a smile and continued, 'When I told him I would accompany al-Khasawneh and Haddadin, Rubinstein raised his eyebrows and said, "Don't you have someone else other than Haddadin?" but I insisted on you. Please be as tactful as you can be.'

'Yes sir, Pasha, I will,' said Haddadin, but he felt he should respond in kind to Rubinstein's resentment of his presence inside the negotiations room.

The proposals for a Common Agenda had been going back and forth between the two delegations since the fourth round in April. Having briefed the members of the delegation, Majali headed to the negotiation room followed by Haddadin and al-Khasawneh. They found Rubinstein with his two colleagues occupying the rear right corner of the room, facing the entrance. At a right angle to their seats, Majali, Haddadin and Khasawneh occupied three seats in that order, with Majali closest to Rubinstein. The working paper was basically the Jordanian proposal for the agenda.

Section A was promptly cleared as it had been agreed upon previously. Section B had the title: 'Components of Jordan–Israel Peace negotiations', and had nine items under it. The first was searching for practical steps to arrive at a state of peace as envisioned in Security Council Resolutions 242 and 338. The second item was 'Security' which had five sub-items. The third was 'Water' and had three sub-items. The fourth was 'Refugees and Displaced Persons' with two sub-items. The fifth was 'Borders and Occupied Lands'. The sixth was 'fields of potential cooperation'. The seventh pertained to phasing the implementation and the establishment of appropriate mechanisms for negotiations. The eighth was the discussion of matters related to both tracks (Jordanian and Palestinian) to be decided upon in common, and the ninth item of Section B addressed the conclusion of a 'peace treaty', something that Majali was eager to entertain in return for Israel softening its positions. There was no third section in the draft agenda at this stage, but one would soon be snuck in.

There was a long debate over a sub-item of 'Security' that addressed weapons of mass destruction, and it was left to be revisited before the end of the negotiations session. The item on 'Water', item 3, was promptly cleared because of previous agreements. A problem erupted when the parties took on item B-5, 'Borders'. The draft, as mentioned above, contained language that defined the borders with reference to the British Mandate borders. At the end of that sub-item were the words, 'Both sides shall respect these international borders.' It was mostly a Jordanian text.

Majali looked at Haddadin and al-Khasawneh to his left with an inquisitive eye; before al-Khasawneh was able to express approval, Haddadin took the floor. 'Ambassador, I have a problem with the word "respect" in this text.'

'But it is a Jordanian text!' protested Rubinstein.

'I realize that, but I have a problem with it.'

'What is your problem?' asked Rubinstein with a resentful tone. Haddadin replied:

> I know that you have borders with Egypt that you respect, I also came to note yesterday's statement by Mr Lobrani, the Israeli head of delegation in the Lebanese track, in which he said that Israel respects its international borders with Lebanon. My problem is that, while you express your respect for those borders, your tanks are running across them every other day!

'What!' exclaimed Rubinstein,

Do you compare Lebanon with Jordan? Lebanon is run by Syria and let me tell you what the Lebanese could not do. I was there during the drafting of the famous Israeli–Lebanese accord of 17 May 1983. The Lebanese agreed to it, but they were never able to have it ratified by their President because of Syrian pressure. Lebanon cannot decide for itself. Lebanon is not a country!

Haddadin was outraged, and thought the time had come to respond to Rubinstein's resentment of his participation. 'Lebanon is as good a country as any other in the region,' he emphasized. 'We do not allow, nor do we accept to hear, statements like this said about Lebanon in our presence. Ambassador, you should apologize!' screamed Haddadin, and leaned over to Majali. 'Pasha, he had Lebanon for breakfast, and he will have Jordan for lunch,' he whispered in Majali's ear to justify his response. Majali nodded.

'Elyakim, this is going way too far,' said Majali. 'We will not allow the scratching of the sovereignty of Lebanon or the dignity of its people. You should retract what you said.'

'I am saying the truth,' Rubinstein insisted, 'and the truth cannot be masked by pretending that Lebanon today is sovereign. Pasha, Jordan is different. Jordan has leadership admired by the whole world. Please do not take offense at what I said.'

'What you said is beyond the permissible levels in any form of diplomacy. You should withdraw what you said.' Haddadin was excited that Majali had concurred with him, but concealed his happiness.

'Pasha, Dr Abdul Salam,' pleaded Rubinstein, 'for heavens sake, do no bring us back to the issue of withdrawal. We have had enough debate over withdrawal under Resolution 242. Now, please, let us get on with our business.'

'If you do not retract what you said,' insisted Majali, 'I am afraid I will not carry on with the negotiations.' After a brief silence, Majali stood up. 'I am going to the men's room,' he said, and walked out of the room. After a while he returned, not to the negotiations room, but to our delegation's room. Majali showed mixed signs of relief and worry.

'What is the matter?' Anani asked him.

'A minor problem,' replied Majali.

'Aren't you going back in?' asked al-Qadi.

'No, no,' said Majali, and continued, 'I left them with Munther throwing stones at them [*mistabeehum fi hjar*] with visible success. I will let him carry on!'

And so it was. Haddadin and al-Khasawneh played complementary roles in concluding an agreement on the Common Agenda. Haddadin acted the tough senior, while al-Khasawneh pleaded with him to be a bit more lenient at times, upon which Haddadin would accept the wording that al-Khasawneh proposed!

The last sub-item (number 9) in Section B spoke of concluding a peace treaty after agreement on the 'above items' (the other eight items contained in Section B) was reached. Al-Khasawneh held the view that the negotiations could culminate in some 'legal instrument' that would bind the two countries to the terms agreed upon. Actually, the Jordanians felt that a peace treaty should be the culmination of the peace process in its entirety, i.e., when comprehensive peace was reached. The Israelis, on the other hand, wanted a peace treaty to be the culmination of the successful negotiations between Israel and Jordan, regardless of the outcome on the other tracks.

In a sneaky move, and without being detected by anyone, Haddadin wrote the letter C over the number 9 of Section B. That move created a third section in the common agenda. Section C stated that after agreement on the above items was reached, a peace treaty would be concluded. However, 'the above items' would now include Section A – the achievement of a just, lasting and comprehensive peace, as well as the eight items of Section B. The meaning was thus altered to become that a peace treaty would be concluded only after agreement on Sections A and B was reached instead of on the items under Section B only. The Israeli delegates did not take note of this change because of the corrections made to the draft in several places.

This marathon session lasted five hours. When Haddadin started rewriting the agreed agenda to produce a clean one for typing, Rubinstein came around, and followed the writing very closely. When this was completed, Rubinstein suggested that the draft be initialed. But before this was done, Haddadin asked for Abdul Rahman al-Hamad, the Palestinian delegate on the Jordanian track, to join the group. 'Abdul Rahman,' Haddadin addressed his colleague, 'this is now the text of the Common Agenda. It differs from the draft you have in some specific few points. Please read it and inform me if you have any comments before we initial this final draft.'

Al-Hamad read the handwritten text carefully, and said: 'I only have one comment, but it does not involve Israel. It is a matter between us, Jordanians and Palestinians.'

'Shall I initial the handwritten draft? Do you have any objection?' Haddadin asked.

'No, no. It is a bilateral matter between us, and it can be resolved,' Al-Hamad said.

The door of the room was opened, a sign of the completion of the session. Majali entered with the rest of the delegation. He read the text, consulted with both Haddadin and al-Khasawneh, and was clearly very pleased.

The handwritten text was initialed and sent to be photocopied. Haddadin kept two copies including the original, and Rubinstein got two copies. It was after 9:00 p.m. by then, and the press was waiting for the usual briefing by the heads of delegations. Majali headed towards the C-Street entrance, followed by the rest of us. Haddadin stayed behind to talk to al-Hamad. He took him into the Palestinian section of the joint delegation room. 'What is it that bothered you in the Common Agenda?' Haddadin asked.

'Oh, nothing, it is just item B-4 "Refugees and Displaced Persons"' said al-Hamad.

Haddadin understood the dilemma, and assured Al-Hamad that the item, as it read, called for resolution of the *bilateral aspects* of the problem of refugees and displaced persons in accordance with international law. 'We will only negotiate the bilateral aspects,' remarked Haddadin. 'Besides, you have had this text since last April, six months ago. Why haven't you raised a single question since then? Is this now the proper time to raise questions – six months later?'

'Why should Jordan negotiate for the refugees and displaced persons?'

'The bilateral aspects refer to the refugees in Jordan, and as you well know they all carry Jordanian citizenship. If Jordan did not speak for them, who do you think would?'

'The PLO,' replied al-Hamad.

That was the bottom line! Haddadin was deeply disappointed.

I agree with you but only with one condition. You and I would go door-to-door knocking in all the refugee camps in Jordan to ask them whom they want as their representative. Those who choose the PLO to speak on their behalf are entitled to their choice. You will have to buy them and their families one-way tickets to Tunis, where the PLO resides. And what you have just heard, you can relate.

So Majali had his great moment. Finally, a breakthrough had been achieved under his leadership before the first anniversary of the Madrid Conference dawned. His briefing to the press betrayed his pleasure despite his attempts to conceal the achievement. The governments in Jordan and Israel had to be informed, and their approval of the text of the Common Agenda had to be secured.

Back at the presidential suite that Majali occupied at the Willard, activity was intense that evening. People were on the phone, others drafting reports, and Anani took it upon himself to draft the daily report to the government. For the first time since negotiations began, the report to Jordan commended persons in particular. It commended Haddadin and al-Khasawneh for their efforts in concluding the agreement on the Common Agenda. Inserting recognition of Haddadin and Al-Khasawneh did not appeal to the rest of the members of the delegation. Some thought, rightfully, that it was not within the norms of reporting, and recommended it be taken out. Majali overruled, and the cable was sent about midnight. At the end of the report, Majali put a question to the Prime Minister in Amman: 'In our press conference to break the news of the agreement on the Agenda tomorrow, what is your instruction? Shall we play it with a low, medium or high pitch?' There was no question in Majali's mind as to the need to break the news before October 30, the Madrid Conference anniversary; the question was how to present the news in the absence of similar progress on the other tracks of negotiations.

Majali got busy with Marwan Muasher, our delegation's spokesperson, on making arrangements to break the news in a joint press conference where Majali, Rubinstein and Djerejian, the US Assistant Secretary of State, would jointly appear. Majali asked Muasher to organize and work out the details of that press conference. After midnight, when the delegates were gone from Majali's suite except for Haddadin and Marea, Haddadin looked at Majali and wondered aloud: 'Don't you think, Pasha, that our public in Jordan should hear the news from our own media, and not through the international press? I say so in particular because we have Jordanian press correspondents accompanying the delegation.' Majali looked at Haddadin with a big smile and nodded.

On the way to his room, Haddadin came across Caroline Faraj in the hallway. She was the correspondent of the wide circulation Jordanian paper, *Al-Rai*. He handed her a copy of the handwritten Common Agenda at about 1:00 a.m. Wednesday morning, and asked her to keep it until further instructions. Haddadin passed by the room of the correspondent of Petra, the Jordan News Agency, and left him a similar copy under his door at that late hour after midnight, and retired for the day.

The next track meeting was scheduled at 4:00 p.m. the following day, Wednesday. At about 10:00 a.m., Marwan Muasher came into Majali's suite with disturbing news from the region. Israel had been shelling and bombarding towns in South Lebanon and the mood in the region was one of anger. For how dare the Israelis commit such atrocities while, at the same time, negotiating peace with the Arabs including Lebanon. Muasher was of the opinion that a press conference of the type Majali was proposing would not be in Jordan's best interests in light of these developments, especially as no progress had been achieved on any of the other Arab negotiations tracks. We all debated the subject but reached no conclusion. It sounded like Majali was eager to break the news of the Common Agenda despite the deterioration in the region, at least through his regular briefing of the press after the track session. The mood in the delegation was not easy. Haddadin called the Jordanian press correspondents to whom he had given a copy of the Common Agenda and instructed them to freeze everything until they received a call from Muasher or himself from inside the State Department during the track meeting.

We were getting ready to depart to the State Department for the track meeting at 4:00 p.m. By 3:30 there was no news from Amman, which was unusual. Haddadin went to Majali's suite to follow up on the matter. '*Sidi*,' he said, 'we have received no response from the Prime Minister in Amman to our cable of last night. It is important that we get his approval of the announcement to be made about the Common Agenda.'

'I know, but what could we do more?'

'Pick up the phone, please, pick up the phone and call the Prime Minister. It is now 3:35 p.m. here, or 8:35 a.m. in Amman.'

'I do not know what to make out of this. I tried to call the Prime Minister earlier and he would not take the call. Now he has not yet answered a very important cable we sent him last night. What should I do?'

'Please try, Pasha, please try.'

Majali walked over to the telephone in his bedroom, dialed a number, stayed on the phone for a short while, and then came back with a solemn face.

'What is it?' Haddadin asked.

'They approved the Common Agenda, but he does not want us to disclose the agreement to the press.'

'Very strange indeed, but why?' Haddadin wondered.

'I do not know. Let us go, we are a bit late.'

The motorcade left for the State Department. Haddadin used Muasher's mobile phone and called Caroline Faraj to confirm that the Common Agenda was not to be released under any circumstance, and he did the same to the Petra correspondent. In the track meeting, the two parties reviewed the Common Agenda, now typed in neat form, and made sure it coincided with the handwritten one. The meeting approved it and mutually agreed not to leak a work about it to the press. The Jordanians were suspicious of the Israeli media to which all the Israeli delegation news was frequently leaked.

Early Thursday morning, Majali was awakened by a call from Kamel Abu Jaber, the Minister of Foreign Affairs. Abu Jaber was upset as he told Majali that the Common Agenda, over which no word was to be leaked, was published in full in the *Jordan Times*, and was translated and published by *Al-Rai* newspaper. Majali was surprised that such a thing could happen despite the commitments made in the negotiations room the day before. Haddadin had already left for a meeting in Virginia on the environment to which he'd been invited by USAID. He returned around 5:30 p.m. to find the atmosphere at the Willard tense and unhealthy. 'What the hell is going on?' Haddadin asked Quosous.

'The *Al-Rai* correspondent is barred from entering any of the floors where delegation members reside. She betrayed us, she got hold of the Common Agenda and had it published in *Al-Rai* newspaper. Amman is very upset, and Majali is recalled to Amman for consultation. I am fixing his plane reservations now.'

Haddadin hurried to Majali's suite, and asked him for a word alone. 'I am sorry I was away all day at a meeting on the environment. I feel most sorry to have heard just now what has happened.'

'The press did it for journalistic interests, not considering the interest of the country. We are embarrassed in front of the Israelis, and we are more embarrassed in front of our own Prime Minister. I wonder who gave Caroline a copy of the Common Agenda.'

'I certainly did shortly after I brought up the subject with you Tuesday evening, Pasha,' replied Haddadin.

I am sorry I was not here in the early morning to tell everyone that. I did it in good faith so that, as I told you, our people would hear the news not from the international press, but from our own media. This is a Jordanian day for the Jordanian press that has accompanied us for seven long rounds of negotiations. But I told Caroline in person, with no ambiguous terms, that she had to freeze processing of the news until further notice, and I told her later by a phone call that not a word should be mentioned about the Common Agenda. I am surprised she violated the trust that she has always been worthy of. The Petra correspondent apparently abided.

'This is what is at hand; the mood of our superiors in Amman is not good. I am to report to them immediately,' Majali said.

'I am sorry again to be behind this embarrassment. Please tell Amman the details that I just told you. I will look for Caroline and find out what the heck happened.' It did not take a long time to locate Caroline Faraj. Haddadin took her and a friend of hers to dinner, calmed her fears and asked her what had happened.

'Aktham Quosous interrogated me and insisted to know where I got the copy of the Common Agenda. I refused to disclose my sources. I have not told anyone, and I am under no obligation to do so,' Caroline said.

'I am your source so you do not have to be suspicious of me. I also disclosed your source to Dr Majali an hour ago. Now everyone knows. Just tell me, what happened. I told you not to process anything. What happened?'

Caroline, with an apologetic tone,

Well, you gave me the copy at about 1:00 a.m. Wednesday morning. It was about 8:00 a.m. Wednesday morning Amman time. I faxed it from my room immediately to the Chairman of the Board, the Editor-in-Chief in Amman. He was very happy. Then I contacted him at 2:00 p.m. that same day, or 9:00 p.m. his time, and told him to freeze the processing until further notice like you asked me to. He said he was willing to wait until 11:00 p.m. his time before the press closes on the issue of the following day. When I called him two hours later to tell him of your instruction banning any publication, he said to tell you that he was nowhere to be found. He went ahead and published the Common Agenda. This is what happened.

'We cannot do much about it. It is done. It is irresponsible of your boss to embarrass us like that. You have a lot of fences to mend with the delegation,' Haddadin said.

The publication of the Common Agenda was a big surprise to all. Most surprised was Fayez Tarawneh who was in Paris heading the Jordanian delegation to the meeting of the multilateral group, REDWG. As he came out of the meeting for a recess, the press was waiting for him. 'Dr Tarawneh, how did you come to agreement with the Israelis on the Common Agenda?' Tarawneh was able to make out the question amidst a confusing shower of words.

'What Common Agenda? What agreement?' Tarawneh responded.

'Sir, it has been published, Jordan and Israel agreed to a Common Agenda for negotiations,' said a correspondent.

'Really? Seriously?' asked the bewildered Tarawneh, who was supposed to be the deputy to Majali; another embarrassing situation indeed.

Rubinstein was very unhappy. While he denied any substantial progress with the Jordanians, *Al-Rai* newspaper carried the news to the contrary, and the Israeli press was up in arms because they were denied an equal opportunity. On the morning of October 29 in Washington, the Israeli delegation received both the good news that the Israeli Cabinet had approved the draft agenda, and the bad news that the Jordanian newspapers had published the complete draft in English, as well as its unofficial translation in Arabic. Rubinstein strongly hoped that the Jordanian government would approve it, as the Israeli government would give grave consideration to any lack of action on the part of the Jordanians. When Rubinstein and his colleagues returned home that day, their pleasure had been reduced to symbolic gestures.

The publication of the agenda invited a great deal of criticism from the PLO and the political opposition inside Jordan. Tayyeb Abdul Raheem, the Palestinian Ambassador to Jordan, forwarded a worrisome message to the Jordanian authorities from Chairman Arafat, which he orally and hurriedly delivered to Kamel Abu Jaber, Jordan's foreign minister. The Palestinian opposition to the draft agenda rested on four main points. The first was that Jordan should not move that fast in negotiations with Israel because that would hurt Palestinian chances of achieving progress. The second point was that the Palestinians were worried about their rightful share of water in the Jordan River basin. The third point concerned their objection to Jordan's negotiation of the issue of refugees and displaced persons since these issues were the direct responsibility of the PLO in accordance with the Arab Summit Conference decision of 1974 acknowledging the PLO as the sole legitimate representative of the Palestinian people. Even if that notion did not apply to the refugees in Jordan on the grounds that they all held Jordanian citizenship, any settlement of the bilateral issues concerning those refugees in Jordan would undoubtedly prejudice the outcome of negotiations over the other refugees outside Jordan when the PLO took on the issue in the Final Status negotiations with Israel. The fourth point was the language of the saving clause in item B, on borders and territorial matters, which read: 'without prejudice to the status of the territories presently under Israeli military government control'. According to the Palestinians, this clause handed East Jerusalem to the Israelis who had annexed Jerusalem officially in 1967 and did not consider it as falling within the 'territories presently under Israeli military control'.

Dr Majali, who returned to Jordan on October 31 after receiving a fax from Amman inquiring about these Palestinian positions, did not agree with any of the four points. According to him, the Jordanians were not in a hurry in their negotiations with Israel, and the Palestinians' surprise at the progress was not justified because they always had two delegates actively observing and occasionally participating in Jordanian–Israeli negotiations. Moreover, the Palestinian delegation was handed early copies of all documents exchanged between Jordanian and Israeli delegates. 'What has been achieved is more than a list of items, but it is not a peace agreement. Negotiations usually start with an agenda. It is only now that we will begin negotiations on substance,' Dr Majali told Haider Abdul Shafi before departing Amman.

On the other points, the Jordanian government agreed with its delegation that the issues of water and refugees were purely Jordanian concerns, as Jordan would negotiate the bilateral nature of these two items as clearly stipulated in the Common Agenda. However, some Cabinet ministers agreed with the PLO's need to change the saving clause of the item on borders in a way that would preclude even the remotest notion that Jordan would enter into any understanding which would give Israel a better bargaining position on Jerusalem. The *Jordan Times* reporter Ayman al-Safadi, in the November 8, 1992, issue, reported the reaction of the Muslim Brotherhood bloc in the Jordanian Parliament. Safadi wrote: 'In a strongly-worded statement against what it called "the Jordanian–Israeli agreement", the parliamentary office of the bloc said the informal draft agreement reached by Jordanian and Israeli negotiators in Washington on October 27 bodes ill for our national unity and inter-Arab relations.' The bloc's statement refused the draft agenda, calling it purposefully 'an agreement to surrender Arab rights in Palestine, squander the rights of Palestinian refugees and help realize the Zionist dream'. These statements by the Muslim Brotherhood parliamentary bloc were made while leading Palestinian leaders were reviewing the text with the Jordanian government. On November 8, Jordanian Prime Minister Zaid Ibn Shaker received a Palestinian delegation consisting of Yasser Abed Rabbo, Yasser Amro, Suleiman Najjab and Faisal al-Husseini. The meeting was the seal of a series of earlier meetings that had taken the draft agenda to task, going over every detail.

The Common Agenda crisis in Amman coincided with yet another crisis that the government had to face. It was the trial of two deputies in the Parliament who had been held in custody on charges of involvement with underground organizations that practised violence to achieve their goals. According to the Ministry of Interior, elected member Yacoub Qarrash, originally from the West Bank, 'was arrested for his involvement in leading the group calling itself the Shabab al-Nafier [Clarion Call Youth], which was found to possess weapons and explosives'. After a few days, another elected member, Laith Shbeilat, was arrested and charged with allowing his car to be used for transporting explosives. Shbeilat was the most outspoken critic of the government in the Parliament. He had led a heated debate in the Parliament on corruption charges against a former Prime Minister and two of his ministers. The trial of Shabab al-Nafier or the Clarion Call Youth had captured Jordanian public interest to a level comparable with the O.J. Simpson trial in the United States. When the draft agenda news broke out in November, the trial was in its final stages and the verdict was to be taken by the three-man military tribunal that usually handled similar cases. The eruption of the news regarding the draft agenda put the government between a rock and a hard place, especially because there were some gross errors in the translation. It was easier for the Jordanian government, at the time, to suspend approval of the agenda in the light of the opposition to it coming from the PLO and the political opposition. Majali's efforts to convince the government to have it approved fell on deaf ears.

Majali was dismayed that the government did not opt to endorse the Common Agenda that the Jordanian delegation had labored to conclude. He particularly felt the lack of support for his leadership of the delegation as the government allowed others to second-guess him. 'While we fight the battle of peace,' Majali thought, 'our backs are vulnerable and the government is lending ears to the PLO and is mindful of the domestic political opposition.' It was then that he contemplated resignation because he thought that the effort that he and the delegation had exerted was being squandered at the political convenience of those who did not appreciate it.

When the second leg of the seventh round resumed on November 9, Majali was still making every effort in Amman to have the Common Agenda endorsed. Without such endorsement, the delegation could hardly conduct productive negotiations, and it would be in an awkward position. Majali asked Tarawneh, his deputy apparent, to lead the delegation in his absence. Tarawneh did not find it difficult to conduct the talks as he was strongly supported by his colleagues.

The outcome of Majali's struggle for approval of the Common Agenda culminated in a precondition made by the government to please the PLO emissaries. The precondition was to amend the language of the saving clause in the item of borders and territorial matters. The text that read 'without prejudice to the territories presently under Israeli military control', should be amended to read 'without prejudice to the status of any territories that came under Israeli Military Government control in 1967'. When Majali arrived a few days after the second leg started, he explained all the circumstances that had led to the delay in the

Jordanian government's approval of the agenda. Majali, however, thought that the clause as originally agreed better served the Palestinian interest because he thought that all territories over which Israel exercised control beyond the legitimate boundaries delineated in the partition Resolution 181 of 1947 were, in fact, territories under Israeli military control, and not merely the West Bank territories only.

Rubinstein was deeply unhappy because he considered both parties to have worked out a magnificent peace negotiations document. Furthermore, he believed that the peace treaty concept included in the draft agenda was a precious gain that was similar, but not equal to, Israel's success in arriving at peace accords with Egypt 13 years earlier when Rubinstein served as a young and promising negotiator. However, it escaped Rubinstein that the treaty provision, contained in Section C of the agenda, was conditioned upon achieving the other two of its sections, the first of which was achieving comprehensive peace. 'You know, Pasha, our government has approved the Common Agenda,' said Rubinstein to Majali. 'I want to admit now that the Jordanian text is stronger than the requested amendment of the saving clause. I will support the amendment because it will pull me out of a deep hole dug by the original text, the issue of legitimacy and military occupation.'

'Then there will be no problem,' remarked Majali.

'In the meantime,' said Rubinstein, 'I do not think it pays to engage in a language battle, nor would it change the current status. It will take a decision of our government to accept the amendment, and I think that will be forthcoming.'

The two sides agreed, instead, to break into non-official expert groups to continue the discussion on a range of bilateral issues such as security, water, environment, energy, economic cooperation and the reopening of Jordanian banks in the West Bank. This last issue was enjoying fast progress, but the Israeli side, which still felt bitter about Jordan's failure to approve the Common Agenda, was not willing to end negotiation on any topic with positive conclusions.

The morale of Dr Majali and his colleagues was low as they felt that, although they had been doing a good job, reporting to Amman regularly, and receiving instructions, the result of their work was subject to second-guessing by the PLO and to the whims of political opposition at home. The conversations of the delegation gave way to sighs of bewilderment, the jokes had become old and stale, and the card games, which Majali enjoyed as much as watching wrestling games on television, had become frustrating, time-killing exercises, rather than a pleasurable pastime. News from home about the vicious attack on the delegation and its head on account of the Common Agenda added to their deep-felt agony, especially when no government officials made a statement in defense of the delegation. Actually, in a hideous way, the government was happy that the delegation was the target of the anti-peace movement smear campaign. Their spirits were lifted only when the King stepped in and sent a public message to Majali full of appreciation and praise for Majali and his colleagues in the peace delegation. The King's message commended the honorable soldiers of peace, praised their ethical and moral qualities, and expressed great appreciation for their powerful performance in the negotiations. He bestowed on Majali the Renaissance Medal, usually given to Prime Ministers. Anani was asked to draft an answer on behalf of the delegation to the King, *Sayyedna*. The emotionally charged letter was an honest expression of Majali's feelings, and those of his colleagues. Majali's greatest gratification stemmed from the implicit suggestion that he could be a prospective Prime Minister although he was at the time careful not to divulge this to anyone. It was Anani, the veteran minister who had served under four previous prime ministers, who picked up the royal hint.

Anani brought Majali the final, edited letter to the King for his signature. Majali signed it almost without looking at its content and whispered his thanks. Anani told him that he should have read the letter before signing it because it did not include any special thanks to the King for nominating Majali to serve as the next prime minister of Jordan! Taken by surprise, Majali's immediate response was to throw one of the cushions at Anani, a reaction that betrayed his deep pleasure at finding someone who could speak his language and read his mind, and to whom he could confide his inner thoughts. Majali and Anani, with the former talking and the latter interrupting, stayed up until 5:00 a.m. talking about the things that a Majali government would do and ought to do, provided, of course, that they had not overread the royal letter.

In the United States, the young presidential candidate, Bill Clinton, defeated the incumbent, George Bush, who was once thought set to win a second term in office. Worries harbored by the Arab delegations about a possible erosion of interest on the part of the United

States in moving the peace process along proved to be without foundation. The President-elect soon confirmed his interest in supporting the process. In the November 10 issue of the *Boston Globe*, Pam Constable wrote an analysis of the US presidential transition on Middle East peace negotiations. She quoted William Quant as saying, referring to the outgoing administration: 'There will be an inevitable lame-duck quality to anything this Administration proposes. Baker would not have much arm-twisting capability.'

Yet, a lesson was learned. The events in South Lebanon and inside the Occupied Territories intensified the frequency and degree of violence and counter-violence, and all of these setbacks poisoned the negotiations atmosphere. Men of influence in pushing the negotiations forward like Secretary Baker, or in deterring them like Prime Minister Shamir, come and go. Success and failure in negotiations respectively generate optimism and pessimism. But, in the final analysis, peacemaking succeeds in maintaining itself as an ongoing process – irreversible and determined on its path until it achieves its goal.

Shortly after his arrival in Amman with the rest of his colleagues, Haddadin was called by Dr Abu Jaber, the Minister of Foreign Affairs. 'I asked to see you, Dr Munther,' said Abu Jaber, 'to ask you who you recommend to replace you in the delegation. I am sorry to have to do that, but it is [others] that are to be blamed for this.'

'Please do not feel bad about it. I am but a soldier in service of my country in these difficult times. You tell me to get in, I abide, and you command me to get out, I abide too, without asking questions.'

'I am really sorry,' said Abu Jaber, 'because you are one of the most efficient and effective members of the delegation. By the way, you will stay as head of the Jordan delegation to the Water Resources Working Group at the multilateral talks.'

Haddadin nominated Omar Abdallah Dokhgan, a Jordanian who knew the details of the conflict with Israel inside out.

It turned out that the Jordanian government was embarrassed by the publication of the Common Agenda on account of the dissatisfaction of the PLO. Haddadin was blamed for it and was therefore asked to step down from the delegation. He promptly wrote a detailed report to Majali on the status of the progress of his share of the negotiations with Israel, and outlined the Jordan position on water and the basis on which that position was taken. Majali was pleased with the report and bid his delegate farewell.

The Council of Ministers formed the delegation for the eighth round of negotiations as it had for each of the preceding rounds. Dokhgan and Mohammad Saleh Keilani, a former water minister, replaced Haddadin on the delegation. The eighth round started on December 7 and ended on December 17, 1992 without substantive negotiations. The round was effectively aborted by the deportation of some 418 Palestinian activists to Marj al-Zuhour in Southern Lebanon. The folding of the round coincided with the break for the Christmas and New Year holidays and was also convenient in the sense that not until January 20 of the following month would the new US administration be instated. Haddadin was at the airport to receive his daughter, Sumaya, who was coming home for Christmas when the delegation arrived on the same flight on 20 December, 1992. He met with Dokhgan and the other delegates, and received a short briefing on their activities in Washington. They said it was not much to speak of in practical terms.

The Common Agenda, however, was the subject of subsequent deliberations to remove from it any ambiguity related to Jerusalem. The saving clause, i.e., the no prejudice provision in item 5 addressing the borders, would be applied to Jerusalem as part of the Occupied Territories. The official initialing of the Common Agenda awaited progress on the Palestinian track, such progress surprising the world from Oslo in early September, 1993. The PLO–Israel Accord was arrived at through secret negotiations outside the format of the peace process. The Oslo Accord was signed between the PLO and Israel on the White House lawn on September 13, 1993, and the Common Agenda for the Jordanian–Israeli track of negotiations was initialed in the US State Department on September 14, 1993 (see Appendix 3).

# 10

## More PLO Involvement

How could rational, negotiating adversaries agree to resolve a paradoxical situation if they continued to operate in vicious circles? What Palestinians call their basic right to resist foreign occupation, the Israelis would label as terrorism. What the Israelis describe as security measures taken to ward off terrorism, the Palestinians stigmatize as abuses of human rights. This circular futility became an issue of urgency in a period of violence that marred the peace process during the months of bilateral rounds of negotiation. In a way, the negotiating process was frustrated by violence on the ground that Israel said was masterminded by the Islamic movement which believed that fighting was the only solution to the whole Palestinian question and the Arab–Israeli conflict. Hamas and al-Jihad al-Islami movements had been relatively incognito as resistance forces, especially when compared with the PLO factions of the sixties and the seventies. Moreover, Hizbollah, the Iran-backed guerilla movement in South Lebanon, constituted a major security concern to Israel and a threat to its northern settlements. Hizbollah resumed shelling of northern Israel from mobile bases in Southern Lebanon in November 1992 after almost a three-year lull. The paramilitary activities of these resistance movements pushed the new Labor government in Israel against the wall. The Israeli opposition was critical of the rise in Israeli casualties and the re-emergence of 'terrorism' in the Occupied Territories. The Labor government had to counteract the activities of those resistance movements through stringent security measures.

Leading Palestinian participants in the peace process like Haider Abdul Shafi, Faisal al-Husseini, Hanan Ashrawi, Saeb Ereikat and other personalities saw a chance to force the hand of the outgoing US administration of President Bush. They insisted that their participation in the eighth round scheduled for December 7–17, 1992, hinged on the approval by Israel of certain Palestinian demands, and they requested US leverage to have Israel respond favorably. These demands were, reportedly, as follows:

The US should commit itself to securing an Israeli pledge to respect the human rights for Palestinians in the Occupied Territories; the US should reaffirm the right of the Palestinian people to exercise authority with full jurisdiction over the Occupied Territories, including East Jerusalem, and secure Israeli commitment to respect this Palestinian right during the interim phase; the US should ensure that Israel produce new ideas other than those presented during the last round of negotiations; and the US should pledge to transform its promises into action.

Looking closely at those four direct demands of the US, or derived demands of Israel, one could see the Palestinians' deep agony. However, Majali and Anani thought that the Palestinian delegation aimed through the demands to lure both the US and the Rabin government into dealing directly with the PLO.

However, Rabin's determination to make peace was handicapped by a few Palestinian factors. On the one hand, he had a hot potato in his hand that he needed somehow to dispense with. It was the Israeli law that prohibited Israelis from talking to the PLO; on the other, and with the premise that the Palestinian–Israeli track succeeded in arriving at mutually accepted arrangements, who would sign that agreement? What authority and legitimacy, if any, did the Palestinian delegation have? Would Dr Abdul Shafi sign an agreement with Israel, and what commitment could he deliver on? These factors were springing up in the minds of the American officials as well. Rabin had to do something to allow contacts with the PLO. He first had to deal with the Israeli law that prohibited Israeli talk with the PLO.

To demonstrate the seriousness of their position, the Palestinians sent only four delegates to the eighth round, putting an end to any hopes by the outgoing administration of achieving some tangible results in the peace process before its term ended in January of 1993. Meanwhile, the Jordanian government saw fit to refrain from pursuing any progress in the negotiations with Israel and to slow down the pace of negotiations until the Palestinians and the Israelis achieved similar progress. On the other side, on December 6, Rabin made an optimistic statement that Reuters carried. Rabin said: 'I am convinced that in 1993 an agreement will be reached, if not with all the delegations, with some of them.' If the wording 'some of them' was carefully used, Rabin was actually sending a clear hint that he meant the Palestinians in particular. When the eighth round opened in Washington, Hanan Ashrawi suggested in a public statement that the United States could work out 'three-way trilateral discussions to overcome some of the basic obstacles'. The Palestinians thus were inviting the US actively to participate in their track with Israel. However, Yossi Gal, the Israeli spokesperson, refused the direct participation of any of the sponsors, claiming that 'once a third party steps in, then all the rules of the game are changed'. To him, the best route, that had no alternative, was to hold face-to-face bilateral negotiations.

On Monday, December 7, when the eighth bilateral round of negotiations started as usual at the US State Department, three Israeli soldiers were killed by Hamas activists near Gaza, and, in retribution, Israel sealed Gaza off and prevented Palestinian workers from crossing to Israel. The four Arab delegations to the bilaterals decided to impose a one-day suspension of negotiations on Wednesday, December 9, in remembrance of the Intifada's fifth anniversary. That decision angered both the United States and Israel. 'We regret this decision,' said Richard Boucher, the State Department's spokesperson. 'In our view,' he continued, 'no opportunity should be lost in the engagement of the parties to advance the Arab–Israeli peace talks.' Israeli delegations to the negotiations with Syria and Lebanon were not informed of the Wednesday suspension of talks directly by their counterparts, but indirectly through US officials.

By the third day of the eighth round, it became very obvious that the Israelis wanted to remove the United States and Russia from the negotiations, while the Palestinians wanted a more active US inter-mediation role. These differences of opinion were strongly reflected in a press conference held by Nabil Sha'ath, the prominent PLO executive, who was not a participant in the face-to-face negotiations as per the rules agreed upon, but accompanied the Palestinian delegation and was overtly overseeing the negotiations without any protest by the Israeli delegation or Embassy. On December 9, both Reuters and the *Washington Post* quoted Sha'ath advocating the involvement of the peace sponsor:

> All the ambiguity that was built in the peace process needed impasse-breakers . . . The absence of the American role as a real sponsor should not be underrated because the peace process was built around that sponsorship . . . Unfortunately, the sponsor, since

Mr Baker got out, was doing nothing but patting people on the back and saying – keep on, keep on, keep on.

Meanwhile, some voices, low but sensible, were questioning the virtue of Israel's policy not to talk directly to the PLO. In an article published in the *Christian Science Monitor* on Friday, December 11, Alon Ben-Meir argued in favor of direct Israeli–PLO talks:

> The advent of the Labor government in Israel and a new administration in Washington offers new opportunities for major developments, if not a breakthrough, in the Arab–Israeli peace process. Prime Minister Yitzhak Rabin, who promised to abolish the law that made it illegal for Israelis to talk to PLO members, should apply the same commitment to his own government. It is an illusion to think that the PLO has been, or can be, excluded in the future from representing the Palestinians.

One event soon led to another. On December 13, an Israeli policeman named Nissim Toledano was kidnapped in Israel. The Izziddin al-Qassam military wing of the Islamic resistance movement Hamas declared its responsibility for the kidnapping and demanded that Israel release the long-jailed spiritual leader of Hamas, Sheikh Ahmad Yassin, in return for Toledano's safe return. Otherwise, Toledano would be killed in the evening of that same day. The reason for this swift action and short notice was to deny Israeli any chance of mounting a rescue operation. Rabin had his worst security nightmare. He responded with a relatively conciliatory note to the kidnappers while stressing that their aim to abort the peace negotiations would not be realized. Rabin said, 'Not stones nor petrol bombs nor gunshots will deter me from continuing peace negotiations . . . As was already publicized, we requested a sign that Toledano is living as a condition for dialogue with them [the kidnappers], and I stress dialogue.' Mohammad Nazzal, a spokesperson for Hamas in Jordan, declared that Hamas would be willing to talk if there was willingness to free Sheikh Yassin.

The ripple effect of the kidnapping reached Washington. In unusually strong language, Elyakim Rubinstein condemned the kidnapping and called upon the Palestinian delegation to push ahead with negotiations. On December 14, Reuters quoted Rubinstein as saying, 'there are those fanatics, those crazies, those murderers, those assassins who have just blood on their minds and they are continuing their efforts to bring destruction to their people . . . The main point is to encounter this by negotiating, by making progress. The peace process is there. It must be there for our sake and for everybody's sake.' Rubinstein asked the Palestinian delegation to denounce the kidnapping. Both Majali and Ereikat denounced violence and the killing of innocent people and insisted that the best response was to stop stalling and foot-dragging and to make progress in the resolution of substantive issues through the negotiations. Majali said, 'Jordan would never condone violence. We in Jordan had our ambassadors killed, borders closed, officials shot at . . . We also know that violence is a product of despair. Let us work to give people hope by achieving real progress.'

Meanwhile, King Hussein paid a visit to the White House on Wednesday, December 11, where his brains were picked over ways to bolster the faltering peace negotiations. The King assessed the negotiations on the Jordanian track as 'slow but steady' without making commitments as to the time when he would meet with Rabin or the date when the Jordan government would approve the Common Agenda. At the same time, President Hafez al-Assad of Syria was marking the first anniversary of the start of the resumption of the bilateral talks by stressing a 'do not be in a hurry' theme. On December 15, Reuters reported President al-Assad's interview with *Time Magazine*. In that interview, President al-Assad responded to a question regarding the need for him and Rabin to meet. President Al-Assad said, 'we are enemies who have been fighting for more than 40 years. We have a mound of martyrs, blood and devastated wealth and possessions. There are lands occupied and millions of refugees . . . In the shadow of that, do you think there can be any human attraction in such a meeting?' Surprisingly enough, the same Reuters report quoted Shimon Peres, Israel's Foreign Minister, as saying on another subject: 'We reject him, yes, because of a man who gave orders to kill 22 children at school; in our memory we shall never forget.' The man who was rejected by Peres was Yassir Arafat. Peres made the statement during a meeting with five advocates of the Camp David Accord and top members of Egypt's intellectual elite who argued for the need to create direct dialogue between Israel and the PLO.

Chairman Arafat, on the other hand, was reported to be pointing his finger at Syria, with which his PLO had deep rifts since 1982. Some of Arafat's close aides believed that Syria, which harbored splinter PLO organizations opposed to peace, was also encouraging Hamas to mount violent acts against Israelis in an effort to defame the PLO which had failed to score on the peace front.

By the end of the second week of negotiations, Nissim Toledano was killed by his kidnappers. His death presented Rabin with an opportunity to act swiftly and on a scale that would convince the Israeli public that he was a man with an 'iron fist'. The Israeli Cabinet met and decided to deport 418 Hamas and Jihad activists to a strip north of the Israeli-claimed security zone in South Lebanon. The area was devoid of any Lebanese presence. Jordan had alerted Israel that it would not receive Palestinian deportees any more. On December 17, after it had been corroborated by the Israel's Supreme Court, the 418 people were deported to a place called Marj al-Zuhour (the flower range), which gained international fame. The language of the deportation decision was crafted in a way that did not make it possible for the Israeli Supreme Court to reject it as it had done on similar occasions during the Shamir government. The decision was taken in the light of the declared state of emergency to preserve the safety of the Israeli public and of its land. The decision also stated that, 'temporary removal will not exceed two years', and that, 'whoever is to be removed in this manner will be eligible within 60 days to appeal'. The words 'emergency', 'temporary' and 'appeal' helped a great deal in giving the decision a cloak of legitimacy which the Israeli Supreme Court could not refuse. Compared to the inability of his predecessor and of the Likud government to deport 11 Palestinians, Rabin's move gave him the popular support and the toughness certificate he needed to take the other important measure for peace.

The deportation decision, made on December 15, was the subject of immediate condemnation throughout the Arab world and in Washington. Rabin justified the act by his need 'to do it in quantity, in time, and quickly'. President-elect Bill Clinton expressed his understanding of Israel's frustration and outrage over the killing of the Israeli policeman, but said, 'I am concerned that this deportation may go too far and imperil the peace talks.' In the December 18 issue of the *New York Times*, Thomas Friedman wrote, 'Mr. Clinton's statements were consistent with the policy of the Bush administration, which also condemned the deportations.'

Arab delegates, angered by the Israeli government's decision, decided to boycott the December 16 bilateral sessions. However, on the same day, President Bush had already scheduled separate meetings with all five delegations to push the peace process forward and to bid farewell to the negotiators. Only four Presidential invitations were sent at the beginning of the eighth round, and one of them was forwarded to the joint Jordanian-Palestinian delegation. According to the invitation, each delegation would send four of its delegates to the meeting with the President, and the joint Jordanian-Palestinian delegation was treated as one delegation. Majali resented that treatment and informed Ed Djerejian of the State Department that he would not attend unless the White House invitation included four Jordanians and four Palestinians, each in parity with the other delegations. At the White House, Secretary Baker had initially refused the idea of having the President meet separately with the Palestinians and with the Jordanians. However, after the King's visit with President Bush, the White House arranged to hold a joint meeting with an eight-man joint Jordanian-Palestinian delegation for one hour, to be followed immediately by a 30-minute meeting with the Jordanian delegation alone. During the meetings, most of the discussion focused on the deportation of the Hamas and Jihad activists to Marj al-Zuhour.

'Mr President,' said Majali, 'I cannot understand how the Israeli government deports "418 terrorists" to Lebanon where it claims terrorism thrives, when we know that Hamas, to which these deportees supposedly belong, was initiated by Israel.'

President Bush looked at James Baker and asked him, 'Is that true?'

'Yes, Mr President.'

'Where are they financed?'

'From Muslim countries, primarily Saudi Arabia, through official and non-official sources. The official sources have stopped, and the non-official sources are on their way to stop,' answered Baker. The President was understanding of Arab feelings, but leaned on the Arab parties to continue with the process.

Rabin then moved to annul the law that prohibited contacts with the PLO. He had already told the Israelis to forget about Greater Israel. He started setting the stage for progress in the peace negotiations.

The eighth round ended on December 17 without any of the tracks scoring tangible success, with the exception of the Jordanian track. On the last day, the Israeli delegation submitted a language for the disputed agenda item B-5 entitled 'Borders and Territorial Matters'.

Throughout the eighth round, the two delegations held only one official meeting, and the rest of the meetings were confined to informal experts' discussions. The Jordanian delegation pressed for a reconsideration of the Israeli refusal to change the saving phrase. Rubinstein's reason for refusing to change this phrase was not because of its substance, but because the change was instigated by the PLO. Rubinstein's goal was to assert to us that he was not willing to tolerate an enhanced PLO influence on either the Jordanian or the Palestinian tracks. Moreover, he was worried that the Jordanian and Palestinian delegations could combine forces to place more pressure on the Israeli delegation to grant additional concessions. Majali, Anani, al-Khasawneh and Tarawneh agreed among themselves that the new Israeli language was acceptable but decided not to reveal their position until the Jordanian government approved it. Since it was the last day of negotiations, the whole matter had to be postponed until a future round, and no one knew when, where or how that round would convene.

On Thursday evening, the evening before our departure from Washington, we were in a cheerful yet sorrowful mood because we did not know whether the eighth round would be our last. Anani mimicked everyone, including Majali, who laughed from the bottom of his heart. Majali's policy of talking with a straight, unassertive and commanding approach, in addition to his always open suite, made him very special to all delegates. Even when he became angry at someone, he was only mad for a short period, and once the steam was off, he would forget the whole matter, leaving the victim of the outburst stewing for a long time, wondering what punitive action Majali would take. When Anani shouted like Majali, everyone laughed.

Anani moved to mimic Tarawneh and asked him sharply, 'Why did Naef al-Qadi call you Ambassador Tarawneh the other day? Does he know something that we do not?'

Tarawneh and al-Qadi were taken aback for a few seconds and then both said, almost at the same time, 'We do not know what you're talking about. You are hallucinating.' Well, Majali quizzed Tarawneh on the matter, and eventually Tarawneh spilled the beans.

'Well, Pasha,' said Tarawneh, 'remember when I went to London at the beginning of this month to attend the multilaterals' Steering Committee? Well, I saw there the Prime Minister Sherif Zaid Bin Shaker who told me that His Majesty had selected me to be his ambassador in Washington.'

'Congratulations!' said Majali in a reproachful tone. 'When would the assignment start?'

'In due time,' said Tarawneh. 'Of course, I was pleased at the news. Actually, it came as no surprise to me. Dr Abu Jaber, the Foreign Minister, had approached me with the offer, but I thought that the decision rested with His Majesty.'

Majali, who did not like to see one of his team members reassigned without him being consulted, slumped into a deep silence. When everyone but Anani and Tarawneh left, Majali shouted, 'I am really disappointed, not in the Foreign Minister or the Prime Minister . . . No, I am disappointed in you, eloquent Fayez Tarawneh. Here you are, my friend, trustee, and team member, making it appear like I am the husband of the adulteress, the last to know. Why?'

Tarawneh told him that he had tried more than once to tell him but could not find the right time. Tarawneh said that he would still remain a member of the delegation anyway, and, maybe, would even be in a better position in Washington to serve the delegation. Majali's anger at the time, however, was too deep to be erased by Tarawneh's persistent cajoling. Anani finally decided that he himself had caused this rift by raising the question in the first place. He therefore felt he should work to mend the fences. He looked at Majali and said, 'If I were Tarawneh, I would be very upset with you. You never told Fayez that you would be the next Prime Minister. Now his chances to return as a Minister have been wiped out.' Both laughed. Tarawneh indicated that his wife, Ruwaidah, and he had long ago decided that living four years in Washington would be very good for them and the children. Both had previously lived for five years in Los Angeles when Fayez was working on his MA and PhD at the University of Southern California.

President Clinton assumed his post in January 1993 and set about appointing his staff and members of the National Security Council. It became apparent that the American peace team remained essentially the same. Dennis Ross was reinstated as the coordinator for the Middle East peace process. Martin Indyk, Director of the Washington Institute for the Near East Policy, and a close watcher of Middle Eastern affairs, was appointed to the National Security Council with responsibility for the Middle East file, and was succeeded at the Washington Institute by Dr Robert Satloff. Eventually Ed Djerejian was appointed Ambassador to Israel, and Robert Pelletreau, the former Ambassador to Tunis who made the first US contact with the PLO, took over as Assistant Secretary of State for Middle East and North African affairs, replacing Djerejian. Wesley Egan, a fine diplomat and a smooth operator, replaced Ambassador Harrison, the American Ambassador in Amman.

As for the Palestinian deportees in Marj al-Zuhour, they enjoyed unparalleled international press exposure. In the early days of their relocation, the international media followed every word they said and every gesture they made. They were often seen walking in a long, tidy line towards the Israeli self-proclaimed security zone, where they would try to cross but would be stopped by Israeli soldiers. Their spokespersons, Abdul Aziz Rantissi and Mahmoud al-Zahar, made regular appearances on television news programs. Viewed as heroes in the Arab world, in the eyes of the rest of the world they were seen as individuals with a mission. Israeli officials claimed that their deportation weakened the Hamas and Jihad movements and decreased the frequency of 'terrorist acts'. When winter came and brought snow, the Palestinians in Lebanon and their Lebanese supporters carried food, tents, clothes and utensils to the deportees. CNN carried these pictures daily and round the clock, with coverage reminiscent of their daily reporting from Baghdad during the Gulf War. The emphasis in the coverage began to shift from the political dimension to the human suffering of the deportees. A Jordanian physician, Dr Abdul Raheem Malhas, wrote an article in Jordan's daily newspaper, *Al-Rai*, drawing attention to how good the deportees had it: everyone was sending them food and clothing, while there were many more deserving Palestinian refugees who did not have anybody rush to their assistance. The article had a profound effect on the Jordanian and Palestinian public, who believed that the deportees should put up with suffering like the children of the Intifada. A popular suspicion grew that the deportees' plight had become strictly political and not humanitarian.

Fresh diplomatic efforts were mounted after the holidays of Christmas and New Year to convene the ninth round of negotiations. New US Secretary of State, Warren Christopher, and his Middle East peace team intensified their efforts to put the peace process back on track, and their efforts generated heated activity among diplomats in the Arab World. The US and Russian sponsors issued a joint letter of invitation to each negotiation party, setting April 20, 1993, as the start date for the ninth round. The Palestinians were busily engaged in an effort to strike a deal to free Palestinian prisoners whom Rabin had promised to release at the outset of his term in office, and to return the Marj al-Zuhour deportees. The Israelis did not respond favorably despite American promises to have only some of the Palestinian demands fulfilled. One week before the scheduled beginning of the ninth round, the Palestinian deportees at Marj al-Zuhour urged the Palestinian population in the West Bank and Gaza to prevent Palestinian negotiators from leaving for Washington. A day later, four masked gunmen entered Saeb Ereikat's house and told his wife they would kill him if he went to Washington.

Meanwhile, Yassir Arafat and President Hafez al-Assad of Syria, assisted by the intermediation of Saudi Arabia and Egypt, agreed to meet. The two men met in the northern Syrian city of Latakia on April 19, while a foreign ministers' meeting of the four Arab negotiating parties and Egypt was in session at the Royal Cultural Center in Amman. The ministers delayed making a decision to attend the negotiations until the end of the Syrian–Palestinian Summit. The summit was the first since the PLO accused Syria after the sixth negotiation round of having covertly made a separate peace deal with Israel. In the meeting of foreign ministers, the Palestinian delegate, Farouq Qaddumi, alluded to the matter. 'Is it true, Mr Minister, that you are very advanced in your negotiations with Israel?' he asked Share' of Syria.

'Do you expect me to place the fate of the Syrian people in your hands and wait for you to finish your negotiations after five years? Each party should remove the thorns in his palm with his own hand,' Share' responded. He was obviously referring to the Final Status negotiations the Palestinians were scheduled to conclude with the Israelis in five years. That answer was not very far from the understanding reached in a similar coordination meeting held in Damascus the year before, where it was decreed that each negotiation track had its own particularities, and its own speed and acceleration.

The April 20 issue of the *Washington Post* reported that the Saudis promised financial aid to the Palestinians and asked other Gulf States to do the same. Prince Saud al-Faisal, Saudi Arabia's Foreign Minister, was keen to see the Palestinians return to negotiations. The decision that the five foreign ministers took that same day, April 20, under PLO pressure, was to postpone the negotiations until April 27. It was a compromise between the conferees: Jordan and Egypt who wanted to hold the negotiations on time as set by the invitation (April 20), Syria and Lebanon who were lukewarm regarding the matter, and the PLO who wanted to place conditions on the decision. Our delegation had already arrived in Washington on April 18 before that decision was taken. We were weary of the repeated maneuvers of some Arab parties before every round that would coerce our country, Jordan, the other side of the so-called joint delegation, into positions on which it had not been previously advised, notified or consulted.

The dynamics of events were bound to raise the following set of questions, which if answered honestly, would all point to one major conclusion. How could you ensure a reasonable degree of success on the Palestinian–Israeli front without the PLO? How could media exposure be avoided so that negotiations could take place inside closed rooms and not in front of cameras? How could you isolate negotiations from the poisonous effect of violence on the ground? How much would the American mediation role be missed if it were only reconciliatory and not assertive? Are there other Israelis and other Palestinians who would be willing to conduct confidential negotiations in parallel to the ongoing negotiations in Washington? These were real impediments to shifting the Palestinian–Israeli negotiations to higher places, and the answer to all these questions would logically lead to one conclusion: lure the Israelis and the Palestinians to negotiate secretly in a place where no one would suspect.

Meanwhile, our delegation was getting prepared for more substantive engagement with the Israelis, especially now that the Common Agenda was all but completed. Offices were prepared for the delegation on the fourth floor of the Ministry of Foreign Affairs, and Majali conducted meetings for the delegation, gave press interviews and received guests in those quarters. On April 8, 1993, the Foreign Minister, Kamel Abu Jaber, asked Haddadin to join the bilateral delegation again. Haddadin responded without hesitation:

> Remember, Excellency, what I said the last time I was here? I said I was a soldier, and I still am. You told me to join the delegation in November 1991 and I did. A year later you told me get out, and I did. Now you tell me get back in and I will. I am but a soldier in service of my country. I just have one favor to ask of you.

'Yes,' said Abu Jaber, 'what is it?'

'For this soldier to fight with all the courage and power of morals, may I know why it is that you issue such repeated orders of in and out?' asked Haddadin.

'May God punish the cowards who were behind it. It is them to blame,' said Abu Jaber, and he did not elaborate any further.

'If you are unable to elaborate, then I want to see the Prime Minister in your company,' said Haddadin.

'Okay, I will ask for an appointment,' said the Minister, 'but please, could you join the delegation promptly. Majali is on the fourth floor downstairs, please report to him.'

On the way, Haddadin met Abdallah Toukan, and Haddadin briefed him on what happened. 'I knew they would ask you back in. It is because His Majesty was not happy about the reports of the eighth round, and he directed them to bring you back in,' said Toukan.

Ten days later, the Foreign Minister accompanied Haddadin to the Prime Minister's office. Majali was there and also Abdul Ilah al-Khatib, Director of the Special Office of the Foreign Ministry, and Secretary of the High Committee on Negotiations. After shaking hands and a few nice words of welcome, the Prime Minister said to Haddadin, 'Well, you are a senior member of the delegation. We hope you will avoid falling into pitfalls like the one that caused us embarrassment. I am referring to the publication of the Common Agenda without our permit. You should not have leaked it to the press, and you know that.'

Haddadin listened with concentration and refused to drink the Arabic coffee that the attendant brought in, a sign of dismay. It was Haddadin's chance to put the record straight, and he took it:

I am, surprised, sir, I am really surprised for two reasons. First, I am surprised at the way we are treated as members of the delegation. It looks like you are telling us 'Go in the company of your God and enter battle. We are sitting and watching.' If we score victory, the credit goes to you. If we make a mistake, then death is our reward! Second, Your Excellency, I am surprised that you, in particular, would entertain an idea that leads you to think I am a rookie and not a pro. You, among all Jordanians, know for a fact how I managed the water dispute with Israel for over ten years, and not a single word leaked out. My wife did not know at the time what I was managing, nor did she know of the risks I had exposed myself to in performing my duties. You, sir, as General Commander of the Armed Forces in the eighties, know what I went through in that connection, and yet, not a single leak throughout those long years. For you, sir, to think for a moment that I would leak sensitive information is a gross misconception of my abilities that you know only too well.

Haddadin then recounted the details of what had happened with the Common Agenda and how it was given, not leaked, to the correspondents and published. He asked Majali to correct him if he reported anything inaccurately, and Majali never interrupted or corrected any part of Haddadin's report.

'Okay,' said the Prime Minister, 'you are now back in and I am sure you will do a very good job. Be assured of my support and the support of His Majesty.' On the way out, Abu Jaber said that he thought Haddadin did a good job in clearing things up. The impression the King and the Prime Minister had, he said, was that Haddadin leaked the Common Agenda knowing that he should not. 'That impression,' Abu Jaber made clear, 'is now corrected.'

The following day, Majali showed up briefly at the Ministry of Foreign Affairs, before leaving to get ready for the trip to the US via London, where he had an audience scheduled with His Majesty King Hussein who was on a private visit to the British capital. That meeting soon triggered rumors that Majali was the upcoming Prime Minister of Jordan.

## Water Resources Working Group, Geneva

The third round of the multilateral talks was also organized to take place in late April. The Water Resources Working Group would hold its meetings in Geneva, Switzerland. Haddadin headed the Jordanian delegation, and arrived at the Intercontinental Hotel in Geneva on the evening of April 25. Upon arrival, Haddadin left a note for the Palestinian delegation with his room number and a reminder to meet and coordinate. He stayed up until the early hours of the following day waiting for a Palestinian hint that they had arrived, but none was received. On the following morning, the two delegations came across each other in the breakfast restaurant. '*Himdillah Assalamah!* [Thank God for safety!]' Haddadin said to Dr Riyadh al-Khudary, head of the Palestinian delegation. 'When can we meet to coordinate?'

'Oh, yes, we have Abu Ala' with us. He is upstairs, let me contact him for the purpose,' said al-Khudary. Abu Ala' (Ahmad Qurei') was a leading figure in the Executive Committee of the PLO from the ranks of Fatah. He later was elected Speaker of the Palestinian Parliament in 1996. Al-Khudary went to the phone and came back to the breakfast table. 'He is asleep, should I wake him up?' al-Khudary asked Haddadin.

'Oh, no, no. Palestine's case can wait, but sleep presses and cannot wait,' answered Haddadin. He got busy after breakfast with arranging a coordination meeting among the Arab delegates, the Palestinians included. The Saudi delegation showed unqualified support to the Jordanians and Palestinians. The other Arabs followed suit. They entrusted Haddadin with the leading role. On Monday, the first day, and after the delegations carried out the registration procedures, the gavel-holder had the usual meetings with the delegations. Haddadin brought up the subject of having a separate sign in front of the Palestinian delegation, and, to his surprise, the request was heeded before the day was over. Israel did not object, an unusual event indeed.

The proceedings of the third round were not without problems. The Palestinians presented their case and said that they knew nothing about the development of their own water resources, and that Israel withheld data and information. They also insisted on having the issue of water rights discussed in the multilaterals. The confrontation became hot and the three delegations, Jordanian, Palestinian and Israeli, monopolized the discussion. It was more of a fight between the Israelis and the Palestinians. Haddadin watched and made positive interventions to facilitate the progress of the Group's work. The gavel-holder called for a break without specifying a time to reconvene.

'You know, Munther' said Dr John Hayward, the World Bank observer, 'it will not be encouraging for the rest of the delegations to attend the meetings of the Working Group if this goes on and on.'

'Well, John,' said Haddadin, 'the Palestinian dismay is quite understandable. They ought to have access to data, and they ought to be advised as to what is being done with their water resources. Besides, the issue of water rights is basic to them, and to us.'

'But is this the place to have it negotiated? You know more than anyone else here,' said Hayward.

'To be honest, no. This is not the forum for a water rights debate. The forum is the bilateral negotiations. But the Israelis are confining their negotiations with the Palestinians there to the issues of the interim arrangement, and they claim that water comes in the negotiations for Final Status.'

'Can you do something to get over this high bump?'

'It appears that the gavel-holder is conducting talks with both delegations, the Israeli and the Palestinian. I can help if they all ask.'

The delegates helped themselves to coffee and biscuits, and Haddadin came across Ambassador Amos Ganor of the Israeli delegation. 'Good morning, Ambassador,' greeted Haddadin.

'Good morning my friend,' said Ganor, 'are you over that Palestine syndrome?' Ganor was referring to the confrontation in the Washington round between Haddadin and the Israeli delegation over 'Judea and Samaria' versus 'Palestine'.

'I will be as soon as you guys get over the syndrome of Judea and Samaria!' snapped Haddadin.

The two men exchanged jokes until Alan Kieswetter, the gavel-holder, came out of the room in which he was trying to get the Palestinians and the Israelis to work out their differences. He asked Haddadin to join him upon the invitation of the Israelis and the Palestinians. Haddadin went into the room with Kieswetter, and there was Avraham Katz-Oz, head of the Israeli delegation, and Riyadh al-Khudary, head of the Palestinian delegation. 'We consider you a rational, knowledgeable and neutral party,' sadi Katz-Oz.

'Thank you for the compliment and the confidence. But neutral? I doubt. I want you to know from the very beginning that when the chips are down, I will side with my Palestinian brother. I would be fooling you if I claimed otherwise,' said Haddadin.

'We know, we know. And we still need your assistance,' said Katz-Oz.

Haddadin labored to come up with a solution. He finally drafted a text that would commit Israel to taking on the issue of water rights in the bilateral negotiations in the round that was then just commencing in Washington. The Israelis wired the text to Tel Aviv, and waited for an answer from their Ministry of Foreign Affairs. They were on the phone most of the four hours that the recess took. Finally, an affirmative answer came from Tel Aviv.

'Good, very good,' whispered Haddadin in al-Khudary's ear. 'This will be a pleasant surprise to your delegation in Washington, DC. I am going there the day after tomorrow.'

'I cannot approve the text on my own,' said al-Khudary. 'I have to get the consent of Abu Ala'. He is upstairs. Can you please come with me?' he asked.

Haddadin thought for a moment, and agreed to go to Abu Ala' to convince him to accept that text, which offered a clear advantage for the Palestinians. He took the elevator with al-Khudary, and they headed for a corner suite. 'Come in please, come in,' said one bodyguard politely. Haddadin and al-Khudary walked through a guard's room into a reception room. Both rooms had bodyguards in them. Abu Ala' received Haddadin with a nice welcome. Haddadin looked around the premises and compared them in his mind with the room he was occupying, with hardly enough room for him to sit at a modest desk to write his reports, and no bodyguards! After the exchange of courteous words of welcome they started to discuss their business.

'I am glad to tell you, Abu Ala', that the Israelis agreed to a text I wrote in which they commit themselves to put the water rights on the agenda of their bilateral negotiations with the Palestinians. Here is the wording of the text.' Haddadin extended a sheet of paper to Abu Ala', whose response disappointed Haddadin:

> I have seen it, Riyadh brought it to me. I just do not trust the Israelis. They are full of tricks. There is no way we can come to terms with them. I have issued my instructions to Riyadh not to accept this and to keep pressing for including the water rights on the agenda of this Working Group, and we count on your support.

Haddadin thought to himself and wondered why Abu Ala' was declining a clear advantage to the Palestinian delegation in Washington. Could it be pressure to show the Israelis and the Americans that the PLO could stall the multilaterals? Could it be there was competition between the Palestinians themselves such that the officials in charge of the multilaterals wanted to outdo those in charge of the bilaterals? Could that be a prelude to putting the PLO on the front line of negotiations soon? Haddadin could find a good reason for Abu Ala's rejection. 'Well, Abu Ala',' said Haddadin,

> you can always count on our support where it is meaningful. But let us face it. You have nothing to lose. The PLO has been described with many adjectives in international circles among

which 'terrorists' is a familiar word. Well, I have a country behind me and I am obliged to uphold its reputation. A respected Jordan is a better supporter to your cause. I am sorry. In this case, if the duel over water rights is resumed, all I can offer in terms of support is silence. I do not agree with your reasoning.

'Please do not be displeased with me. I have just come from Oslo where I oversaw the meetings of the Refugees Group. The Israelis are impossible,' said Abu Ala' who, it later became known, was in on the continuing secret talks with the Israelis in Oslo.

'I am not trying to change your mind. You know your interests a lot better than I do. I just wanted to help the best I can,' said Haddadin.

The meeting reached no positive conclusion on water rights, even though a final upbeat communiqué was issued. Surprisingly, the text Abu Ala' rejected was approved by the Palestinians two weeks later. Haddadin got the word that a cable came from the PLO instructing al-Khudary, who was attending a meeting for the regional committee of the Working Group in Washington, to accept it. He communicated the Palestinians' approval to Kieswetter. It was a bit late then to have it included in the Palestinian bilateral agenda with Israel.

## Refugees Working Group, Oslo

The third meeting of the Refugees Working Group of the multilaterals was held in Oslo, Norway. It was agreed that there would be separate signs in front of the Jordanian and the Palestinian delegations with the name of each delegation clearly written on it; a small step, but one with great symbolic value. The overseer of the Palestinian delegation was Abu Ala' (Ahmad Qurei') who spent most of the time in his hotel room. Whenever the negotiations were complicated, Anani worked it out with him. The meeting was also closely monitored by the Norwegian Foreign Minister, Bajoulet. In that meeting, a Norwegian Study Center, FAFO, presented the results of a thorough study it had conducted on the socio-economic status of the Palestinian refugee camps in Gaza. Bajoulet presented his findings and said that he needed more time to give a fully detailed report on Israeli and Arab policies and practices towards the issue of family reunification. The report was modest and inadequate and was not worthy of the big debates that had taken place over it in the previous rounds.

Delighted with the results of the meetings, the Norwegian Foreign Minister insisted on inviting the Palestinian delegation, including Abu Ala', the Jordanian delegation, and the FAFO experts to a superb smoked salmon dinner. Anani was soon engaged in a discussion with Norway's Deputy Foreign Minister over the Arab explorer, Ibn Fadhlan, who arrived ten centuries ago in the Scandinavian territories and wrote about the life there. Abu Ala' sat laughing and giggling with ease and familiarity with the Foreign Minister, his wife, and their small boy, as if they were buddies. Anani took note of the intimacy shown to Abu Ala' and informed his own Foreign Minister about it in the final report of the delegation. However, it did not look like that incident registered with the Jordan government nor was any attention paid to it. About a hundred days later, the world's capitals, including Jordan's, were surprised by headlines carrying the news of the Oslo Accord, the result of secret PLO–Israeli negotiations informally held at the house of Norway's Foreign Minister and in which Abu Ala' was deeply involved.

# 11

# Ninth, Tenth, Oslo, Eleventh

The ninth round of bilateral negotiations was scheduled to start on Monday, April 27, 1993. The Willard Hotel and all other decent hotels in Washington, DC were fully booked because of the Gay Rights Convention. Our delegation was put up at the Ritz Carlton Hotel by Tyson's Corner in Virginia.

That ninth round generated optimism. On the Jordanian–Israeli track, negotiations focused on Israel's position towards amending the saving clause of item B-5 on the Common Agenda. The two parties agreed on a text, but upon Jordan's request, also decided to keep it undisclosed until the time came when the two sides could go public with their agreed Common Agenda, and that was, in our view, when progress had been achieved on the Palestinian track. We proceeded to address the mechanism of discussing the agenda items on the premise that they had been mutually accepted. Prioritization was a problem for both sides, not of the items themselves, but of the sub-items, on which our priorities differed. Finally, upon Majali's insistence, we agreed to have three different working groups, or, as Rubinstein preferred to call them, subcommittees. We would negotiate the different items of the Common Agenda as arranged into three different baskets. The first would deal with borders, territorial matters, security and arms control; the second addressed refugees and bilateral cooperation; and the third handled water, energy and the environment.

Haddadin arrived from the multilaterals in Geneva on the afternoon of Thursday, April 30, and met with Majali in his suite for the first time since they had met with the Prime Minister in Amman about two weeks earlier. They had a friendly chat, and Majali briefed Haddadin on the developments of the past four days of negotiations with the Israelis. Majali told Haddadin to head the group on water, energy and the environment. The next morning, Friday, Haddadin joined Nayef al-Qadi for breakfast. Nayef was sitting alone when Haddadin entered the restaurant of the Ritz Carlton Hotel. 'What do you know!' said an excited al-Qadi: 'It appears that the Pasha will be our next Prime Minister.'

'Really? How did you come up with this? Did Majali say anything to that effect?' asked Haddadin.

'No he did not, and will not. But it is 90 percent sure if not more,' said al-Qadi, 'and he will take with him Dr Jawad Anani from our delegation for a ministerial portfolio.'

'How can we be sure?' asked Haddadin.

'I have an idea,' replied al-Qadi, and he then worked out with Haddadin a scheme to force Majali to show his hand.

Friday was a day reserved for a general meeting of the delegation. Majali sat at the head of the table, Tarawneh to his right, Marea to his left, Haddadin to Tarawneh's right followed by Hassan Abu Ni'meh, al-Qadi and the others. 'Before we start, Pasha,' said al-Qadi, following the plan he had agreed with Haddadin over breakfast, 'I want to speak about a rumor we heard, not from ordinary people or off the street; we heard it from the ranks of the Israeli delegation.'

'What is it about, our agenda?' asked Majali.

'No, sir, Pasha, they say that you will soon be our Prime Minister, and very soon there is going to be that Cabinet change in Jordan. His Majesty will ask you to form the next cabinet,' al-Qadi said.

Haddadin looked at al-Qadi, and, playing his part, said, 'Nayef, for heaven's sake, how can you entertain stories from Israelis? What do they know? They don't know about our own affairs.'

'No, no, they do know, they do,' Majali interjected, and that was the first indication from Majali that he would be the next Prime Minister.

After the delegation meeting, Haddadin went to his room and drafted the sub-agenda on water, energy and the environment. He gave this non-paper the number 001, implying that he was prepared to submit 999 proposals for such a sub-agenda. He called for a meeting of the team in Majali's suite to review the draft.[1] By Sunday, the draft sub-agenda took its final shape and Majali approved it.

## Water, energy and the environment

On Monday May 4, the Jordanian and Israeli teams met in the negotiation room of the Jordan–Israeli track.[2] The two sides agreed to prepare a draft for a sub-agenda for their detailed negotiations over the topics of their group. Haddadin suggested that he would present a draft proposal and invited the Israelis to submit a proposal as well.

In each working group the discussion was as ever directed at priorities: what to tackle first, the substantive points of contention as we Jordanians insisted, or the areas of bilateral cooperation, as the Israelis preferred. The hottest debate evolved in the water group. On Tuesday, the Israelis submitted a draft sub-agenda they had informally given us in the eighth round, that Haddadin did not attend. He read in the Israeli proposal an item calling for the suspension by Jordan of the construction of the Karama dam.

The Karama dam was being seriously considered for construction in the floor of the Jordan valley. Haddadin discovered the site in the Middle Ghors in 1982 as he was taking a morning walk with his seven-year-old son, Yezan. Storage behind a dam in the Mallaha depression could be proven compatible with the Johnston Plan of 1955. It would impound floods brought to it from the Yarmouk River via the King Abdallah Canal. The Israelis based their objections to the construction of the dam on the fact that the dam would impound Yarmouk floods before agreement was reached between Israel and Jordan on sharing of the Yarmouk water. Haddadin explained that the dam would impound flood waters from the catchment of the Mallaha depression, from side wadis inside Jordan, and the excess waters in the King Abdallah Canal (implicity meaning the Yarmouk waters).

On Wednesday, May 5, Haddadin had his proposal for the draft sub-agenda, but kept it to himself for the time being. 'Do you have your proposal for a sub-agenda?' asked Kinarti.

'Well, we still have time, let us probe our own views first,' answered Haddadin. Kinarti gave the floor to Uri Shamir.

'We are still of the opinion that Jordan should call off the construction of the Karama dam,' said Shamir.

'Listen Professor Shamir,' responded Haddadin, 'this is a sovereign Jordanian decision. The dam will be built on Jordanian soil, with Jordanian money. We would appreciate non-interference in our own affairs; I would further appreciate it if you keep your opinions to yourself. This decision of Jordan is non-negotiable; and anyone who tries to interfere in Jordan's affairs will have his hands cut off!' Haddadin voice was loud and decisive.

Deafening silence loomed in the room. Mahasneh wrote a note and passed it over to Haddadin via Abu Ni'meh as the rules of our delegation required. The note said, 'How many F-15 fighter planes are supporting your blitz on these guys? How many tanks and heavy guns? What are you depending on?' Haddadin read the note, looked at Mahasneh while the Israelis watched, and nodded his head in a show that the note carried full support! Kinarti did not know what to do. Haddadin took advantage of the bewilderment and went on to deliver his own views on what the water agenda items should contain.

'Just give us your proposals so that we can study them,' said Kinarti.

'I will, when the time is ripe,' answered Haddadin.

'If you do not want to negotiate our own viewpoints, and will not give us the sub-agenda as you promised a few days ago, what are we going to negotiate? We will walk out of the room,' said the upset Kinarti.

'Well, you are free to do whatever you want,' said Haddadin.

Kinarti walked toward the door. His colleagues rose and followed him. Haddadin rose and met Kinarti at the door before he exited, and handed him a copy of the sub-agenda. Kinarti took it without thinking and left the room with his team. Haddadin kept the door open so that he could watch what went on across the hallway in the Israeli room. He was delighted that it was, for the first time ever, the Israelis who were walking out of a meeting with Arabs. All too often Arab delegates had withdrawn in protest from meetings, leaving Israelis free to take center stage. 'Stay put in your seats,' he ordered his colleagues in the delegation as he took his seat with the door wide open. 'None of you is allowed to leave his seat, not even to go to the men's room.'

Kinarti and his colleagues circled around Rubinstein and were having serious talk as their gestures showed. Rubinstein sent for the American representative, who hurried to the hallway where the Israelis were assembled. 'We have a problem with Dr Haddadin,' Rubinstein said to the US representative.

'What is it?' asked the US representative.

'He is impossible. He would not negotiate over our viewpoints, nor would he bring any of his own. He promised to present the meeting with a proposal for a sub-agenda, but he did not,' said Kinarti.

'What is this document that you have?' asked the US representative. Kinarti gave him the document that Haddadin had handed to him before he left the room. The US representative read the title on the first page. It read: 'The Jordan–Israeli Track. Non-Paper 001. Draft Common Sub-Agenda for Water, Energy and the Environment.'

'But this is a proposal for the common sub-agenda,' said the US representative. The Israeli delegates and the US representative then went into the Israeli delegation room. After a short while, the US representative came out, and so did Rubinstein. He went straight to Majali and complained about Haddadin anyway.

'Look here,' said Majali angrily, 'Haddadin does not seek your permission before he talks. He does not clear his language with you to conform to the tone that you favor. He is the head of our team on that group, and he operates within his area of jurisdiction,' he added with a decisive tone.

'But, Pasha, how can we negotiate if we cannot communicate. The two sides should have an understanding regarding a decent way of communicating with each other; no negotiation without communication!' said Rubinstein.

'Look here! Haddadin and the rest of our team are a lot more decent than you are trying to insinuate. Be careful in the choice of your words when you talk to me,' Majali responded, and walked away from Rubinstein. He then sent for Haddadin, who soon came into the delegation room with his colleagues and explained the conflict they had with the Israelis over the Karama dam and the sub-agenda. Later the meeting went well.

Over the weekend, al-Khasawneh arrived from Amman, and related to Majali the approval of the Common Agenda. Al-Khasawneh was very pleased with His Majesty's reaction to the Common Agenda. 'You know, Munther, His Majesty had several consultations with expert British lawyers that he knew. He wanted to make sure that the document was foolproof,' Awn confided in Haddadin.

'How were the reactions?'

'Very good, excellent.' Al-Khasawneh described one such reaction from a prominent Jewish lawyer in London. To the King's question whether or not he should approve the agenda, the lawyer replied: 'The lawyer in me says yes, but the Jew in me says no!' which was testimony to the triumph we scored in concluding the Common Agenda.

Over that same weekend, Majali took Aktham Quosous, Haddadin, and Mousa Majali, his bodyguard out to a pizza restaurant. 'I see, Munther, you have been negotiating without a clue on who lost the 1967 War with Israel,' said Majali as they sat down to two large pizzas.

'You are right, Pasha, I care less now who won that war because I feel I am in a new round of a different war. It is a series of battles for peace. I concede I would lose if I were to confront the Israelis in a hot war today; but I am here for the battle of peace, and I am determined to win, and I shall.'

'Very good spirit. In the process it looks like you have shaken up your opponents. You have achieved good progress, be careful and tactful because you will consolidate your gains and achieve more progress,' advised Majali.

'Sir, I know when to explode in their faces; only when they make a mistake, after which I show them stars in midday! One more thing, I intend to have my colleagues in the group develop better guts when they negotiate with the Israelis. I intend to show my colleagues that the Israelis are not the breed that cannot be defeated.'

'God bless your efforts; we all intend to come up with a result that His Majesty will be proud of, and our own people will be glad to accept,' said Majali.

On May 4, the Israeli delegation handed the Palestinians a new self-government proposal that they termed a 'draft framework agreement for the negotiations'. It was rumored that the Palestinian delegation had somehow leaked a copy of it to the *Jordan Times*, because the newspaper published it in its May 10 issue. It was interesting to note that no comments were raised about its publication compared to the hell that broke loose over the publication of the Common Agenda of the Jordan–Israeli track in October 1992. The draft proposal was fashioned after the Jordan–Israeli draft agenda, and contained nine points. Although it fell short of what the Palestinian delegation had been asking for, it contained some principles they had been struggling for since the beginning of the peace negotiations. One of these was the linkage between the interim and the Final Status stages of the peacemaking process.

Another principle was the acceptance of an elected Palestinian Executive Council (PEC) that would assume executive, judicial and legislative responsibilities – the three areas of authority that the Israelis had previously refused on the grounds that it would constitute the nucleus of a Palestinian state. The PEC would have its own police force, but overall security during the interim period would continue to be an Israeli responsibility. The most important concept was the unity of the territories in accordance with terms to be mutually determined in the 'permanent status' negotiations.

The PLO's first reaction to the proposal was to refuse it, but it soon amended its position as its representatives stated that 'it deserves a second reading'. Hanan Ashrawi gave a similarly lukewarm response. The only basic problem with the offer was the fact that it did not contain the principle of unity between Palestinians in diaspora and those in the Occupied Territories. Such a linkage would carry a de facto recognition of the PLO as the negotiating partner. US diplomats intervened to present a form that would be more appealing to the Palestinian delegation, the main noticeable change being the replacement of the word 'empower' with 'transfer of authorities'. However, the Palestinians gave a long list of amendments to Ed Djerejian, who labored in vain to convince both sides to issue a joint statement on agreed principles.

On the Syrian and Lebanese tracks, movement was slow. The security versus withdrawal debate persisted. The Lebanese complained of Israel's insistence on forming a joint military committee to discuss security measures on the borders, thus ignoring Lebanon's demand for the implementation of Israel's withdrawal from the Lebanese occupied territories. The round ended prematurely on May 13, 1993. Despite the problems, Ed Djerejian's evaluation of the ninth round was encouraging. He was quoted in the *Washington Post* as saying there had been 'movement forward on substance', which he attributed to the 'full partner' role played by the US in this round. In fact the US, under the new administration, wanted to assert its commitment to move the negotiations forward. The suspicion that the Clinton administration would show less interest in the peace process turned out to be misplaced.

## A new government

Upon the return of our delegation to Amman, Majali met Prince al-Hassan and King Hussein. In his audience with the King, Majali was asked to form a new government.

The King usually acts upon the mood of the public in their desire for a change of government. When he decides the time is ripe for a change he normally entrusts a public personality of his choice to form a new government. The chosen person looks to those he knows and respects to fill Cabinet posts. He usually observes the long tradition of pluralism in Cabinet membership, selecting ministers from diverse social groupings, geographic origins and ethnic and religious affiliations. The Prime Minister designate seeks approval of his candidates from the King and the King usually concurs with the Prime Minister's choice. The new ministers take the oath of office before the King, and a Royal Decree is issued appointing the new ministers, and another accepting the resignation of the outgoing Cabinet. It is a swift operation.

Majali sent for Anani and they consulted over the potential candidates, a list of whom both had prepared back in the eighth round of negotiations. Anani was appointed as Minister of State for Prime Ministry Affairs, and was in charge of the negotiation delegations. Another minister who participated in the negotiations was the Minister of State for Foreign Affairs, Talal al-Hassan. Majali's response to His Majesty's letter of appointment included a very strong commitment to peace.

The new government was good news for the negotiating teams. General Abdul Hafez Marea, a member of our delegation to the bilateral rounds, was promoted and appointed Chief of Staff of the Armed Forces. Thus, members of the peace team were well placed to influence the direction of the peace process without inhibition, hesitation or fears. In June, 1993, after the government's formation on May 29, a decision was taken to appoint Ambassador Fayez Tarawneh as head of the Jordanian delegation to the peace negotiations, replacing Dr Majali in that post. Marwan Dodeen was to replace Anani, General Tahseen Shurdum to replace Marea, and Tayseer Abdul Jaber to substitute for Tarawneh in the delegation. Later, Drs Safwan Toukan and Michael Marto were selected to strengthen the economic expertise of the peace team.

The political opposition to peace did not wait to shower the new government with criticism on the grounds that it was a 'peace government'. Islamic parliamentarians spearheaded the attack. Member of Parliament, Sheikh Abdul Mun'em Abu Zunt from the Muslim Brotherhood Movement, called it a 'government of surrender and not of peace'. Parliament, however, was not in session at the time the government was formed but was on its annual recess. Accordingly the battle for the vote of confidence would not be on until December 1993 when the next session of Parliament convened.

Chairman Arafat made several visits to Jordan in 1993. He made a visit to some Gulf States in June and followed that with a visit to Jordan. His main concern was to find the financial support that would help him train a police force to go into Gaza. Anani received Arafat at the airport. On their way to the VIP guest quarters in Jebel Amman, Arafat was furious. First there was his undeclared frustration with the low-level reception he had received at the airport. Although Anani was a senior minister, Chairman Arafat expected the Prime Minister to welcome him at the steps of the plane. Also there was his declared reason for being upset, namely his inability to convince some of the Gulf Emirs and Sheikhs to contribute funds. His anger almost exploded in frenzy:

> I asked the bastard for my money, and he lectures me about Arab nationalism . . . Jawad, I only wanted the 5 per cent tax the Palestinian employees pay on their salary that those governments withhold for the benefit of the PLO. I am not begging them for any money, I am asking for my own money. You are an economist, Jawad, you must have read the United Nations report. The economic situation in our land is very bad. I swear to God, it is very bad. How can I make peace when my people are suffering? The situation inside the Occupied Territories is bad and there are no institutions, no infrastructure, no water, and no jobs. Do they expect me to do miracles?

Anani suggested that he should have more confidence in Jordan and begin to coordinate with its leaders, but Chairman Arafat's face showed feelings of agony and humiliation.

He met with the King at the al-Hashimyyeh Palace, west of Amman. During a luncheon given in Arafat's honor, the King told Arafat that

> some reports have been suggesting that my popularity is widening in the West Bank. I would like to assure you that I have no ambitions whatsoever in the West Bank or Gaza. We in Jordan believe that the

PLO, under the leadership of my brother Abu Ammar [Chairman Arafat], is the sole and legitimate representative of the Palestinians. The importance is placed on the land and the people. You and I are not immortal, but Jerusalem is. How do you want history to judge us if we miss this opportunity of peace? Let us coordinate and work together. We also hear that some of our brothers [PLO officials] suggest that we should declare a confederation from now, and our position on this is very clear. When the Palestinian people gain their right to self-determination and free will, we can make arrangements for a confederation or whatever they want and the people in Jordan will agree. So, if my brother *al-Raees* Abu Ammar has any doubts or questions about our intentions or motives, please say them now so we can attend to them.

Chairman Arafat looked around the table to see who could have leaked to the King any information of his dissatisfaction, and raised his hands up in the air and said:

Your Majesty, you are my big brother, we always come to you for support and advice. Of course, we should work together. What is the difference between us? Your success is my success; your people's success is my people's success. Actually they are the same people, Your Majesty. Yes, the same people and they are waiting to see what Your Majesty and I are going to do. They will judge both of us. You know the police issue; we need training.

The King looked at the Prime Minister, Dr Majali, and nodded his head asking for immediate action. 'At once, Your Majesty,' Majali replied.

The King then looked very intently to Arafat and asked about the PLO's evaluation of a statement Rabin had made. Rabin was quoted as saying 'Let Gaza sink in the sea.' Rabin had made that statement when violence was escalating to high levels and the residents of two Israeli settlements were demanding protection from the government. Chairman Arafat was taken by surprise and said, 'I do not need Gaza. What can I do? I do not have the means to take care of it. I think that he wants to embarrass me.'

The King suggested that this matter should be pursued with the Americans. He shared Arafat's view that dumping Gaza on the Palestinians would reveal the PLO's inability to shoulder the responsibility and would weaken their bargaining power with Israel. The King warned Arafat to be prepared for the possibility of Israel's sudden withdrawal from Gaza. 'The man is seriously frustrated with Gaza. You'd better be careful,' said King Hussein.

A tenth round of bilateral negotiations was scheduled to take place at the US State Department from June 15 to July 1, 1993. This round was driven by the American determination to see a breakthrough on the Palestinian–Israeli track. A Palestinian delegation with both the leader Dr Abdul Shafi and Faisal Hussaini arrived ahead of time to open an intensive dialogue with the American Mid-East staff before the arrival of the Israeli delegation. Faisal Hussaini called the tenth round the 'Jerusalem Round', and he emphasized that without clarifying the future of East Jerusalem, the Israeli–Palestinian negotiations would not go very far. But Secretary Warren Christopher and Dennis Ross, the Middle East Peace Coordinator, knew only too well that the issue of Jerusalem was a non-starter for the Israelis, despite the Palestinians' insistence. Instead, the Americans worked on the two drafts proposed by the Israelis and the Palestinians for a declaration of principles between the two parties. Aaron Miller, Dan Kurtzer, Martin Indyk, in addition to Ross and others, burned the midnight oil to work out a formula that both parties could then be pressured to accept. American attempts failed when the Palestinian delegation insisted that the Americans' final version was based on the Israeli proposal, and was biased in favour of it.

The Jordanians meanwhile reached a final agreed language to item B-5 of the Common Agenda (see Appendix 3). They continued to discuss future cooperation scenarios in the various fields. The three working groups that they had formed in the ninth round began working on detailed agendas of their own. Jordan, however, insisted on freezing the agreed agenda until progress was achieved on the Palestinian track. Israel, in return, voiced its refusal to discuss the return of Jordanian territory except in the context of a final treaty of peace. As outlined earlier, the delegation composition had changed from the team of the first nine rounds under Majali. Al-Khasawneh left the delegation and was promoted to be a legal advisor to His Majesty. Dr Mohammad Bani Hani was no longer part of the delegation and was not replaced.

Muwaffaq Allaf and Itamar Rabinovich on the Syrian–Israeli track practised their usual polite bickering, and, as reported by Allaf in the Arab coordination meetings, achieved little progress. The Israeli delegation insisted that the Syrians define the 'nature' of genuine peace for genuine withdrawal. No Israeli official had ever made the promise of total withdrawal from the Golan Heights. Israeli statements had been made regarding withdrawal on the Golan, or in the Golan, but never from the Golan as a whole. To the Syrians, such language was completely unacceptable because the prepositions 'on' and 'in' meant, in reality, Israeli troop redeployment, and not genuine withdrawal. Allaf would not explain what Syria's definition of total peace meant, and Rabinovich would not commit his delegation to 'total withdrawal'. As a matter of fact, Allaf reported to the Arab coordination meeting that Rabinovich had recently described the Syrian non-paper on the 'vision of peace' presented in the sixth round as a bluff. Rabinovich, who had been happy with that same non-paper in the sixth round, apparently changed heart and expressed dissatisfaction with it. He said that the non-paper called for ending the state of war and not for making peace. The full withdrawal–full peace formula revolved in an endless dialogue.

The tenth round was Tarawneh's first as head of the Jordanian delegation. He and Rubinstein got along very well, and they developed an amicable working relationship. They continued the Majali–Rubinstein tradition of one-on-one meetings before their delegations met. In the final report on the tenth round, Tarawneh evaluated that round as successful on the Jordanian track and, judging from Allaf's reports to the Arab coordination meetings, as unsuccessful on the Syrian and Lebanese tracks. Despite American and Israeli attempts to push negotiations on the Palestinian track, Tarawneh said, 'the Palestinians showed an unusual resistance'! Furthermore, Tarawneh noted that the Palestinians appealed to the media as if they had been pushing for a formula different from the Madrid Invitation. Again, this remark by Tarawneh was not fully explored further in Amman, but its significance was to become clear a couple of months later that, at that time in July, 1993, the secret Palestinian–Israeli negotiations in Oslo were going full blast.

## Secret talks in Oslo

Did the Americans know about those Oslo negotiations? Was this the reason for their insistence on a successful outcome in Washington? Or were there two schools in Israel, one which supported secret negotiation with the PLO away from the Madrid Invitation and its terms, and another which believed that the Madrid formula should be maintained? The second school had supporters in the US State Department who knew about the secret talks but never took them seriously. According to Mahmoud Abbas (Abu Mazen), who played a major role in arranging and conducting the Oslo talks, the whole Oslo affair started as an exercise between academics and researchers on both sides. Prime Minister Rabin and Chairman Arafat were kept fully abreast, on a day-to-day basis, of the developments therein. As a matter of fact, the Oslo affair was akin to an investment in 'venture capital' that yielded the right product, something the Washington labs could not deliver. The difference, of course, was that Oslo put the PLO and Israeli officials face to face, and the Washington bilaterals had not overtly included the PLO in the negotiation rooms. When talks in Oslo succeeded, no one was willing to let the opportunity pass by. Even those who had no prior knowledge of them could not afford to admit that they had been kept away from them.

Arafat came for a visit to Amman before the Oslo news broke out. He was received by Majali and Anani at the airport. When the plane landed at the Queen Alia Airport, Majali was told to wait with his guest, and to keep the press waiting until His Majesty arrived by helicopter from the Royal Palace about 15 miles away. Majali and Anani engaged Arafat, Abd Rabbo, Tayyeb Abdul Raheem and others in a conversation about the economic situation in both Jordan and the Occupied Territories until the King's helicopter arrived. It landed about 100 yards away, and Chairman Arafat outran everybody towards the King to salute him. The Palestinian Ambassador Tayyeb Abdul Raheem joked, 'The *khityar* [old man] can run.'

Over dinner, the King and Arafat evaluated the status of the peace negotiations and the direction they were taking. The King briefed Arafat on his recent visit to the United States and about his encouraging meeting with President Bill Clinton, Secretary Warren Christopher and the Congress. According to the King, President Clinton was fully committed to the peace process and was appreciative of Jordan's steady and irreversible march towards democracy, political freedom and economic structural adjustment to bring the Jordan economy to an open, free-market system. Arafat continued to complain of his narrowing financial means. He thanked the King for his support of the Palestinian police training program, particularly for the special bodyguards who were trained in high defensive and martial arts. Arafat lingered in Amman until the following day.

The news about the secret talks in Oslo became public on Sunday August 29, 1993. The Oslo draft declaration and its initialing between Ahmad Qura'i of the PLO and Uri Savir, the Director General of Israel's foreign ministry, were in print. The Palestinian Ambassador in Amman was summoned to Anani's office in the Prime Ministry for more news. The Ambassador swore that when he saw Abu Ammar (Arafat) some days earlier, Arafat assured him that he would inform the King about Oslo. On the occasion of Arafat's visit to Jordan a few days earlier, the Ambassador asked Arafat at the airport if he had told the King. Arafat said he could not, and asked the Ambassador to tell the Jordanians the way he saw best. 'The news,' said the Ambassador, 'broke before I could tell you.'

The King's immediate response was anger because he expected a prior briefing from Arafat on how things had progressed, not to be kept in the dark. He reiterated his dissatisfaction with the lack of coordination among Arab negotiating teams, especially between Jordan and the PLO, despite Jordan's relentless efforts to promote it. There were close associates in the Royal Palace that fueled the King's anger. Majali, on the other hand, advised the King to let the matter pass. He convinced the King that it was good omen that Jordan was not involved in such a decisive event for Palestinians and that the PLO acted in its own capacity as the sole legitimate representative of the Palestinian people. Majali thought the Oslo Accord was a big gain for the Palestinians. In the first place, Israel recognized the existence of the Palestinian people. Furthermore, this implied recognition of their unity as manifested by its recognition of the PLO. The Palestinians inside the Occupied Territories and outside of them were thus one people. Three days later the King relaxed his opposition. He said that Jordan would stand behind the Palestinians and support them to the end as long as this was their choice.

On Saturday, August 28, the day before the Oslo talks became known, the delegations to the bilateral negotiations were on their way to Washington, DC to attend the eleventh round. Haddadin met with Saeb Ereikat in the Royal Jordanian lounge at Queen Alia Airport. They chatted before boarding. 'This trip is going to be tiring,' said Haddadin. 'The aircraft does not have a first class compartment, and all the seats are economy.'

'I am taking it to Amsterdam only, and I will switch to a KLM flight to Washington, DC direct,' said Ereikat.

'So you will leave me to suffer for seven more hours to New York, and from there I will take the shuttle to Washington the next day.'

'I will actually meet up with Hanan Ashrawi and Faisal Hussaini in Amsterdam Airport, and we will go on the KLM flight together.'

On the plane, Haddadin and Ereikat exchanged views on the level of coordination between their respective delegations. They expressed dissatisfaction with the prevailing coordination and its lack of effectiveness. 'Okay, Saeb,' said Haddadin, 'the party who stands to gain most is the Palestinian delegation. We should put in more effort to coordinate between our two delegations.'

'Yes Munther, I know; and I know there is a collective gain in coordination among us. What do you think can be done?'

'Let us take over that responsibility; you will be responsible for it in the ranks of the Palestinian delegation, and I will work it so that I am responsible for the coordination in the Jordanian delegation.'

'Good idea. Deal,' said Ereikat.

'Deal as far as I am concerned. I also take it that nothing, absolutely nothing, will be hidden by one delegation from the other,' said Haddadin.

'No, nothing.'

'I will get to the Willard on Sunday, tomorrow. You are invited to come to the Willard for dinner on Monday. I will invite Fayez, our head of delegation, and we will talk further.'

'And you are invited to come to dinner at the Grand Hotel the following evening, on Tuesday, and we will seal our deal there,' said Ereikat.

Haddadin continued to New York, stayed overnight there, and headed the following morning, Sunday August 29, to La Guardia Airport to take the shuttle to Washington. He grabbed the *New York Times* from a news-stand, and was very surprised to read the headline across the front page about the Oslo success. 'So much for the close coordination!' he thought.

In Washington, our delegation was in confusion. Tarawneh could not formulate an official position despite his contact with Amman. He spent a great deal of time with the delegation consulting on what could be done in the round that was about to start. The Oslo tremor would change the direction of the entire peace process. 'Here we are,' said

Tarawneh, 'working genuinely in conformity with the Madrid Invitation and formula. The Palestinian delegation is doing the same. But a bomb is detonated from Oslo in a deal that was born outside the framework of Madrid. Where does this put us all?'

'I think we should stick to our own guns,' said Marwan Dodeen. 'We are empowered to negotiate within the formula of Madrid, and we should continue in that manner.'

'What would happen to the joint delegation?' wondered Haddadin. 'I also wonder if the Palestinian delegation had the rug pulled out from under their feet.' He went on to tell Tarawneh of his exchange with Ereikat on the way to Amsterdam. Ereikat never showed up for the dinner at the Willard, nor did Haddadin go to the dinner at the Grand Hotel as he had agreed with Ereikat.

On Tuesday morning, August 31, we went to the State Department to commence the eleventh round. No one from the Palestinian delegation was there to participate. Soon Ereikat appeared, a little late. He made his way down the hallway towards our room. 'By God I did not know! By God I had no idea!' he yelled to Haddadin, in reference to the Oslo talks.

'Neither did I, nor anyone else in the Jordanian delegation,' responded Haddadin, and they both talked about the published text of Oslo. Haddadin had some doubts:

> Look, Saeb, this provision of 'free passage' between the West Bank and Gaza does not translate into a *mamar* [corridor] as I have heard some reports claim. They could have used the word corridor if they meant it to describe the linkage between Gaza and the West Bank. But they used the words 'free passage'. This means just that, passage. One day Palestinians are assured free passage between Gaza and the West Bank through Beer Sheba, and another day through Jenin to the coastal highway down to Gaza, to give an example.

'I honestly do not know. We have to study the thing carefully. I was informed about it by Hanan Ashrawi whom I met in Schiphol Airport after I left you. I swear I knew nothing about the whole deal,' Ereikat answered.

'I believe you, let us just hope for the best.'

The negotiating delegations did not meet. Rubinstein was equally uninformed about the Oslo deal. The working groups met and ironed out some differences. The water group agreed to negotiate the Jordanian draft, and started to do so. The group on security scored some progress, and that on banking did too.

A new gavel-holder, John Herbst, succeeded Alan Kieswetter for the Water Resources Working Group of the multilaterals. Haddadin, upon Herbst's request, went to meet him on the sixth floor on Wednesday, September 8. Herbst came out of his office as soon as he was alerted that Haddadin was there. 'Ahlan wa sahlan,' said Herbst in Arabic, meaning welcome. Haddadin was impressed, thanking Herbst and following him into his office. 'You are going to participate in signing the Oslo Accord on the law of the White House on Monday September 13. Arrangements are being made for that,' Herbst said as the two were entering his office.

'Not to my knowledge,' said Haddadin. 'As a matter of fact, you are the first to inform me that there will be a signature of the Accord in the White House.'

'You *will* sign the Accord along with the Palestinians.'

Haddadin felt both embarrassed and offended. 'This could be an American desire, but my guess is that Jordan will not be a party to the deal. This is a purely Palestinian–Israeli agreement.'

'No, but you will be a party to it,' Herbst insisted.

'Aren't you going to ask me to sit down?' asked Haddadin.

'Oh, please, have a seat.'

It had been a poor start. Their 35-minute conversation was overshadowed in Haddadin's mind by the arrogance of Herbst's tone, and the insinuation that Jordan would have to follow what the Americans design. 'Even if that was the case,' Haddadin thought, 'Herbst should be discreet about it and more appreciative of Jordan's willingness to abide.' The chemistry between the two men never improved, and this was reflected in the works of the multilateral Working Group on Water Resources later on.

Haddadin reported the exchange to Tarawneh. 'Do you think, Fayez, we are likely to sign along with the Palestinians?'

'I doubt it, but your guess is as good as mine. Let us wait and see.'

'If we are made to sign, count me out of the whole peace process!' Haddadin insisted.

'Let us wait and see!' insisted Tarawneh.

On Thursday evening, the King contacted Tarawneh from London. He instructed him to attend the ceremony of signing the Oslo Accord at the White House, and to initial the Common Agenda with the Israelis the following day. On the following day, Tarawneh received a call from Majali, now Prime Minister. In essence, Majali instructed Tarawneh to have the Jordanian delegation leave Washington. 'No delegate, except the two of you who are stationed in Washington, should stay behind,' said Majali.

The Oslo Accord contained a new Palestinian–Israeli Declaration of Principles (DOP), a copy of which was handed to Anani on September 3. It was of great importance to the Palestinians. It recognized the PLO as the representative of the Palestinians and the new negotiating partner. The PLO, on the other hand, had to amend its Charter to delete every reference to the destruction of Israel. Moreover, the DOP ensured the linkage between the interim and Final Status negotiations, the unity of the Palestinian identity in the Occupied Territories and the exile, and the unity of Palestinian lands once these lands were determined in the process of the Final Status negotiations.

The DOP singled out four major areas as topics to be taken up in the Final Status negotiations. These were: refugees, Jerusalem, Israeli settlements in the Occupied Territories and borders. Each of these issues had direct bearing on Jordan's existing responsibilities and negotiating position with the Israelis. For instance, postponement of the issue of borders meant that Jordan could not finalize the delimitation or demarcation of its borders with Israel until the Final Status. Moreover, the postponement of the demarcation of final borders with Jordan put a dent in Jordan's ability to trade freely with the West Bank and Gaza because Israel was still in control of the territories across such borders. On Jerusalem, Jordan had been administering the Islamic holy places in Jerusalem through al-Awqaf, Jordan's religious affairs ministry, and the Israelis have been respectful of this long tradition. The DOP did not refer to the Jordanian role, even though Jordan always argued that it would give up its jurisdiction to the Palestinians when they were ready and not to the Israelis. On the delayed issue of refugees, Jordan had already framed the terms of reference on this hypersensitive issue in its Common Agenda with Israel. The PLO's agreement to postpone this issue until Final Status negotiations handicapped Jordan's ability to finalize the bilateral aspects of refugees and displaced persons before a peace treaty was concluded. Any settlement of the bilateral aspects of refugees and displaced persons between Jordan and Israel would undoubtedly prejudice the outcome of the Final Status negotiations between the PLO and Israel on these matters.

The DOP also included the formation of a quadrilateral committee (Jordanian-Israeli-Egyptian-Palestinian) to agree on the modalities of allowing Palestinians displaced or barred from returning home since June 1967, to return. The other multilateral issue in the DOP was the agreement between Israel and the PLO in the Oslo Accord to study the implementation of the old Mediterranean–Dead Sea canal, which would not tally with the preliminary agreement between Jordan and Israel to build the Red Sea–Dead Sea canal instead. These salient features constituted the main observations of Jordan on the DOP, a copy of which was handed to Anani on September 3.

Negotiations in the eleventh round on the Syrian and Lebanese tracks did not pick up any momentum. The new Palestinian–Israeli accord stole the show completely and froze any progress in the other arenas. Preparations were actively made for the signature of the Palestinian–Israeli Accord in the White House. Christopher asked on Thursday, September 9, to meet with the Jordanian Ambassador and head of delegation Fayez Tarawneh. Both Martin Indyk and Dennis Ross attended the meeting. Christopher informed Tarawneh that Monday, September 13, would be the expected day for the official Palestinian–Israeli signature at the White House. Contacts had been made with the Syrians and the Lebanese, and both had agreed to attend the signing ceremony through their ambassadors in Washington. However, Christopher thought that His Majesty the King, His Royal Highness Prince al-Hassan, or, at least the Prime Minister, should attend. Last, but not least, Christopher asked Tarawneh to probe Amman's reaction to signing the Jordanian–Israeli Common Agenda on that same day. Tarawneh said on the spot that he would immediately get in touch with the Jordanian officials to seek their directives. But he suggested that the ceremony on Monday should be a Palestinian day. Moreover, it was important for reasons of their own for the Jordanians to sign after the Palestinians. After the meeting, Tarawneh immediately went to the Embassy and used the scrambler telephone to talk to King Hussein. After a long wait, His Majesty came to the phone and agreed that Tarawneh, in his capacity as Ambassador, would represent Jordan.

Both Jordanian and Israeli legal experts in Washington sat down to put the final touches on the text of the Common Agenda in a legally accepted language. Papers were flying between Amman and Washington, and most definitely between Washington and Jerusalem. The High Committee of the Negotiations – Prince al-Hassan, Majali, Anani and Talal al-Hassan – were in continuous session. When the work was done, it had to be typed and properly sealed at the Ministry of Foreign Affairs and couriered to the Jordan Embassy in Washington. Dr Majali convened a Cabinet meeting on Saturday, September 11, to get their approval of the Common Agenda. After a short debate, the agenda was approved.

On Monday, September 13, Mahmoud Abbas from the PLO and Shimon Peres signed the historical accord. It was ambiguous in many ways, deficient in others, but, in the final analysis, it served as a bridge to the future. It was a testimony made before the whole world that Israelis and Palestinians acknowledged each other as people with inalienable rights to exist, live and let live. The image of the shy, reluctant but honest Rabin extending his hand for an ephemeral shake with Arafat became part of a new legacy. Arafat in the White House as a guest of honor. Who would have dreamed of such an event just two years before that?

At the State Department on September 14, Christopher, Ross and Indyk witnessed the signature of the Common Agenda for the Jordanian–Israeli negotiations. (See Appendix 3.)

The Israeli right resented the Oslo Accord. Rabin tried to bolster his popularity through signing a peace agreement with Jordan. He proposed the same old approach: sign a treaty now and work out details later. The Jordanians refused that approach and rightfully thought it would lead them into a dark tunnel with no end in sight. That stand was proven right when observers analyzed the outcome of the Oslo Accord, and the many other agreements between Israel and the Palestinians that had to be worked out later. However, it took drastic events to make progress each time. The massacre at the Ibrahimi mosque in Hebron on Friday, February 26, 1994, triggered efforts to conclude an agreement under the Oslo Accord in Cairo in May of the same year.

## NOTES

1 Haddadin headed the team and its members were Dr Hani Mulki; Dr Duraid Mahasneh, Director General of the Ports Corporation and an expert on the environment; Ambassador Hassan Abu Ni'meh, Jordan's ambassador to Italy; Dr Mohammad Bani Hani.; and a legal expert on environmental law.
2 Noah Kinarti headed the Israeli team and its members were Professor Uri Shamir; Dr Uri Sagi, the Director General of the Ministry of the Environment; Dr Robby Sabel, and others.

# 12

## The Process Accelerates

The conclusion of the Oslo Accord and its signature at the White House signaled the beginning of a new era. The PLO surfaced as the sole legitimate representative of the Palestinians, not only in Arab eyes, but also in the eyes of the rest of the world including Israel. President Clinton was enthused by the occasion that registered as a triumph in American foreign policy despite the credit due to the Norwegians for it. He called for a conference of donor countries to be convened in Washington, DC shortly after the signature of the Accord. The conference was scheduled for the end of October 1993 and had as its agenda the provision of international assistance to the Palestinians. Jordan had been a major contributor to the sustenance of Palestinians and Palestinian refugees, and was at the top of the list of invited countries. Prince al-Hassan Bin Talal was named the royal delegate to the donors' conference in Washington, to be accompanied by a high-level delegation including Jordan's Minister of State for Foreign Affairs, Talal al-Hassan, and other senior officials. Israel was also invited to attend. Its Foreign Minister, Shimon Peres, would lead the Israeli delegation.

Syria and Lebanon were dismayed at the surprise Oslo Accord. They suspended the bilateral negotiations that had been going on since 1991. To them, the Madrid Conference was the basis for negotiating a Middle East peace, and not any other formula. They felt the PLO and Israel had concluded an accord outside that framework, and wondered if the Madrid formula would be workable thereafter. The two countries were not in favor of the substance of the Oslo Accord and were critical of Arafat's approval of its ambiguous language. Syria had been critical of Arafat's leadership since the Israeli invasion of Lebanon and supported PLO factions opposed to Arafat and splinter groups from Arafat's Fatah organization.

President Clinton was more than eager to maintain the momentum of the peace process and to boost it in every way possible. The donors' conference was one aspect of his drive for peace. He thought that a parallel progress on the Jordanian–Israeli track, pursuant to the signing of its Common Agenda, would be desirable. He adopted a proposal that would open up a parallel forum for that track in the form of a Trilateral Economic Committee. The USA, Jordan and Israel would jointly probe the potential for trilateral economic cooperation that would help reinforce and consolidate peace when it was reached, and would focus on joint projects between Jordan and Israel. The President thought that an opportune time to announce the establishment of such a committee would be on the occasion of the donors' conference. He thus invited Crown Prince al-Hassan and Minister Shimon Peres of Israel to a joint meeting with him to discuss the idea and announce the establishment of that committee. That meeting at the White House was Prince al-Hassan's first appearance with Israeli officials. It was also the first such appearance for a Jordanian official outside the negotiation meetings. Officials accompanying the Prince spoke of his deep thoughts and of how tense he was before the meeting. A Trilateral Economic Committee was set up with the USA as chair. Its mandate was outlined in broad terms along the above lines.

The Palestinian delegation to the bilaterals, bypassed by Oslo secret talks, felt short-circuited and tricked by its own PLO. Dr Haider Abdul Shafi resigned. Negotiations thereafter were conducted between the PLO and Israel, and the joint Jordanian–Palestinian delegation ceased to exist.

To address the Syrian and Lebanese suspension of negotiations, Secretary Christopher proposed, and the parties accepted, to have consultation rounds with the US to explore the potential for resuming the bilaterals. Two rounds were held in Washington, and the resumption of negotiations took a lot of time and effort. The format of coordination among Arab delegations was upset. The Syrian and Lebanese delegations consulted with America separately, and did not inform the other delegations of what went on. The consultations eventually brought the Syrians and the Israelis back to the negotiation table in Wye Plantation, Maryland. The Syrian Ambassador to Washington, Walid Mu'allem, headed the Syrian delegation. Their negotiations proceeded well until the spring of 1996, and were stalled thereafter because of the change in the Israeli government when Shimon Peres lost the election, and was succeeded as Prime Minister by Benjamin Netanyahu, leader of the Likud.

## The Water Resources Working Group, Beijing

However, the momentum of the multilaterals acquired new energy with the signature of the Oslo Accord. The fifth round for the Water Resources Group met in Beijing, China in November of 1993. It was the first round for the new gavel-holder, John Herbst of the US State Department. In his consultation meetings with the heads of delegation, he was bent on having them approve moving the venue of the talks to the region, an objective the Israelis had always sought. Herbst invited Haddadin for lunch, their first meeting since their unpleasant encounter in Washington on September 8, 1993. 'We are entertaining the idea of moving the meetings to the region,' said Herbst. 'What do you think?'

'I think,' replied Haddadin, 'that it is too early on the one hand, and it would be contrary to the role of the multilaterals on the other.'

'How is that?' asked Herbst, with a tone of dismay.

'Well, the multilaterals are meant to reinforce the bilaterals, and to provide them with motives to make progress, not the other way around. Moving the multilateral talks to the region will short-circuit the bilaterals and prove the point that Syria and Lebanon have been making all along.'

'What have they been saying all along?' asked Herbst, while he held his spoon full of dessert.

Well, their thesis about the multilateral talks is that they are a sneaky way to normalization with Israel before peace is arrived at. You must be new to the maze of Middle Eastern politics. Note that Israel will be a participant in the meetings, and thus will have to send a delegation to that country of the region where the round is supposed to be held.

'What is wrong with that?' asked Herbst.

To you, nothing. As a matter of fact, it falls within the preferences of the sponsors. They feel that such a move would pacify Israel's fears concerning Arab intentions, and serve as a confidence-building measure. To us, every bit of this move is wrong. How can I overlook the state of war that has been prevailing between us and Israel, and agree to receive an Israeli delegation in an Arab capital before the state of war is ended, not to say anything about peace?

'Well, I have instructions to have the meetings moved to the region. I need your support, or, at the very least, I hope you will not object,' said Herbst.

'Thank you for lunch, and let us cooperate for the best.' That afternoon, Haddadin put all his efforts into consolidating an Arab unified stand against moving the talks to the region. He first approached the Saudi delegation. 'Say, Khalid, are you prepared to receive an Israeli delegation in Riyadh shortly?' he asked the Saudi head of delegation.

'Why do you ask a question like that? Well no, we are not and we will not,' answered Khalid, 'but why do you ask?'

'It looks like the gavel-holder intends to solicit an invitation from a regional party to have the next round convene in their country.'

'Maybe he has his eyes on Oman, I kind of heard a rumor to that effect.'

'Well, remember, if they penetrate the region through Oman, the next attempt could be Saudi Arabia.'

'No way,' said Khalid.

'Then let us put our heads together. You talk to the delegations of the Gulf Cooperation Council, and I will talk to the others. You also better secure the support of Egypt, and I will too,' said Haddadin. The contacts with the Arab delegations went well. The Omani delegation said they had instructions to go along if the sponsor demanded Muscat as the venue, but they would be happy if the joint effort of other Arabs thwarted that plan. The next task for Haddadin was to think of an alternative host country for the next round. He decided to approach the Canadian head of delegation to that end. 'Canada is the wealthiest country in the world per capita in renewable freshwater resources, and it also faces serious water environmental problems,' Haddadin observed to the Canadian head of delegation as they lunched together. 'Why don't you propose to host the next round of talks; we sure can learn a lot from Canada's water experience.'

'We can't host a round like this before the new fiscal year starting in April because we do not have appropriations for this purpose in our budget,' responded the Canadian head of delegation.

'Mid-April should be a good enough timing for the next round. So, why don't you make that proposal in the committee meeting to convene shortly?'

'Good idea. I will,' undertook the Canadian head of delegation, who apparently was not appraised of American intentions.

Haddadin was also busy coordinating with the German delegation. The German Foreign Ministry had contacted the office of Crown Prince al-Hassan and solicited support for a German–Jordanian joint presentation in the forthcoming meeting of the Water Resources Working Group to highlight Germany's assistance program in the field of water resources in Jordan. They had in mind to make a presentation on a water manage-ment and automation project that Germany was financing through the technical assistance program. Haddadin proposed a different topic that could strike a chord in the multilaterals. He proposed that Germany initiate a study on the demand for and supply of water in the core party countries (Lebanon, Syria, Jordan, Palestine and Israel). The study would also examine ways of closing the growing deficit between supply and demand in future years and would identify projects to achieve that objective.

On the first day of the meetings, Haddadin's idea was presented by the German delegation, and Haddadin praised the proposal and enumerated its advantages for the multilaterals. It was generally very well received by the other delegations, with the exception of the Israelis. The German proposal could not be passed without Israeli consent. In the evening, the committee on the selection of the venue met. The Omani delegation, although not part of the committee, attended the meeting, apparently at the invitation of the gavel-holder so that the Omanis could offer Muscat as a venue for the following round. The gavel-holder began to state the purpose of the meeting, but Haddadin asked for the floor before Herbst could bring up the subject of the next venue. He thanked the Chinese for hosting the current round, and thanked the hosts of the previous venues. 'The Canadian delegate has something to say in this regard,' said Haddadin.

The Canadian delegate took the floor before the gavel-holder had a chance to comment.

'My country would be honored to host the next round of talks of the Water Resources Group,' said the Canadian delegate, taking the floor, 'I hope it will take place there after the first of April, the beginning of our fiscal year.'

'Thank you, sir,' said Haddadin, 'Canada is an active participant in the multilaterals; it is the richest country in the world in water resources per capita; and Ottowa is a beautiful place. I move to accept the Canadian invitation if no one has any material objection.'

'I second that,' said the Saudi delegate.

'I second that too,' said al-Khudary, the Palestinian delegate.

Herbst looked annoyed, and found himself cornered. The other delegates were in favor of accepting the invitation, and the Omani delegate did not compete! After dinner, the Arab delegates assembled in Haddadin's suite and expressed their pleasure at the performance of the Jordanian delegation. 'The credit goes to all of you, especially the Saudi delegation,' Haddadin assured them. 'It was late when Haddadin retired to bed. At about 3:00 a.m. his phone rang.

'Good morning,' said the caller.

'Is it morning already?' asked a sleepy Haddadin.

'Wake up, sorry to wake you up, this is Jawad in Amman.'

'Oh, Your Excellency, I am up and ready.'

'Listen, I am talking to you after His Majesty called from Paris where he is visiting. Apparently, your gavel-holder out there has complained to the State Department that you are making his life miserable,' said Jawad Anani, now a Minister of State.

'Jawad, he is making his own life miserable. He wants to move the talks to the region and we are just not ready for that.'

'You are doing the right thing, but can you make his life less miserable?' asked Anani.

'Why? Give me one good reason.'

'Aqaba,' said Anani, 'Aqaba.' Anani was referring to the American Navy blockade of Jordan's only port, which had been causing Jordan economic losses. Efforts had been continuous to stop the US Navy inspecting every ship that called at the port of Aqaba, and from diverting at will those ships that had questionable cargo. Jordan had been pleading with the United Nations and the United States to have that blockade lifted.

'Okay, I get the point, and I will abide by what you direct; the cause is worth it.'

The following morning Haddadin could not bring himself to go to the gavel-holder and to reverse positions. He went to breakfast with the rest of the Jordanian delegation. While he was having breakfast, Herbst walked in and saved Haddadin's day. 'Could I have a word with you, Dr Haddadin?' asked Herbst.

'Yes of course, as soon as I am done with breakfast.'

'I will be in the meeting room downstairs.'

'Okay, I will join you soon. Have some coffee with us,' invited Haddadin.

'I just had breakfast and I have lots to do. Thank you.'

The conversation set the atmosphere for a friendly meeting. Haddadin asked Ali Ghezawi, a member of the Jordanian delegation, to accompany him to the meeting. 'The best I can do,' said Haddadin to Herbst, 'is to forget about Canada now if you are prepared to forget about Oman and the region.'

'What are your thoughts?' asked Herbst.

'I suggest that we do not decide right now on the next venue, and leave it to the Steering Committee of the multilaterals to decide. It will meet next month and our position will, in the meantime, be reassessed.'

'Fine, so be it,' said Herbst. The confrontation ended, and the decision on the next venue was left to the Steering Committee. The next challenge for Haddadin was to get the Israelis to agree to the 'German' proposal so that it would be included in the final statement of the works of the round. He worked hard on the Israelis until they came around, and Katz-Oz agreed to the German study.

The Steering Committee of the multilaterals was to hold its meetings in Tokyo in December 1993. Tarawneh and Haddadin headed for Tokyo to be joined by the Jordanian Ambassador there, Farouq Qasrawi, to form the Jordan delegation. Majali and Anani were in Tokyo on a separate visit after the government won a vote of confidence in the newly elected parliament. Majali invited Tarawneh and Haddadin to his hotel suite one evening. He was waiting for two other visitors. They were Dr Yossi Beilin and Ambassador Elyakim Rubinstein who wanted to give their congratulations to Majali in person on his appointment as Prime Minister of Jordan. After all, Majali and Rubinstein had spent nine rounds of bilateral negotiations confronting one another, and it was time that they dealt with each other in a different context. Anani, Tarawneh and Haddadin attended, and the exchange of ideas over the multilaterals was both meaningful and helpful. 'We should not carry the ladder crossways,' said Majali. 'If Oman wants to host the next round of multilaterals for water, why should we stand in their way? It is convenient that we, as Jordan, did not initiate the convening of multilateral rounds in our territories.'

'I was only mindful of opening the Arab capitals to Israelis before a peace agreement with them is reached,' said Haddadin. 'What would be left, after such normalization, as an incentive for Israel to make peace?'

'Lots of things remain,' said Anani. 'Holding a round of talks or a seminar in an Arab capital does not mean establishing diplomatic relations, nor does it mean normalization entailing the free movement of commodities, capital and labor.'

'Munther was adamantly against moving the talks to the region,' said Tarawneh. 'He had a showdown with the gavel-holder in Beijing over the issue.'

'I know, I remember,' said Majali.

'And I remember too,' said Anani, 'I was in the middle of it, and was on the phone with Munther to get the issue resolved.'

'Pasha, that was my own personal reading of where we, as Jordan, stood. Now that I have the benefit of checking with the Prime Minister, I am at your disposal. I, of course, will go along with what my government instructs,' said Haddadin.

'And how about what your head of delegation instructs?' asked Tarawneh jokingly.

'Of course,' said Haddadin, 'this will have to come first, maybe even before the instructions of the Prime Minister! If the Pasha permits, that is,' Haddadin joked backed.

The meetings of the Steering Committee of the multilateral talks went well. More countries applied to join the multilaterals. Romania, Korea and others wanted to join, and their applications were looked upon favorably. The German delegation advised Haddadin, Tarawneh and the US gavel-holder of the Water Resources Group that Germany had been informed of the willingness of Israel to support the study of supply and demand of water in the core countries. An Israeli group would go to Frankfurt, and Germany favored a trilateral meeting with them and the Jordanians before Christmas. Majali approved the trilateral meeting. Haddadin flew from Tokyo to Frankfurt on December 17, and was met there by Ali Ghezawi, the advisor to the Minister of Water and Irrigation and a member of the delegation to the Working Group. On the evening of his arrival in Frankfurt, Haddadin sat in his room at the Intercontinental Hotel and drafted the terms of reference for a study on the supply and demand for water in the region.

The following day, a trilateral meeting took place at the Intercontinental Hotel. Katz-Oz and Ilan Baruch of the Israeli delegation had arrived and checked into the Intercontinental Hotel. The parties approved the draft terms of reference document with very little modification. The representative of the German GTZ, *Gesellschaft fuer Techniche Zusamenarbeitung* (Corporation for Technical Cooperation), took the draft document and had it typed in final form and distributed to the core parties. It needed a little persuasion in the Israeli ranks, and some convincing in the Palestinian ranks before it was finally approved in April 1994.

On the same occasion, Haddadin talked to Katz-Oz about the development of the Jordan Rift Valley. He spoke of its backbone, the Red Sea–Dead Sea Canal. Katz-Oz was supportive of the idea of integrated development of the Rift Valley as outlined by Haddadin, but mentioned other alternatives to the linkage of the Dead Sea with the open seas. 'You know, Avraham, there is more to the linkage than just power generation,' said Haddadin.

'What is up your sleeve?' asked Katz-Oz. Haddadin responded:

The crucial objective is to control the level of the Dead Sea. The recession of its level results in an increased inflow of freshwater into the Dead Sea from the adjacent mountain aquifers. I have been around the Dead Sea shore on the eastern side, and have seen fresh water leaking from the aquifers into the Dead Sea itself. The lower the level goes, the more the driving pressure will be, and the more valuable ground water we lose to the Dead Sea. If we bring back the level of the Dead Sea to where it had been historically, the confining pressure that will stop the flow of ground water will help us preserve this very valuable resource in the adjacent mountain aquifers.

'We never thought of it that way,' said Katz-Oz. Haddadin continued to explain:

One more thing, and I am confident that your guys must have thought of it. We do not have to generate power and then use it to generate sweet water. We can go direct from the potential head to reverse osmosis plants in which that potential head drives the salty Red Sea water through membranes and produces freshwater. The leftover potential head can be used to generate electricity to pump the water up to the urban centers east and west of the Rift.

'Maybe our guys have thought of that. I have an idea of what to call the developed Rift Valley. Call it the Valley of Peace,' said Katz-Oz.

'We will not disagree on the name, just let us get this integrated development idea going, campaign for it, and make it a reality,' said Haddadin.

'You have my support.'

'Thank you, and I will put my ideas in a paper and will have it discussed in the proper peace forum.'

Back in Amman for Christmas and New Year, Haddadin got busy after the holidays documenting the outcome of the meetings that had taken place. He also started putting on paper his ideas of the integrated development of the Jordan Rift Valley. His work was interrupted by a call from the office of the Crown Prince asking him to fly to London the following day. The Crown Prince was leaving for London where His Majesty King Hussein was on a private visit, and he had asked for members of the negotiations teams. Haddadin flew to London on Friday, January 8, 1994 to join Crown Prince al-Hassan and other delegates to work on several issues that touched on the peace negotiations, and the positions that Jordan should take to protect its vital interests. The team worked very hard, and developed position papers for Jordan to be considering, both whilst undertaking peace negotiations and during the peace era. Crown Prince al-Hassan steered the work, and when it was finished, he called upon King Hussein to come and listen to a presentation at the Jordan Information Bureau in London. Haddadin, al-Khasawneh, Michael Marto, and Safwan Toukan briefed the King, each in his own field of competence. The presentation went well, and His Majesty commended the work and the effort of the Crown Prince.

When he got back to Amman, Haddadin focused on the concept of integrated development of the Jordan Rift Valley. He put his ideas on paper in an organized way and submitted them to the Crown Prince, and to Anani, the Minister for Prime Ministry Affairs. Anani called for a meeting at the Prime Ministry to discuss the contents of the paper. Crown Prince al-Hassan showed up at the meeting and directed the debate. Soon, Prime Minister Majali arrived in traditional Arabic costume and joined the meeting. The Prince made valuable comments and was supportive of the effort. His ideas and the comments made and approved by the meeting were incorporated by Haddadin and put in the final paper. He made six copies, and packed them to take with him to

Washington, where a meeting of the Trilateral Economic Committee was to convene on February 23, 1994. The meeting would be preceded by a meeting of the group on water, energy and the environment, and Haddadin left with his team members on February 14, 1994.[1] The occasion was used to convene meetings of the group on borders and security as well. Dr Abdallah Toukan and General Tahseen Shurdum, who were in that group, joined the team traveling to Washington, DC.

The team on water, energy and the environment worked diligently with their Israeli counterparts, and all but agreed to the common sub-agenda. Kinarti, Sabel and Sagi were on the Israeli side. The Israelis took advantage of the occasion and arranged to show a video they had brought with them showing the the intensity of houseflies on the Israeli side of the Dead Sea southern shores, a resort area full of hotels and other tourist facilities. Dennis Ross, the US coordinator, and his staff, attended the show. Also attending were Elyakim Rubinstein and Fayez Tarawneh. The Israelis blamed the intensity of houseflies on the Jordanian agricultural practices and system of garbage disposal. Their bottom line was that, through cooperation, the problem of houseflies could be overcome. 'Okay, folks,' said Haddadin, 'we concede to the unhygienic methods of Jordanian horticulture and garbage disposal . . . Could someone, then, tell me why the houseflies take the trouble of flying over to the clean Israeli side when they have it all made on the Jordanian side?' The Israeli argument was diffused, and the teams went back to work on their sub-agenda.

In the negotiations room, the Jordanian team gave the Israelis a proposal of a text over water sharing which they wanted included in the sub-agenda. The Israeli team left the room to consult with each other and with their boss. The door was kept open, and an American man appeared in the hallway. 'Is this the Jordan delegation?' he asked. Since outsiders never intruded on the delegations and their rooms, it was clear that this man must be an insider.

'Yes it is,' said Haddadin.

'I am looking for Dr Fayez Tarawneh.'

'Well, he is upstairs on the sixth floor. What can we do for you?' asked Mulki.

'I am Wesley Eagan, the US Ambassador designate to Jordan.'

'Oh! You are very welcome by Jordanians already. Please come in,' invited Mahasneh. Eagan visited the Jordanian team for about half an hour and exchanged visiting cards with them.

About the same time Awn al-Khasawneh was in Geneva attending the meetings of the UN International Law Commission of which he was a member. On February 19, Awn was contacted by the office of the Crown Prince and asked to proceed to Washington and join Anani there. Anani and the Jordan Ambassador, Fayez Tarawneh, would define the mission to him. Once in Washington Awn joined Minister Anani and Ambassador Tarawneh for a meeting at the State Department. Ed Djerejian, Dan Kurtzer, and Aaron Miller represented the American side. The purpose of the meeting was to discuss the merits or otherwise of signing a peace treaty with Israel, a matter that Rubinstein had been raising in almost every round of negotiations with the Jordanians. Majali's response and Tarawneh's after him had been a sustained 'No'. In that meeting, Kurtzer was generally the one who did the talking for the Americans. 'Why don't you sign the peace treaty with Israel now and work out details later?' he asked, with visible signs of impatience.

'Dr Kurtzer,' said Awn, 'we have agreed with the Israelis in the Common Agenda that all of its elements would have to be resolved before we sign a peace treaty. Why do you want to upset that delicately worked-out balance?'

Arguments for and against the idea went back and forth until Kurtzer seemed to lose patience.

'Listen,' said an irritated Kurtzer, 'I am working my ass off for you people to get $35 million from Congress as a grant to Jordan, and you tell me you are not going to sign?'

'His Excellency Minister Anani of course speaks on our behalf and at any time he wants, but I cannot leave this issue without an answer,' snapped Awn. 'Dr Kurtzer,' he continued emphatically, 'if you think we are going to sacrifice Jordan's higher national interests for your $35 million, you know what to do with them.'

Everyone was stunned at this point. Kurtzer, who had been sitting on the arm of a sofa, walked out. Five minutes later, Secretary Christopher, who obviously had been briefed about the conversation, called the group into his office. Awn dreaded the pressure that Jordan could be put under in order to coerce it to sign a peace treaty with Israel before the items on the Common Agenda were settled. USA relations with Jordan and the rescue of Jordan's economy depended to a large extent on what the USA could do for Jordan, not only bilaterally, but also through its influence with its allies in the Paris Club and the London Club for external debt rescheduling. As the group walked out to meet with Christopher, the press was there in full alert. It looked like they were expecting an important announcement, maybe along the lines of Jordan's willingness or consideration to sign a treaty with Israel; that, at least, was what Awn feared. 'Had this happened,' Awn later confided in Haddadin, 'we would have gone into another Oslo dark tunnel,' referring to the Oslo Accord that the PLO had signed with Israel.

Secretary Christopher received the delegates, and was kind and understanding. Obviously Kurtzer had briefed him on the stubbornness of the Jordanians, and the Secretary did not force the issue. On the following day, February 24, a meeting of the Trilateral Economic Committee was held in the State Department. Tarawneh, Haddadin and Fayez Khasawneh represented Jordan, and Rubinstein headed his team. The American presence, with Ambassador Dennis Ross heading the delegation, was strong and high level. Rubinstein took the floor and expressed Israel's dismay at Jordan's reluctance to sign a peace treaty with Israel. He poured criticism on Jordan's stand.

'Ambassador Rubinstein,' said Haddadin after he was given the floor, 'I get sick and tired of your repetitive expression of your desire to have Jordan sign a peace treaty with Israel now and work out details later. I challenge you, Ambassador, to come and sign the peace treaty tonight, the treaty that I have drafted.' Rubinstein did not expect this answer, nor was Haddadin aware of what had gone on the day before at the State Department between the Jordanians and the Americans. But that was the last time Haddadin heard Rubinstein speak of a peace treaty, at least in public.

Also in that meeting, Haddadin made a presentation of the Jordan Rift Valley integrated development. He basically presented the paper he had prepared and which was approved by the Ministerial Development Committee. The paper was very well received and the US delegation, composed of at least a dozen people, was taking notes. Before the coffee break, Dennis Ross praised the Jordanian presentation. During the break, he approached Tarawneh, saying 'I have been involved in the peace process for some time now. This is the first time I heard anything with meat on it.'

'Thank you,' said Tarawneh, 'this is very kind of you. I am sure Haddadin will be pleased to hear that.'

'Please tell him that, and I would appreciate it if I could have a copy of the document.' Tarawneh promised him a copy and when the session was over, approached Haddadin. 'Congratulations,' he said, 'the Americans were very pleased with your presentation, and so were the Israelis. Dennis Ross, who very seldom has a complimentary comment for anyone, praised it. He wants a copy. May I have one to give him and one for myself?'

'Yes of course, but in due time,' responded Haddadin.

'What do you mean?'

'I mean whatever we give to Ross or the Americans will find its way to the Israelis. In my presentation I did not read everything in the document. It carries our position on the Rift Valley development. I want to see the Israelis' position before I make my own paper public.' Tarawneh did not like Haddadin's answer.

On Thursday evening, Tarawneh came to Haddadin and told him that he had obtained Amman's approval to give Ross a copy of the document on the integrated development of the Rift Valley. Haddadin conceded the point and promised to hand Tarawneh a copy on Monday. On Friday morning, we heard of the brutal attack by an Israeli settler on the Ibrahimi mosque in Hebron, and the killing of over two dozen Palestinian worshippers while they were performing Ramadan prayers. The delegation was instructed by Amman to interrupt their round and to head back to base on Sunday, which they did. Haddadin was spared the task of handing over his document.

On March 1, Dennis Ross followed the delegation to Amman. The Prime Minister called for a meeting on March 2 with the visiting American delegation at the Prime Ministry. Ross praised the Jordanian Rift Valley paper and asked for a copy of it. Majali looked at Haddadin. 'Give the gentleman a copy,' he ordered in Arabic.

'Yes sir,' said Haddadin, and walked over to Anani and gave him the copy. Anani, in turn, handed the copy over to Ross. On the following day, March 3, 1994, Ross crossed over to Israel and the West Bank in an attempt to contain the damage done to the peace process by the savage crime. He had with him the document on the Jordan Rift Valley. On

March 25, Anani sent an envelope to Haddadin containing the Israeli reaction to the Jordanian paper, and some ideas on the development of the Rift Valley. Haddadin read it and made comments. It was not up to the expected standard, and was definitely inferior to the Jordanian presentation. 'How did you find the Israeli paper?' Anani asked Haddadin on the phone.

'No at all impressive,' said Haddadin, 'I believe ours is superior.'

'I did not think it was impressive either,' responded Anani. About ten days later, another Israeli paper about the Rift Valley arrived with Anani. It was better than the first one, but the impact of the Jordanian paper on the second Israeli paper was detectable.

'It looks like there are two separate groups in Israel working on the issue,' Haddadin told Anani in one of their meetings in Anani's office at the Prime Ministry.

'I think so,' said Anani, 'one group works closely with the Foreign Minister, Peres, and another works closely with the Prime Minister, Rabin.'

'In either case, Jawad, I am confident we will produce better quality and be ahead in this competition.'

A short while later, Peres' book on peace came out, and in it he included the vision of the integrated development of the Jordan Rift Valley. It contained ideas parallel to those presented in the Jordanian paper.

The demands of the peace process during April and May 1994 were immense. The hard work fell on the shoulders of Anani, Awn al-Khasawneh and Haddadin. Preparations were underway to crystallize Jordanian positions toward expected Israeli proposals, and to prepare Jordanian proposals to throw at Israelis when the time became ripe. While these tasks were ongoing, Haddadin was called to the Prime Ministry on Saturday evening, on May 28, 1994. 'Get ready, *Jalalet Sayyedna* [i.e. His Majesty the King] wants to see you and Michael Marto in London tomorrow,' said Majali.

The following day, Haddadin was surprised to see the rest of the Jordanian delegation to the bilaterals at the airport ready to leave for London. 'What is going on?' Haddadin asked General Shurdum as they met at the VIP lounge at Queen Alia Airport. Tahseen Shurdum was as bewildered as the rest of the delegates.

In London, our delegation was met by Embassy staff with limousines to take us to our hotel. The next day, Monday, June 30, Anani joined us from Amman, and Toukan and Tarawneh joined from Cape Cod and Washington. At the same hotel, there were other high-ranking officials including the head of intelligence in Jordan and others. On Wednesday, June 1, the delegation was ushered to the Claridges Hotel in London to meet with His Majesty King Hussein and Crown Prince al-Hassan. His Majesty spoke of times present and to come; nothing definitive but one could tell there was something in the atmosphere. 'Dr Munther, can you please brief us again about our strategy in the water negotiations?' the King asked. Haddadin was taken by surprise. He had never discussed the strategy in public, nor with anyone in detail except the Crown Prince, and in memos forwarded to the King. He looked around and saw the audience waiting for the answer.

'Well, *Jalalet Sayyedna*,' said Haddadin,

> I have been after the water rights of the Hashemite Kingdom in the Jordan River basin as they stood back in 1955, i.e., the West Bank included. This is not to mean that Jordan wants to keep the waters of the West Bank to itself. Each Palestinian now living in Jordan whose rights are counted in the deal can take his water rights with him across the River when he exercises the right of return.

'Please, *ya Akhi*, take note of the decision of disengagement with the West Bank. As such, the rights of the West Bank are not ours to secure,' said the King.

'But, Sire, I think that Palestinian water would be much safer in Jordanian hands than leaving it in Israeli hands,' Haddadin responded.

'The West Bank and Gaza have their own men to defend their rights,' said the King.

'But, Sire, I am taking that water to serve Palestinians in Jordan with domestic water. No Palestinian now living in Jordan brought with him a bucketful of water when he or she came over from Palestine. Whoever goes back, I thought, can take his water share with him,' Haddadin argued.

'But there is parched land in the West Bank and it needs to be irrigated,' said the King, 'and, unlike people, that land was not displaced across the River.' Haddadin appreciated the King's patience in arguing the separate West Bank rights, and the need for Jordanians fully to recognize that the Palestinians were in charge of defending their rights against Israel. He agreed to follow King Hussein's instructions.

The King and the Crown Prince took Tarawneh aside and spent some time talking to him. A round of trilateral talks was to convene soon in Washington and the delegation would leave for Washington in a couple of days. As it turned out, the conversation had something to do with moving the negotiations venue to the region. The King then bid the delegation farewell, and left the hotel.

The delegation continued with the meeting under the chairmanship of the Crown Prince. As they sat down, the Crown Prince looked at Haddadin who was sitting to his left, deep in his thought. 'I can tell,' said Prince al-Hassan, 'from the look on your face that you are not convinced by what His Majesty has instructed.'

'But who am I, sir, not to be convinced? I am but an emissary to defend the policy of the Kingdom and to have it implemented. I have heard the instructions from the source of the spring. My job is to abide and implement,' said Haddadin. He started thinking of separating the water rights of the West Bank, basing his thoughts on the words of the Technical Committee of the Arab League between 1953 and 1955.

The delegation flew over to Washington to attend the trilateral round of negotiations. Some bilateral topics were negotiated and the common sub-agenda on water, energy and the environment was agreed upon, and there was talk on cooperation in the field of the Rift Valley development and on joint cooperation on tourism on and around the Dead Sea. The American Parks Authority participated in the talks, and it was felt that 'someone' was pushing to have cooperative efforts started before the signing of a peace treaty.

On June 6, 1994, Tarawneh announced at the end of the Trilateral Economic Committee meeting that the negotiations between Jordan and Israel would be moved to the region. They would be held on the truce line between the two countries. This marked an end to our attempt to keep the talks away from the region until progress was achieved. The following rounds of talks would be conducted in alternating venues in Israel and Jordan.

## NOTE

1   The members were Dr Duraid Mahasneh; Dr Hani Mulki, Dr Fayez Al-Khasawneh (a relative of Awn Al-Khasawneh), Dr Ibrahim Badran.

# 13

## Implementation

———————

July 18 was set as the date for the first round of negotiations between Jordan and Israel to take place in Wadi Araba on the truce line between the two countries. Dr Tarawneh arrived from Washington, DC to head the Jordanian delegation to those negotiations. Our delegation was expanded and dispatched to Aqaba on July 17. Army tents were pitched in an area about ten kilometers north of Aqaba, at the location where the border with Palestine, adjusted in 1946, met with the original Mandate border. The main tent was long and wide with zipper doors to it on both the western and eastern sides, and had its center on the truce line. The tent had several compartments to accommodate the several working groups: water, energy and the environment; borders and security, and economic cooperation. The site had been prepared and access roads to it built by the Royal Engineers Corps on the Jordan side, and by the Israeli Defense Forces on the Israeli side. Work was going on around the clock to make the site ready for the occasion. The Jordan protocol staff of the Ministry of Foreign Affairs cooperated with the ranks of the Royal Engineers Corps to arrange the Jordan side of the site, and supervise the seating arrangements and the supplies.

Our delegation checked into the Holiday Hotel (formerly the Holiday Inn) in Aqaba, and senior members were assigned suites on the third floor, a welcome change from single-room arrangements at the Willard. On July 18, the delegation headed to the new negotiations venue north of Aqaba. Haddadin headed the group on water, energy and the environment, and was also asked to keep an eye on the borders issue taken up by the second group.

The opening meeting was seen as historic. The Israeli press in particular was very excited. They took pictures and videos of Tarawneh shaking hands with Rubinstein across the meeting table. The meeting was ceremonial, and soon broke up into the working groups. Haddadin headed toward the negotiations tent followed by the members of his delegation. As he entered the tent, he found the Israeli delegation, headed by Noah Kinarti, sitting on the western side of the meeting table, and he took the seat in the middle of the eastern side – the Jordan side of the border. Haddadin sat down, and remembered that Jordan had not yet recognized the State of Israel. 'It is my pleasure,' he said as the meeting convened, 'to welcome you to Jordan for this very first meeting of our group held in the region, and I give our guests the floor.' The guests were actually sitting on their own soil. The Israeli head of delegation did not get the nuances of this welcome, and responded with words of courtesy. He then asked to give the floor to Professor Uri Shamir of Technion, Israel Institute of Technology sitting to the far left of Kinarti. Shamir spoke English with an American accent. He had triggered angry reactions from Jordanians in the Washington, DC meetings when he asked that the construction of the Karama dam be suspended. In his new submission, Shamir emphasized bilateral cooperation, and brought examples on how Jordan and Israel could cooperate in the field of designs and research in water resources.

Haddadin had new delegates with him, and he wanted them to be free from any inhibitions when they talked to the Israelis or negotiated with them. He had to deflate Shamir in the best possible way. 'Are you through, professor?' Haddadin asked as Shamir finished some ten minutes of talk.

'Yes, Dr Haddadin, and we would like to hear your reaction to my proposal,' answered Shamir.

> Do you think you are in a classroom? Haddadin shouted back. And if you do, you should recognize who the professor in this classroom is. What is this? Who gave you the right to set the agenda of the talk? I consider such an attempt an infringement on our common sub-agenda. As a matter of fact I take it as an insult to presume that we are prepared to talk cooperation with you before we score progress on water sharing. To be honest with you all, it does not honor me to share a negotiation table with you!

Haddadin hit the table with his fist, stood up, turned his back and headed toward the eastern door of that Army tent. 'Where should I go?' thought Haddadin to himself. 'There is nothing but desert stretches all around.'

Shamir saved Haddadin's day. 'I am sorry,' he said politely before Haddadin got halfway to the door. 'I did not mean to upset you.'

'And I accept your apology,' said Haddadin as he turned back to head the delegation. By that time, all the delegates of the other groups had gathered around the group on water, energy and the environment. They hurried to see what was behind all that shouting. Haddadin was deeply glad inside that he did not have to leave the tent and spend the day in the desert alone.

When the time came for lunch, it was served in the Israeli side of the compound. 'How come you are not eating? It is all kosher,' remarked an Israeli press correspondent to Haddadin. 'Or are you afraid there could be poison in your food?'

'Israelis poison atmospheres, not food,' Haddadin answered. 'I have stomach problems and acidity; the best way to deal with it is less food intake.'

That first encounter was conducive to better communication between the two delegations, and diplomatic language prevailed thereafter. The talks were inching forwards over the substance of water sharing, and on ways to mitigate the negative impacts of droughts. That evening was eventful. It was announced that Shimon Peres, the Foreign Minister of Israel, would come to attend a meeting of the Trilateral Economic Committee the following day in a hotel on the east shore of the Dead Sea. Secretary Christopher would also attend, and Dr Majali, the Prime Minister and Foreign Minister, would head the Jordanian side. The Jordanian team involved in the work of the Trilateral Economic Committee got ready.

It was the first time an Israeli Foreign Minister had paid an official visit to Jordan. His company crossed the Jordan River via the King Hussein Bridge near Jericho, and proceeded by bus to the hotel, the Dead Sea Spa Hotel on the east shore of the Dead Sea. Prime Minister Majali came by car from Amman, and so did Secretary Christopher, who had arrived in Amman the night before. Peres flew in by helicopter from nearby Jerusalem, and the chopper landed in the hotel parking lot; another landed on the highway next to the hotel. Peres was met as he disembarked by Talal al-Hassan, the Minister of State for Foreign Affairs, who escorted him to the hotel. The hotel was jammed with reporters and with security men from all three countries: the USA, Jordan and Israel.

A plenary meeting was held in the ground floor of the hotel. It was very well organized. After the opening plenary in which speeches were made by the heads of the three delegations, the parties retreated to a meeting on the second floor of the hotel. They touched on the bilateral negotiations. Anani, Tarawneh, Haddadin, and Safwan Toukan, the Secretary General of the Ministry of Planning, accompanied Majali in this meeting. Minister Peres was accommodating of our concerns over the slow progress in the bilaterals. The parties then declared their intention to accelerate the negotiations and to do their best to overcome any obstacles. The event made history, and witnessed the first official Israeli visit to Jordan, not to the capital city as official visits normally are, but to a spa hotel on the east shore of the Dead Sea.

Shortly after lunch, Foreign Minister Peres left the way he came in – by helicopter, and Secretary Christopher left for Amman Airport, Majali and Tarawneh leaving at the same time to bid him farewell at the airport. Majali asked Haddadin to head the Jordan delegations to the various working groups of the Trilateral Economic Committee, and he did. Tony Verstandig of the State Department chaired the plenary after Secretary Christopher left, and the various working groups got to work. Most of the Jordanians were witnessing their first encounter with the Israelis, and so were most of the Israelis with the Jordanians. Haddadin spent his time moving from one working group to another to lend support to the various Jordanian teams. He urged them to be brave, careful and considerate. He issued directions to anyone who asked for them. The Trilateral Economic Committee continued work on the following day, July 20, 1994, and agreed to hold its next meeting in Eilat in September.

Another historic day fell on July 25, 1994. His Majesty King Hussein and Prime Minister Yitzhak Rabin met at the White House under the auspices of President Clinton. They issued the Washington Declaration, ending the state of war between the two countries, and expressing their intent to make peace in the Middle East. The two leaders addressed a special joint session of the US Congress on July 26, and were received with a standing ovation. King Hussein shone, expressing Jordan's intentions and appearing as a true champion of peace in the Middle East. The world media carried the event, and the world began to expect positive developments in the bilateral negotiations. The two leaders pledged that they would attend in person to all the obstacles and difficulties facing their respective negotiating teams.

The bilateral negotiations venue then alternated between the Moria Plaza Hotel on the western shore of the Dead Sea in Israel, and the Dead Sea Spa Hotel on the eastern shore in Jordan. Three Jordanian helicopters carried our delegation to Moria Plaza when the negotiations were held there, and a bus carried the Israeli delegation over the King Hussein Bridge when the negotiations were conducted in the Dead Sea Spa Hotel. Each venue hosted the negotiations for one working week (Sunday through Thursday).

## Water, energy and the environment

In the meantime, Haddadin got busy preparing a document needed to take a further step on the trail of the Rift Valley integrated development. He started drafting 'Terms of Reference for Consulting Services'; a document needed to invite competitive bidding between qualified consulting firms to perform the necessary pre-feasibility and feasibility studies. He headed the Jordan Rift Valley (JRV) team in addition to the tasks assigned to him in the bilateral and multilateral negotiations. Haddadin was seriously overworked and sometimes wondered whether it would be to no avail.

The meetings at the Moria Plaza Hotel in Israel were conducted in the midst of worldwide press coverage. In the lobby, there was a big hall where the press correspondents were accommodated and were served free coffee. Up on the sixth floor, there were the negotiation rooms for each group, and another room for more free donuts, coffee and tea. The negotiations went well, but the Jordanians were annoyed by the Israeli lack of discretion. Almost everything raised in the negotiation rooms was broadcast on their public media on the same day, and repeated the following morning. In one such broadcast, Israel radio spoke of the talks on the integrated development of the Jordan Rift Valley, a concept proposed and formulated by Jordan. The radio elaborated on the concept and attributed the credit for it to the Israeli Foreign Minister, Shimon Peres. 'It is well known,' said the announcer, 'that the concept of the development of the Jordan Rift Valley was proposed by Israel; Mr Shimon Peres, the Foreign Minister was the author of this concept.' That was not true. The concept should have been credited to Jordan. Its chief promoter was Crown Prince al-Hassan during the preparation sessions for the Madrid Conference, and Haddadin was the author of the concept paper that was presented to the Trilateral Committee in February in Washington. By July, the credit had gone to Shimon Peres!

On the way to Amman airport to take the helicopters to Moria Plaza, Fayez Tarawneh shared a limousine with Haddadin. Fayez was buoyant but Haddadin was solemn. 'You are not yourself, Munther,' noted Tarawneh. 'Is something the matter?'

'These Israelis always want more. They always will demand more, and will go about getting it in any way.'

'Why do you say that? Anything new?'

'I heard on their radio this morning that Peres is the author of the concept of the integrated development of the Jordan Rift Valley.'

'But that is a big lie!' exclaimed Tarawneh.

'They took Palestinian land, Palestinian homes, and claimed Palestinian costumes as their own, the falafel dish that is now sold in New York as an Israeli dish, and now they claim our ideas to be their own,' said Haddadin grimly. 'I am going to deal with it today.'

'Please be careful. Rock the boat but do not overturn it.'

> You will feel how strongly the boat is rocked, I assure you. You were a witness to my presentation of the JRV concept paper in Washington last February. I cannot claim the credit for myself. *Sidi* Hassan [Crown Prince al-Hassan] was the primary architect of the whole thing and chaired the final meeting that approved the document carrying the concept. Remember Fayez, remember when I refused to give you a copy of our position paper to forward to Dennis Ross in Washington right after the presentation? I was sure he would hand it over to the Israelis and I was afraid they would claim the great idea for themselves.

The reception on the Israeli side was good as usual. After donuts and coffee, the groups headed for the meeting rooms. 'There will be no meeting today on the Jordan Rift Valley; all Jordanians can join me in the meeting of the water group,' said Haddadin.

'But why?' asked Rafi Benvenisti, a senior member on the Israeli JRV team.

'Because, Rafi, and I speak to all Israelis here now, because your radio is distorting facts. They announced this morning that the concept of the JRV development is attributed to your Foreign Minister, a totally false statement,' said Haddadin.

'Well, you know how the correspondents are, and how the press is,' said Yossi Vardi, a leading Israeli expert on the JRV.

'How can we build trust with you if you commit such mistakes and deny Jordanians their dues? I expect a clarification from your Ministry of Foreign Affairs before we proceed with the Jordan Rift Valley meetings.'

The meeting was called off. When Rubinstein was made aware of Haddadin's decision, he rushed to Tarawneh to save the day. Tarawneh said that Haddadin handled his own affairs as far as the Jordan Rift Valley was concerned. After lunch, a statement was issued by the office director of the Israeli Minister of Foreign Affairs and was distributed to the press. The press release acknowledged that the concept of the integrated development of the JRV originated in Jordan and that Jordanians engineered the outline of the scheme too. The JRV meetings were resumed the following day.

In that round of negotiations at the Moria Plaza, another unusual development occurred on water issues. Over morning coffee on Tuesday August 9, 1994, Kinarti approached his counterpart, Haddadin. 'I want to talk to you by myself,' said Kinarti. 'Can you talk to me alone?'

'Yes, I am authorized to conduct the talks alone or jointly with others, the way I see fit.'

'I do not want our delegates to know that I am meeting with you,' said Kinarti.

'Fine with me, I will not publicize the matter.'

'Where can we meet?'

'We first have to get our guys busy,' said Haddadin. In his own thinking, he ruled out the use of one of the negotiations rooms for his meeting with Kinarti because word would spread, and the secrecy that Kinarti wanted would be violated. After the delegations were given topics to negotiate, the two heads of the water group were ready to meet one on one. 'Follow me,' Haddadin told Kinarti, and headed for the hallway of the sixth floor toward the elevators.

They took a crowded elevator down to the lobby and headed for the coffee shop through the press hall. In the coffee shop, they sat at the only table that was unoccupied. Haddadin looked around and recognized a group of Jordanian journalists sitting at the next table. One was Caroline Faraj from *Al-Rai* newspaper, who had accompanied the delegation in the bilateral negotiations since they began and had been the one to leak the Common Agenda, albeit inadvertently. 'Caroline,' said Haddadin, 'come here.' He saw the look in her eyes, a look that suspected that an important meeting must be in the offing. She knew that the two men were not good buddies who would go out for coffee and a chat at a time when the talks were supposed to start upstairs.

'Yes, sir,' said Caroline as she approached the table.

'Give me this laptop computer of yours, and go get us two cups of hot black coffee from the next hall for free.'

'Do you want anything with it? Cream? Sugar?' she asked.

'No, just black.'

Caroline left her laptop and came back with two cups of coffee as requested. They thanked her kindly and Haddadin told her to please leave them alone and stay as far away from them as she possibly could. She left the coffee shop, went out into the lobby, and watched the two delegates across the big glass window, hoping to lip-read.

'The least suspected secret meeting is the one held in a public place like this,' Haddadin told Kinarti.

'I want to talk serious business,' said Kinarti. 'Are you prepared to talk serious business?'

'You mean water business?'

'Yes.'

'I have never been more ready,' said Haddadin.

'Tell me,' said Kinarti, 'how much water do you want from the Jordan River?' Haddadin answered quietly:

> Before we get into this, I want to put on record that whatever we negotiate is a purely bilateral matter between Jordan and Israel; whatever we agree to should not be construed as infringing on the rights of other riparian parties, particularly the Palestinians. We are not authorized, nor am I willing, to speak on their behalf. They will speak for themselves. We, Jordanians, stand prepared to give them all the support that they might need when they ask for it.

Kinarti argued to include the Palestinian rights in the talks. Haddadin was adamant in refusing that notion. After all, the instruction of His Majesty the King in London a few weeks earlier was very loud and clear. The King's words rang in his ears: 'You are to observe the disengagement decision.' Finally Kinarti agreed, and Haddadin created a new file on the laptop he had borrowed from Caroline Faraj. He divided the file into two columns, the first of which was reserved for Jordanian suggestions and/or reactions to Israeli proposals, and the second reserved for Israeli reactions to Jordanian proposals and suggestions.

'It is so strange,' said Kinarti; 'you are defending their independence and support their side, but they are not taking your side.'

'What do you mean?' Haddadin asked, suspecting Kinarti of trying to precipitate a clash between Jordanians and Palestinians.

'Before I came here, one of their leading figures came to me and asked me to negotiate on their behalf,' Kinarti said.

'Are you serious?'

'Yes, very serious.'

'Who was it that came to you and authorized you to speak on behalf of the Palestinians?' asked Haddadin. Kinarti smiled and did not answer. Haddadin wrote in the Israeli column what Kinarti said, and looked up to check on Caroline. She was still there, in the lobby, looking at the two. 'Having now agreed to discuss only bilateral matters,' said Haddadin, 'let us now talk about Jordanian rights, I stress, Jordanian, nothing to do with anything Palestinian.'

'How much water do you need from the Jordan River?' repeated Kinarti.

Haddadin was surprised at the question because, with Palestinian rights ruled out of the discussion, Jordan was left with no water rights on the Jordan, just the Yarmouk tributary.

'I would be willing to settle for 200 mcm from the Jordan River alone. This does not include any other source, like the Yarmouk,' answered Haddadin.

'This is too much,' protested Kinarti.

'I have too many people to serve with domestic water,' noted Haddadin. 'I am not taking the water to use it in irrigation or to throw it away. I need it for people to drink.'

'It is still too much.'

'Is it too much to pacify the thirst of your neighbor with whom you are trying to make peace? Remember, a thirsty neighbor is not a good neighbor,' explained Haddadin.

'Zero is very little and 200 is just too much. Your share will be somewhere in between.' The conversation went on and on, and no agreement was reached over the Jordan River.

The East Bank, the name given to today's Jordan before the disengagement decision with the West Bank, had its water rights in the side wadis that discharge into the Jordan River from the east and are totally within Jordanian territory (they average 175 mcm per year), and in the waters of the Yarmouk that Jordan shares with Syria and Israel. Jordanian water rights are satisfied from these sources, and not from the course of the Jordan River itself. The Technical Committee of the Arab League between 1953 and 1955 made that ruling. The Committee further accepted that Israel's share from the Yarmouk would be 25 mcm per year, and that the rest of the Yarmouk flow at Adassiya (after deducting 90 mcm for Syrian uses) belonged to the Hashemite Kingdom. Actually, the total rights of Jordan from the Yarmouk were 296 mcm per year to be added to the side wadis of 175 mcm, and 8 mcm from wells to produce a total of 479 mcm per year, the irrigation requirement for 33,490 hectares. The West Bank had its water rights in the side wadis and springs that discharge into the Jordan River from the west and are totally within West Bank territories (52 mcm), from wells in the basin (8 mcm), an estimated 81 mcm from the Yarmouk as a residual user, and 100 mcm from the Jordan River to be abstracted from Lake Tiberias. The total Palestinian rights would then be 241 mcm, the irrigation requirements of 15,232 hectares. Kinarti's question was, in effect, giving Jordan an opportunity to get some kind of share from the Jordan River.

At the end of the meeting, a printout of the minutes was made and the two delegates signed it. The results of this first 'business' meeting were good and would be related in detail to the Crown Prince.

The negotiations appeared to develop a distinctive flavour, unlike the rounds in Washington, DC. On the following day, Haddadin and Kinarti had a one-on-one meeting again. Kinarti asked to have the minutes of the previous day amended. 'What is there to amend?' asked Haddadin.

'Well, it is about what the Palestinians told me,' said Kinarti. 'They did not say negotiate on our behalf, rather, they said "do not forget us when you negotiate with the Jordanians"; that is the amendment I want to introduce.'

'But I read it to you two times yesterday, and I stressed its contents about the Palestinians, and you maintained it was true. What made you change your mind?'

'Well, I want the minutes amended,' insisted Kinarti.

The minutes of the day before had been kept with the official register along with other important negotiation records. 'They are there, in the record,' thought Haddadin, 'and there is no harm in making Kinarti's comments part of the record of the new day.'

'Okay, Noah,' said Haddadin, 'I will not let something like this stand in our way to an agreement. I am willing to make the amendment, provided you tell me who it was from the Palestinian leadership that came to you and told you whatever he told you.'

'Well,' said Kinarti, and he mentioned the name.

## Borders and security

The water talks came to a break, as Haddadin was required to attend the presentations on borders. The wording of the Common Agenda item on borders was very clear. They were to be demarcated and delineated in accordance with the Mandate borders. The Mandate borders definition referred to a line originating from a point on the Gulf of Aqaba, defined at a certain distance from the last house on the western edge of that town at the time. The line would extend up the *center* of Wadi Araba. The Israelis went out of their way to prove that the center of Wadi Araba was not the line of lowest points in the wadi (thalweg line), but rather was the median between the highest points on the adjacent escarpments to the east and the west of the wadi.

Our group made an analytical presentation supported by maps and historical references, but the Israeli presentation was more impressive. The Israeli Defense Forces did one part, the experts at the Ministry of Defense did another, and there were at least four international law experts sitting on their side of the table. The Israeli delegation was headed by Rubinstein, and the Jordanian by Dr Tarawneh. To his left sat Haddadin, and to his right sat General Tahseen Shurdum. More delegates sat on the Jordanian side, and two of them were international law professors. After the presentations were made, the floor was opened for discussions. 'That point on your map,' inquired Haddadin as he pointed to a point in Wadi Araba, 'how far is it from the burned tank west of Qa' Sayediyeen?' Rubinstein was stunned. Haddadin sounded like he knew every inch of that border.

'What Qa' Sayediyeen?' asked a uniformed Israeli Army officer.

'Well, let me put it in a different wording; how far is that kink on your map from the landing strip in Wadi Araba that the allies used in World War II?'

That made Rubinstein even more surprised. 'What is this, Dr Haddadin, were you raised there? How come you know all these details that experts here do not?' asked Rubinstein.

'I was in charge of the development of that region along with the rest of the Rift valley. I did not do deskwork only. I had to familiarize myself with the terrain and the people of the area I was in charge of.' He then walked up to the map, looked at the scale, and estimated the distance he was after.

Other questions were considered by both sides. The part of the Mandate border between the coastline of the Gulf of Aqaba and the current location of the Aqaba airport was adjusted back in 1946. The adjustment was the result of an exchange of correspondence that started in December 1945 and lasted until September 1946 between the British Director of the Department of Lands and Surveys in Transjordan and his British counterpart in Palestine in December 1945. More correspondence took place later between officials of the Transjordan government and those of the British administration in Palestine, including the High Commissioner, and the Ministry of the Colonies. In the course of those exchanges, Jordan became an independent Kingdom with a Basic Law in May 1946. The agreement to adjust those borders was concluded in September 1946, after Transjordan was proclaimed an independent country under the name 'The Hashemite Kingdom of Jordan'.

Haddadin was fascinated by the Israeli account of the border adjustment, which was correct. Israel, however, was not established until two years later, on May 15, 1948. 'I have another question, if I may,' said Haddadin.

'Please, go ahead,' answered Rubinstein.

'My question is simple and pertains to the adjustment of the borders in 1946; where do you propose to put Israel in all of this?'

Rubinstein gave the floor to one legal expert, whose answer did not have much of a bite. Another legal advisor tried to respond, but seemed to differ from the first. A third legal advisor interrupted. 'I will answer you by the word of international law,' he said, as he flipped through a file he had in front of him. 'Israel's involvement is rooted in the rule of . . .'

'The rule of Succession of States,' interrupted Haddadin.

'Exactly,' said the legal advisor.

'And, on behalf of Jordan, I accept this reasoning. I just want it on record that Israel abides by the rule of Succession of States.' This meant that Israel inherited the rights and obligations of the predecessor government, that of the Mandate administration. This was a serious matter for Israel. Haddadin wanted, through upholding the rule of Succession of States, to invoke the responsibility of the successor government for the population of the land, thereby bringing to the fore Israel's responsibility to repatriate Palestinian refugees and their right to citizenship. That would be in addition to UN resolutions pertaining to the rights of Palestinian refugees.

A fourth legal advisor tried to dig the Israeli delegation out of their hole. He floundered for a while before Rubinstein interrupted. 'Dr Haddadin,' said Rubinstein, 'we will take what you said as a joke, laugh at it for a minute and then change the subject.'

Haddadin became furious. The Israeli side of the table had some twelve civilians, and behind them sat over 18 uniformed high-ranking officers of the Israeli Army. That did not deter him. He shouted,

> What! Ambassador, have you forgotten why I am here? Do you think I am here to listen to your jokes? Have you forgotten we are all here for the settlement of a serious dispute between our two countries? Besides, isn't it insulting to presume I was joking? I am dead serious, and I demand that you reciprocate. I sure do reciprocate; because in as much as you gave yourself the right to unilaterally change the subject, I hereby exercise the same right. Meeting adjourned!

Haddadin thumped the table with characteristic passion and stood up as he announced the end of the meeting. The rest of our delegation stood up, and followed Haddadin out of the room.

'That was tough, real tough,' said Tarawneh as the two entered Tarawneh's room, 'but he asked for it.'

'I take that as a compliment,' said Haddadin. There was a knock on the door. It was General Tahseen Shurdum.

'General Uzi Dayan came to me,' he said. 'The Israeli military is protesting at Haddadin's remark. They take it that Haddadin does not recognize the State of Israel.'

'He is right, I do not, nor does any Jordanian. There has not been mutual recognition between the two States yet,' said Haddadin.

'But they are furious. They are very mad. They are assembled in the hallway,' said Shurdum.

Haddadin did not answer. He left the room, strolled down the hallway amidst a crowd of angry Israelis. He went up and down, looking them all straight in the eye. The crowd was so silent that Haddadin was sure he scored his own point. He then went back to Tarawneh's office. He had hoped that he would have the chance to engage in a heated argument with some Israeli officers that would lead to a fight in which he would be overwhelmed by so many Israeli generals. That would have made headlines the world over; unfortunately the situation did not materialize.

The dramatic clash outlined above took place on a Monday, and tension hung over the talks on Tuesday and Wednesday. On Thursday morning, Tarawneh managed to get Rubinstein and Haddadin together for a heart-to-heart talk, and normal communication resumed.

The delegations took a break for one week before they were to convene on August 28 in the Dead Sea Spa Hotel on the Jordan side of the Dead Sea. Haddadin worked hard to finalize the 'Terms of Reference for Consulting Services' for the JRV integrated development. The document would be the reference point for qualified consulting firms bidding for contracts on the project. He had pledged to forward the proposal to the next meeting of the Trilateral Economic Committee on August 27. The Israelis were supposed to come up with a parallel proposal at that meeting too so that a joint document could be prepared using the ideas the two proposals encompassed. Four days before the meeting was due, Haddadin received an instruction from the Crown Prince's office: His Royal Highness would like you to travel to Germany, to join a meeting on the Mediterranean Sea–Dead Sea Canal. A German group, an Israeli group and a Japanese banking group are meeting to appraise an Israeli study of the Med–Dead Canal. His Royal Highness wants you to participate and defend the Jordanian preference of a Red–Dead Canal.

The meeting was to take place on Monday, August 28. As the Trilateral Economic Committee meeting was to be on August 27, and to resume in Washington, DC on 31 August, Haddadin arranged to skip the regional part of the meeting and to join the continuation of the Trilateral meeting in Washington.

The meeting in Germany brought together the Israeli Military industry with three German construction firms. The Japanese financiers did not arrive in time for Haddadin to meet them. The Med–Dead

Canal project was handicapped by potential environmental hazards, and by the storage system for desalinated water. The project proposed to store desalinated water in a big open reservoir to be set up in the Jordan valley, where evaporation rates would cause the loss of valuable water, and pollution would necessitate retreatment of the water. The disposal of brine was also another problem. Haddadin advised the groups in the meeting to devise engineering measures that would pre-empt environmental hazards, and to calculate the cost of the project accordingly. The brine that the project proposed be dispensed with in the course of the Jordan River should be kept away from that culturally very important river, and, instead, be transported to the Dead Sea in a closed conduit running parallel to the Jordan River and west of it. With measures like this incorporated, the project would turn out to be more expensive than the alternative, the Red–Dead Canal.

In Washington, the meeting of the Trilateral Economic Committee convened in the State Department on the morning of August 31.[1] A few days earlier, at the Dead Sea Spa Hotel in Jordan, the Committee had looked into the 'Terms of Reference' for the study as proposed by Jordan and by Israel. In the course of presenting the results of that initial meeting, the Israeli, Yossi Vardi, asked for the floor. 'I am not a diplomat, nor am I famed for my diplomatic language. I want to say this in front of all of you to Dr Haddadin,' he said. 'Dr Haddadin,' Vardi continued as he looked at him and held a copy of some three pages of loose papers, 'you made us ashamed of ourselves when we compared this proposal by Israel with the proposal you sent to the meeting. Your proposal is superior, and we are embarrassed.'

That was the first time ever that Haddadin had heard an Israeli public confession that a Jordanian product was superior to an Israeli competitor. The participants then adopted the Jordanian proposal as a joint proposal of the Committee.

'What could be the next step?' asked Dennis Ross as he looked to Haddadin for advice.

'Jordan and Israel do not as yet have a legal joint identity, and therefore cannot legally act as an employer to the consultants who would do the study,' said Haddadin. 'I suggest that we, jointly, ask the World Bank to act on our behalf as the employer.' Ross approved and the Israelis concurred. Ross sent for Caio Kochwesser, Vice-President of the World Bank, who came to the State Department promptly, accompanied by the Director of the Middle East Department, Ram Chopra. They accepted the assignment gladly on behalf of the Bank, and alerted a team they already had in the region to get ready to perform the needed task. The Jordanian and Israeli teams agreed to have a bilateral meeting on September 8 to have the joint document carefully reviewed and put into final form. Haddadin took with him Dr Hani Mulki and Dr Ibrahim Badran to Beit Gibrael in Israel, along with a military liaison officer. The Israeli team had Vardi, Benvenisti and others. The document was slightly modified and put in the form of a final draft.

The following round of bilateral negotiations was due to convene at Beit Gibrael on the southern shore of Lake Tiberias on September 12. Tarawneh attended as head of delegation. Awn al-Khasawneh joined after a long period of interruption. The talks became active on all the critical items of the Common Agenda. Water, borders, security, and other topics were being discussed. Haddadin chaired the JRV group, attended by a World Bank representative, John Hayward, and a representative of the USAID Mission in Amman. Haddadin would shuttle between the JRV group and the bilateral negotiations meeting in the same complex. Tarawneh al-Khasawneh and Tahseen Shurdum, joined by Haddadin, represented our side, and Rubinstein, Moshe Kochanovsky and Noah Kinarti comprised the Israeli side. The issues of water, borders and security were being linked together for the first time. Jordan had favored linkages in previous months, but Israel had preferred separate consideration of each topic. Rubinstein brought up the issue of a peace treaty in which most of the issues could be resolved. That was a departure from the previous Israeli approach, supported by the USA at times, to sign a peace treaty first and then work out the details. A draft treaty was being prepared by the Israelis that would have room for the new approach.

During a coffee break in a private lounge in the Beit Gibrael complex, Rubinstein asked, 'Dr al-Khasawneh, what do you want to do after this is over?'

'I want to retire and look after my farms.'

'You are too young and talented to retire.'

'I do not have brothers to help with my private concerns, I have to take care of them,' replied Awn.

'How about Ali?' asked Rubinstein, referring to Awn's son.

'Ali is still too young for that.'

Rubinstein then turned to Fayez Tarawneh, who was enjoying his coffee. 'And what would you like to do, Fayez, after this thing is over?'

'I hope to be Prime Minister!' Fayez joked.

The conversation gave the impression that 'this thing' would be over soon.[2]

The Israelis had a nice set-up for lunch on a boat that cruised on Lake Tiberias. On one such cruise, Rubinstein told the gathering: 'When I proposed to Prime Minister Rabin to hold the negotiations in Beit Gibrael, and mentioned that we would organize a luncheon in such a boat that would cruise on the Lake, Rabin said, "Are you out of your mind? This will only increase Haddadin's appetite for Israeli water!" I assured him I would handle the matter.'

'How do you propose to handle it?' asked Tarawneh.

'Dr Haddadin,' said Rubinstein, 'this is not water!' and he pointed to the surface of the lake, while everyone laughed.

The coverage by the Israeli press was extensive. The correspondent of the *Jerusalem Post* interviewed Haddadin, who did not share the excitement over those meetings. The paper came out the following day with a headline 'The Ice Cube in the Jordanian Delegation' and carried the interview with Haddadin.

That month of September witnessed various turning points in the Jordanian–Israeli negotiation. Crown Prince al-Hassan was scheduled to arrive in New York to deliver Jordan's speech to the annual session of the United Nation's General Assembly. Several Jordanian officials and non-officials were to accompany him. During the visit to New York, Jewish dignitaries planned to call on the Prince and businessmen had asked to give a reception in his honor. Shimon Peres was scheduled to address the General Assembly too, and the two were likely to meet on that occasion. Prince al-Hassan would also pay a visit to Washington, DC for talks with the US administration. The Jordanian Minister of Transport, who had been Minister of Water and Irrigation, needed to formulate a position paper on transportation for Jordan to present to the Israelis.

'You know, Munther,' said Samir Kawar, the Minster of Transport, 'I looked everywhere in the Ministry of Transport, but could not find one person who would formulate a position paper on transport that we can use in our talks with the Israelis.'

'It does not take a genius to formulate such a paper. Just give me the strategy of the Ministry, and I will write the position paper.'

'But we do not have a strategy for transport!'

'Okay, then we start by formulating one; you give me one guy from the Ministry to work with me as a gofer. Also cover my meals while I do the work in your office in Jebal Amman,' said Haddadin. 'The time we have to accomplish the task is less than a week, and there is no time to waste.'

Haddadin produced a position paper on transport and gave it to the Minister. The Minister had to leave before the Crown Prince because he had things to attend to with the EU in Brussels. On Friday September 23, 1994, Haddadin flew from Amman to New York to join the entourage of the Crown Prince there. Mrs Randa Kawar, the Minister's wife, was on the same flight, and so were the Crown Prince's staff.

They landed in Amsterdam for refueling and more passengers. As soon as the aircraft came to the gate at Schiphol Airport in Amsterdam, the Royal Jordanian manager came in to talk to the staff of the office of the Crown Prince: 'We got a message for you from Amman: you are to go back from here. The visit of His Royal Highness to America has been postponed.'

'What!' exclaimed Haddadin. 'Is it postponed or cancelled? Who asked for the postponement? Us or them?' The manager had no further information.

A perplexed Haddadin arrived at his home in Amman about ten hours after he had left it. On the following morning he called the Prime Ministry and the office of the Crown Prince but no one had a clue as to what the story was. Haddadin resolved to go to Cairo on a mission for the Food and Agriculture Organization (FAO), to attend a meeting on water at the Arab League. He had turned down the mission earlier because of the New York trip.

In Cairo, Haddadin also met with the Jordan Ambassador, the former colleague in the negotiation with Israel, Ambassador Nayef al-Qadi. They chatted about the developments in the peace process over a dinner that al-Qadi hosted at the Gazeera Sheraton.

'I feel something is happening, Nayef, but I do not know what it is,' Haddadin told his host.

'I share your feelings. I just hope that we can stick to our grounds, and maintain our strong ties with the Arab countries. We cannot afford to spin off,' said al-Qadi.

The Egyptian paper, *Al-Gumhuria*, carried surprising news on Tuesday morning. The headline read: 'Peace Treaty Between Jordan and

Israel' and the front-page story spoke of a peace treaty in the making, and stated that it would be a matter of days before Jordan and Israel would sign it. The Egyptians were eager to see other Arabs join them in making peace with Israel.

Haddadin took the afternoon flight back to Amman on Tuesday September 27. He received a phone call shortly after he was home. 'Hi, this is Ali Shukri,' said the Chief Communications Officer for His Majesty the King.

'Well, hello,' said Haddadin.

'What are you doing?'

'Eating French fries, would you like to join me for some?'

'No, thank you. But would you be surprised if I told you that you are needed?'

'Not at all, I would not be surprised.'

'You did not ask when.'

'Okay, when?' asked Haddadin as requested.

'Right now!'

'I am not surprised either.'

'You did not ask me where you are needed.'

'Okay, where?'

'In Aqaba. There is a C-130 plane waiting for you at Amman Airport, and it will fly you and General Shurdum to Aqaba.'

The C-130 had three Air Force officers in the cockpit. Haddadin and Shurdum joined them for the 45-minute flight to Aqaba. They were whisked to the home of the Crown Prince where they arrived at about 10:00 p.m. In the living room were the Crown Prince, the Prime Minister, the Commander-in-Chief of the Armed Forces, Ambassador Awn al-Khasawneh, two legal advisors (Professor James Crawford, an Australian teaching at Cambridge, and Professor Bernard Graefrath, a German), and Dr Ahmad Mango, Advisor to the Crown Prince. The group stayed up late. It became evident to Haddadin and Shurdum that there was a draft of a peace treaty that was being debated amongst the Jordanians, and that an Israeli team was expected the following morning. The group members were given chalets in the compound of the King's palace in Aqaba. It was around 3:30 a.m. when they were able to retire for the night.

The Israeli team arrived the next morning headed by Rubinstein. It included, for the first time, General Ihud Barak, Chief of the General

Staff of the Israeli Defense Forces. A big breakfast was served, and the Jordanian group, who had just had a big breakfast at the King's palace next door, had to eat another one. Work started after breakfast. Awn al-Khasawneh, assisted by Graefrath, Crawford, Haddadin and Shurdum, comprised the working Jordanian group. Other talks went on between Barak, the Crown Prince and Prime Minister Majali. In the Israeli draft treaty, there were some four or five clauses that demanded of Jordan to mind its security obligations toward Israel, and gave that obligation priority over any other security commitment that Jordan might have. In essence, those clauses would have neutralized Jordan's commitment towards Arabs, and put Israel's security as top priority. Jordan could never concede to that.

'Look here, Mr Barak,' said Prime Minister Majali, 'I am extending this hand to make peace with Israel,' and he extended his right arm. 'This arm,' he added, 'is part of this body and can function normally. Now, what good will this arm be to you if it is cut off from its body?'

The message was loud and clear. Barak excused himself, and went out to use his cellular phone. He came back a short while later. 'Okay,' he said, 'we can forget about these clauses.'

The working team continued to negotiate the articles of the treaty. They had two drafts to work on; one looked Israeli and the other Jordanian. The Jordanian team was able to sway the Israelis toward the Jordanian text. Haddadin drafted and negotiated Article 6 over water, and inserted a reference to an annex that would spell out the details of agreement over water. 'What is going on?' Haddadin asked Awn al-Khasawneh after lunch.

'I want to tell you what happened the day before yesterday,' al-Khasawneh told Haddadin. 'It is for your own ears and not for the tongue to remember it. I just want you to be aware.'

'What happened?'

We were given the Israeli draft treaty. The legal advisors and myself studied it carefully. The three of us asked for an audience with His Majesty. Present in the meeting were Crown Prince al-Hassan, the Chief of the Royal Court, Sherif Zaid Bin Shaker [later made Prince Zaid Bin Shaker], and Marwan Kassim, His Majesty's advisor.

'Your Majesty,' said Crawford, the legal advisor, 'we Australians are known to be frank to the point of crudeness. If you do not like what I have to say, Sire, you have yourself to blame because you hired me. We cannot, in good conscience, advise you to accept this text advanced by the Israelis because this is tantamount to capitulation, and we should not forget that they need a treaty partner.'

'Fine, thank you,' said His Majesty, 'please go and do your job.'

We immediately started working on a counter-proposal. The three of us worked until the early hours of the following morning and produced a counter-proposal for a treaty. We sent it to the Israelis. The Israelis did not show up the following morning as they were supposed to. There was speculation in our ranks, and there was official worry. General Ali Shukri made contact, and the Israelis showed up at about 11:30 a.m. and were in a bellicose mood. Obviously, Rubinstein was unhappy with the Jordanian counter-draft, and he asked the Crown Prince for a word with him alone. He told the Crown Prince that it appeared as though the lawyers had taken over. His Royal Highness conveyed Rubinstein's concern to me.

'If this is true,' the Crown Prince said to me, 'it would be good to keep in mind who is working for whom.'

'*Sidi*,' I replied, 'if lawyers are a problem, why then is half of the Israeli delegation made up of lawyers?'

The work on the two drafts continued. It soon became clear that the issue of Palestinian refugees was a sticky issue. The Israelis were deadly determined not even to talk about it. Rubinstein would avoid a confrontation with al-Khasawneh over the issue, and preferred to talk to the Crown Prince who, as royalty, would be much safer to talk to without fear of receiving sharp answers. The Crown Prince listened to Rubinstein carefully and then convinced him to at least listen to what al-Khasawneh had to say. Rubinstein's arguments regarding the refugees advocated dropping the issue altogether. The group sat to listen to al-Khasawneh who made a 12-minute presentation on the issue, explaining why there should be a reference to the refugee problem.

The Crown Prince, in an attempt to have the views of Rubinstein heard by the Jordanian side, took Awn to one side. 'Thank you Awn for the wonderful presentation,' said the Crown Prince, 'but I need to reinforce my convictions with some of your legal arguments. To play a devil's advocate, why should we restate the obvious? The right of return is non-alienable as you say.'

'*Sidi*,' said Awn, 'if we do not have it confirmed in the Treaty, it will get lost.'

The Crown Prince liked Awn's justification, and went back to the group, accompanied by him. Al-Khasawneh made the following points in demanding that the issue be addressed in the treaty:

a) The issue is a primary subject as agreed to by both sides in the Common Agenda signed on September 14, 1993 at the State Department. (It was item number 4 on the Agenda.)

b) The Israelis agreed with the Palestinians in the Oslo Accord that the issue would be negotiated in the Final Status. To Jordan, the treaty is a Final Status negotiation, and now is the time to have the bilateral aspects of refugees and displaced persons addressed and resolved.

c) The issue is of direct legal interest to Jordan because it affects the survival of Jordanians and their rights.

d) The parties cannot claim that they have arrived at peace without at least resolving the problem of Palestinian refugees, which, admittedly, is a complex problem. As an element, however, it should not be missing from a treaty of peace.

When al-Khasawneh was done, Rubinstein, who had quit smoking some years back, looked at him and said, 'Can I have a cigarette?'

'Okay,' he said after lighting up, 'I will relay these arguments to Prime Minister Rabin.'

Professor Crawford, who listened to al-Khasawneh's presentation and to Rubinstein's response very attentively, confided in Awn at that point, 'These have been the most dramatic 12 minutes in my professional life, including my appearances before the International Court of Justice.'

The working group continued to do more work on the drafts. The group on borders split and used the annex to the Crown Prince's house, where a meeting table was provided, and a desert cooler kept the air a bit moist and cool. By Thursday September 29, the teams had achieved progress on some articles, but had not covered as much ground as was hoped. Eight of the Treaty articles were finalized including Article 6 on water. Its language was general, leaving the details to an annex. In the afternoon of that day, it was announced to the working teams that Prime Minister Rabin would come to visit in the evening and meet with His Majesty King Hussein in an attempt to overcome obstacles in the way of concluding a treaty.

The meeting between the two leaders was convened in the King's palace. Dinner was served, and the press was alerted to the meeting. Haddadin wrote the press release and had it cleared and distributed to the press: 'In compliance with the commitments the two leaders undertook in their Washington Declaration, they have met to iron out differences over issues in the bilateral negotiations between the two countries.' In fact, the two leaders talked of the difficulties facing the negotiators and each stuck to his grounds concerning the resolution of the refugee problem. Rabin claimed it would be suicidal for Israel to accept the right of return for the Palestinian refugees, and the King argued that peace could not be just and comprehensive without recognizing that right.

The Jordanian team, led by the Crown Prince, was flown back to Amman after midnight on the King's plane, which continued on to New York a few hours later on Friday September 30. The flight had several officials on board. Jawad Anani, Munther Haddadin, Hani Mulki, Awn al-Khasawneh, and others. There were support staff, mainly those who had been turned back from Amsterdam exactly a week earlier. The group was checked in to the Saint Ridges Hotel, a few blocks south of Central Park in New York.

On the following morning, Saturday October 1, the Crown Prince chaired a meeting of senior members in his delegation. Awn al-Khasawneh did not attend, but came into the meeting and asked Haddadin out for an important word with him. 'I think you should start working on the water annex you referred to in Article 6 of the treaty draft,' said Awn.

'Why now? Who issued the instruction?' asked Haddadin.

'*Sidi* Hassan did,' answered Awn.

'Okay, right after the meeting is over.'

After the meeting, Haddadin went to the office of the support staff, borrowed a laptop, and went down to his room. He had no references, no documents of any kind, but had to write the water annex, which he did. By Sunday afternoon, the annex was ready, and he had four copies printed out, giving one to each of the legal experts: Awn al-Khasawneh, Graefrath, and Crawford. He asked for a meeting with the three that same evening to hear any comments. The comments were all positive. The draft of the water annex was approved with only a presentational minor change.

'You cannot convince me, Dr Haddadin, that you do not have a law degree,' said Professor Crawford; 'the language of the annex reveals that.'

'I would not even try,' said Haddadin whose college education, graduate work and experience had all been in civil engineering and economic and social development.

On Monday October 3, 1994, the Jordanians accompanied Prince al-Hassan to the United Nations where he delivered Jordan's speech to the annual session of the General Assembly. The following day, the Crown Prince took Awn al-Khasawneh and others with him for his visit to Washington, and meetings with the administration. He met with President Clinton, and with Secretary Christopher and other officials, and returned to New York the same day. On the following day, Tuesday October 4, the Crown Prince met with an Israeli delegation headed by Shimon Peres at the Saint Ridges. As the meeting of the two sides started in a hall in the hotel basement, Minister Kawar came to Haddadin and asked: 'What do I do with the position paper on transport? Shall I give it to *Sidi* Hassan or what?'

'Give a copy to *Sidi* Hassan, give three other copies to Ambassador Fayez Tarawneh over there, and keep a couple for ourselves. Do not forget to tell Tarawneh to hand over two copies to Peres,' Haddadin suggested.

Kawar did as advised. Shimon Peres looked through the document, said a few nice words about it, and the meeting addressed general topics of mutual interest, including the Red–Dead Canal of the Jordan Rift Valley development. Peres' presentation exhibited the philosophical approach for which he was famous, and Prince al-Hassan responded with eloquence. That same evening, Haddadin asked permission of the Crown Prince to attend to some family obligations in the United States. The Prince asked him to be in Amman on Sunday, October 9, at the latest. When Haddadin arrived at his home on the evening of Sunday October 9, there were numerous messages, and an instruction to proceed to Aqaba the same evening. He checked in at the Aqua Marina II Hotel in Aqaba, and found a considerable number of Jordanian experts who were set to negotiate with the Israelis: in agriculture, tourism, environment, security, water, the Jordan Rift Valley, borders, transport, and other matters. Haddadin was given the additional tasks of supervising the work of agriculture, and tourism in addition to water, the JRV and borders. Tarawneh was there leading the troops, and so was Awn al-Khasawneh. On Monday September 10, 1994, the Jordanian teams traveled to Eilat by bus taking the newly opened crossing point north of Aqaba that had been inaugurated two weeks earlier by Prince al-Hassan and Minister Shimon Peres.

The negotiations on the first day gathered momentum, and our teams had in-house sessions in the evenings to appraise the work of the day and set the strategy for the following day. The Prime Minister and Dr Anani in Amman were in almost continuous contact with Tarawneh, and issued the necessary directions whenever Tarawneh asked for them. The Common Agenda was the document that guided the negotiations.

The set-up at the Moria Plaza in Eilat was convenient, and the logistics worked well. The teams on transport struggled to come to terms with the altitudes that the Royal Jordanian Airline would be allowed to fly in Israeli airspace. The issue of security and Israeli Air Force requirements for training became a stumbling block. Murdachai Gur, retired Israeli Air Force commander, came to Eilat to explain Israeli Air Force concerns. Work on agriculture proceeded without major hitches. The Israelis gave good presentations, especially on fish farming. Veterinarian concerns were addressed and the rules of quarantine reviewed. The team also discussed the potential for bilateral cooperation. Dr Mukhlis Amareen of the Jordanian delegation excelled in his presentations.

On Tuesday October 11, Noah Kinarti came up to Haddadin in the hotel lobby just before lunch. 'What do you say to you and I sitting down to write the water annex to the treaty?' asked Kinarti in an unusually friendly manner.

'Of course,' said Haddadin, 'I figured it would be needed and have made preparations for it. Here is a copy of a proposal for the annex. I did it because I thought we could save a lot of time.' That was a surprise to Kinarti.

The talks of the various teams proceeded. Everyone was excited by the occasion, and listened to each other with respect and interest. Yet still no progress was achieved on the major issues of water, borders and refugees. A turning point came on Wednesday October 12. The negotiation teams at the Moria Plaza in Eilat broke for lunch. Over lunch, the views of the two sides on the potentials and methodology of the JRV development were exchanged. Haddadin walked over to join Rubinstein and Tarawneh who were still having lunch. With them sat Yacov Rosen, the Jordan Desk officer in the Israeli Foreign Ministry. 'How are things going?' asked Haddadin.

'Dr Haddadin,' said Rubinstein, 'I read your annex. It gave me a heart attack and I fainted.'

'Oh no! This is the last thing we would ever want to happen to you. Anyway, we have good cardiologists in Jordan and we can send for them right now.'

'I actually need a heart specialist and also a psychiatrist.'

'I do not know if we have the right shrink, but maybe we all can help!'

Someone came in to talk to Rubinstein who excused himself and went to the phone. A short while later, the Israeli teams started to file out of the restaurant and walked out of the hotel to their bus. The Jordanians did not know what was going on. This movement attracted the press correspondents, and many came to Tarawneh and Haddadin, who were walking out of the restaurant wondering what was happening. 'Dr Tarawneh, why are the Israeli teams walking out?' asked several correspondents.

'I do not know.'

'Is it true that Dr Haddadin is behind this walkout? Is it true that he made them very upset?'

'No, nothing of the sort.'

'Dr Haddadin, what sort of challenge did you pose to the Israelis this time? Why have they walked out?' asked several other correspondents.

'No challenges and no bad feelings. We are proceeding with satisfactory progress. I do not know why they walked out. Your guess is as good as mine,' said Haddadin.

Tarawneh looked around for the other senior members of the delegation, and noticed that Awn al-Khasawneh wasn't there. 'Where is Awn?' he asked Haddadin.

'I do not have the vaguest idea.'

'Have you seen Awn, Caroline?' Tarawneh asked the *Al-Rai* newspaper correspondent.

'Yes, I saw him leave the hotel about a half hour ago. He had with him Nidal Saqarat, the guy from the Geographic Center.'

'Where do you suppose he is going?' Tarawneh asked Haddadin.

'I do not know, but judging by the speed with which Rubinstein left without even a message tells me something very important is happening.'

The Jordanians went back to Aqaba, still wondering what the matter was. That Awn would leave without telling Tarawneh was odd but not unexpected. It was strange that Nidal Saqarat, the technical assistant to Shurdum, would leave the hotel in Eilat without a word.

The 8:00 evening news on Jordan television helped the delegation understand what had happened. The news bulletin started with a tape of His Majesty King Hussein receiving Prime Minister Rabin at al-Hashimyyah Palace west of Amman. A high-level meeting was convened that afternoon with Peres, Barak, Rubinstein and others participating from the Israeli side. Crown Prince al-Hassan, Prime Minister Majali, Dr Anani, General Marea, Sherif Zaid Ben Shaker, Marwan Kassim, Awn al-Khasawneh, Hani Mulki, and Nidal Saqarat participated from the Jordanian side. A breakthrough was in the making.

'Do you like what you just saw?' a dismayed Tarawneh asked Haddadin.

'I take it as a good sign and a good omen. I only wish that you were called in to participate too.'

'Well, His Majesty and His Royal Highness are all that count in a serious event like this. I am sure it will be for the sake of progress in the negotiation. I just wish we had been alerted to it.'

'It could be worse, Fayez,' said Haddadin; 'we could have heard the same news, not from our own television station, but from the Israeli broadcast!'

## NOTES

1   The American delegation was led by Ambassador Dennis Ross, and members were Tony Verstandig, Aaron Miller and others. Tarawneh led the Jordan delegation and members were Haddadin and Fayez Al-Khasawneh, who were joined in the afternoon by Awn Al-Khasawneh and Hani Mulki. The Israeli delegation was led by Elyakim Rubinstein and members were Itamar Rabinovitch, Yossi Vardi and Rafi Benvenisti, among others.

2   Both men achieved their goals some time after the 'thing' was over. Awn al-Khasawneh retired in February 1998 to take care of his farms after he had served as Chief of the Royal Court for two years, and Fayez Tarawneh became Prime Minister in August 1998 after he had served as Minister of Foreign Affairs under Majali for one year and replaced Awn as Chief of the Royal Court for a few months.

# 14

## The Peace Treaty

### At al-Hashimiyyah Palace

The atmosphere was relaxed as His Majesty King Hussein welcomed his Israeli guests to al-Hashimiyyah Palace. All were seated on comfortable sofas in the ground floor reception hall. His Majesty had a few words to one side with Rabin, and then both joined the other delegates. Diplomatic niceties, coupled with words of welcome and appreciation were exchanged. The group then launched into the subject.

'Your Majesty,' said Rabin, 'I do not have any designs to take an inch of your territory, nor to take a drop of your water.'

'Thank you, Prime Minister. This really sets a good tone for our two sides to come to an agreement soon,' commented the gracious Hussein.

'We accept the notion of reciprocal minor adjustments in the borders, so that you take from Israel exactly the same area Israel has used in farming on border areas of Jordanian territory,' said the Prime Minister.

'We thought, Your Majesty, that this would be only fair. There is absolutely no truth to the rumors that circulate to the effect that Israel wants to keep land and water that belong to Jordan,' interjected Shimon Peres.

'This is reassuring,' said His Majesty. Peres resumed:

We want to offer you a water package of three components that will resolve the water stand-off. Each of the three components has fifty million cubic meters per year. The first component of fifty million cubic meters will come from what Israel has been using of the Yarmouk flow; the second fifty million will be from dams that we will jointly build; and there is a third component of fifty million.

Peres did not specify the source of this last component. The King looked at the Crown Prince with a gesture signalling the need to have this followed up.

Other talk went on over the need to arrive at a comprehensive peace, and the need to stop wars and bloodshed. 'The region has had enough suffering; we have wasted many opportunities,' remarked the King. 'I believe we should work toward comprehensive peace, and toward the improvement of the lives of our peoples. History will judge us by what we do. I certainly for one intend to have history be with us and not against us.'

'We share your vision, Your Majesty,' said Rabin, 'and we hope to shorten the time needed to arrive at comprehensive peace. We certainly want the well-being of our people, and intend to cooperate to rid the region of the dangers of war.' There was more talk over the problems facing the negotiators. Crown Prince al-Hassan flew to Aqaba the next day as did Marwan Kassim, Awn al-Khasawneh and Nidal Saqarat. The negotiating teams spent Thursday morning in Eilat with their Israeli counterparts. In the afternoon, the Jordanian delegates went back to Amman for the weekend, and Tarawneh, al-Khasawneh, Haddadin and Shurdum stayed behind. The Crown Prince sent for them.

'How are you folks!' greeted the Crown Prince as he parked his jeep.

'*Al-Hamdu Lillah, Sidi,* [Praise be to God, Sir] we are happy when you are happy,' Tarawneh said.

The Crown Prince disembarked, and walked with the group to his house. He gave them a briefing on what had happened at Hashimyyah. He then asked Haddadin to step outside with him into the backyard. They strolled along, coming to a halt under a tall palm tree at the southwest corner of the porch. 'They are offering us a water package of three components, fifty million cubic meters each,' said the Crown Prince. 'It is thought that this package may be suitable.' He explained the above package to Haddadin.

'*Sidi,* I am happy with the last fifty million component. As for the first and second, I think I can get better results through negotiations. I just do not know the source of the third fifty million.'

'Evidently Rabin does not know either,' said the Crown Prince. 'When one Israeli asked Rabin where this fifty million would come from, he threw both his hands in the air in a sign that meant he did not know.'

'I hope we will soon find out.'

'They are coming soon, tonight. So be prepared,' said the Crown Prince.

The Prince explained the deal on the minor adjustment of the borders. 'This is good news,' said Haddadin; 'at least they now recognize that the line of lowest points in Wadi Araba, the thalweg line, is its center as the Mandate line is described. They tried to throw that line to the geographic mean, which would have taken quite a bit of Jordanian territory.'

'Rabin said he was not interested in one inch of our land nor in one drop of our water,' said the Crown Prince.

'We will soon have that tested, *Sidi*.'

In the early evening, the Israeli delegation of five men arrived by bus at the home of the Crown Prince. Negotiations started to get the various issues settled.

## The water annex

Haddadin and Kinarti occupied the eastern of the two tables on the back porch facing the beach.

'I suggest that we go over the draft annex that I gave you the day before yesterday,' said Haddadin.

'Yes, but I noticed that you did not pay attention to our need for ground water in Wadi Arava,' said Kinarti.

'Easy, we can accommodate whatever we agree on and have it inserted in the text. Let us just start.'

'You propose here, in Article I (a) that Israel's share of the Yarmouk will only be 25 million cubic meters each year. We do not recognize that. This quantity is our share during the summer months only. An additional amount of 20 mcm is our share during the rest of the year; so our annual share is 45 mcm,' said Kinarti. Haddadin replied:

> Listen, Noah, we can play this kind of music forever, but we should save time. Your share was based on the contribution of the Yarmouk to the irrigation needs of the Yarmouk Triangle in Israel. The Triangle has frontage on the Jordan River, on Lake Tiberias, and on the Yarmouk, and therefore the balance of its irrigation needs would have to come from the other two sources.

'True, but Israel never conceded to the 25 mcm figure. Show me one piece of evidence for that.'

> I have two pieces of evidence, Noah. The first is the declaration by the Prime Minister of Israel, Levy Eshkol, in the Knesset in 1964 that Israel accepted the Johnston Plan, and the second is the Plan itself. Check it and you will see that Israel's share is 25 mcm per

year. I have a third, but verbal piece of evidence that is just out of the oven, fresh and smells good. Prime Minister Rabin said yesterday that Israel was not interested in a single drop of Jordan's water. You put two and two together, and there you go.

'But the Israelis never accepted that share, and you say that asking for our share of 45 million is infringing on Jordan's water?'

'Yes, exactly, this would be infringing on Jordan's water, not by my own claim, but by what the US emissary ruled in September 1955. So let us not waste time.'

Haddadin knew that the Israelis had never conceded to the 25 mcm in their talks with Johnston over the period 1953–5, and had demanded 40–45 mcm as their annual share from the Yarmouk. The minutes of the meetings of those talks reveal their position. The two delegates argued for a long time. Haddadin knew that the Israelis needed to use more of the Yarmouk water because of the dependency they had created on it since the early seventies. There were areas in their Jordan valley that could be watered only from the Yarmouk. 'Okay Noah,' he said, 'I am willing to help you with this. I can let you have the additional 20 mcm from the winter flow of the Yarmouk provided you give us in return 20 mcm from Lake Tiberias in the summer.' What Haddadin offered Kinarti was a winter flow that Jordan could not capture or use simply because of the absence of a dam on the river to impound the winter flow and regulate it. Even when a dam would subsequently be built it would be at Maqarin leaving the flows downstream unregulated. The agreement to his proposal was a big gain for Jordan: trading unusable winter flows with much needed summer water.

Haddadin thus traded 20 million cubic meters per year of winter water in the Yarmouk for an equivalent amount of water from Lake Tiberias delivered to Jordan during the dry months, May 15 through October 15 of each year. This equated to virtual storage of the Yarmouk floods for Jordan's benefit. The Israeli share outside this trading was only 25 mcm, the amount that the Arab Technical Committee agreed to in its negotiations with Eric Johnston in the mid-fifties. The remainder of the Yarmouk flow, after deducting 90 mcm for Syria, the Committee had decreed, belonged to Jordan. And that was the essence of the agreement with Israel over the Yarmouk. It was a major achievement that Jordan, after a series of Arab defeats since the mid-fifties, was able to reinstate its water agreement with Israel as accepted by the Arabs back then.

Haddadin tried to double the quantity of winter flow that would be traded with summer flow from Lake Tiberias: up to 40 mcm. Kinarti gave no consent and wanted to switch to Wadi Araba and ground water there. He knew that Israel would pull back from the Jordanian territories it had occupied since 1949. There were wells Israel had drilled in the Jordanian territories it had occupied in Wadi Araba, and the Moshavs (Israel's agricultural settlements) there needed more water to upgrade the cropping patterns and to expand their farms; they partially depended on the well water in the Jordanian territories. 'I demand that the existing wells inside the Jordanian territories be the property of Israel after the borders are finalized,' said Kinarti.

'What! Who do you think you are to set demands with a tone like that? There shall be no conceding to Israel of any well there, nor any inch of territory without reciprocity and mutual agreement.'

'If you do not agree, I will not negotiate with you,' said Kinarti.

'Listen, Noah, if you think I am in a hurry, you are mistaken. I have all the time in the world.' Apparently Kinarti was under the impression that, after the Hashimiyyah meeting, every issue would fall into place!

Kinarti stood up in protest, and walked toward the second table where Rubinstein sat with Tarawneh and others. He said something to Rubinstein, who hurried across and talked to the Crown Prince. The Crown Prince summoned Haddadin, and stood with him under the same tall palm tree by the southwest corner of the porch that they had stood under earlier. The Israelis were watching but could not hear the conversation.

The Crown Prince comprehended the water conflict and had trust in Haddadin's ability to defend Jordan's rights. He exchanged a few words with him and confirmed that the results of the negotiations had to be acceptable to the Jordanian public. The two men strolled toward the beach. 'I am confident, *Sidi*, said Haddadin, 'that if you are happy with the results that I come up with, it will be acceptable to the majority of Jordanians, and His Majesty will be very pleased with them too.'

'Will you be able to convince the Government?'

'Yes, *Sidi*, I will.'

'Including Dr Abdul Salam Majali?'

'Yes, *Sidi*, including the Prime Minister, Dr Abdul Salam Majali.'

'Bless your efforts, now show me how you can have the negotiations resume.'

'Don't worry, *Sidi*, Kinarti and I have got used to each other, and I will get him back to talk.'

By that time the two had reached the beach, and they turned back to the porch where the other negotiators were sitting, with the exception of the security and border group that occupied the annex to the house. The stroll with the Crown Prince helped a great deal in leaving the impression among the Israelis that the Prince gave his support to Haddadin. It also helped Haddadin to get Kinarti back to the negotiations table. The rest of the evening did not produce much progress. Kinarti questioned Haddadin about the brackish water on the Jordanian side of the Jordan valley. He was trying to make such water a source for the third 50 mcm component of the Israeli package, but did not get anywhere.

The following day, Friday September 14, the talks went a bit smoother but without much progress. Kinarti had with him a colonel in the Israel Army (dressed in civilian clothes), Daniel Reisner. The issues were known, the stands of each party were known, and each was trying to make the best out of the preparedness of their two leaders to remove obstacles. Awn al-Khasawneh insisted that the issue of refugees be addressed in the treaty, and then he confronted the Israelis with the need to address the settlement of disputes. The Israelis, after they had lost in the Taba arbitration with Egypt, were adamantly against arbitration as a means of settling disputes. They insisted that disputes be resolved amicably between the parties through negotiation. Al-Khasawneh insisted in return that the disputes be resolved through arbitration. That exhausted the negotiators, and consumed time, but neither party would budge. Decent progress was achieved on the delineation of borders following the principle that Jordanian border lands developed by Israelis in irrigated agriculture would be traded with an equal area of Israeli land across the border.

In a short break after lunch, the team drank coffee at the western table on the porch. 'Say, Fayez, our Foreign Minister, Mr Peres, brought back with him from New York a good piece of work by Jordanians. It was a document on transport. We never thought that Jordanians could produce such quality work,' said Rubinstein, referring to the document that Minister Kawar handed over to Tarawneh and on to Minister Peres in New York.

'Thank you,' said Tarawneh.

'Who wrote it in Jordan?' asked Rubinstein.

'Dr Haddadin did,' answered Tarawneh. At this moment, Rubinstein almost choked on his coffee! He made no further comments.

Kinarti and Haddadin clashed again over the Wadi Araba ground water and the ownership of the wells that were located in the occupied Jordanian territories. Kinarti solicited the support of Rubinstein but that got him nowhere.

The negotiations went on and on with modest success concerning the basic water issues. Part of the text of the annex was cleared where there was agreement and the points of difference were postponed until later. The issue of the settlement of disputes remained unresolved. The reference to the problem of refugees was inserted in the treaty. In this regard, the Jordanians recognized that a Jordanian resolution of the bilateral issues of refugees with Israel as stipulated in the Common Agenda would definitely prejudice the resolution of the Palestinian refugees issue elsewhere (West Bank, Gaza, Lebanon, Syria and Egypt). These were areas for which the PLO was responsible and could be taken up with Israel only at the Final Status negotiations. As such, it was agreed between the two parties, Jordan and Israel, that the issue of displaced persons be resolved through the framework of a quadrilateral committee (Jordan, Israel, PLO and Egypt) as stipulated in the Oslo Accord. The issue of refugees, it was also agreed, would be resolved through bilateral negotiations, or otherwise concurrent with the PLO–Israel negotiations on Final Status, in accordance with international law.

## Aqaba

The teams took a break on Friday October 14 and returned to work on Sunday 16 at the house of the Crown Prince at Aqaba. The group on borders and security continued its delineation of the borders without problems.

'Careful,' al-Khasawneh said to Haddadin, 'history will not pardon any of us if we commit a mistake or compromise any of the basic rights.'

'Don't you worry. In my case, I am handling the water issue the way I should. I wish you good luck.'

Al-Khasawneh stuck to his guns, and so did Haddadin. The Israeli negotiator, Daniel Reisner, was a real gentleman and a knowledgeable lawyer. The Jordanian side continued to be represented by Haddadin, solo.

On Sunday the water negotiations table was changed. It shifted to the table on another porch facing Eilat. The talks covered a lot of ground on the issues of pollution and protection of water resources, but agreement was not forthcoming. At one point, Kinarti exhibited his favorite reaction, that of going to Rubinstein to complain. 'He wants to talk to you,' said Kinarti as he was walking back to the table, referring, Haddadin thought, to a higher official.

'I am here to negotiate with you,' shouted Haddadin. There was silence for a few minutes before Dr Ahmad Mango, advisor to the Crown Prince, appeared from around the corner. He noticed the silence and the tense atmosphere, and signaled to Kinarti, who excused himself and walked to talk to Mango. The two stood under the tall palm tree at the corner of the two porches.

'This Haddadin is driving me crazy,' said Kinarti. 'He must be crazy too. You see, he does not listen to the Crown Prince.'

'You have not seen much,' said Mango, who saw an opportunity to disarm Kinarti. 'I have seen Haddadin say no to his Majesty face to face.'

'I cannot negotiate with him,' resumed a surprised Kinarti. 'Why don't you bring Dr — —?'

'It is too late, we cannot do anything about this. I am afraid you have to find your own way with Haddadin,' said Mango.

'Can you help bring us back to talking terms?'

'I will try.'

Mango came and sat next to Haddadin. Daniel Reisner, who was witnessing all of this for the first time, looked puzzled and did not know what to make of it. Mango tipped Haddadin in Arabic and was able to bring the negotiations back on track. From that morning on, negotiations went smoothly and a lot was accomplished by noon as the teams assembled for lunch. Work resumed immediately after lunch with an intention to achieve more. The negotiators were told that His Majesty and Prime Minister Rabin would arrive at around 5:00 p.m., and the negotiators should be ready for briefings. By 5:00 p.m., Haddadin and Kinarti had made further progress. However, the plan to meet with the leaders changed, and the teams took a C-130 plane from Aqaba to Amman Airport from where they boarded two helicopters to fly over to al-Hashimiyyah Palace.

## Al-Hashimiyyah again

As the teams arrived, the three Jordanian principal negotiators (Shurdum, al-Khasawneh, Haddadin) and Tarawneh went into conference with Crown Prince al-Hassan. He reviewed with them the extent of their progress. Before they were finished, King Hussein arrived and joined the meeting. The Crown Prince wanted to offer the King the seat at the head of the table, but His Majesty declined and insisted on al-Hassan retaining the seat of the chair.

'How is it going?' asked the King.

'Pretty well,' said the Crown Prince, and asked the negotiators to brief His Majesty. Awn al-Khasawneh made a briefing and identified the major problem he was facing, that of the settlement of disputes. His Majesty asked Shurdum for a briefing, and Shurdum gave a concise presentation and singled out the problem they were facing in the border adjustments. It was a piece of developed land, about 300 hectares in area, that was located about four kilometers east of the Mandate line inside Jordanian territory. To adjust the borders there was not easy without having the borderline look odd and funny. His Majesty turned to Haddadin for a briefing on water, and he gave a short resumé.

'Things are going well, Sire,' concluded Haddadin.

'Are you happy?' asked His Majesty.

'Yes Sire, I am. We have finished about 70 per cent of our work, and I hope to finish the remaining 30 per cent tonight.'

'Good, bless your efforts, all of you young men!' said the King.

There was a break for dinner. The visiting delegation from Israel comprised Prime Minister Rabin, Minister Shimon Peres, and Ihud Barak, in addition to the negotiation team, headed by Rubinstein, that arrived from Aqaba. The conversation over dinner helped create a good atmosphere with the visiting delegation from Israel.[1]

The official meeting between the two sides started with a warm welcome from the King, who soon gave the floor to Prime Minister Rabin. 'Your Majesty,' said Rabin, 'I am told that Dr al-Khasawneh is putting an obstacle in the way of reaching an understanding. It does not look like his attitude is helpful to have us reach agreement.'

Haddadin was pleased in a way that the Israelis were complaining about someone in the Jordanian delegation other than himself, but thought that his turn would be next. His Majesty gave the floor to al-Khasawneh. Awn defended his case very politely and in a highly presentable manner. His focus was on arbitration as the method of resolving conflicts arising out of the implementation of the Treaty. Rabin did not comment further, but took the floor again. 'And, Your Majesty, we are not sure if Dr Haddadin has been helpful either. He has been putting obstacles in the way of negotiations, so much so that we are not sure he wants peace.'

The King looked at Haddadin, who was the fourth person to his left, and signaled him over. Haddadin walked over and put his head in between the King's and al-Hassan's to his left. 'What is this that I am hearing,' said Hussein, 'I thought you were happy.'

'I am, *Jalalet Sayyedna*. It is him who is obviously not happy.'

'What is it all about?' asked the King.

'Sire, they pledged to your Majesty fifty million cubic meters per year in the third component of their water package; and they have been trying to pull out of that pledge. They shall deliver if we are to come to an agreement.' The King nodded his head with a visible smile, and Haddadin took it as a sign of support. He decided to go all the way.

The King was very supportive. He said that the negotiators should be given more time to come to acceptable terms. The Israelis were not as decorous as were the Jordanians in the presence of royalty. They interrupted one another and took the floor without discipline. The Jordanians were disciplined, polite and ordered. Finally, King Hussein proposed to go over to the hall across the corridor where the maps of Wadi Araba were displayed to try to find a solution to the remaining problem in the border adjustment, that of the isolated 300-hectare Israeli farm inside Jordanian territory. The two delegations crossed the corridor over to the opposite hall. The map showing the 300-hectare land developed by the Israelis inside Jordan was laid on a large coffee table. Rabin stood to the right of the King, and to his left stood the Crown Prince, Haddadin, Majali, Marea, Shurdum and the others. Some stood behind in a second row.

'If we adjust the border to give that piece to the Israelis,' whispered Majali as he leaned toward Haddadin, 'it would look like the long penis of a donkey!' Majali was obviously not happy with the idea of modifying the border at that location (Zofar/al-Ghamr). Rabin did his best to persuade the King to have the borderline adjusted, but the King did not favor the idea.

'Why don't you, Your Majesty, lease it to us for some time?' asked Rabin.

'The notion of lease is not on the table,' said the King, 'but for how long do you want to stay in it?'

'Say, 25 years, renewable by mutual consent.'

The King looked to his left. 'What is the opinion?' he asked, without addressing the question to anyone in particular. There was a pause. A condition flashed into Haddadin's mind. It was a condition contained in *Al-Uhda al-Omariyyah* (the Pledge of Omar) issued to the Patriarch of Jerusalem by the Caliph, Omar Ibn al-Khattab, in the year 637 as he rode from Madeena in Hijaz to be handed the keys of the gates of Jerusalem: 'No Jews shall be our neighbors in Eliyya [Jerusalem].' As such, Jews were allowed into the city during the day, and were not to stay in it overnight. Haddadin broke the pause: 'With one condition, Your Majesty.'

'What is it?' asked the King.

'That they cross into our territory and out of it during the day only. They shall not stay in it overnight, and shall therefore not build houses on that plot of land.' The King looked at Rabin, and the Prime Minister accepted the condition, and the obstacle was overcome. The deal was not that of a lease; it was a Jordanian permission for the Israeli farmers to keep utilizing that plot of land for 25 years, renewable by mutual consent. After that resolution, the groups went off to complete their work.

### The water annex

The water group occupied a meeting room on the south side of the Palace. The other teams occupied rooms on the northern side of the Palace. The rest rooms were on that side too. For a water negotiator to go to the rest room, he had to walk across the lobby, to which a pleasant terrace, facing Jerusalem, was attached. Every time Haddadin made that trip to the rest room, he saw Danny Yatom, the Deputy Director of Mossad, who had accompanied the Israeli delegation, standing on that terrace with his cellular phone pressed to his ear.

The teams worked through the night. At about 4:00 a.m., al-Khasawneh passed by Haddadin. 'I am through with the articles of the Treaty, and I need to get a few hours of sleep. The borders group is not progressing well. I was instructed to ask you to take care of Annex I (a) to the Treaty that handles the borders. They are across the hall, you know where they are.'

'Yes, I know where they are. I will attend to that piece of work as soon as I am through with Annex II, the water annex,' said Haddadin.

'Please. It is important. Give it all that it takes.'

'Don't you worry; have a good sleep.'

By 6:15 in the morning the water annex was done. With the issue of the 300-hectare farm resolved as above, the use of those wells drilled in Jordanian territory that supply Israel with ground water was allowed to continue under Jordanian sovereignty. Israel agreed to supply Jordan with 10 mcm of desalinated water in the north, and Jordan agreed to let Israel increase the abstraction of ground water in Wadi Araba by 10 mcm per year pursuant to a determination through a specialized study to ensure that the increased abstraction would not harm the aquifer. Until the desalination was operational, the 10 mcm due to Jordan would be supplied from Lake Tiberias. On the issue of the third 50 mcm, it was agreed that the two countries would cooperate to find the source of supply within one year. No agreement was reached on paying the costs of capital projects, and it was agreed to forward that non-agreement to the leaders as soon as they were ready that morning. The two leaders finally resolved this issue to the satisfaction of the negotiators. They said that donors from friendly countries would be happy to pay the cost of development.

## The borders annex

Haddadin then hurried to attend to the issue of borders. On one side of the table, facing the door, was Nidal Saqarat. Opposite him were three Israeli negotiators headed by Moshe Kochanovsky. 'Where are the rest of the Jordanians?' asked Haddadin.

'They went to sleep. They were told that you would take over,' answered Saqarat.

Haddadin looked at the draft annex, and started to correct its English. It needed a lot of editing. 'Who wrote this?' Haddadin asked Saqarat, who was educated in France.

'Don't ask me please. My English is hardly enough to get me home if I were lost!'

'And how come you did not go to sleep like all the others?'

'This is a heavy responsibility. I was afraid if I did, someone might tamper with our documents and the annex.'

'Good for you, and bless your heart. I wish the country had many more like you,' said Haddadin, who had not slept one minute.

There was a very important issue regarding the borders. The West Bank has a frontage on the Jordan River that extends between Wadi Yabis in the north to the middle of the Dead Sea in the south. The rest of Jordan's western borders are abutting Israel proper. The issue had been debated with the Israelis earlier, and Jordan had succeeded in having a disclaimer inserted on the maps to indicate that the status of occupied territories was not prejudiced. The disclaimer, describing the line separating the West Bank and Jordan, started with the words 'This international line . . .'

'Who wrote this disclaimer?' Haddadin asked Saqarat in Arabic.

'Awn al-Khasawneh and the legal advisors,' Saqarat answered.

Haddadin asked for a break, left the room and headed to the reception room next to the lobby to look for Awn al-Khasawneh. He found him in a meeting with the Crown Prince, and signaled to him for a word. Al-Khasawneh came.

'I am afraid I cannot live with the text of this disclaimer,' said Haddadin.

'I know what you mean; but this was the best we could do.'

Awn, when you refer to the line as 'international' it means there is a state on each of its two sides. We know Jordan is a state on the east side of the line, but, to me, there is no sovereign state on its west side, not unless Israel is recognized as that state; and that is what will be construed from this text. This will put us in trouble with so many Arab parties, on top of the PLO.

'I agree. Well try your best.'

Haddadin proceeded to the office of the King's secretary and used her desktop computer to try to come up with a language for the disclaimer that he could live with and convince the Israelis to accept. 'What do you think of this text?' he asked al-Khasawneh. The new wording described the line with the West Bank as the line that separated the governorates of the Hashemite Kingdom of Jordan before the 1967 war. Al-Khasawneh read it carefully, and cleared it as the legal expert of the delegation. Haddadin then went back to the negotiation room and had the meeting called to order. Two more negotiators, including Daniel

Reisner, joined the Israelis. He embarked on a few details of the text before he came to the important point. 'Now we come to the disclaimer. Here is our proposal for it,' said Haddadin as he handed over one hard copy to Moshe Kochanovsky.

The two sides went through hard negotiations as the time for lunch approached, and that particular issue was the only one remaining before the treaty could take its final form. Finally, the text was agreed and the disclaimer statement was jointly signed. 'Thank you all,' said Haddadin, 'I think we can call this a success, and call it a day or a night!' He invited the group to coffee, socialized with them and then hurried to al-Khasawneh, saying 'Here it is, Awn, I had good luck.' Awn could not believe it. He was very happy and he explained the development to the King.

'It appears that the draft treaty will be initialed today, Awn,' said Haddadin.

'Yes, I have been so advised.'

'We have successfully completed item B of the Common Agenda, but what about item C that stipulates that a treaty would be concluded after the achievement of items A and B? Item A as you know, has the comprehensive peace provision,' said Haddadin. Awn al-Khasawneh gave a considered response:

> Remember the Arab coordination meeting in Damascus in 1992, and the one in Amman in 1993? It was agreed there that each party could proceed at a different pace with Israel. Syria was quoted as saying: 'Each party shall take out its own thorns with its own hand.' The second paragraph in the preamble of the Treaty, however, confirms the goal of comprehensive peace.

'I am afraid we have to brace ourselves for increased Syrian criticism, and for criticism from the PLO and its supporters,' said Haddadin.

'We did not criticize Oslo, and we will be happy for a peace treaty between Syria and Israel.'

Before noon on Monday, October 17, 1994, al-Hashimiyyah Palace started to receive more Jordanian officials. All the King's advisors arrived, and the senior staff of the Royal Court. The Prime Minister arrived at about midday, and spoke to Tarawneh and Haddadin who were standing close to the entrance:

'How did things go?'

'Very well,' said Tarawneh.

'Is the Treaty ready?'

'Soon it will be, sir.'

'Do you have any comments on it, Munther?'

'No, Pasha, it is good. It is finally in good shape.'

'Who is supposed to initial it?' asked Majali.

'You, as Foreign Minister, and Shimon Peres,' said Tarawneh.

'*Ala Barakat Illah* [With God's blessing],' said a very brave Majali.

The dining hall downstairs was set up for the occasion. Shortly after lunch the ceremony of initialing the Peace Treaty would take place. The press correspondents filled the room. A limited number of chairs were put out to seat the Jordanian and Israeli officials on the two sides of the table on which the Treaty was to be signed. Haddadin went downstairs with the others to attend the ceremony. He looked for his name on the chairs set for the Jordanians, but did not find a chair for him. As he was retreating, the Chief of the Royal Protocol, Ayman Majali, insisted on adding another chair at the back for him.

King Hussein appeared with Prime Minister Rabin, and Prime Minister Majali with Minister Peres. The dignitaries took their seats. Haddadin looked for the negotiators, for Awn al-Khasawneh, for the guys who had labored all these years to make this conclusion possible, but he could not see them. At some distance, he spotted Awn in the midst of the crowd of press correspondents, not giving press interviews, but looked like he was one of them!

After the ceremony ended at about 4:00 p.m., Haddadin and Michael Marto headed for the door to go home and get some sleep. They spotted Anani sitting on a bench by the door, very tired and dozing off as he sat. The Crown Prince stood at the door to say goodbye to the Israeli guests. Haddadin approached him.

'Congratulations, *Sidi*,' said Haddadin.

'*Ye'teek al-Afiah* [May God give you the vigor]!' Then Haddadin said:

I have an apology to make; I think we have been a burden on your home in Aqaba for over a week, and you have been very gracious with us despite our clashes with the guests. I have screamed at a guest in your house, and I feel sorry for that. No one can be insulted in a Hashemite house. But you know *Sidi*, I was doing what I did for the sake of the country, nothing personal.

'You know,' said the Crown Prince, 'I used to hear about how tough you were in negotiations with the Israelis; but hearing is not like watching you in action.'

'*Al-Hamdu Lillah* [Praise be to God] it is over.'

'Not yet, you are to appear at the Royal Court at six this evening to brief the advisors to His Majesty, ministers and parliamentarians. I guess there is no time to sleep!' said the Crown Prince.

'Don't worry, *Sidi*, I will be there.'

The negotiators arrived at Basman Palace at 5:30, briefed the officials in the main meeting hall, and answered their questions.

That was on Monday, October 17, 1994. The Treaty was initialed and the news was carried on all the wires. It was a day to celebrate for many, but was not good news for some others. Some Arab states, like Syria and Egypt, picked on reporting errors, especially those talking about 'leasing' Jordanian lands to the Israelis. There was not a lease arrangement in the Treaty, and leasing of Jordanian lands was not on the table.

On Sunday, October 23, 1994 an Israeli team crossed over to Amman to have both sides proofread the Treaty before its signing, scheduled for Wednesday, October 26. The work was done at the Jordan Geographic Center in Jubeiha, west Amman. Tarawneh headed the Jordanian side that included Haddadin, Shurdum and Dr Abdallah Toukan. The work continued the following day. A few disagreements over the format of maps, and names of places were resolved; the Treaty was made ready for its final signature.

On Tuesday, October 25, an Israeli team, composed of Yossi Vardi, Rafi Benvenisti and Oded Eran, who later served as Israel's Ambassador to Jordan, crossed over to Jordan to resume talk over the Jordan Rift Valley. The meeting was held at al-Hashimiyyah Palace, and the two sides agreed on the next steps to be taken. After lunch, Haddadin decided to show them Amman, as it was their first visit ever. He took them on a drive to the Amman Citadel. From there, they overlooked the Roman amphitheater across the wadi. As the group looked across to the amphitheater, they could hear the slogans of a modest demonstration in Hashimiyyah Plaza in front of the amphitheater. It was basically an anti-peace demonstration shouting slogans against Israel and the Peace Treaty. It must have been some 1,000 people, audible at the Citadel. Haddadin drove his guests down toward the amphitheater, stopped for a while to watch the protest, and then drove them off for tea at his home. They were later driven to the bridge on the Jordan by a Jordanian army officer.

## The signing of the Peace Treaty

The next day was historic. Arrangements were made for a major ceremony in Wadi Araba north of Aqaba for the signing of the Peace Treaty between Jordan and Israel. It was not readily acceptable to sign the Treaty in either Amman or Tel Aviv; nor was it viewed appropriate to have it signed in the territories of either country. A border point was the more suitable location, and, obviously, it would be difficult to have it on the centerline of the Jordan River, or the Dead Sea. On the other hand, the desert-like terrain of Wadi Araba would trigger the interests of the leaders to support the integrated development of the Jordan Rift Valley. The location, chosen to the north of the Aqaba Airport, was the location where the first negotiation session in the region was conducted in July.

Aqaba Airport received more planes that day than ever before. Three planes left Amman Airport for Aqaba carrying Jordanian dignitaries and their wives to attend the event, which was very well orchestrated. King Hussein led the official Jordanian group to the signing. Crown Prince al-Hassan, Prime Minister Majali (also Foreign Minister) and Fayez Tarawneh were on the stage. From Israel, Israeli President Ezra Weizman, Prime Minister Rabin, Foreign Minister Shimon Peres, and Elyakim Rubinstein were on the same stage. Majali and Rabin signed the Peace Treaty. President Clinton, and the foreign ministers of Russia, Germany and the United States, also attended. The signing ceremony was conducted; bands from the armed forces of both countries played each other's national anthem; veterans of Jordanian–Israeli wars faced each other and shook hands; whilst overhead doves were released. President Clinton made a speech in appreciation and support of the Treaty, and spoke of transforming the arid lands of Wadi Araba into a Valley of Peace.

## Reactions and explanations

On the following day, Haddadin left for Germany, as instructed by the Crown Prince, to give a joint briefing with the Israelis on the Peace

Treaty to German officials. Michael Marto joined him in Bonn. The two represented Jordan in a presentation to the German Foreign Ministry and Chancellery. They then left for Casablanca via Berlin, London and Tangiers to join the Jordanian delegation to the first Economic Summit for the Middle East and North Africa. Crown Prince al-Hassan Bin Talal headed that Jordan delegation.

Our delegation did very well at that conference. Jordanian delegates gave presentations on economic cooperation, the Jordan Rift Valley, water and the environment, and transport and trade. Attendance was so high that there were not enough seats for all the delegates, nor were the good hotels of Casablanca sufficient. The EU delegation was eager to hear about the water agreement, and Haddadin presented it in the presence of Dr Hisham Khatib, Jordanian Minister of Water and Irrigation. The EU expressed readiness to support the study on the water peace projects.

The summit was the first of its kind for the region and offered an excellent opportunity to bring people, businesses and projects together. It was considered a big success and gave further momentum to peace.

After the Casablanca Summit, Haddadin took a flight to Athens where the multilateral Water Resources Working Group was to convene shortly. In the same hotel complex, there was a seminar organized by the University of California at Los Angeles. He was invited to that seminar, the principal topics of which focused on peace in the Middle East. There he met an Israeli acquaintance who confided in him that he had been contacted on the evening of October 16 for clues as to what points of weakness Haddadin might have. Israeli negotiators needed help in winning the water debates. The Israeli acquaintance had advised the caller that Haddadin had guts enough to tell the Syrians off over the Yarmouk waters. 'Any Jordanian who is tough with Syria over the Yarmouk will not be kind to Israel over the same issue!' he had advised. Haddadin remembered the cellular phone fixed to the ear of Danny Yatom that evening of October 16 as the teams were busy negotiating at al-Hashimiyyah Palace.

In that seminar, an American Jew made a presentation that was skewed in favor of Israel, and threw suspicions at the stand of the Arabs. It was similar to the presentation made by Jews and Israelis before the Peace Treaty was concluded. 'I can see that our job in making peace with Israel is not complete,' responded Haddadin. 'It looks like we ought to extend our efforts to make peace with Jews all over the world!' he added.

The Palestinian delegation arrived for the multilateral peace talks. They, too, were unhappy with the Jordanian Treaty. They had told the EU, and had published in their newspapers, that the Jordanians recovered their water rights at the expense of the Palestinians, a claim that was totally unfounded. Haddadin sat down to talk to the Palestinian delegation. No one in their delegation knew the bases of Palestinian water rights in the Jordan River basin. They just talked of Palestinian water rights but were not able to define them properly. In their session with the EU before the multilaterals, the Jordanian delegation was briefed on the Palestinian complaints about the water rights in the Jordan–Israel Treaty. The EU delegates said that they received these complaints from the highest Palestinian authority. When pressed, they admitted they had heard the complaint from President Arafat himself.

The Jordan–Israel Treaty was forwarded by the Jordanian government to the Parliament for approval and enactment into law. Abdul Karim Kabariti chaired the committee on Foreign Affairs, and was in charge of explaining the terms of the Treaty. They wanted an explanation of the water annex, and Kabariti sent questions by fax to Haddadin while he was in Casablanca. More questions came to Athens, and Haddadin answered them. The vote in the Lower House of Parliament on the Treaty was 54 votes for and 25 votes against with one member absent, and the Treaty was approved to be put into law. The Upper House of Parliament also approved the Treaty, and it was issued into law by a Royal Decree. The Treaty was ratified by the two countries in a ceremony at Beit Gibrael on the southern shores of Lake Tiberias on November 11, 1994. (See Appendix 4.)

## Public interest

Jordanian negotiators were invited onto several TV shows, and gave interviews to the foreign press, explaining the Treaty, and responding to questions. They gave speeches all over the country, especially on campuses and in social clubs. The Treaty was generally well received and the approval rates were reportedly very high. The press carried analyses of the Treaty, and columnists contributed to its appraisal. There was an acceptance by the elite that Jordan had extracted more from Israel than had been expected under the circumstances.

'So what did the Treaty bring us in Jordan?' asked a caller to one of the TV shows.

'If you can bear with me, I will explain it very briefly,' said Anani, appearing on the show with Haddadin and al-Khasawneh:

> First, Jordan has recovered every inch of territory that was controlled or occupied by Israel. Israeli farmers are permitted to continue their activities in two farms under Jordanian sovereignty and Jordanian law.
>
> Second, Israel's borders with Jordan have been defined for the first time, and that will put an end to the aspirations by Israeli extremists to expand eastward at Jordan's expense.
>
> Third, Jordan has recovered its rightful share of water at a time when we are badly in need of more water.
>
> Fourth, we have obtained confirmation of the rights of Palestinian refugees and displaced persons in accordance with international law.
>
> Fifth, there is consolidation of collective security in the region, and the stabilization of peaceful relations. Such a state will attract foreign investment, reduce unemployment, and lead to the establishment of a Regional Development Bank.
>
> Sixth, we have achieved foreign debt forgiveness, especially of our debts to the United States. Debt rescheduling with other lenders will be a lot easier.
>
> Seventh, there is now cooperation in the integrated development of the Jordan valley. The majority of the benefits from there will accrue to Jordan.
>
> Eighth, we have ended a state of siege under which we have been since the Gulf War of 1990. We can reach out now with ease to other countries in the region and in the world at large.

A second caller put another question: 'Is Israel committed to the implementation of the UN resolutions concerning the refugees and displaced persons?' Anani asked al-Khasawneh to take that question and he answered:

> The Treaty stipulates, as indeed did the Common Agenda, that the bilateral aspects, i.e. the Jordan–Israel component of the issues of refugees and displaced persons, will be resolved in accordance with international law. There was a Security Council Resolution 236 in 1967 requiring that displaced persons be allowed to return to their homes and properties, and there is a score of General Assembly resolutions confirming the rights of the 1948 refugees. These resolutions are part of international law.

'Why should we allow the Israelis to stay in Baqura and the other piece of land in Wadi Araba, for 25 years?' asked another caller. Haddadin replied:

> The other piece is a 300-hectare area developed by the Israelis and is called al-Ghamr. But let me address the Baqura area, if I may.
>
> Baqura and another stretch of land next to it on the east side of the Jordan River and on the west side of it has been owned by the Jewish Palestine Electric Company since 1926. Land pockets in Baqura proper have been owned by Jews since the twenties and thirties. We, in Jordan, respect private property, and we have assigned a guard to this 'enemy' property since 1949 so that no one trespasses on it. We expect the Israelis to reciprocate. If we do not respect Jewish property inside Jordan, Israel would be happy to reciprocate and forget about the property rights of Jordanians inside Israel, and there is a lot more Jordanian property there than there is Israeli property inside Jordan.

'What did we get in terms of water compared to our water rights?' asked another caller. Anani asked Haddadin to take that question. Haddadin responded:

> Our rights, pursuant to the disengagement decision, are those of the East Bank as defined by the Technical Committee of the Arab League in their work on the subject in the mid-fifties. We have been required to leave the rights of the West Bank for the PLO to defend and recover. Our rights, then, are in all the side wadis that discharge in the Jordan River from the east, and in the Yarmouk River. No one shares with us the flows of the side wadis, but the Yarmouk River is shared with Syria and with Israel. It is important to remember that the negotiations and the Treaty were concluded with Israel, and that we do not in this context address any Syrian-Jordanian differences over the Yarmouk. The Treaty addresses only Jordanian–Israeli affairs. The Arab Technical Committee finally gave its consent in 1955 to an Israeli share in the Yarmouk at 25 million cubic meters per year, and said that the balance of the Yarmouk flow is for Jordan. Syria, the Committee decreed, is entitled to 90 mcm of water from that river upstream. What we have achieved is:
>
> First, we confined Israel's share to 25 mcm per year; a figure exactly equal to what the Arabs said in 1955 should be Israel's share.
>
> Second, we allowed Israel 20 mcm of winter water in the Yarmouk that we cannot use, and obtained 20 mcm from Lake Tiberias in the summer, the time when we need the water most.

This is analagous to storage of Yarmouk flood water to use it in the summer without any loss to evaporation.

Third, we have also traded 10 mcm per year of ground water of marginal quality in Wadi Araba with an equal amount from Lake Tiberias, which is of superior quality.

Fourth, we have become entitled to 50 mcm of water of drinkable quality from sources in Israel to be defined through cooperation between the two countries.

Fifth, we succeeded in sharing the remaining flow of the Jordan River, excluding the flow of the Yarmouk of course, in equal amounts with Israel along our borders with it.

Sixth, we succeeded in getting Israeli acquiescence to the building of a diversion/storage dam on the Yarmouk River at the Adassiya tunnel location, something we have been trying to do for ages without success.

Seventh, we got Israel to agree that we build a dam or two on the Jordan River to store any excess flood for the benefits of Jordan, and also to store such floods off the course of the River.

Eighth, the two parties undertake to protect the water resources against pollution and against tampering with the installations on their respective territories that belong to the other party.

Sir, it is worthwhile to note that point one above comprises the water rights of Jordan, i.e. the side wadis and the Yarmouk residual flow after the Syrians and the Israelis take their respective shares. All the other points above have been wrestled with Israel through hard bilateral negotiations. None of our points would prejudice the rights of any other party, particularly the Palestinians.

'May I interject?' asked al-Khasawneh. 'A primary achievement is the security undertakings in the Treaty. The two sides undertake not to use force or the threat of using it against each other, and the two sides undertake to work together to make the Middle East an area free from the weapons of mass destruction.'

One last thing, sir,' added Haddadin; 'note that, after a series of Arab defeats since 1955, Jordan was able to achieve in this Treaty more than the Arabs said would be our water rights.'

'There are many more corollary achievements and potential achievements for Jordan. I think we have entered a new era. Thanks to the efforts of His Majesty King Hussein, and to the efforts of His Royal Highness Crown Prince al-Hassan,' concluded Anani.

The hopes for progress on the Palestinian track became high as the Treaty gave the peace process a shot in the arm. The same hopes were also attached to the Syrian and Lebanese tracks so that it seemed possible that the goal of comprehensive peace would be achieved. It was not long before Syria and Israel resumed bilateral negotiations at Wye Plantation in Maryland, and information leaked from there indicated good progress. It was soon known that the two parties agreed that Israel would 'withdraw' to the lines of June 4, 1967. Other arrangements were to be worked out pertaining to security and Israeli settlements on the Golan. It was, however, hard to tell how successful the negotiations on the other tracks would be.

Jordan and Israel started working out detailed agreements on various fronts, as provided for in the Treaty. Eighteen agreements were concluded in such fields as transport, agriculture, trade, aviation, health, education, information, tourism and others. The borders between the two countries were demarcated and border markers installed. In the field of water, the annex had enough details to start implementation. A joint Water Committee was established, and two subcommittees were set up under it. The meetings of the joint Water Committee alternated between Israel and Jordan. A pipeline was installed to convey water from Lake Tiberias to the King Abdallah Canal in Jordan, and the King inaugurated the project on July 5, 1995. The water sharing in the Yarmouk River was adjusted to conform to the Treaty articles. The water thus gained enabled Jordan fully to operate the water system supplying Amman with municipal water from the King Abdallah Canal.

The multilateral working groups also received a shot in the arm as a result of both the Cairo Agreement between Israel and the PLO, and the Jordan–Israel Peace Treaty. The Water Resources and the Environment Working Groups held a joint meeting in Amman in June 1995 that was addressed by Crown Prince al-Hassan. The other groups scored progress too, and the atmosphere was conducive to peace-related activities.

His Majesty King Hussein bestowed medals on the Jordanian negotiators commensurate with their respective ranks in government, or the equivalent if they were in the private sector. The heads of the delegations, Tarawneh and Rubinstein, were honored in Beit Gibrael by the two leaders on the occasion of the ratifying of the Peace Treaty and the commencement of its effectiveness on November 11, 1994. They received financial awards and Tarawneh donated his to the Ministry of

Social Development of Jordan to be spent on the orphans and the needy. On the return flight from Beit Gibrael, Tarawneh missed his helicopter ride and had to come home in an Army jeep.

'So you went there without even asking for your colleagues to attend the ceremony with you,' Haddadin said to Tarawneh after he congratulated him. 'Eleven members of Parliament were taken, senators too, but not a single member of the delegation!'

'It was never my arrangement, nor was I consulted,' Tarawneh assured him.

'Were there any Israeli negotiators in that ceremony?'

'Yes, practically all of them that we know; many asked about their counterparts. Noah cannot wait to see you!'

'I bet! At least their government remembers them. Blessed be Awn al-Khasawneh who once told me that this could be a thankless job. I hope we will not end up as defendants for what we have achieved for the country.'

'Come on, you must be kidding.'

'I could be, but someone out there may not be!'

The negotiators disappeared from the political scene for a while, and others took over. Majali and Anani left government in January 1995, Haddadin left the process in March 1995, and Awn left it by the time the Treaty was signed. They all came back to the political scene, but exited from it a short while later. King Hussein himself passed away on January 7, 1999. People changed but the Treaty survived.

## NOTE

1 The Jordanian delegation consisted of the King, the Crown Prince, Prime Minister Majali, Sherif Zaid Bin Shaker, Dr Anani, Marwan Kassim, General Marea, Dr Haddadin, Awn al-Khasawneh, General Shurdum, and Dr Ahmad Mango. Behind sat Dr Michael Marto.

# 15

# Implementation Overview

The state of war that had prevailed between Jordan and Israel since May 15, 1948 was ended on July 25, 1994 when King Hussein met with Prime Minister Rabin under the auspices of President Clinton at the White House and issued the Washington Declaration. The bilateral negotiations acquired new momentum and the joint efforts culminated in the conclusion of the Peace Treaty that was signed in Wadi Araba on October 26, 1994 and came into effect on November 11, 1994.

Almost immediately after the Treaty was signed, crews from Jordan and Israel worked jointly to install border marks in Wadi Araba. Joint work between the military on both sides assured the implementation of Annex I on borders. Access gates in the border fence were opened for the northwest area of Baqura that was returned to Jordan's sovereignty, and to the Israeli farm in Wadi Araba at al-Ghamr. Border crossing points were opened at Jisr Sheikh Hussein in the northern Jordan valley and at the location where the Treaty was signed in Wadi Araba. The crossing point at King Hussein Bridge is not a border-crossing point for the nationals of Israel because the borders there separated Jordan from the occupied West Bank and not Israel. Embassies were opened for each country in the land of the other, Israel's Embassy being stationed in a hotel until a suitable building was found. The same was done for the Jordanian Embassy in Tel Aviv.

The joint Water Committee, stipulated in the water annex, was formed promptly. Haddadin was appointed as head of the Jordanian side and Kinarti as head of the Israeli side. The Committee met as early as November 1994 and agreed to the steps to be taken to implement the provisions of the water annex. A pipeline was to be built to convey water from Israel (Jordan River immediately upstream from the Degania gates, which is Lake Tiberias water) to Jordan's King Abdallah Canal in the Jordan valley. There was an existing Israeli pipeline and pump station at that location, and the end of the pipeline was about two hundred meters shy of the Yarmouk River. A connecting pipeline, about 3.2 kilometers in length, needed to be built to connect with the King Abdallah Canal in the Jordan valley. The connecting pipeline was designed and built, and water started flowing on July 5, 1995. Part of that water was pumped to Amman for drinking, and it helped relax a tight water budget for western Amman.

The two sides met in Amman and discussed a draft prepared by Haddadin on the 'Terms of Reference' for consulting services to conduct the studies needed for the water projects under the Treaty. A joint document was produced, taken jointly to Brussels and presented to the EU for possible financial assistance. Prince al-Hassan Bin Talal headed the Jordanian team and Israel's Foreign Minister, Shimon Peres, headed the Israeli team. The EU allocated a total of 10 million towards the studies stipulated in the 'Terms of Reference', and a selection of consultants started late in the summer of 1995.

Teams were organized under the chairmanship of Dr Hani Mulki to draw up agreements under the various articles of the Treaty to regulate relations between the two sides in several matters. Eighteen such agreements were concluded organizing relations in education, culture, health, drugs traffic, agriculture, trade, aviation, and others.

The peace process was dramatically interrupted by the assassination of Prime Minister Yitzhak Rabin in Tel Aviv on November 5, 1995. A Jewish extremist student from Bar Ilan University fired shots at the Prime Minister at close range and killed him. Shimon Peres succeeded Rabin as Prime Minister. During his short tenure violence erupted on the Lebanese front and hundreds of civilian casualties fell, despite them taking refuge in United Nations barracks. New general elections were called in Israel, and the incumbent Prime Minister, Peres, lost to his competitor, Benjamin Netanyahu of the Likud, by a very narrow margin. The ascent of Likud to power in Israel was not very good news for the peace process. The multilateral talks were totally stalled, and talks between the Palestinian Authority and Israel had a bumpy ride. King Hussein was instrumental in overcoming many of the difficulties that those talks faced. However, the impact of the shift of power in Israel's government on the Treaty with Jordan was minimal. It was known that the Knesset members of the Likud voted for the ratification of the Treaty with Jordan.

On the Syrian track, talks had resumed under United States sponsorship at the Wye Plantation when Rabin was in power. These talks soon faced difficulties because of a lack of agreement on total Israeli withdrawal from the occupied Syrian Golan and on the security arrangements.

In Jordan, Prime Minister Majali was entrusted with the task of forming the Jordanian Cabinet on March 19, 1997. He brought with him key figures from the Jordanian delegation to the bilateral negotiations with Israel in a gesture aimed at accelerating the implementation of the Peace Treaty and accelerating the peace process. Anani became Deputy Prime Minister and Minister of State, Haddadin became Minister of Water and Irrigation, Mulki became Minister of Trade and Industry and Minister of Supply, and Tarawneh became Minister of Foreign Affairs. The Majali government worked diligently to accelerate Jordanian–Israeli relations in peace time. Haddadin established a dialogue with his Israeli counterpart, General Ariel Sharon, and was able to agree with him on more water flow from Israel to Jordan on account of an item in the water annex. They also agreed on the construction of a diversion weir on the Yarmouk at Adassiyya, a structure that Jordan had badly needed since 1960, but had never been able to build because of Israeli objections. The Peace Treaty enabled Jordan to have that weir built and completed in December 1999. Minister Haddadin won the approval of Minister Sharon and Commissioner Meir Ben Meir for a 60 mcm storage facility in Lake Tiberias for Jordan to use annually. Unfortunately, this part of the agreement was not followed up for implementation after the Majali Cabinet left office.

Mulki's efforts with his counterpart, Nathan Sharansky, yielded several agreements on trade and Jordan's cement started to be shipped to the West Bank and Israel. Joint efforts on the preparation of the Jordan Rift Valley project for implementation resulted in a pre-feasibility study and better definition of the project components. Joint work was underway to achieve the use of the Jordanian airport of Aqaba by both countries as a common airport, and contacts were sustained for the improvement of relations.

Jordanian–Israeli relations suffered a serious setback when Israel's Mossad attempted to assassinate Khalid Masha'al, a Hamas leader, in daylight, as he was entering his office in West Amman. Hamas, a Palestinian Islamic Movement (*Harakat al-Muqawamah al-Islamiyyah*), opposes peace with Israel. The attempt by the Israeli agents to run away was thwarted by Masha'al's driver, who chased the assassins and fought with them in the street. The police arrested the assassins and discovered their real identity. They had entered Jordan with Canadian passports. King Hussein saved Masha'al's life when he personally insisted that the Israelis bring the antidote to the drug they had injected in Masha'al's body, which they did. He also had the Israelis release Hamas leader, Sheikh Ahmad Yassin, from jail in exchange for the Mossad agents that were in Jordan's custody.

In June 1998, King Hussein left Jordan for medical checks at the Mayo Clinic in Rochester, Minnesota, and cancer of the lymph nodes was diagnosed. He passed away on January 7, 1999 after he had decreed his eldest son, Prince Abdallah, as Crown Prince, replacing the King's brother, al-Hassan. King Hussein was succeeded by his son, King Abdallah II Ibn al-Hussein. The death of the King was a big loss for Jordan and the region, but the peace process was the biggest loser.

Elections in Israel were called again in the summer of 1999. General Ehud Barak of Labor was elected Prime Minister and he tried hard to put the peace process back on track. The Likud that ruled Israel under Netanyahu (1996–9) had been instrumental in derailing the process. Talks with Syria were resumed but got nowhere because of the commitment that Syria sought from Israel to withdraw to the June 4, 1967 lines, and the security commitments and arrangements Israel sought from Syria. To improve Israel's image and end its losses in southern Lebanon, Ehud Barak worked intelligently within Israeli ranks and took the unprecedented step of voluntarily implementing a unilateral withdrawal from South Lebanon in May 2001. Disagreements after withdrawal erupted over the Shaba'a farms that Israeli forces retained, with Lebanon claiming them as part of Lebanon, and Israel, supported by United Nations maps, insisting they were part of Syria and as such would be included in the talks over the Golan Heights with Syria.

Majali's second government came to an end in August 1998, and Dr Fayez Tarawneh formed a new Cabinet. After the King's death, caution was exercised in Jordan as to the speed with which the country could normalize relations with Israel. The preamble to the Peace Treaty with Israel referred to it as part of a comprehensive peace that should be reached between Israel and the Arabs. However, the peace process suffered yet another major setback in the stalling of the talks between Syria and Israel, despite attempts by President Clinton to move them forward. Clinton convened a summit meeting on March 26, 2000 with

President Hafez Assad of Syria in Geneva, but the summit failed for the same reasons that the Israeli–Syrian talks had always failed. On June 9, 2000, President Assad of Syria passed away and was succeeded by his son, President Bashar Assad. The talks with Israel never got restarted.

There was worse in store for the peace process. In late September 2000, a new Palestinian Intifada erupted in response to a daring visit by General Ariel Sharon, head of the Likud, at that time the opposition party in Israel, to al-Aqsa Mosque in Jerusalem. Muslims, particularly Palestinian Muslims, feared that Israel intended to tear down that holy shrine and replace it with the Jewish Temple. Despite the absence of any archaeological evidence that the Jewish Temple ever existed there, Jewish leaders insist that the Temple was situated on the site of al-Aqsa Mosque. The Palestinians' second Intifada gradually embarked on violent means, and Israel responded in kind. Egypt, the first Arab country to initiate and conclude a peace treaty with Israel, called its ambassador back from Tel Aviv, and Jordan, the second Arab country to conclude such a treaty, did not send a new ambassador after the term of the serving ambassador expired.

When Israel called for general elections, Barak, who had tried but failed to reach a deal with Arafat at Camp David under the auspices of President Clinton in the fall of 2000, was unseated by Ariel Sharon, who did not look favorably on the Oslo Accords signed with the Palestinians in September 1993. He adopted a tough policy towards the Palestinians and was eager to annul the Oslo Accords and erase its effects. Violence escalated and target killings became a norm of Israeli military behavior. Many Palestinian activists were assassinated and war planes were called to bomb Palestinian cities. Israeli forces reoccupied towns and cities under the administration of the Palestinian Authority. The Palestinian militant factions, especially those opposed to the peace deals with Israel, resorted to more violence and suicide bombing took hold. The stance of the new United States administration inflamed the situation. President George W. Bush, to the surprise of the Arabs and most of the world, called Sharon 'a man of peace' at a time when the Israeli Defense Forces were engaged with the Palestinian cities and civilians in military operations of grave proportions. Jenin refugee camp was invaded by Israeli tanks and atrocities were committed by Israeli soldiers. Gaza camps were raided as well and many civilian casualties fell. On the other side, many Israeli civilians, including schoolchildren, were killed in suicide bombing operations. Violence drew violence, and the voices of moderation were silenced. Gone were the days when the American role was that of an 'honest broker' in the peace process; the US administration called for the removal of President Yassir Arafat.

The situation in the region deteriorated further in the wake of September 11, 2001. The war against terror declared by the United States tainted Muslims and the Palestinians with the stigma of terrorism. Israel succeeded in drawing an analogy in the minds of Americans between al-Qaeda and the Palestinian Authority, and between Yassir Arafat and Osama Bin Laden. The region kept boiling, and the world showed less and less concern.

As we finish this chapter, meager hope exists in the hearts of the optimists. The basis of hope is an initiative taken by the United States Administration, the United Nations, the EU, and the Russian Federation in which a solution of two states living side by side is adopted. A 'Road Map' has been drawn up and given to the parties. The Palestinians accepted the Road Map but Israel lodged over a dozen reservations. Follow-up by the United States, the UN and the EU to have the Road Map implemented has been met with Israeli reservation and no progress has been made.

To impose a settlement on the Palestinians, Prime Minister Sharon proceeded with the construction of a separation wall between Israel and the Palestinians. The path of the wall infringes on occupied Palestinian territories and separates thousands of Palestinians from their means of livelihood, their farm lands. The International Court of Justice, upon the request of the General Assembly of the United Nations, decreed in the summer of 2004 that the separation wall is illegal.

Prime Minister Sharon, in his efforts to impose a settlement, announced he would implement a unilateral withdrawal from Gaza and a couple of Israeli settlements in the West Bank. The parties to the Road Map supported his move in the hope that it would be the first step toward implementing the Road Map. However, the unilateral withdrawal, due to start next year, created more problems than it solved: problems such as who would be responsible for the Gaza Strip after Israel's withdrawal; what would be the role of neighboring Egypt in securing the borders with Sinai, and other domestic Palestinian problems.

In the midst of all the killing that has dominated the scene in Israel and the Palestinian territories, the Road Map initiatives provide much-needed hope for a breakthrough. There is no way out of the long suffering of the peoples of the Middle East other than peace in which all parties will be the winners, finally able to enjoy a long-awaited era of harmonious co-operation.

# Appendices

---

(Sent to the parties by Secretary of State James Baker)

Begin message:

- As you recall in Madrid, I made it clear publicly and privately that I was prepared to see the parties themselves try to sort out the venue and timing of the next round of direct bilateral negotiations.
- Since then, I conveyed to you several ideas from Israel on how to resolve this issue. However, the Israeli suggestions were not approved by any other party.
- I understand the complexities involved in sorting out the procedural aspects of this issue. I do not minimize them, but neither do I believe they should become, in and of themselves, reasons to block further discussions between the parties on the substance of the negotiations.
- In this message I want to address three issues: finding an acceptable venue for the next round of negotiations; determining the best date to hold the next round; and beginning to foreshadow the kinds of issues that each of you might decide to take up in order to make the negotiations most productive.

## Venue and timing

- It is clear that Madrid will not be an acceptable venue for the next round. It is equally clear that there is no agreement yet to hold talks in the region.
- I want to make clear the view of the United States that, over time, there is no reason to exclude holding negotiations in the region.

Many successful talks have been held in the region in the past and a regional venue would allow close proximity for the negotiators to consult with their political leadership. But I understand we will not resolve this issue now.

- We have consulted on this matter with the Soviets and we agree that the most important issue now is to resume the direct bilateral negotiations as soon as possible.

- Accordingly, I am pleased to invite each one of you to come to Washington to start negotiations on Wednesday, December 4.

- In order to begin preparations for these negotiations, I will need your affirmative response no later than Monday, November 25.

- The United States will arrange the sites for the talks and other administrative issues; the talks will take place here in Washington.

- Each delegation will be expected to assume all other costs associated with the negotiations such as transportation, lodging, staff support and the like.

- We will not be in a position to meet delegations on arrival but, with advance notification on arrival time, we will alert airport authorities to your planned arrival.

- The delegations to these direct bilateral negotiations need not be the same as those that attended the Madrid Conference. In order to ensure, however, that the terms and conditions agreed upon for this process remain, we need to know in advance the composition of each delegation. Our intention would be to notify the composition of each delegation to all other delegations in advance of negotiations.

- In addition, we envisage no particular credentialing for the delegations. However, since the negotiations are likely to be held in US Government buildings, access to those buildings will be available only to those declared as delegates. Other advisors and staff will not be permitted at the sites of the negotiations, but should plan to remain in whatever offices are set up by the delegations themselves.

- Similarly, we plan to provide no press facilities, and any press activity by delegates will have to be arranged by the delegations themselves.

# Substantive negotiations

- As all of us expected, the first round in Madrid covered little substantive ground, and thus provided no real direction as to where the negotiations might now head.
- It is not the intention of the US or the Soviet Union, as co-sponsors, to suggest to you what to do in the negotiations. However, we thought you might find it useful for us to share some preliminary thinking on which approaches to negotiations might help get them launched successfully.

## Israel–Jordanian/Palestinian talks

- In the case of the negotiations between Israel and the Jordanian/Palestinian delegation, there are two distinct sets of issues that need to be discussed.
- Jordan has notified us and presumably Israel, that there are a number of border issues unrelated to UN Security Council Resolution 242 which need to be discussed. We see no reason why these issues should not be raised early in the negotiations so that experts can get to work to examine respective claims and historical background.
- At the same time, Israel and Jordan could profitably discuss a number of other bilateral issues, such as the nature of peace, the resolution of maritime problems in the Gulf of Aqaba, joint management of waste water facilities, joint production of potash, tourism, civil aviation and the like, which could form the essential building blocks of a final settlement, once the elements of a final settlement begin to fall into place, or alternatively as interim arrangements or unilateral measures to serve mutual interests and improve the atmosphere and process of negotiations.
- As we understand it, it is the expectation of both sides that in these negotiations between Israel and Jordan, Palestinians from the joint Jordanian/Palestinian delegation would also attend in order to maintain the integrity of the joint delegation in negotiations with Israel.
- With regard to issues related to the West Bank and Gaza it is similarly our understanding that Palestinians would take the lead but would be accompanied by Jordanians as part of the joint Jordanian/Palestinian delegation.

- In these negotiations there is already agreement that the first phase will focus on interim self-government arrangements.
- Having experienced several years of negotiations on these issues in the late 1980s, it is our considered view that both Israel and Palestinians should avoid as much as possible a protracted debate on such principles as the 'source of authority, nature of the interim self-government authority', and the like.
- Rather, Israel and the Palestinians might agree that each would present in this or the next session a proposed model of interim self-government authority.
- Such models are likely to be quite different; they will vary widely in terms of the scope of authority and jurisdiction that they anticipate extending to Palestinians. Nonetheless, they will provide both sides with some potentially useful starting points to begin hammering out the powers and responsibilities that will be assumed by Palestinians during the transitional period, as well as the issues that need to be defined and negotiated during the period ahead.

**Israel–Lebanon talks**
- With regard to the negotiations between Israel and Lebanon there are clear differences as to how to proceed.
- In our view it might be most productive for both sides to start engaging on the most practical issue that they both confront: namely, how to unlock the current stalemate in Jazzine.[1]
- By this, we do not mean in any way a departure from principles of an overall settlement to substitute a Jazzine settlement for a resolution of the underlying issues between the two countries. However, since the Jazzine issue involves the complex of political and security issues that will be required in order to deal effectively with the problems that extend throughout Southern Lebanon and Northern Israel, it can represent a useful first step and it can demonstrate to both parties that negotiations can produce practical solutions to problems on the ground.

## Israel–Syria talks

- With regard to the negotiations between Israel and Syria, the five-hour talks held November 3 indicated that neither side will find it easy to proceed until key issues of principle are recognized by the other side. While not diminishing the significance of these principles to each party strict adherence to them could lead to early stalemate in the negotiations.

- One way to proceed, in our view, might be to probe the other side's position in certain hypothetical circumstances. For example, Syria might ask, hypothetically, what the Israelis' position on withdrawal would be if Syria were prepared, as part of a comprehensive settlement, to sign a peace treaty with Israel, exchange ambassadors, and work out mutually acceptable security arrangements. Alternatively, Syria might ask whether under such circumstances Israel would exclude withdrawal and return to Syrian sovereignty over Golan.

- Israel, for its part, might ask hypothetically what Syria's position on a peace treaty, full normalization and diplomatic relations would be if Israel were prepared to undertake withdrawal. Alternatively, Israel might ask whether under such circumstances Syria would exclude a treaty of peace, full normalization and diplomatic relations.

- While this kind of dialogue does not adequately overcome differences of principle, it could permit the sides to begin exploring some of these issues raised during these presentations.

Baker

## Jordan's Informal Draft Agenda[2]

### A. Goal
The achievement of a just, comprehensive and lasting peace.

### B. Items
1. Implementation of Security Council Resolution 242 in all its aspects.
2. Israeli Settlements.
3. Borders and Occupied Lands.
4. Refugees and Other Displaced Persons.
5. Water.

## Israel's Informal Draft Agenda[3]

### A. Goal of the negotiations
Israel–Jordan Treaty of Peace.

### B. Israel–Jordan peace negotiations
1. Peace Treaty [changed to read Vision of Peace]: components of peace.
   (1) Termination of the status of war and establishment of peace, including full diplomatic relations.
   (2) Security.
   (3) Borders.
   (4) a. Normalization, including various spheres (trade, civil aviation, culture etc).
       b. Areas of cooperation for special attention: water, energy environment and economy.
2. Possible preliminaries for peace (during the course of negotiations):
   (1) Liaison arrangements.
   (2) Opening of borders and mutual visits.

(3) Liaison system between the two militaries.

(4) Non-political exchanges in spheres of mutual interest, including cooperation in the areas of water, energy and environment and economy.

## C. Matters which may relate to both tracks and to the General Meeting

1. Economic matters.
2. Legal matters.
3. Coordination Mechanism.
4. Rehabilitation of refugee camps in Jordan and in the territories.

## D. Possible Committees (e.g.)

1. Israel–Jordan bilateral security arrangements.
2. Israel–Jordan civilian relationship-normalization.
3. Israel–Jordan cooperation in specific areas (water, energy, environment).
4. Legal matters.
5. Economic matters.

# The Bilateral Peace Negotiations
## Jordan–Israel Track Common Agenda[4]

## A. Goal
The achievement of just, lasting and comprehensive peace between the Arab States, the Palestinians and Israel as per the Madrid Invitation.

## B. Components of Jordan–Israel Peace Negotiations
1. Searching for steps to arrive at a state of peace based on Security Council Resolutions (242) and (338) in all their aspects.
2. Security:
   a. Refraining from actions or activities by either side that may adversely affect the security of the other or may prejudice the final outcome of negotiations. Threats to security resulting from all kinds of terrorism.
   b. i. Mutual commitment not to threaten each other by any use of force and not to use weapons by one side against the other including conventional and non-conventional mass destruction weapons.
      ii. Mutual commitment as a matter of priority and as soon as possible, to work towards a Middle East free from weapons of mass destruction, conventional and non-conventional weapons; this goal is to be achieved in the context of a comprehensive, lasting and stable peace characterized by the renunciation of the use of force, reconciliation and openness.
      **Note:** The above (item b–ii) may be revised in accordance with relevant agreements to be reached in the multilateral Working Group on Arms Control and Regional Security.
   c. Mutually agreed-upon security arrangements and security confidence-building measures.

3. Water:
   a.   Securing the rightful water shares of the two sides.
   b.   Searching for ways to alleviate water shortage.
4. Refugees and Displaced Persons:
   Achieving an agreed just solution to the bilateral aspects of the problem of refugees and displaced persons in accordance with international law.
5. Borders and Territorial Matters:
   Settlement of territorial matters and agreed definitive delimitation and demarcation of the international boundary between Jordan and Israel with reference to the definition under the Mandate, without prejudice to the status of any territories that came under Israeli Military Government control in 1967.[5] Both parties will respect and comply with the above international boundary.
6. Exploring the potentials of future bilateral cooperation, within a regional context where appropriate, in the following:
   a.   Natural Resources:
   Water, energy and environment.
   Rift Valley development.
   b.   Human Resources:
   Demography
   Labor
   Health
   Education
   Drug control
   c.   Infrastructure:
   Transportation: land and air.
   Communication.
   d.   Economic areas including tourism.
7. Phasing the discussion, agreement and implementation of the items above including appropriate mechanisms for negotiations in specific fields.
8. Discussion on matters related to both tracks to be decided upon in common by the two tracks.

**C. It is anticipated that the above endeavor will ultimately, following the attainment of mutually satisfactory solutions to the elements of this agenda, culminate in a peace treaty.[6]**

# Preamble

The Governments of the Hashemite Kingdom of Jordan and of the State of Israel:

Bearing in mind the Washington Declaration, signed by them on 25th July, 1994, and which they are both committed to honor;

Aiming at the achievement of a just, lasting and comprehensive peace in the Middle East based on Security Council resolutions 242 and 338 in all their aspects;

Bearing in mind the importance of maintaining and strengthening peace based on freedom, equality, justice and respect for fundamental human rights, thereby overcoming psychological barriers and promoting human dignity;

Reaffirming their faith in the purposes and principles of the Charter of the United Nations and recognizing their right and obligation to live in peace with each other as well as with all states, within secure and recognized boundaries;

Desiring to develop friendly relations and co-operation between them in accordance with the principles of international law governing international relations in time of peace;

Desiring as well to ensure lasting security for both their States and in particular to avoid threats and the use of force between them;

Bearing in mind that in their Washington Declaration of 25th July, 1994, they declared the termination of the state of belligerency between them;

Deciding to establish peace between them in accordance with the Treaty of Peace;

Have agreed as follows:

## Article 1 – Establishing Peace

Peace is hereby established between the Hashemite Kingdom of Jordan and the State of Israel (the 'Parties') effective from the exchange of the instruments of ratification of this Treaty.

## Article 2 – General Principles

The Parties will apply between them the provisions of the Charter of the United Nations and the principles of international law governing relations among states in time of peace. In particular:

1. They recognize and will respect each other's sovereignty, territorial, integrity and political independence;
2. They recognize and will respect each other's right to live in peace within secure and recognized boundaries;
3. They will develop good neighborly relations of co-operation between them to ensure lasting security, will refrain from the threat or use of force against each other and will settle all disputes between them by peaceful means;
4. They respect and recognize the sovereignty, territorial integrity and political independence of every state in the region;
5. They respect and recognize the pivotal role of human development and dignity in regional and bilateral relationships;
6. They further believe that within their control, involuntary movements of persons in such a way as to adversely prejudice the security of either Party should not be permitted.

## Article 3 – International Borders

1. The international boundary between Jordan and Israel is delineated with reference to the boundary definition under the Mandate as is

shown in Annex I (a), on the mapping materials attached thereto and coordinates specified therein.

2. The boundary, as set out in Annex I (a), is the permanent, secure and recognized international boundary between Jordan and Israel, without prejudice to the status of any territories that came under Israeli military government control in 1967.

3. The Parties recognize the international boundary, as well as each other's territory, territorial waters and airspace, as inviolable, and will respect and comply with them.

4. The demarcation of the boundary will take place as set forth in Appendix (D) to Annex I and will be concluded not later than 9 months after the signing of the Treaty.

5. It is agreed that where the boundary follows a river, in the event of natural changes in the course of the flow of the river as described in Annex I (a), the boundary shall follow the new course of the flow. In the event of any other changes the boundary shall not be affected unless otherwise agreed.

6. Immediately upon the exchange of the instruments of ratification of this Treaty, each Party will deploy on its side of the international boundary as defined in Annex I (a).

7. The Parties shall, upon the signature of the Treaty, enter into negotiations to conclude, within 9 months, an agreement on the delimitation of the maritime boundary in the Gulf of Aqaba.

8. Taking into account the special circumstances of the Baqura/ Naharayim area, which is under Jordanian sovereignty, with Israeli private ownership rights, the Parties agree to apply the provisions set out in Annex I (b).

9. With regards to the Al Ghamr/Zofar area, the provisions of Annex I (c) shall apply.

## Article 4 – Security

1. a. Both Parties, acknowledging that mutual understanding and co-operation in security-related matters will form a significant part of their relations and will further enhance the security of the region, take upon themselves to base their security relations on mutual trust, advancement of joint interests and co-operation, and to aim towards a regional framework of partnership in peace.

b. Towards that goal, the Parties recognize the achievements of the European Community and European Union in the development of the Conference on Security and Co-operation in Europe (CSCE) and commit themselves to the creation, in the Middle East, of a Conference on Security and Co-operation in the Middle East (CSCME).

This commitment entails the adoption of regional models of security successfully implemented in the post World War era (along the lines of the Helsinki Process) culminating in a regional zone of security and stability.

2. The obligations referred to in this Article are without prejudice to the inherent right of self-defence in accordance with the United Nations Charter.

3. The Parties undertake, in accordance with the provisions of this Article, the following:

a. to refrain from the threat or use of force or weapons, conventional, non-conventional or of any other kind, against each other, or of other actions or activities that adversely affect the security of the other Party;

b. to refrain from organizing, instigating, inciting, assisting or participating in acts or threats of belligerency, hostility, subversion or violence against the other Party;

c. to take necessary and effective measures to ensure that acts or threats of belligerency, hostility, subversion or violence against the other Party do not originate from, and are not committed within, through or over their territory (hereinafter the term 'territory' includes the airspace and territorial waters).

4. Consistent with the era of peace and with the efforts to build regional security and to avoid and prevent aggression and violence, the Parties further agree to refrain from the following:

a. joining or in any way assisting, promoting or co-operating with any coalition, organization or alliance with a military or security character with a third party, the objectives or activities of which include launching aggression or other acts of military hostility against the other Party, in contravention of the provisions of the present Treaty;

b. allowing the entry, stationing and operating on their territory, or through it, of military forces, personnel or materiel of a third party, in circumstances which may adversely prejudice the security of the other Party.

5. Both Parties will take necessary and effective measures, and will co-operate in combating terrorism of all kinds. The Parties undertake:

a. to take necessary and effective measures to prevent acts of terrorism, subversion or violence from being carried out from their territory or through it and to take necessary and effective measures to combat such activities and all their perpetrators;

b. without prejudice to the basic rights of freedom of expression and association, to take necessary and effective measures to prevent the entry, presence and operation in their territory of any group or organization, and their infrastructure, which threatens the security of the other Party by the use of, or incitement to the use of, violent means;

c. to co-operate in preventing and combating cross-boundary infiltrations.

6. Any question as to the implementation of this Article will be dealt with through a mechanism of consultations which will include a liaison system, verification, supervision, and where necessary, other mechanisms, and higher level consultations. The details of the mechanism of consultations will be contained in an agreement to be concluded by the Parties within 3 months of the exchange of the instruments of ratification of this Treaty.

7. The Parties undertake to work as a matter of priority, and as soon as possible, in the context of the Multilateral Working Group on Arms Control and Regional Security, and jointly, towards the following:

a. the creation in the Middle East of a region free from hostile alliances and coalitions;

b. the creation of a Middle East free from weapons of mass destruction, both conventional and non-conventional, in the context of a comprehensive, lasting and stable peace, characterized by the renunciation of the use of force, and by reconciliation and goodwill.

## Article 5 – Diplomatic and Other Bilateral Relations

1.  The Parties agree to establish full diplomatic and consular relations and to exchange resident ambassadors within one month of the exchange of the instruments of ratification of this Treaty.
2.  The Parties agree that the normal relationship between them will further include economic and cultural relations.

## Article 6 – Water

With the view to achieving a comprehensive and lasting settlement of all the water problems between them:

1.  The Parties agree mutually to recognize the rightful allocations of both of them in Jordan River and Yarmouk River waters and Araba/Arava ground water in accordance with the agreed acceptable principles, quantities and quality as set out in Annex II, which shall be fully respected and complied with.
2.  The Parties, recognizing the necessity to find a practical, just and agreed solution to their water problems and with the view that the subject of water can form the basis for the advancement of co-operation between them, jointly undertake to ensure that the management and development of their water resources do not, in any way, harm the water resources of the other Party.
3.  The Parties recognize that their water resources are not sufficient to meet their needs. More water should be supplied for their use through various methods, including projects of regional and international co-operation.
4.  In light of paragraph 3 of this Article, with the understanding that co-operation in water-related subjects would be to the benefit of both Parties, and will help alleviate their water shortages, and that water issues along their entire boundary must be dealt with in their totality, including the possibility of trans-boundary water transfers, the Parties agree to search for ways to alleviate water shortages and to co-operate in the following fields:

    a. development of existing and new water resources, increasing the water availability, including co-operation on a regional basis, as appropriate, and minimizing wastage of water resources through the chain of their uses;

b. prevention of contamination of water resources;

c. mutual assistance in the alleviation of water shortages;

d. transfer of information and joint research and development in water-related subjects, and review of the potentials for enhancement of water resources development and use.

5. The implementation of both Parties' undertakings under this Article is detailed in Annex II.

## Article 7 – Economic Relations

1. Viewing economic development and prosperity as pillars of peace, security and harmonious relations between states, peoples and individual human beings, the Parties, taking note of understandings reached between them, affirm their mutual desire to promote economic co-operation between them, as well as within the framework of wider regional economic co-operation.

2. In order to accomplish this goal, the Parties agree to the following:

a. to remove all discriminatory barriers to normal economic relations, to terminate economic boycotts directed at the other Party, and to co-operate in terminating boycotts against either Party by third parties;

b. recognizing that the principle of free and unimpeded flow of goods and services should guide their relations, the Parties will enter into negotiations with a view to concluding agreements on economic co-operation, including trade and the establishment of a free trade area or areas, investment, banking, industrial co-operation and labor, for the purpose of promoting beneficial economic relations, based on principles to be agreed upon, as well as on human development considerations on a regional basis. These negotiations will be concluded no later than 6 months from the exchange of the instruments of ratification of this Treaty;

c. to co-operate bilaterally, as well as in multilateral forums, towards the promotion of their respective economies and of their neighborly economic relations with other regional parties.

## Article 8 – Refugees and Displaced Persons

1.  Recognizing the massive human problems caused to both Parties by the conflict in the Middle East, as well as the contribution made by them towards the alleviation of human suffering, the Parties will seek to further alleviate those problems arising on a bilateral level.

2.  Recognizing that the above human problems caused by the conflict in the Middle East cannot be fully resolved on the bilateral level, the Parties will seek to resolve them in appropriate forums, in accordance with international law, including the following:

    a. in the case of displaced persons, in a quadripartite committee together with Egypt and the Palestinians;

    b. in the case of refugees,

        i. in the framework of the Multilateral Working Group on Refugees;

        ii. in negotiations, in a framework to be agreed, bilateral or otherwise, in conjunction with and at the same time as the permanent status negotiations pertaining to the Territories referred to in Article 3 of this Treaty;

    c. through the implementation of agreed United Nations programs concerning refugees and displaced persons, including assistance to their settlement.

## Article 9 – Places of Historical and Religious Significance and Interfaith Relations

1.  Each Party will provide freedom of access to places of religious and historical significance.

2.  In this regard, in accordance with the Washington Declaration, Israel respects the present special role of the Hashemite Kingdom of Jordan in Muslim Holy shrines in Jerusalem. When negotiations of the permanent status will take place, Israel will give high priority to the Jordanian historic role in these shrines.

3.  The Parties will act together to promote interfaith relations among the three monotheistic religions, with the aim of working towards religious understanding, moral commitment, freedom of religious worship, and tolerance and peace.

## Article 10 – Cultural and Scientific Exchanges

The Parties, wishing to remove biases developed through periods of conflict, recognize the desirability of cultural and scientific exchanges in all fields, and agree to establish normal cultural relations between them. Thus, they shall, as soon as possible and not later than 9 months from the exchange of the instruments of ratification of this Treaty, conclude the negotiations on cultural and scientific agreements.

## Article 11 – Mutual Understanding and Good Neighborly Relations

1. The Parties will seek to foster mutual understanding and tolerance based on shared historic values, and accordingly undertake:
   a. to abstain from hostile or discriminatory propaganda against each other, and to take all possible legal and administrative measures to prevent the dissemination of such propaganda by any organization or individual present in the territory of either Party;
   b. as soon as possible, and not later than 3 months from the exchange of the instruments of ratification of this Treaty, to repeal all adverse or discriminatory references and expressions of hostility in their respective legislation;
   c. to refrain in all government publications from any such references or expressions;
   d. to ensure mutual enjoyment by each other's citizens of due process of law within their respective legal systems and before their courts.
2. Paragraph 1 (a) of this Article is without prejudice to the right to freedom of expression as contained in the International Covenant on Civil and Political Rights.
3. A joint committee shall be formed to examine incidents where one Party claims there has been a violation of this Article.

## Article 12 – Combating Crime and Drugs

The Parties will co-operate in combating crime, with an emphasis on smuggling, and will take all necessary measures to combat and prevent such activities as the production of, as well as the trafficking in illicit drugs, and will bring to trial perpetrators of such acts. In this regard, they take note of the understandings reached between them in the above spheres, in accordance with Annex III and undertake to conclude all relevant agreements not later than 9 months from the date of the exchange of the instruments of ratification of this Treaty.

## Article 13 – Transportation and Roads

Taking note of the progress already made in the area of transportation, the Parties recognize the mutuality of interest in good neighborly relations in the area of transportation and agree to the following means to promote relations between them in this sphere:

1. Each party will permit the free movement of nationals and vehicles of the other into and within its territory according to the general rules applicable to nationals and vehicles of other states. Neither Party will impose discriminatory taxes or restrictions on the free movement of persons and vehicles from its territory to the territory of the other.

2. The Parties will open and maintain roads and border-crossings between their countries and will consider further road and rail links between them.

3. The Parties will continue their negotiations concerning mutual transportation agreements in the above and other areas, such as joint projects, traffic safety, transport standards and norms, licensing of vehicles, land passages, shipment of goods and cargo, and meteorology, to be concluded not later than 6 months from the exchange of the instruments of ratification of this Treaty.

4. The Parties agree to continue their negotiations for a highway to be constructed and maintained between Egypt, Jordan and Israel near Eilat.

## Article 14 – Freedom of Navigation and Access to Ports

1. Without prejudice to the provisions of paragraph 3, each Party recognizes the right of the vessels of the other Party to innocent passage through its territorial waters in accordance with the rules of international law.

2. Each Party will grant normal access to its ports for vessels and cargoes of the other, as well as vessels and cargoes destined for or coming from the other Party. Such access will be granted on the same conditions as generally applicable to vessels and cargoes of other nations.

3. The Parties consider the Strait of Tiran and the Gulf of Aqaba to be international waterways open to all nations for unimpeded and non-suspendable freedom of navigation and overflight. The Parties will respect each other's right to navigation and overflight for access to either Party through the Strait of Tiran and the Gulf of Aqaba.

## Article 15 – Civil Aviation

1. The Parties recognize as applicable to each other the rights, privileges and obligations provided for by the multilateral aviation agreements to which they are both party, particularly by the 1944 Convention on International Civil Aviation (The Chicago Convention) and the 1944 International Air Services Transit Agreement.

2. Any declaration of national emergency by a Party under Article 89 of the Chicago Convention will not be applied to the other Party on a discriminatory basis.

3. The Parties take note of the negotiations on the international air corridor to be opened between them in accordance with the Washington Declaration. In addition, the Parties shall, upon the exchange of the instruments of ratification of this Treaty, enter into negotiations for the purpose of concluding a Civil Aviation Agreement. All the above negotiations are to be concluded not later than 6 months from the exchange of the instruments of ratification of this Treaty.

## Article 16 – Posts and Telecommunications

The Parties take note of the opening between them, in accordance with the Washington Declaration, of direct telephone and facsimile lines. Postal links, the negotiations on which having been concluded, will be activated upon the signature of this Treaty. The Parties further agree that normal wireless and cable communications and television relay services by cable, radio and satellite, will be established between them, in accordance with all relevant international conventions and regulations. The negotiations on these subjects will be concluded not later than 9 months from the exchange of the instruments of ratification of this Treaty.

## Article 17 – Tourism

The Parties affirm their mutual desire to promote co-operation between them in the field of tourism. In order to accomplish this goal, the Parties – taking note of the understandings reached between them concerning tourism – agree to negotiate, as soon as possible, and to conclude not later than 3 months from the exchange of the instruments of ratification of this Treaty, an agreement to facilitate and encourage mutual tourism and tourism from third countries.

## Article 18 – Environment

The Parties will co-operate in matters relating to the environment, a sphere to which they attach great importance, including conservation of nature and prevention of pollution, as set forth in Annex IV. They will negotiate an agreement on the above, to be concluded not later than 6 months from the exchange of the instruments of ratification of this Treaty.

## Article 19 – Energy

1. The Parties will co-operate in the development of energy resources, including the development of energy-related projects such as the utilization of solar energy.
2. The Parties, having concluded their negotiations on the inter-connecting of their electric grids in the Eilat-Aqaba area, will implement the interconnecting upon the signature of this Treaty. The Parties view this step as a part of a wider binational and regional concept. They agree to continue their negotiations as soon as possible to widen the scope of their interconnected grids.

3.   The Parties will conclude the relevant agreements in the field of energy within 6 months from the date of exchange of the instruments of ratification of this Treaty.

## Article 20 – Rift Valley Development

The Parties attach great importance to the integrated development of the Jordan valley area, including joint projects in the economic, environmental, energy-related and tourism fields. Taking note of the Terms of Reference developed in the framework of the Trilateral Jordan-Israel-US Economic Committee towards the Jordan Rift Valley Development Master Plan, they will vigorously continue their efforts towards the completion of planning and towards implementation.

## Article 21 – Health

The Parties will co-operate in the area of health and shall negotiate with a view to the conclusion of an agreement within 9 months of the exchange of the instruments of ratification of this Treaty.

## Article 22 – Agriculture

The Parties will co-operate in the areas of agriculture, including veterinary services, plant protection, biotechnology and marketing, and shall negotiate with a view to the conclusion of an agreement within 6 months from the date of the exchange of instruments of ratification of this Treaty.

## Article 23 – Aqaba and Eilat

The Parties agree to enter into negotiations, as soon as possible, and not later than one month from the exchange of the instruments of ratification of this Treaty, on arrangements that would enable the joint development of the towns of Aqaba and Eilat with regard to such matters, *inter alia*, as joint tourism development, joint customs posts, free trade zone, co-operation in aviation, prevention of pollution, maritime matters, police, customs and health co-operation. The Parties will conclude all relevant agreements within 9 months from the exchange of instruments of ratification of the Treaty.

## Article 24 – Claims

The Parties agree to establish a claims commission for the mutual settlement of all financial claims.

## Article 25 – Rights and Obligation

1. This Treaty does not affect and shall not be interpreted as affecting, in any way, the rights and obligations of the Parties under the Charter of the United Nations.
2. The Parties undertake to fulfill in good faith their obligations under this Treaty, without regard to action or inaction of any other party and independently of any instrument inconsistent with this Treaty. For the purposes of this paragraph, each Party represents to the other that in its opinion and interpretation there is no inconsistency between their existing treaty obligations and this Treaty.
3. They further undertake to take all the necessary measures for the application in their relations of the provisions of the multilateral conventions to which they are parties, including the submission of appropriate notification to the Secretary General of the United Nations and other depositories of such conventions.
4. Both Parties will also take all the necessary steps to abolish all pejorative references to the other Party, in multilateral conventions to which they are parties, to the extent that such references exist.
5. The Parties undertake not to enter into any obligation in conflict with this Treaty.
6. Subject to Article 103 of the United Nations Charter, in the event of a conflict between the obligations of the Parties under the present Treaty and any of their other obligations, the obligations under this Treaty will be binding and implemented.

## Article 26 – Legislation

Within 3 months of the exchange of the instruments of ratification of this Treaty, the Parties undertake to enact any legislation necessary in order to implement the Treaty, and to terminate any international commitments and to repeal any legislation that is inconsistent with the Treaty.

## Article 27 – Ratification and Annexes

1. This Treaty shall be ratified by both Parties in conformity with their respective national procedures. It shall enter into force on the exchange of the instruments of ratification.
2. The Annexes, Appendices, and other attachments to this Treaty shall be considered integral parts thereof.

## Article 28 – Interim Measures

The Parties will apply, in certain spheres to be agreed upon, interim measures pending the conclusion of the relevant agreements in accordance with this Treaty, as stipulated in Annex V.

## Article 29 – Settlement of Disputes

1. Disputes arising out of the application or interpretation of this Treaty shall be resolved be negotiations.
2. Any such disputes which cannot be settled by negotiations shall be resolved by conciliation or submitted to arbitration.

## Article 30 – Registration

This Treaty shall be transmitted to the Secretary General of the United Nations for registration in accordance with the provisions of Article 102 of the Charter of the United Nations.

Done at the Araba/Arava Crossing Point this day Jumada Al-Ula, 21st, 1415, Heshvan 21st, 5755 to which corresponds 26th October, 1994 in the Arabic, Hebrew and English languages, all texts being equally authentic. In case of divergence of interpretation, the English text shall prevail.

For the Hashemite Kingdom of Jordan      For the State of Israel

Abdul Salam Majali             Yitzhak Rabin
Prime Minister               Prime Minister

Witnessed by

William J. Clinton
President of the United States of America

# List of Annexes, Appendices and Other Attachments

**Annex I:**
(a)  International Boundary
(b)  Baqura/Naharayim Area
(c)  Al-Ghamr/Zofar Area

Appendices (27 sheets):
I.    Wadi Araba (10 sheets), 1:20,000 orthophoto maps
II.   Dead Sea (2 sheets), 1:50,000 orthoimages
III.  Jordan and Yarmouk Rivers (12 sheets), 1:10,000 orthophoto maps
IV.   Baqura Area (1 sheet), 1:20,000 orthophoto map
V.    Al-Ghamr Area (1 sheet), 1:20,000 orthophoto map
VI.   Gulf of Aqaba (1 sheet), 1:50,000 orthoimage

**Annex II:   Water**
**Annex III:  Crime and Drugs**
**Annex IV:   Environment**
**Annex V:    Interim Measures**

**Attachments: Agreed Minutes A to D**

## NOTES

1 Jazzine is a town in southern Lebanon where the occupying Israeli forces were confronting Lebanese militias belonging to Hizbollah. Israel unilaterally withdrew from southern Lebanon in a move made by Israeli Prime Minister Ihud Barak in May 2000.

2 Submitted to the Israeli Delegation in the afternoon of Tuesday, January 14, 1992.

3 In response to the Jordanian draft agenda, the Israeli delegation submitted their counter-proposal for a Common Agenda later the same day, January 14, 1992.

4 As negotiated and agreed on Tuesday, October 29, 1992. Jordan was represented by Dr Abdul Salam Majali, Dr Munther Haddadin and Awn al-Khasawneh; Israel was represented by Elyakim Rubinstein, Dr Robby Sabel and Ahaz Ben-Ari.

5 As amended in the ninth round of April–May, 1993. The original draft, agreed on October 29, 1992, read: '. . . without prejudice to the territories presently under Israeli military administration'.

6 Item C was inserted in lieu of the number 9, a continuation of the numbering of items under item B above, as the draft agenda stipulated. Thus, the treaty of peace culmination became conditional upon the achievement of a just and lasting peace as stipulated in item A.

# Index